The State Of Judaism

JUDAISM 3.0

JUDAISM'S TRANSFORMATION TO ZIONISM

by

GOL KALEV

 Mazo Publishers

Judaism 3.0
Judaism's Transformation To Zionism

Softcover ISBN: 978-1-946124-81-4
Hardcover ISBN: 978-1-946124-84-5

E-mail: comments@judaism-zionism.com
website: www.judaism-zionism.com

Published by

Mazo Publishers
www.mazopublishers.com
mazopublishers@gmail.com

*Zionism is the return to Judaism, even before
the return to the land of the Jews.*

Theodor Herzl

Contents

Contents

Contents

Contents

Contents

Terminology

Zionism
The national expression of the Jewish nation-religion.

Rabbinic Judaism
The religious expression of the Jewish nation-religion
for the last 2,000 years.

Biblical Judaism
The original religious and national expression of
the Jewish nation-religion until the 1st century CE.

Judaism 3.0
Zionism is the organizing principle of Judaism
(2020s –)

Judaism 2.0
Rabbinic Judaism is the organizing principle of Judaism
(1st century CE – 21st century)

Judaism 1.0
Biblical Judaism is the organizing principle of Judaism
(Inception to 1st century CE)

Timeline

1948
The establishment of the State of Israel.

1897
Theodor Herzl launches the Zionist movement, a Jewish national
political movement that aspires for the re-establishment
of the Jewish state.

1st century CE
The Jewish Temple is destroyed; Jews are exiled from Jerusalem and
eventually from other parts of Judea.

I

Introduction

What is Judaism, and who is the Jew? The answer to these questions was clear to both Jews and the outside world until merely a century ago. It was clear during Biblical times when Jews lived in Judea and it was clear during the Jews' long exile, when Jews lived in insular communities. But today, there is a confusion that stems from unprecedented changes in Jewish circumstances:

- The Jewish state was re-established.
- Jews became secular, abandoned their insular communities and began marrying non-Jews.
- More than 98% of Jews have immigrated during the last 150 years, primarily moving from Europe and the Middle East to America and Israel.

Those radical changes altered the state of Judaism and have been leading to a transformation, which is now beginning to become evident. Judaism, which has been a nation-religion since its inception, can be viewed through its two primary contexts:

- Its religious context – Rabbinic Judaism is the religious expression of Judaism, through all its streams including Orthodox, Conservative and Reform.
- Its national context – Zionism is the national expression of Judaism. Israel is the physical manifestation of Zionism.

Judaism 3.0 is a recognition that the organizing principle of Judaism has shifted from its religious element (Rabbinic Judaism) to its national element (Zionism). This shift is occurring without any compromise to the religious aspect of Judaism, and indeed only strengthens it. As this book shows, Zionism is increasingly becoming the relevant conduit through which Jews relate to their Judaism and the prism by which the outside world perceives the Jews. This is both through positive and increasingly through negative connections; whether by one's action or passively through affiliation. Indeed, Zionism is where a Jew meets his Judaism. It is the aspect of Judaism that evokes passions and emotions – for Jews and non-Jews alike.

This is not the first time the organizing principle of Judaism has changed. Judaism successfully transformed about 2,000 years ago. Its original organizing principle was the Temple and the physical presence in Judea (Judaism 1.0). When the Temple was destroyed and the Jews exiled, Judaism adopted a new organizing principle – Rabbinic Judaism: The synagogues replaced the Temple, the prayers replaced the sacrifices, the insular ghetto replaced the insular life in Judea, and the yearning to return to Zion replaced the actual presence in Jerusalem (Judaism 2.0).

Judaism 2.0 was not just a better reflection of Jewish realities of the time, but also a more suitable construct to address new threats to Judaism. Similarly, Judaism 3.0 is not only the most accurate reflection of contemporary Jewish life today, but it is also the right framework to counter the emerging threats to Judaism. First and foremost, the existential threat of Israel-bashing which, as discussed in the book, has replaced anti-Semitism as the manifestation of age-old European opposition to Judaism.

The seeds for Judaism 3.0 were planted in the late 19th century by Theodor Herzl, the father of political Zionism, whom I have been researching for many years. This book ties his original vision to today's Judaism and shows that just as he predicted, Zionism has turned into the vehicle for the return of Jews to Judaism.

The transformation to Judaism 3.0 is not a call to action. It is a diagnosis of the contemporary state of Judaism. It is happening in one's consciousness – in one's basic approach to Judaism. Recognizing that Judaism has transformed and is now in Judaism 3.0 would lead to a more genuine relationship of the world with the Jews, and to a greater sense of Jewish belongingness and pride. It would provide Jewish clarity.

The years 2020-2021 challenged conventional thinking: About the way we socialize, work and prioritize; about our relationship with the state, community, police, religion and race; about existential dangers, about democracy, and about identity. It also gave us better tools to comprehend change and recognize transformations. Therefore, the outset of these pivotal years is a great time to delve into an inevitable conversation that has been brewing under the surface for over 120 years, since Herzl published that short book he titled *The Jewish State*.

The ideas in this book have been in the works for over a decade, and perhaps for much longer. I have developed them through my articles in *The Jerusalem Post*, position papers I wrote in the America-Israel Friendship League Think Tank, as well as through endless interactions and conversations with friends and momentary acquaintances of all strides in Israel, America, Europe and around the world – through life in Judaism

3.0. This book is not academic research, but intertwined observations that deliver the state of Judaism. I hope that even for those who disagree with my observations, the ideas in the book can serve as a basis for conversation. I invite you to delve into the intricacies of Judaism 3.0.

II

The Idea of Judaism 3.0

Judaism today is different from the Judaism of a century ago when Jews were in exile. In those 1,800 years of exile, the Jewish nation-religion has had both an internal glue of religiosity and an external one of complete insularity. Jews miles apart prayed at the same time, in the same manner, practiced the same rituals and adhered to the same Jewish laws. This was complemented by the closed nature of Jewish life. A Jew had no viable option to exit Judaism.

But starting in the 19th century, and mostly during the 20th century, there has been a steep decline of Jewish religious observance (from arguably close to 100% to less than 10% today). At the same time, the outer walls that confined Judaism have crumbled. As a result, Judaism has been losing its organizing principle.

Yet, just as the Jewish religious connector has faded, the Jewish national connector has been dramatically augmented: The Jewish state was re-established, and after 70 years, a new organizing principle of Judaism has emerged: Zionism.

The re-establishment of the Jewish state provides a physical point of orientation and tangible mechanism to relate to Judaism – for Jews and non-Jews alike. This is true also for those who are avid critics of Israel. They too engage with Judaism through Zionism. In fact, for many American Jews, criticism of Israel has become their primary Jewish-related activity.

The success of Israel allows a Jew to connect to his Judaism in a natural and willing manner. He can choose from the broad range of Israeli products and experiences suitable to him – be it consuming Israeli wine, criticizing Israeli military actions in Gaza, celebrating Israeli gay culture or following Israeli high-tech innovations. An organic connection to Judaism through choice replaces the reluctant connection to Judaism through no-choice that existed when Jews did not have a path out.

In addition, while Zionism is defined quite simply as the national expression of the Jewish nation-region, the mere mention of the term triggers emotions to the good and the bad. No other aspect of Judaism evokes such a degree of passion, anger, love, fear, pride and dissent, underscoring that the Jew's most relevant connection to Judaism is occurring through Zionism. Indeed, Judaism has transformed and Zionism is now its organizing principle.

The transformation of Judaism did not occur upon the establishment of the State of Israel. It takes time for transformations of such magnitude to materialize, and there were insurmountable hurdles that prevented it from occurring. Those included Zionism's exaggerated association with secularism, Israel's economic and survival hardships, the fierce objection to Zionism by ultra-Orthodox Jews, American Jews' fear of dual loyalty accusations, and overemphasis on the practical aspects of Zionism – immigration to Israel. As shown in this book, the various hurdles are now removed and the path is clear to recognize that Judaism has transformed.

Indeed, the 120-year-old process of the transformation to Judaism 3.0 can be viewed as occurring in three phases:

1. Inception of the Zionist movement in Europe by Theodor Herzl in 1897 and its ultimate recognition by the world nations as a representative of the Jewish people (1897-1935).

2. The takeover of the Zionist movement by Jewish immigrants to Palestine in the 1930s; the establishment of the State of Israel in 1948 and its survival through tough military and economic challenges (1935-2010s).

3. A change in the stature of the Jewish state, from being poor and fragile to being strong and a contributor to humanity. This while there is a steep erosion in legacy connectors to Judaism in the Diaspora (2010s).

Herzl famously said, "at Basel, I founded the Jewish state." He immediately clarified that the "state" he founded was not only a geographical representation, nor a collection of citizens who happen to live in a given territory – but that it was an ideal. He explained: "A territory is merely the concrete basis. The state itself, when it possesses a territory, still remains something abstract." This abstraction, this ideal, is now turning into the organizing principle of Judaism.

Nowhere are the realities of Judaism 3.0 more evident than in the Jewish state that Herzl envisioned.

Israel – Anchored In Zionism

Israel is the most profound expression of Jewish life and the most relevant conduit to Judaism. This is not only because it is the national homeland of the Jewish people and the only place in which Jews live in Jewish sovereignty, but also because over the last few decades, Israel has become the world's largest Jewish community, and has experienced astonishing success.

No longer facing the paralyzing economic hardships that accompanied it through the turn of the 21st century, Israel's perception has shifted from being a "charity case" that depends on the generosity of the "rich American uncle" (trees, the JNF blue box), to being a beacon to the world. Israeli technological innovations improve livelihood around the globe and save lives.

Merely 120 years since the State of Israel was conceived in the mind of Herzl, and 70 years since its establishment, Israel is thriving. Confidence levels are high, quality of living is amongst the world's highest, and the sense of personal safety is strong despite terrorism. Same goes with the sense of medical safety. All Israelis have access to health care and there is subsidized elderly care. No doubt, there are ample challenges and hardships, but the traumatic motto of the early years – "the last person out, turn off the lights" – is gone.

Zionism is the ideological bedrock in which Israeli Jewish society is rooted. There are ample policy debates within Zionism, but not about Zionism. Indeed, the strength of the Zionist ideal enables the numerous points of division in Israel to be argued passionately yet safely.

Buying into the Zionist ideology, and taking pride in being part of the Jewish nation remains high across all sectors and political strides of Israeli Jewish society, including the secular, traditional, National-Religious and ultra-Orthodox, who are very much Zionists in practice if not by definition.

There are small exceptions, most notably amongst elements in the media and academia, as well as fringe groups within the ultra-Orthodox community, but as a whole, Zionism serves as the Israeli Jewish consensus. About 99% of Israeli Jews consistently vote for Zionist parties. The large left-wing party, that at times was falsely accused of not being as enthusiastically Zionist as the rest of Israel, renamed itself in 2015 "the Zionist Camp."

After losing his quest to become prime minister, the Zionist Camp leader, Isaac Herzog, then proceeded to become the head of the Jewish Agency – the flagship of Zionist institutions, and in July 2021, proceeded to become President of Israel.

One of the highest-rated broadcasts in Israel each year is television coverage of the annual Independence Day ceremony that takes place by Herzl's grave – a fulfillment of Herzl's Zionist vision.

At the pinnacle of such Zionist success comes a Jewish revival in Israel. Regardless of one's observance level, Israelis breathe Judaism as they step on the streets. Zionism provides the unison of Judaism that Herzl dreamed about: the "tight connection between the most modern elements of Judaism with the most conservative."

But this was not the case in Israel's first 70 years. The way Zionism evolved prevented this from happening until recently. In the 1930s, a revolutionary secular stream won elections to the Zionist institutions and subsequently consolidated power. This group, led by David Ben-Gurion, was in power for 40 years and reshaped the Zionist ethos. Hence, Israel's independence and formative years were characterized with a particular flavor of Zionism.

Under those Zionist leaders a new society was formed in the Land of Israel: A new language, a new culture, a new dress code, a new pattern of thinking, a new hope. This was not about continuing Diaspora Judaism back home in Israel – on the contrary. Ben-Gurion and his colleagues orchestrated a divorce from the past. That included a divorce from the religious past.

As a result, Zionism evolved to be a staunchly secular movement that was even perceived to suppress Jewish religiosity. This was a primary hurdle that prevented Zionism from becoming the organizing principle of Judaism. An ideology that is associated with the rejection of religion cannot serve as the anchor for Judaism. Yet, there were other hurdles as well. This includes the fierce objection to Zionism by the Haredis (ultra-Orthodox), who are a significant portion of the Jewish world and of Israel's citizens.

In addition, Zionism evolved to be a socialist movement at the time when a significant degree of the world Jewish population was capitalist and outright rejected socialism. Also, Israel was poor and under existential military threat, which prevented Zionism from being an anchor of Judaism. Finally, given its daunting challenges in the early years, Israel put a halt on the topic of Israel's religiosity by locking in a status quo. The status quo deferred any discussion about the Jewish nature of the Jewish state to an unspecified later date. Those hurdles have now been removed.

Israel has been experiencing a religious resurgence amongst its secular community. The Jewish religion has become popular in recent years in those same secular circles that once utterly rejected it. Israeli seculars are increasingly engaging with the Jewish religion while staying secular. They are not on a trajectory towards becoming observant – they do not keep Shabbat, put on tefillin every morning, wear a kipa, attend synagogue or keep kosher. But they shifted from the previous generation's suppression of religiosity, and are engaging with the Jewish faith selectively – whether by studying the weekly Torah portion, attending Jewish religious classes or observing rituals, like the Shabbat kiddush. Thus, a new Israeli secular has emerged: The Datlaf, a Hebrew acronym for "sometimes religious." The Datlaf consumes religious experiences a-la-carte, while staying secular.

In a sense, Israeli seculars are rebelling against the rebels. While the country's founders revolted against the previous generation's religiosity, today's generations of Israelis are revolting against the founders who robbed them of Jewish religious experiences and went too far in stripping Judaism from Zionism.

In addition, there is a de-sectorization of Israeli society. This includes the blurring of old demarcations between seculars, traditionals, National-Religious and ultra-Orthodox. This allows an Israeli to consume experiences previously available only to members of other sectors, including religious experiences. As a result, Israeli seculars increasingly engage in, and are exposed to religious experiences. There has also been a shift of power from the secular minority that ruled Israel since its founding, to the religious/traditional majority, estimated to be about 60% of the population. This group has historically been under-represented in government, civil service, the media, legal system and academia, and hence, had less of a say in shaping Zionism's ethos. That is now rapidly changing. Perhaps symbolic of this change is the election in June 2021 of a religious person, Naftali Bennett, as the prime minister of Israel.

In addition, shifts within Israel's religious communities contribute to the greater role of the Jewish religion in Zionism. The National-Religious community is today a leader in military service, community volunteering and Zionist education. To a large degree, it is holding the baton of ideology and optimism that was held in the early days by the socialist seculars. The emergence of the "religious-lites," who are more integrated with Israeli secular society than others in the religious community, sprinkles the Israeli experience with more of a Jewish feel, and transplants a boost of ideology and of optimism.

At the same time, the ultra-Orthodox (Haredi) are no longer anti-Zionist. In fact, while staying insular, they have turned into a "poster-child" of Zionism. This is reflected in a de facto embrace of Zionist ideology, the centrality of the Jewish nation in theology, in physical settlement of the Land of Israel, as well as in Haredi contribution to Israeli society, such as through motorcycle medics who save hundreds of Israeli lives each year. Diaspora Haredi Jews travel to Israel much more frequently than other Jews and connect to one another through Israel. It is fair to say that today all sectors and groups in Israeli Jewish society pivot around Zionism in one way or another.

In addition, the greater engagement between Israeli Jewish and Arab populations provides tailwind to the transformation of Judaism. Israeli Arabs are going through a process of Israelization, but not Judaization. Their interaction with the Jewish state and Jewish society is through the national aspect of Judaism, certainly not the religious one. While Israeli Arabs are not Zionist, they are an emerging elite in certain sectors of the Jewish state – such as in medical professions, the pharmaceutical industry as well as in culture and entertainment. Similarly, the rising Arab-philia in Israeli Jewish society – on the left and right alike – allows for a mutual celebration of the particularity of each society, as opposed to negation, as the case is in Europe.

Israeli Jews celebrate Arab particularity through consuming Arab art, culture, and cuisine. For example, Arab hip-hop music is heard in popular Tel Aviv cafes and bars. The political conflict does not negate the cultural fondness. This is portrayed, for example, in Israeli TV shows *Fauda* and *Tehran*. The trend of embracing Middle Eastern culture in Israel is also a byproduct of the shift in Israeli ethos and power previously discussed. The shift from the secular minority to the religious/traditional majority shadows a shift from the old European Ashkenazi elite, to Israeli Jews of Middle Eastern Sephardi ancestry.

The Israeli ecosystem supports the transformation of Judaism, as there is also a gradual shift of power and cultural ethos from Tel Aviv to Jerusalem. While Tel Aviv remains a beacon of creativity and innovations, it has been associated with a culture of cynicism that hindered such transformation. The shift to Jerusalem is a shift from a tone of skepticism to one of optimism, from complaints about the half-empty to great appreciation of the half-full, as well as to a greater focus on religiosity and ideology that is associated with Jerusalem.

Herzl predicted that the Jewish state would exist because it would be a necessity of the world. Israel today is becoming that necessity in Herzl's prediction. This is due to its technology breakthroughs, medical innovations, daring social experiments, as well as its military strength and much-needed intelligence and cyber capabilities that are shared with allies.

Indeed, Israel's success across multiple fields and industries has turned Zionism to be a "light to the nations" as well as a light to Judaism. Developments in American Jewry, where 80% of Diaspora Jews reside, make it clear that through positive and negative, Zionism has become the most relevant (or for some, the least irrelevant) aspect of Judaism.

America's Jewish Community – Losing Its Old Glues

The core of the American Jewish community is on a path of evaporation. It is reflected in the relatively low engagement with Judaism, and it is a byproduct of the century-old attempt to denationalize the Jewish nation-religion in America.

The fading of old glues that held American Jewry together serve as an impetus for the transformation to Judaism 3.0. A new conduit is needed for Jews to connect to their Judaism. As shown in this book, it is increasingly evident that Zionism is becoming that conduit – both through positive and negative connections.

Over 95% of today's American Jews arrived in the last 140 years. Upon arrival in America, most Jewish immigrants were religious, spoke Yiddish, worked in a profession regarded as Jewish, had a predominantly Jewish circle of friends and married other Jews. Being part of the Jewish nation-religion was at the top of their hierarchy of identities.

But over the years, those American Jews Americanized, assimilated, got out of the Jewish ghetto – physically and metaphorically. A denationalization of the Jewish nation-religion occurred, reducing American Judaism to the "Jewish Church."

This was revolutionary. Judaism has been a closed nation-religion since its inception. An early attempt to denationalize Judaism was made in Western Europe in the 19th century, but it only affected a small percentage of world Jewry. Most stayed in the Jewish ghetto or some form of it in Eastern Europe, the Middle East and even in Western Europe, where the majority of the Jews remained in their insular Jewish communities. America was the first widespread attempt at Jewish denationalization. This attempt has failed.

The Jewish nation-religion in America went through a concurrent process of denationalization, reducing itself to the Jewish religion, and massive secularization, eroding its religious connector.

By the late 20th century, most American Jews connected to their Judaism through temporary replacement glues: the memory of the Holocaust and nostalgia to the Eastern European past. By the third decade of the 21st century, these temporary connectors have all but faded, as the immigrant generation and Holocaust survivors are passing away. The Jewish grandmother served not only as a conduit to one's Judaism but also as a powerful reminder of the duty to stay Jewish: "Do not let the Nazis win."

Today, most grandmothers of young American Jews were born in America after the Holocaust, and do not speak Yiddish. The "Jewish grandmother" has turned into the "American grandmother." The guilt-reminder to stay Jewish has faded.

Not only individual Jews are losing old connection points to Judaism, but also American Jewry as a whole is losing its legacy distinctions. There is a reduction of Jewish influence and perceived power along with dispersion of American Jewish wealth. The rich uncle became the old uncle. Perhaps this is reflected symbolically in the fact that the two Jewish politicians who ran for President in the 2020 elections were close to 80 years old (Bernie Sanders and Michael Bloomberg).

Attempts to connect Jews to Judaism through Tikun Olam (repairing the world) have failed since this is not particular to Judaism. Indeed, a Jew who wishes to help save the environment, advance human rights or help the poor, typically does so without wearing a "Jewish hat," but rather through non-Jewish organizations. Similarly, attempts to glue Jews in through community activities, and various other non-particular and low-octane connectors, have also failed and for the most part have not been sufficiently relevant to the contemporary life of the American Jew.

Increasingly, Jews are now experiencing Judaism, less through their current identity, but more through the traditions of their parents and grandparents: Yiddish culture, nostalgia for the Eastern European past such as through food, memory of the Holocaust, Jewish icons. The secular American Jew today connects to his Judaism primarily through the strong past, because his present association with Judaism is weak. Indeed, for most, Judaism is about tradition, not about vibrancy.

For a small percentage of American Jews, Judaism remains an integral part of life – these are the Orthodox Jews as well as those non-Orthodox who are involved in Jewish causes, such as active involvement in the local synagogue or a Jewish organization. Indeed, these groups are not on the same trajectory of evaporation that the majority of American Jews are, but, as discussed in the book, these are estimated collectively to be well below 20% of American Jews.

When analyzing American Jews, there is a tendency to focus on this minority group within American Jewry. This is where the heart of the Jewish community lies. These are the engaged Jews, and this is where data is available. The majority of American Jews on the other hand – those that are some place on the track of evaporation – are more difficult to analyze since they are not a closed community and their connection to Judaism is not through routine Jewish activities.

For most under-engaged American Jews, Judaism plays a role, but it is subordinate to other elements of their identity. Surveys indicate that 84% of American Jews do not regularly attend synagogue (of any stream), 85% do not keep kosher, and significantly over half do not marry a Jewish spouse (with some estimates being as high as 72% of non-Orthodox newlyweds).

The life of the secular American Jew is culturally similar to that of the American non-Jew. This is manifested in his circle of friends, social networks, activities and culture. He is not a Jew who happens to live in America as much as an American who happens to be Jewish.

Jewish evaporation is a natural progression after a century of Jewish life in America. It is an evaporation track similar to that experienced by other immigrant groups who came to America around the same time, such as the Irish and the Italians. Like them, American Judaism is gradually turning into a pan-American brand, available for consumption by all Americans. This is just like the American-Irish culture, it is now a brand consumed by all Americans. Indeed, Saint Patrick's Day parades are attended mostly by non-Irish. Similarly, Yiddish words are used by all Americans. Katz Deli's customers come from all backgrounds to consume a "Jewish experience." Even Seinfeld's audiences are mostly non-Jewish.

Ancillary cultural differentiation is also gone: Traditional lines between what was regarded as Jewish professions and non-Jewish professions have disappeared and the same goes when it comes to Jewish law firms and investment banks. For example, Goldman Sachs is no longer a Jewish firm and Morgan Stanley is no longer a WASPy firm, as they were perceived to be through the turn of the 21st century.

The bonding through some form of Jewish affiliation, such as membership in a Jewish organization, being a member of a synagogue, or even sending one's children to Sunday School, certainly exists, but such affiliation is not necessarily a key factor in Jewish priorities. Membership is easy and non-exclusive. The secular American Jew is also often a member of a social club or country club, alumni association, or a professional association. Somewhere in this hierarchy, the secular Jew may also hold a Jewish affiliation.

Paradoxically, if such an evaporation of American Jewry continues, then Judaism will turn to Judaism 3.0, since the overwhelming majority of Jews would be in Israel, where, as discussed, Zionism is the connecting ideological thread.

For some, the evaporation of American Jewry is not necessarily a negative. A small minority of Jews would welcome such dissipation. For centuries, the logic goes, Jews sought to integrate, to assimilate, to become German or French, but they were denied. Jews were not permitted to assimilate and were forced by their host nations to stay Jewish. Now they are accepted, now they are free to evaporate.

The majority of Jews, however, do not want to evaporate. The preponderance of American Jews want American Judaism to prevail. To do that, American Jews suddenly need Zionism. American Jews need Israel. A transformation to Judaism 3.0 is the alternative to evaporation of American Jewry and it is already happening.

There is a cultural Israelization of the American-Jewish experience. Israeli culture, cuisine, music, innovations, and vibrancy are replacing bagel and lox, gefilte fish, Holocaust and Yiddish. Wonder Woman is replacing Yentl and Gal Gadot is replacing Barbara Streisand.

This is enabled by the shift in the perception of Israel in the eyes of the American Jew – from poor to fun, from sympathy to admiration.

Indeed, at a time when staying in Judaism is a choice, it should be obvious that the more desirable items there are on the shelves of the Jewish connections supermarket, the more likely it is that a consumer will purchase at least one product. The Israeli supermarket has a wide range of relevant connections, while the old Jewish supermarket is limited and depends on "customer loyalty." An American Jew who is into wine can connect to his Judaism through the growing list of award-winning Israeli wines. An American Jew who is gay can connect to his Judaism through Israel's flourishing gay culture. An American-Jewish innovator can connect through Israel's high-tech industry. The American Jew is the one who chooses when to connect, how often and in what form.

This turns Judaism from a burden, chore and something that is predominantly associated with the past, into an asset, a want, and something that is genuine and relevant to the contemporary life of an American Jew.

Moreover, an American Jew is now able to connect through Israel without living in Israel or even visiting. Unlike a few years ago, Israel is now at his fingertips. He can access Israeli music in the exact same way the Israeli does – since neither of them use radios anymore. He can access Israeli TV shows and join Israel-related webinars. Zionism is no longer in a faraway land with faraway trees, it is in the American Jew's living room and available on demand.

This, in turn, allows an American Jew to have an attractive and accessible point of orientation for his Jewish life and to recenter his Jewish identity around his national connection to Judaism – around Zionism. It is a connection to Judaism by choice as opposed to by duty.

At the same time that Zionism is providing the American Jew with appealing connection points to Judaism, it is also turning into the most relevant Jewish American experience from the negative side. Criticism of Israel by a significant portion of American Jewry is also a form of connection to one's Judaism through Zionism. This too is a demonstration of the Jewish transformation. Such criticism is not against issues relating to Judaism 2.0, but against issues related to Judaism 3.0.

Moreover, for many of those Jews, criticism of Israel is the primary Jewish-related activity they engage in. Orthodox Jews, who are involved in Judaism on a daily basis, tend to be supportive of Israel's policies. For some Jews with low engagement with other aspects of Judaism, such criticism serves as a primary conduit to their Judaism – further evidence of the transformation to Judaism 3.0.

Zionism has become the primary arena in which Jews meet their Judaism, even for those Jews far out on the evaporation track who feel they have no connection to Judaism. Passing by a synagogue does not force a Jew into his Jewish identity. He simply does not go in, just as he does not go into a church. But Israel and Zionism does provide entry to one's Jewish identity.

An American Jew arriving on the college campus or socializing with progressive circles, is often "guilty by association" due to his last name, even if he is unaffiliated and detached from Judaism. This Jewish person might feel no other connection to Judaism, but he meets his Judaism because of Zionism. Hence, it is Zionism that defines his Judaism and not Rabbinic Judaism. It is his national association with Judaism, and not the religious one.

Centering one's identity around Israel was difficult in the past because the "ask" Israel put to American Jews was Aliya (immigration to Israel). However, by the 21st century, the Israeli government, society and even the Jewish Agency softened that expectation and now merely encourages American Jews to strengthen their connection with Israel.

The American Jew can choose from a range of alternative relationships with the Jewish state: Stay at home and consume Israeli experiences through a laptop or phone, be a serial visitor, own a vacation home in Israel or indeed make Aliya.

The shift from Aliya-Zionism, which is unfeasible for most American Jews, to Cloud-Zionism – where one can access Zionism easily, in a non-committal way and through his own choices – allows the American Jew to feel greater inclusion in Zionism and to more strongly connect to Judaism through Israel.

The renewed ability and necessity to connect through Israel comes hand-in-hand with changes in the composition of the American-Jewish community itself. There are more Persian Jews and Sephardi Jews. They not only tend to have stronger ties to Israel, but have more of their Jewish identity intertwined with Zionism. Most importantly, there are more

Israeli Americans in America, and they are more and more accepted by the Jewish community, even taking leadership roles in American Jewry. The Israeli Americans are no longer taxi drivers and movers who "must be kept away from our daughters," instead they are high-tech entrepreneurs, scientists, professors, lawyers, investment bankers and investors. Their on-the-ground presence further contributes to the cultural Israelization of the American Jewish experience, at the expense of legacy Yiddish culture. It also demystifies the concept of Zionism for American Jews. The association of Zionism is shifting away from nostalgia about the film *Exodus,* a blue box and those faraway trees. Indeed, for the previous generation of American Jews, Zionism was often bunched in with other legacy Jewish values that were "shoved down the young Jew's throat:" Holocaust, Lower East Side heritage and indeed supporting Israel.

The American Jews' ability to now see Israelis in their own circles – in restaurants, cafes, workplace, and increasingly even in their own families – provides an immediate identity benchmark. Perhaps symbolic of this Israelization of the American-Jewish experience is the December 2019 speech by President Trump at the Israeli-American Council. The President chose an Israel-related organization to address the Jewish community, and indeed his remarks were directed at American Jews at large, not just Israeli American Jews.

American Jews now have the means to connect to their Judaism through Zionism. This cycles back to the foundation of Zionism. Herzl did not only view Zionism as a movement to rescue the Jews but also as an organic Jewish ideal. It is exactly this aspect of Zionism which turns current developments in American Jewry into a primary enabler of the transformation to Judaism 3.0. Yet, an even bigger impetus to the Jewish transformation lies in the flagship feature of American Judaism: Intermarriage.

An estimated 50-70% of Jews marry non-Jews. For non-Orthodox Jews, the rate is estimated to be 60-80%. The intermarriage reality is far more prevalent than any other commonalities of American-Jewish life (such as routine synagogue attendance at 15%, or ever visiting Israel at 41%). Indeed, intermarriage is the number one common characteristic of American Jewry.

But Judaism 3.0 turns intermarriage from a foe to a friend. The "ask" is no longer Jewish prayer books in your library (unrealistic and a "chore"), but an "Israeli flag in your heart" (attainable and desirable).

Regardless of whether the non-Jewish spouse converts and what type of conversion is chosen, as this book shows, under Judaism 3.0, the non-Jewish spouse is more likely to seek engagement with Judaism and feel included than under legacy Judaism 2.0. This, in turn, will help keep the children and the next generations in the Jewish tent. This is not a halachic change. Recognizing the transformation to Judaism 3.0 does not represent an opinion on whether the spouse or the children are Jewish under Jewish law. It merely suggests that since the organizing principle of Judaism is the Jewish nation, the intermarried family is not excluded. More so, it provides the family with a set of attractive tools to strongly connect to their Judaism, which in turn allows them to be included.

A separate private issue would be the religious choices of such Jewish families. It is perfectly legitimate for a person in the next generation to choose not to marry someone because her mother did not go through an Orthodox conversion. This is just as it is perfectly legitimate for a person not to eat in a kosher restaurant, because its kosher certificate is not of a particular standard (for example, not Glatt kosher). Under Judaism 3.0, just as in the case of the kosher restaurant, the intermarried family is still in the Jewish tent, because they are connected to their Judaism through Zionism. This enables the sidestepping of halachic issues, without compromising them.

One common error made in analyzing American Jewry is the assumption that intermarriage and assimilation are the same. This is not the case. In fact, assimilation out of Judaism commonly occurs in families where both spouses are Jewish.

This is also true historically. The ancient nations that evaporated out of existence, such as the Canaanites, Moabites, and perhaps even the lost ten tribes of Israel, did not assimilate due to intermarriage. Most likely they assimilated because they began looking and acting more and more like their neighbors. They might have still married one another, but one could no longer tell the difference between a Moabite family and an Ammonite family.

Today, one can see the same patterns with American Jews. Non-Orthodox Jewish couples, having Judaism low in their hierarchy of identities, typically do not pass on sufficiently sustainable Jewish connectors to their children. The fact that their great-grandmother spoke Yiddish is not sufficient to prevent intra-marriage assimilation.

On the other hand, a child of an intermarried couple who goes on a Birthright trip and engages with Israel – through positive or negative aspects – is much more likely to stay Jewish than that of an intra-married couple who does not go on such trips and is agnostic about Israel.

While intermarriage has, until now, been a driver for assimilation, under Judaism 3.0 it can be turned around, and serve as a disrupter to assimilation!

More so, assimilation needs to be understood in terms of what the Jew is assimilating to. The American Jew is not assimilating to Christianity or paganism. He is assimilating to Americanism, which, as will be discussed, by its core nature is intertwined with Zionism.

An assimilated American Jew is a Zionist American Jew – not because he is a Jew, but because he is an American.

Herzl's disciple, Chaim Weizmann, said that Zionism is about "Judaizing the Jewish communities." It seems that a century later, Zionism is achieving exactly that for American Jews. Religion and legacy Jewish culture are receding, but instead of evaporation, Zionism enables American Jews not only to cling to Judaism, but indeed to strengthen their Jewish identity. It is the American Jew's ticket to the return to Judaism.

America - A Religious Society Intertwined With Zionism

Shifts in America provide tailwind to the Jewish transformation and to the ability of an American Jew to center his Jewish identity around Zionism.

The contemporary American ethos is arguably more compatible with Zionism being the anchor of Judaism (Judaism 3.0), than it is with a secular version of religious Judaism being the anchor (Judaism 2.0). This is in part because America and Israel are both religious societies, while American Jews are not.

In his Presidential victory speech in November 2020, Joe Biden said, "On eagle's wings, we embark on the work that God and history have called upon us to do." He described America's mission to spread the faith, and in the last sentence of his speech, mentioned God three times. Kamala Harris makes frequent religious references, such as calling the current year, "The year of our lord."

Indeed, America is a deeply religious country, but American Jews are not. In fact, they are perceived to be flag-carriers of secularism in America and at the forefront of efforts to make America feel less religious.

Israel, like America, is a deeply religious country. This is reflected both through its religious/traditional majority and through the increasing consumption of religious experiences by its secular minority.

Zionism allows the American Jew not only to have a relevant conduit to his Judaism but also to be associated with a religious society (Israel), even though he himself is not.

It is not only that Americans are religious, but Americanism has been and remains a religious ideal. Notwithstanding the sacred separation of church and state, America was established as One Nation Under God. On its currency an American motto is clearly stated: "In God we Trust". Hence, there is a perceived structural disconnect between American Jews' secular-phila, and the American ideal.

Once Jews stop defining themselves as a religious minority that does not practice religion (Judaism 2.0), and instead redefine themselves more naturally through their ethnological national affiliation, Zionism (Judaism 3.0), they will be in greater unison with the predominant American ethos. Judaism as Zionism is much more in tune with Americanism than Judaism as secularism

The greater compatibility with Zionism is also a product of the evolving nature of America. In the early days, America was dominated by the homogeneous "Mayflower narrative." Hence, the Jews who wanted to fit in and resemble their patriotic American neighbors felt they had to suppress their Jewish ethnological national identity.

But America has shifted and today there is a broad embrace of multiple cultural branches of Americanism, as long as they are anchored in the strong core American trunk. The patriotic neighbors of the Jews celebrate their own ethnological national affiliation – be it Mexican, Irish or Korean. That is manifested by Vice President Kamala Harris, who is proud of her Jamaican and Indian affiliations.

In addition to the consensus American trend to embrace one's heritage identity, there is also a broad recognition that an American has multiple identities – his profession, sexual orientation, race, state and indeed his ethnological national affiliation.

Therefore, a Jew proudly showcasing his own ethnological national affiliation (Zionism) is a great expression of Americanism.

America and the world are in an age of clarity. Gray is out; being out is in. This includes being clear about who you are, and being proud of your identity.

When protesters throughout America took to the streets in the spring and summer of 2020, they made it clear that they would no longer be defined or profiled by outside "authorities," that the time had come for them to be clear about who they are, and how they feel – to be true to their own identity.

The age of clarity is in part a counter-reaction to the politically correct and overly hedgy cultures that preceded it (saying what you believe you are supposed to say, as opposed to saying what you believe). In this context, an American Jew who suppresses his ethnological national affiliation (Zionism, Israel) is not only out of touch with his Jewish heritage, but is also out of touch with the contemporary American mentality.

Moreover, from its beginning, America was about the renewal of the ancient promise: The establishment of the new Jerusalem, the return to the new Zion, rejection of the oppressive dogmas of the European past, as well as the return to God and freedom of worship. From the onset, Americanism was a form of abstract Zionism. When tangible Jewish Zionism began to take shape, it was synergistic with the American version of Zionism.

Therefore, American Jews proudly showcasing their Zionist affiliation is also a powerful demonstration of the core essence of Americanism. Indeed, an American Jew is naturally drawn to Zionism not only because he is a Jew, but also because he is an American.

In addition, Israel is the most visible Jewish issue for Americans. America's strong and relevant alliance with Israel across a spectrum of arenas, such as the war on terrorism and military cooperation, and the frequent news coming out of Israel, places the Jewish state front-and-center in the American attention span, while issues related to Rabbinic Judaism and cultural Judaism certainly are not. For many Americans, in particular within progressive circles, criticism of the Jewish state turns Israel to be the primary Jewish issue. When presidential candidate Bernie Sanders, a harsh critic of Israel, was asked in 2019 about his Jewish affiliation, he chose to speak about Israel. Most of his supporters are not Jewish and are themselves critics of Israel. Hence, this perhaps is symptomatic of how such supporters as well as Americans in general relate to the Jew: through Israel – whether through support or through criticism.

While Israel serves as a relatable point-of-contact to Judaism, secular American Judaism (Judaism 2.0) is turning to be less and less relevant. This includes Judaism 2.0's association with American liberalism.

Both conservatives and liberals have issues with Judaism 2.0-associated liberalism. Conservatives have growing disdain for liberals, especially as the dialogue and discourse becomes more polarized. This while liberals have been shifting away from what some would perceive as "Jewish liberalism" towards one that outright rejects the previous version of liberalism (Progressives/Black Lives Matter/Occupy movement/Alt-Left). This is perhaps underscored by the June 2020 Democratic primary defeat of Congressman Eliot Engel, a staple of Jewish liberalism for four decades. After 32 years in Congress, he was defeated by Progressive candidate Jamaal Bowman, who represents the new American liberalism.

Judaism 2.0's role in shaping Americanism has eroded, while the outside contribution of Zionism to Americanism only increases.

In some regards, many Americans, in particular in the heartland and in the South, have a similar attitude towards Judaism that Israelis have: Both have developed a lack of fondness on some level to the "Diaspora Jew" (Judaism 2.0). While at the same time, both groups have an absolute admiration for the "Israeli Jew" – the one who fulfills the dream, who returned to his long-forsaken home, who unlike the "Diaspora Jew" is strong, daring, assertive, direct and bold (Judaism 3.0).

The United States and Israel are both countries that are firmly rooted in a bedrock of related ideologies: the United States is rooted in Americanism, Israel is rooted in Zionism.

While both American and Israel are religious countries, their anchor is a national one. This underscores the inevitable reality that most Americans view Judaism through the prism of the Jewish nation – through Judaism 3.0! But this is not just an American reality, it is a global reality as well.

The World – Long Viewed Jews As A Nation

Jews today are integrated into a global society and impacted by worldwide trends. Therefore, the state of Judaism is also a function of global developments and the shifting manner in which the world perceives the Jews.

Jews have been consistently viewed by the outside in a national context – by friends and foes alike. Indeed, the most hostile attacks against Judaism have been directed at Jews as a nation - not as a religion. Such was the case of the liquidation of Spanish Jewry in the 15th century – some by deportation and some by murder. One could not have converted out of the Jewish religion and be safe. On the contrary, conversion placed the Jews-turned-Christians under the jurisdiction of the Inquisition, which became the tool for the genocide of Spanish Jewry.

Similarly, four centuries later, the Holocaust was committed against the Jewish nation, not against the Jewish religion. Secular and atheist Jews were slaughtered alongside religious Jews. Here, too, one could not have converted out of the persecution. Same goes for the multiple deportations of Jews from European countries, the Dreyfus Affair, and the ethnic cleansing of Middle Eastern Jews. These were all directed at the Jewish nation, not at the Jewish religion. The world's treatment of Judaism has historically been a leading indicator to the state of Judaism, and this seems to be the case today as well.

Most notably, this is reflected in the current state of the relationship between Europe and the Jews. This relationship dates back 2,300 years to the Greek invasion of Judea and continued through centuries of Jewish refugees living in Europe. An estimated 80-90% of global Jews lived in Europe during most of the exile years. While there have been periods of peace, or at least containment, the Europe-Jewish relationship has repeatedly cycled back to conflict.

Europe has persistently and continuously objected to Judaism. Whatever form Judaism took, Europe was there to counter it, developing philosophies and mechanisms that were relevant to the evolving condition of Jews and Judaism. Similarly, the nature of European opposition to Judaism was also a function of evolving European realities: In the Middle Ages, when Europe was religious, the opposition to Judaism was manifested in seemingly religious persecution. In the 19th century, when Europe became increasingly secular, it was manifested in ethnological hatred. This hatred was given a new name towards the end of the 19th century: anti-Semitism.

This historical pattern continues today. Judaism evolved: The re-establishment of the Jewish state is the most astonishing development in the last nineteen centuries of Jewish history. As a result, Europe has funneled its entire opposition to Judaism through its relationship with Zionism and, by extension, the State of Israel.

The shift from European opposition to the Jews as individuals to the Jews as a collective is also consistent with European developments. Back when the world was decentralized, each monarch, then empire and then country, had their own relationship with their local Jewish population. The increased centralization and collective European mindset – the EU, the UN, multinational organizations – suggests that a collective approach be taken on the question of the Jews as well.

The establishment of a Jewish state allows a European to have a tangible conduit to express his opposition to Judaism. In this regard, the creation of the State of Israel does great service to the Jew-hater. It does not only provide an address for the opposition to Judaism but also a new vehicle to express it: Israel-bashing.

Israel-bashing has turned into a culture, fashion and code of conduct. The BDS coalition, which calls to boycott, divest and sanction Israel, is just a small part of it. While the hardcore of the Israel-bashing movement might still be on the fringe, its influence has been trickling into Europe's mainstream and from there to the rest of the world. It is expressed for example, in Europe's intense criticism of Israel's right to self-defense, in the intensity of European anger at the American decision to recognize Jerusalem as Israel's capital, and in its votes in a series of UNESCO resolutions that essentially denies Jewish ties to Jerusalem.

Today European anti-Semitism is no longer an existential threat to Judaism. Given European evolution over the past decades, there is no longer the fierce institutionalized objection to Jews nor to the Jewish religion (Judaism 2.0). While there are certainly dangers for Jews as individuals, Jews as a whole do not face the state-sponsored opposition they did in the past. Yet at the same time, there is rising and fierce European objection to Zionism (Judaism 3.0), including state-sponsored opposition.

In other words, Europe has settled its account with Judaism 2.0 and now has a new feud with Judaism 3.0. In doing so, it is helping define Judaism from the outside.

There are startling parallels between the evolution of the previous episode of European Jew-hatred – anti-Semitism, and the evolution of Israel-bashing.

Just like today, during the early days of the anti-Semitism movement in the second half of the 19th century, there was a debate about where to draw the line between legitimate criticism of Jews and outright Jew-hatred. No doubt, the emancipation of Jews in Europe had consequences: Jews were taking jobs from Europeans, they were amassing wealth, and were acting in the stock market in ways that damaged the interest of European miners and laborers. Some Jews no doubt engaged in antisocial behavior, and in manners that were contradictory to European culture. There were anti-Semites who had Jewish friends, and there were anti-Semites who sought to reform the Jews for the Jews' own benefit. Today as well, there is a recognition that much of the criticism of Israel is legitimate – whether one agrees with it or not. Similarly, those critical of Israel's policies must be defended from allegations that they are motivated by hate – indeed many of them have Israeli friends. Yet, one cannot ignore the contemporary European obsession with Israel. The dogmatic political opposition and blood libels ("massacre in Gaza" / "genocide in Palestine") cannot just be dismissed as "criticism" of Israel, just like the 1886 popular book *Jewish France* cannot simply be dismissed as criticism of Jews. Evolving European attitudes towards Jews, then and now, must be analyzed in the context of the contemporary state of Judaism.

Israel-bashing is the current evolution of centuries-old European Jew-hatred. It is much stronger, well financed, and integral to contemporary European culture and global society than previous iterations of Jew-hatred. Indeed, anti-Semitism was a fringe movement in the late 19th century and had fewer resources and buy-in than today's Israel-bashing. Tragically, 70 years since it appeared in Europe, anti-Semitism led to the Holocaust.

There is a clear shift in Europe: from opposing Judaism through anti-Semitism to opposing Judaism through Israel-bashing; from opposition to Judaism 2.0 to opposition to Judaism 3.0.

Yet, recognizing that Judaism has transformed would rob Israel-bashers of their prerequisite assumption: the premise that Judaism is merely a religion. It would clarify that Israel-bashing and Jewish-bashing are one and the same.

Israel-bashing is not just limited to Europe, but it incubates there and then spreads to Europe's sphere-of-influence. In May 2021, we saw how old European blood-libels get applied to the contemporary state of Europeanism and Judaism. Human-rights concepts championed by Europe were used as currency of opposition to the Jewish state. The eviction of eight Palestinian families in a property dispute was labeled by Israel-bashers as "Ethnic Cleansing" and the defensive actions against Hamas terrorists, who fired over 4,300 rockets into Israel, was labeled as "genocide." Social media enabled the anti-Israel poison to spread broad and deep. The ceasefire, after 11 days of conflict, put an end to the rockets coming from Gaza, but not to the anti-Israel hatred coming from the West. Such anti-Israel incitement came from all over the world, but the underlying Israel-bashing ideology has incubated in Europe. This too is consistent with the previous iteration of Europe's opposition to Judaism. The last round – anti-Semitism – was also not just limited to Europe, but it incubated there and exported out.

Then, just like now, it adopted local flavors. This is what Theodor Herzl identified early in his Zionist thinking: "We naturally move to those places where we are not persecuted, and there our presence produces persecution. This is the case in every country, and will remain so, even in those highly civilized."

Same goes for earlier manifestations of European opposition to Judaism. The blood libels that were a popular expression of European Jew-hatred when Europe was religious were not limited to Europe either. In 1840, Jews in Syria were accused of using human blood to prepare Passover Matzahs. The Damascus blood libel that shocked Syria and the Ottoman Empire at the time did not originate with the Arabs. It was orchestrated by French diplomats.

Europe brought this along with other anti-Jewish fables into the Middle East and within decades the ideas were adopted locally in Arab communities. Indeed, religious-based Jew-hatred, just like anti-Semitism and Israel-bashing that followed it, was a European export to the world. Hence, the evolving form of European opposition to Judaism helps define Judaism from outside.

And yet, two events serve as disrupters to those endless cycles of European animosity towards the Jews:
  – The American Revolution (establishment of new Zion) and
  – The founding of the Jewish state (re-establishment of old Zion).

America rebelled against deeply rooted European dogmas. Americans attained new freedoms that were unimaginable in Europe. This included the freedom from Europe's chronic opposition to Judaism. Not only Jews were free in America, but so was Judaism.

This new radical attitude towards the Jews became more significant at the turn of the 20th century, as global power had shifted from Europe to the United States. For the entirety of recorded history, Europe has dominated world affairs and dictated global perspectives, including attitudes toward the Jews. The rise of a new global power meant a disrupter to European opposition to Judaism.

While no longer the globally dominant factor today, Europe still wields disproportionate power over global affairs through multinational organizations that Europe funds and strongly influences. Those institutions' touch points with Judaism are with Zionism, not with religious Judaism. For example, the International Criminal Court is heavily funded by Europe and is housed in Europe. The court is not a threat to the Jewish religion – on the contrary, but it is certainly a threat to the Jewish nation. It has the capability to deliver paralyzing blows to Israel's security, economy and society, such as by threatening to arrest Israeli government officials, military personnel, settlers – in short, all Israelis; in short, the Jews. This is not just a theoretical conspiracy theory about Europe targeting the Jews. This is an ongoing multi-year active investigation, funded by European taxpayers.

The second disrupter, the re-establishment of the Jewish state, redefined Europe's relationship with the Jews. The European-Jewish relationship has never been that of co-equals. Jews were the miserable ones – a nation of refugees with no rights residing in the midst of Europe. In Europe's defense, how could one possibly expect them to swiftly change this attitude towards the Jew? Herzl understood that human psychology: "There is no use in suddenly announcing in the newspaper that starting tomorrow, all people are equal," he warned Otto von Bismarck, Germany's first Chancellor.

After Herzl's time, the situation only got worse: The establishment of the State of Israel meant that the Jew was not only suddenly equal but also suddenly strong. This was too difficult to swallow for Europeans after centuries of indoctrination. Indeed, as the Jews were on track to establishing their own state, European animosity to Judaism intensified to horrific proportions.

In recent decades, the Church's view towards Jews and Judaism radically changed, and indeed religious European Christians today embrace the strong Jew. But sadly, the European-Israeli relationship has cycled back to conflict yet again in part due to the shift from a religious Europe to an atheist Europe. The strong Jew represents an insurmountable problem for the secular European whose religious point of reference is stuck back in the Middle Ages, where the Church's view towards the Jews was hostile.

The astonishing success of the Jewish state in recent years makes this problem even worse. Perhaps a weak State of Israel could have been contained, but in the 21st century, as the Jew went from equal to strong to powerful, the 2,300-year-old European-Jewish conflict is once again escalating.

Historically, European disdain for Jews was amplified whenever there were growing frustrations in Europe. During times of European flourishment, the Jews typically did well. When things went bad in Europe, the Jews were to blame.

Such was the case during the black death pandemic in the mid-1300s, when Jews were massacred in "response" to the plague. Such was the case after France's humiliating defeat to Prussia in 1870, which led to the Dreyfus Affair, and such was the case in Germany's humiliating defeat in World War I, which led to the Holocaust.

Since the end of World War II, Jews in Europe and around the world have been living in yet another Golden Age. But Europe's fortunes are changing. A series of frustrations are emerging that will have an inevitable impact on Europe's attitude to Judaism.

First and foremost is Europe's trench war against Islamic terrorism, which is still in its early stage. Europe is not remotely prepared for the magnitude, cruelty and amorphous nature of this war. European fingers are already being pointed at the Jews, but this time it is specifically pointed at the Jewish state (Judaism 3.0). There is a mainstream European view that the Israeli-Arab conflict is a cause of terrorism around the world. If we "address" the Israeli occupation, the logic goes, Europe would be safer.

The Jewish transformation is not only evident by the evolving nature of the world's opposition to Judaism. There is outright admiration for the Jewish state in Asia, Africa, Latin America, North America, parts of Europe and even the Middle East. Such admiration for Israel translates into renewed admiration of Judaism. This is indicative of a Jewish transformation.

The world seeks an engagement with Judaism. This is particularly true for Christians, many of whom feel they want to "come back home." In part this is driven by intra-Christian movements to understand Jesus better, to feel what he felt living in Judea. This Christian yearning to come back home to Judaism is not possible from a religious point of view. Hence, under the existing Jewish architecture, there remain built-in amicable tensions. But recognizing that Judaism has transformed to Judaism 3.0 would allow Christians to get much closer to Judaism, while staying devout Christians, and without posing a threat to the Jewish religion.

Judaism 2.0 (Rabbinic Judaism) proactively rejects Christianity. It has been doing so since the time of Jesus. Judaism 3.0 (Zionism) on the other hand, invites Christians to get closer. One does not need to be a "member" in order to be a friend.

Being friends of Zionism (Judaism 3.0) is much easier than being Friends of religious Judaism (Judaism 2.0). Moreover, it was the particular manner in which Judaism developed – Rabbinic Judaism – that made a point to emphasize the contrasts between Judaism and Christianity.

Similarly, the Jewish religion does not have the language that would allow such rapprochement. Jewish particularity and religious laws make it impossible for this kind of "coming back home." The Jewish religion discourages Christians and other non-Jews from converting to Judaism. (Conversions in Jewish law are performed under the theory that the converted person is reconnecting to an old Jewish past.)

On the other hand, failure to transform can be dangerous for both religions. The yearning to get closer to Judaism is already manifested in hybrid solutions, such as "Messianic Jews." The transformation to Judaism 3.0 provides a framework for Christians and other non-Jews to "come back home," without any compromises to the Jewish religion or the distinct particularity of Judaism.

Recognizing that Judaism has transformed would dispel Jewish fears that Christians are trying to convert them, and would draw clear lines: Christians are getting close to the Jewish nation, not to the Jewish religion, and moreover, they are doing so without intentions to become part of it.

This is already manifested through various Christian organizations such as Friends of Zion, the League for Friendship, Christians for Israel and various other organizations whose focus is not about being pro-Judaism 2.0, but rather about being pro-Judaism 3.0.

Recognizing the transformation would allow Christians to extend their friendship, not only to the State of Israel and to Israelis, but also by extension to Judaism and Jews as a whole.

The rivalry between Europe and Israel will remain, but recognizing the transformation would end remaining traces of the 2,000-year-old rivalry between Christianity and Judaism – an artificial rivalry that is a byproduct of the European-Israeli conflict. It could lead to a Judeo-Christian front – a form of a confederacy of two distinct and separate sister religions.

Indeed, from the perspectives of both love and hate, from motivation of both support and opposition to Judaism, it is evident that the world is already at Judaism 3.0

Judaism 3.0 – Judaism's Transformation

Judaism is transforming. Rabbinic Judaism (Judaism 2.0) was effective as Judaism's organizing principle during centuries of exile, when Jews were religious and when there was an outer wall to Judaism. Circumstances have now changed.

The following table shows the shift in Judaism's organizing principle:

	Temple, Sacrifices, Jerusalem, Judea	Halacha, Rituals, Learnings, Oral Torah	Jewish Nationalism
Judaism 1.0 Biblical Judaism (10th c. BCE – 1st CE)	**Judaism's organizing principle**	√	√
Judaism 2.0 Rabbinic Judaism (1st c. CE – 20th c.)		**Judaism's organizing principle**	√ (Mitigated due to exile)
Judaism 3.0 Zionism (21st c. –)		√ (Mitigated due to secularization)	**Judaism's organizing principle**

The organizing principle is certainly not the only thread of Judaism. Indeed, Israelis' increased engagement with the Jewish religion facilitates the shift in Judaism's organizing principle from Rabbinic Judaism to Zionism.

Moreover, Zionism does not only draw from the previous organizing principle of Rabbinic Judaism, but it is also inseparable from it. The shift is a natural progression in Judaism's evolution.

"No portion of my argument is based on a new discovery," Herzl stated in the preface to his manifesto *The Jewish State*. Same should be said about the idea that Judaism is transforming and that Jews coming back to their land after 2,000 years and forming a Jewish state is a transformative event in Judaism.

In the early 20th century Rabbi Abraham Isaac Kook spoke about the theological and redemptive context of Zionism. In 1981, Rabbi Irving Greenberg wrote "The Third Great Cycle of Jewish History" and argued that just as the Biblical era of Judaism was shaped by the Exodus from Egypt and the Rabbinic era by the destruction of the Temple, the third era of Judaism is shaped by the Holocaust and the birth of the State of Israel. Others have also argued that the establishment of the State of Israel represents a new period in Judaism.

And yet, recognizing that Zionism is now the organizing principle of Judaism is far from obvious. Indeed, so far this has not been broadly acknowledged. In the previous transformation of Judaism, it took centuries to recognize that Judaism had transformed – that it was no longer about a nation living in Judea; no longer about the Temple and sacrifices.

As described in this book, the transformation to Judaism 3.0 is increasingly evident and is ripe for broad recognition. Just like Herzl described his original vision 120 years ago, today's transformation is the result of an inescapable conclusion, rather than that of a flighty imagination.

Herzl understood that his ideas would encounter both external and internal opposition: "We shall have to endure hard and bitter struggles: with regretful Pharaohs, with our enemies, and above all with ourselves," he wrote.

The recognition of the transformation to Judaism 3.0 addresses the multiple camps of opposition. It allows secular, unaffiliated and religious Jews alike to embrace Judaism while at the same time it provides the vehicle for the world's nations to finally accept Judaism.

In discussing the opposition to Zionism, Herzl once wrote: "How can we tell the power of an idea? – When we see that nobody can ignore it – whether he is for it, or against it."

Zionism today is the one aspect of Judaism that cannot be ignored – not by Jews and not by the outside world. That is because, as this book shows, Zionism has become the organizing principle of Judaism.

III

From Judaism To Zionism

The transformation to Judaism 3.0 needs to be placed in its historical context, recognizing that Judaism has also transformed in the past. The following table is a snapshot of the evolution of Judaism:

		Jewish Population		
		Europe	America	Israel
Judaism 1.0 - Biblical Judaism	10C BCE ↓ 1C CE	0%	0%	~90-100%
Judaism 2.0 - Rabbinic Judaism	1C CE			
	↓	~80-90%	~0%	<5%
	1895	Zionism established		
		Opposition to Zionism	Opposition to Zionism	
	1917	Zionism recognized		
	1935		Zionism recognized	Yishuv takeover of Zionism
	1948			Jewish state established
	↓			
Judaism 3.0 - Zionism	21C CE	~5%	~40%	~45%

1. From Judaism 1.0 to Judaism 2.0

Since early in its establishment, Judaism was associated with the Temple, the ritual of the sacrifices, Jerusalem and the Land of Israel. That was the architecture that bound together world Judaism, as evidenced by the Biblical narrative, archeology and historical accounts. The Temple provided the tangible manifestation of Judaism for the Jew, regardless of whether he actually worshiped there, and was the anchor that kept Jews together. Hence, when the Romans destroyed the Temple in the first century CE, they destroyed Judaism's anchor. Soon thereafter, the architecture that served as the organizing principle of Biblical Judaism collapsed. Not only was the Temple destroyed, and the ritual of sacrifices ceased, but the Jews were also deported from Jerusalem and eventually from the Land of Israel.

Astonishingly, Judaism survived. It did so by going through a dramatic transformation: from Biblical Judaism being the organizing principle of Judaism (Judaism 1.0) to Rabbinic Judaism serving in this role (Judaism 2.0).

2. Two thousand years of Judaism 2.0

Rabbinic Judaism radically shook the core of Jewish life. Moving away from the previous focus on the Temple, the priests and customs based on the physical presence in the Land of Israel, Rabbinic Judaism evolved to accommodate the new realities of the Jewish nation-religion being in exile.

The synagogues replaced the Temple as the Jewish point of orientation. The structured prayers replaced the sacrifices as the method of worship. The insular life in the Jewish ghetto replaced the insular life in Judea. With Jews away from Jerusalem, the yearning to return to Zion became a cornerstone of Rabbinic Judaism.

In addition, the Oral Torah was canonized to complement the Written Torah. The infrastructure for setting rules and laws governing Jewish life was put in place (halacha), and rituals and customs developed.

The transformation to Rabbinic Judaism as Judaism's organizing principle was successful. Eventually, most of the Jews, with the notable exception of the Karaites, adopted Rabbinic Judaism, and Judaism prevailed throughout the next 1,800 years of exile. Consequently, today, the terms Judaism and Rabbinic Judaism are essentially interchangeable.

The Jews stayed a closed nation-religion in their various host countries until modern times. At the end of the 18th century, it is estimated that 80-90% of the Jews lived in Europe, the vast majority of them in Eastern

Europe. [1] Living in insular communities, it was obvious to the Jews, as it was to others, that the Jews are a distinct nation, composed of individuals who are connected to one another, and not to the people amongst whom they reside.

(i) Core to Judaism 2.0: Defined by both Jews and the Outside as a Jewish nation

The complete insularity and rigid walls kept Judaism intact from the outside, and the religious glue of Rabbinic Judaism preserved Judaism from the inside. Jews miles apart prayed in the exact same manner and at the same time, practiced the exact same religious rituals, adhered to the exact same Jewish laws.

Jews throughout Europe and the world were united through the various components that made up Rabbinic Judaism (Judaism 2.0): Shabbat, the religious holidays, the Jewish calendar, halacha, the rituals and study of the Torah. Once a month at the same time, Jews all over the world declared: "All Israel are friends."

The rabbis typically served as both community and religious authorities and usually represented the Jewish interests to the rulers of the areas in which they resided. [2]

The Jewish village, the Jewish ghetto, the Jewish neighborhood, the Pale of Settlement, the Jewish shtetls – through all of these places of residence, Jews were defined by their distinct and closed national identity.

In some ways, Jews seemed like any other nation. Just as other nations at the time did not have a flag, anthem or modern-day national characteristics, neither did the Jews. (Other nations were connected, for example, through loyalty to a king or an empire.)

Until the 19th century, there was a universal external and internal recognition that the Jews had no option or path to meld with the nations where they resided. A Jew living in Austria was obviously more closely aligned with a Jew living in Russia than he was with an Austrian living in Austria. Similarly, there was no such thing as an Austrian Jew marrying an Austrian non-Jew. The Jew will marry another Jew – if not from

---

1 – Benjamin Harshav: "Language in Times of Revolution: The Modern Jewish revolution and the renaissance of the Hebrew Language".

2 – This was done both informally and formally, such as through The Council of Four Lands that represented Jews in the 16th-18th century. For more on Jewish life in exile, see Alex Bein: "The Jewish Question" and Simon Dubnow: "World History of the Jewish People". Visit the book's website (Judaism-Zionism.com) for information and links to books and articles referenced in the book, as well as for additional bibliography.

Austria, then from Poland, Russia or some place else.

While not labeled as such, Jewish nationalism was always organic and obvious to what being Jewish meant. Core to that Jewish identity was an eternal yearning to go back to where they came from – to Judea, the Land of Israel.

(ii) Core to Judaism 2.0: Yearning to Return

Indeed, one of the pillars of the Jewish religion was the yearning to return to the ancestral homeland. Not only was the prayer to return recited three times a day, but also much of the infrastructure and theology of Rabbinic Judaism was built around this yearning. The Romans changed the name of Judea to Palestine, punitively named after the Philistines, the Biblical arch-rival of the Jews, who have long been extinct. But no name change could alter the strength of connection that prevailed through the exile years between Jews and Judea.

For many Jews, the quest to return was not a hypothetical concept. The yearning was so strong and core to Judaism, that it amounted to a belief that one day this return would occur; the exile was temporary. Many viewed the return in a messianic context, waiting for the Messiah to take them back to Judea. Yet, the primary failure to return was not the notion that the Messiah had yet to arrive, it was simply due to inaction.

This is exactly what Theodor Herzl identified as the malaise of Judaism during 2,000 years of exile. He concluded that it was not the persecutions, as much as the absence of united political leadership, that would create the conditions for the return of the Jews to their land.

The lack of united leadership prevented a mass return, but there was also a built-in resignation to the exile. There was a Talmudic determination, core to Rabbinic Judaism, that "because of our sins we have been exiled from our land and sent far from our soil." Jews have been reciting this every Shabbat and holiday in the prayer of Mussaf, and so there was an acceptance that life in exile was a punishment from God. This was synergistic with the concurrent Christian concept of Replacement Theology – indeed the Jews have sinned and therefore they now live in poor conditions in exile. Moreover, Jews living in such conditions must remain as the suffering remnant.

In neither the Jewish rationale nor the Christian rationale, was there an actionable tangible path for the return. Jews prayed for forgiveness for those sins and just waited, hoping their prayers would one day pave a path for their return. Christians offered no path of forgiveness as long as Jews stay Jewish.

Hence, the temporary state of exile was accepted as "permanent temporariness," and no significant efforts were made to change it. The plan to return was replaced by the sanctification of the yearning to return.

The inaction and failure to go back to the Land of Israel was well depicted in the 11th century by Yehuda Halevy in his book, *The Kuzari*.[3] In this book, a rabbi discusses the merit of Judaism with the King of the Khazars. The rabbi can answer every question and challenge about the Jewish religion posed to him, except as to why the Jews are not returning to their land. Indeed, during the long sleepy years of exile (Judaism 2.0), the concept of the return evaporated into a dream.[4]

Furthermore, the concept of a faraway dream became a primary vehicle in which the Jews could connect to God. The dreams resided in the prayers.

While through most of the 1,800 years of exile, the notion of a mass return was not feasible without united Jewish leadership, there were various times in which the possibility to return was not impossible.

Nations migrated through the Middle Ages, and the Jews could have possibly done so as well – the gates to the Land of Israel were at many times open. In fact, when attempting to return as individuals or small groups, those attempts often succeeded. The political hurdles were not in the way, and at times, the rulers of the region even encouraged the return.

In the late 18th century, Palestine was administered by a Jew, Chaim Farahi. Given the power structure and the favor policy that was enacted during his time towards Jews in Palestine, it is likely that a more organized effort to return would have been successful.

When the French conquered Palestine in 1799, Napoleon issued a declaration calling for the Jews to return to their land and labeled them "the rightful heirs to Palestine." While Napoleon was eventually defeated and the French retreated, there was no evidence of Jews getting ready to come to Palestine (just like there were no massive movements over a century later when the British conquered Palestine and invited the Jews to come).

To sum, the lack of return was not primarily due to external reasons, but due to internal Jewish inaction – the lack of political leadership. Yet, some Jews did return.

---

3 – Kuzari, 2:23-24; For commentary on the book of the Kuzari, see Micha Goodman: "The King's Dream" (Hebrew).
4 – Referring to the failure to return to the Land of Israel as a sin, the rabbi makes a comparison to the inaction that was prevalent during the Babylonian exile. He explains that King Solomon, in "Song of Songs," referred to the state of exile as sleep.

(iii) Jews return in small groups

During 1,800 years of exile, Jewish settlements in various parts of Palestine came and went. At times, they grew and flourished. At other times, they were massacred out of existence, such as in the case of the crusades in the 11th century and in the Hebron massacre in the 20th century.

Leading rabbis returned through the Middle Ages individually or in small groups. In the 16th century, Jews began to return in a somewhat more organized way. This was prompted by the Ottoman takeover of Palestine as well as Spain's deportation of its Jews. The incoming Jews tended to settle in the Jewish communities that existed in the big cities: Jerusalem, Tsfat, Tiberius, Hebron and Gaza. Similarly, at the turn of the 19th century, students of one of Judaism's leading rabbis, the Gerah, were encouraged to return to their ancestral homeland, and so they did. Still, all of these were local initiatives of deeply religious Jews and not a pan-Jewish effort to return.

The returnees tended to be supported through donations from the Diaspora Jewish community. This system of Diaspora Jews financially supporting Jews in the Land of Israel was well rooted in the Jewish mantra. It solidified the connection of Judaism to the Land of Israel and amplified the notion that a return to the Land is a core aspect of Rabbinic Judaism. Those returnees were keeping the flame fueled, but it was actually in Europe where the Jewish flame began to recede.

(iv) Judaism 2.0 begins to fracture (1800s)

In the second part of the 19th century, European developments took place which affected the closed Jewish nation-religion. For the first time, Jews in the West were offered emancipation, which included rights and the ability to finally be part of their host nations: To be French, to be German.

But such emancipation, to a large extent, was expected to come along with Jews agreeing to shed their Jewish national affiliation and to narrow Judaism to a religion. This principle was laid out in a French parliament speech by Count Stanislas de Clermont-Tonnerre: "We must refuse everything to the Jews as a nation and accord everything to Jews as individuals."[5] Jews implicitly accepted this guiding principle through Napoleon's Sanhedrin in 1807 as well as in other countries in the West.

At the same time, secularism was on the rise. Those two processes

---

5 – Clermont–Tonnerre, Speech on Religious Minorities and Questionable Professions, 23 December 1789, French National Assembly.

– denationalization and secularization – posed a threat to Jewish sustainability, but the threat was confined to the small Jewish communities of Western Europe. The majority of Jews lived in insularity in the East and were not affected neither by denationalization nor secularization. Neither were the Jews of the Middle East, estimated to be about 10% of world Jewry at the time. They also remained insular and religious. But then came a massive wave of migration that changed this reality – first to Western Europe, and by the end of the 19th century, to the new world – to America. The exposure of the Jewish masses to the secular, emancipated West posed a new challenge to Judaism.

Core to Judaism 2.0 was the unity of the Jewish nation-religion. Due to the discussed processes, this unity began to fracture. These developments contributed to the 19th century split of Rabbinic Judaism into three main streams: Orthodox (the incumbent stream), Conservative and Reform. The latter two, fringe and small in 19th-century Europe, became paramount in the United States, primarily with German Jews who immigrated towards the end of the century. When the large wave of Eastern European immigrants followed, many of those previously Orthodox Jews joined the new streams, resulting in today's American Jewry being primarily Reform or Conservative.

(v) Denationalization of Judaism 2.0

Judaism has been a nation-religion since its inception. But once the Jews began moving to America, they began a process to shed their Jewish national identity and diminish Judaism to a religion. Denationalization and secularization that affected only a small percentage of Jews in Western Europe was now a growing phenomenon with the Jewish masses in the new world.

This was a radical departure from history. Indeed, the 20th century was the first time in 3,000 years of Jewish history, when a large group of Jews no longer perceived themselves as a nation.

(vi) Emergence of Anti-Semitism

The emancipation of Jews in Western Europe led not only to a process of denationalization of the Jewish nation-religion, but it also triggered a European counter-reaction. All of a sudden, Jews were competing with the locals for jobs and business. Jews became successful and some Jews amassed significant wealth and power. This led to the rise of a new popular counter-movement in Europe. Towards the end of the 19th century that popular movement was given a name: anti-Semitism. Suddenly, the centuries-old hatred towards the Jew was not directed towards the Jewish religion, but towards the Jewish nation. This caught Jews and non-Jews alike by surprise. The 19th century mass secularization in Europe led many to believe that European Jew-hatred was over. In a secular Europe, there was no longer a need to defend attacks on the Jewish religion, but suddenly there was a need to defend attacks on the Jewish nation.

(vii) Suppression of national sentiments

Not only did Judaism begin to denationalize in the 19th century, and new opposition to the Jewish nation emerged in the form of anti-Semitism, but Jews in Europe were also under pressure to suppress their Jewish national identity for another reason. This happened as increased sentiment of nationalism rose in the European nations in which the Jews lived. Soon, European nations began engaging in competing land claims and competing narrative claims against one another. Suppressing their own national aspiration was a natural reaction for the Jews. This was surmountable since they had the strong religious element to cling to as Judaism's organizing principle.

Still, the rise of nationalism in Europe trickled into Jewish circles. Various Jewish groups began applying European national concepts to Judaism and fused them with the old yearning to return. Most notably, Chovevei Zion groups were set up in Russia and Poland, and served as platforms for small-scale immigration to Palestine in the 1880s and 1890s. At the same time, in Western European cities such as Koln, Jewish intellectuals began thinking about Jewish nationalism, discussing it and even writing about it, but it was not until the surprise appearance of one man that things began to change.

3. Emergence of political Zionism (1895)

On February 14, 1896, a small brochure was published in Vienna by a small-press publisher – it was called *The Jewish State*, and was written by a relatively unknown journalist named Theodor Herzl. "My life is about to change," Herzl wrote that day in his diary, and indeed it changed, and so has the course of Judaism.

In the following year, Herzl convened the first Zionist Congress, which ratified the Basel Program, an action plan for the creation of a Jewish home in the Land of Israel. The yearning for the return to Zion turned from a dream into an organized movement.

(i) Zionism as a solution to a need

The rejection of emancipated Jews in Western Europe, the rise of the anti-Semitism movement and growing violence against Jews in Eastern Europe contributed to the urgency of finding a solution to the "Jewish question" – What to do with the Jews of Europe? Zionism provided such a solution – resettlement of the Jews back to their ancestral homeland.

That solution was met with warmth by other stakeholders: The German Kaiser viewed it as a way to rid the undesirable elements in his empire, the British establishment viewed it as a way to fulfill an old prophecy, the Russian Czar's government viewed it as a way to address the threatening rise in socialism, and Arabs viewed it as a way to promote Arab aspirations and interests in the Middle East.

Zionism addressed the needs of the Jews and of the world, but as it was designed by Herzl, Zionism was about much more than a solution to a need.

(ii) Zionism as an Infinite ideal

Herzl's Zionism was not designed merely as a process to re-institute the Jewish state. Herzl's Zionism was designed as a Jewish philosophy, an ideal. It remains an ideal.

"There are those who do not understand us properly and believe that the purpose of our effort is to return to our land," Herzl said in a speech in 1899. "Our ideal goes well beyond that. Our ideal is the vision of grand eternal truth; it is an ideal that always moves forward; it is an ideal that is infinite, that forever grows, in such a way that with every step forward that we take, our horizon expands in front us, and in its perspective, we see an even greater and more noble purpose to which we strive."

Indeed, Zionism was designed by Herzl as a vehicle for the betterment of Judaism. The migration to the Land of Israel was a method to achieve this, but not the sole essence of Zionism. With Zionism as its anchor, Jews would once again fulfill their latent potentials, and nations would benefit once more from the ingenuity of the Jews.

"God would not have kept us alive so long if there was not a role left for us to play in the history of mankind," Herzl wrote in his diary as he was drafting his Zionist vision. For Herzl, the purpose and context of the return was clear.

(iii) Zionism as a Jewish concept

Contrary to popular belief, when Herzl established political Zionism, it was by no means anti-religious. The first Zionist Congress was launched with the blessing of *Shehehiyanu* – thanking God for bringing us to this moment. In his inauguration speech launching the movement, Herzl stated: "Zionism is the return to Judaism, even before it is the return to the Land of the Jews."

Zionism as a return to Judaism was a key thread in Herzl's vision. In that same inaugural address that kicked off political Zionism, Herzl said: "Already Zionism was able to achieve something magnificent, that was considered before, impossible: The tight connection between the most modern elements of Judaism with the most conservative."

For Herzl, right from the start, it seemed clear what would connect the various factions of Judaism. What would connect the Eastern-European Jews and the Western-European Jews, the rich and the poor, the religious and the seculars? The connecting thread for Jews around the world was Zionism!

(iv) Herzl

Born in Budapest, Hungary in 1860, Herzl was raised in a secular environment with a strong Jewish awareness. He likely drew a tremendous amount of Jewish content and philosophy from his grandfather, Shimon Leib Herzl, who was an observant Jew and an associate of Rabbi Judah Alkalay – an early Zionism prototype thinker.

Herzl was shaped through tragedy, losing his sister Paulina to Typhus when he was 17. Within a few weeks he and his parents abruptly departed Budapest to Vienna due to grief. A year later, he lost his beloved grandfather and then a few years later, he lost his best friend Heinrich Kana to suicide. This too prompted an abrupt departure and a journey through Europe. Through tragedy and revival, through noise and clarity, a path was carved that eventually culminated in the 1896 publication of *The Jewish State* and the 1897 convening of the Zionist Congress in Basel, Switzerland.

Herzl's path to Basel was not linear: At first, he was a staunch German nationalist. In doing so, he rejected both the rising Hungarian nationalist movement and the notion of an Austrian national identity, so much that as a university student, Herzl joined a fraternity centered on a strong belief in German nationalism, promoting the "German Spirit." Herzl agreed that Jews were antisocial and needed to be reformed. He attributed these characteristics to centuries of oppression and discrimination. In German nationalism, he found a potential answer to the "Jewish question" – assimilation.

This was in the 1880s, as the anti-Semitic movement was beginning to take shape in Europe. Suddenly the Jews were emancipated and could compete with Christians in Europe. Indeed, Jews thrived, and European envy grew.

Herzl quickly realized that the anti-Semitic movement was pivoting away from "reforming" the Jews and urging them to integrate, to outright opposition to the Jews and denying them a place amongst the nations – both as a collective and as individuals.

Herzl noticed how the form of hate evolved. This was no longer about allegations of Jews killing Jesus, or about Jews using the blood of Christian children to make Matzahs. In fact, it was no longer an opposition to the Jewish religion. It was opposition to Jews as Jews. It was the uncompromising rejection of the Jewish nation.

Herzl resigned from his fraternity, and a decade later, redirected the emotions and beliefs he had about German nationalism towards Jewish nationalism.

For Herzl, being German was about the German nation – not about Christianity, which was protected but not a prerequisite for German nationalism. Hence, Herzl himself could be a proud German.

Similarly, being Jewish was about the Jewish nation. Just like a German could be a subject of a political entity other than the German Empire – such as the Austro-Hungarian Empire, or later a citizen of Austria or the Czech Republic, so could a Jew.

Herzl later observed similar patterns in France. He spent four years there, starting in 1891, as the Paris correspondent of the prestigious Viennese newspaper *Neue Freie Presse*, owned by Jews and championing European liberalism. Spending time in the halls of power, Herzl internalized the French model of the state, which was anchored in French nationalism, and hence, could include members of various religions.

Yet, in both the German and French cases, Herzl also observed the utter rejection of Jews from those nations. Jews became German patriots and French patriots, and this, in turn only increased the opposition and hate toward them.

Herzl understood that European attitudes towards Judaism are not about the Jewish religion. The Jewish question is a national question, he concluded, and hence, the response to the chronic age-old European opposition to Judaism must be on the national level.

Jews having a state of their own would provide an answer to the dual issues:
- the opposition to Jews (external) and
- reforming the Jews (internal, driven by external pressure).

It would not only solve the "Jewish question," it would also unleash the tremendous Jewish potential, suppressed for 1,800 years, which in turn would benefit humanity as a whole.

Herzl therefore planted the seeds for a transformation of Judaism. He led a shift from having the religious aspect as Judaism's organizing principle and the rabbis as its leaders, towards having the national aspect as its organizing principle, and the Jewish state as its geographical expression. [6]

(v) Zionism's early debate: Politicals vs. Practicals

Debates immediately ensued in the Zionist movement between political Zionists, who sought to fulfill the Basel program through diplomatic means and practical Zionists, who sought to fulfill it through land purchase and settlement.

Herzl opposed infiltration of Jews to Ottoman-controlled Palestine. He maintained that Zionism's objective could only be achieved through diplomacy, building international coalitions and assuring the return in agreement with world nations. He viewed this kind of return as a grand act of a nation returning home, not just of individuals immigrating.

In that realm, Herzl was skeptical about the benefit of building Jewish settlements in Palestine until such diplomatic inroads were completed. "A colony is a small state," he told Edmond de Rothschild, who was the patron of the settlements, "a state is a big colony."

The political Zionists' major hurdle was the Ottoman Empire's unwillingness to cede Palestine. Herzl worked tirelessly at attempting to convince the Turkish Sultan to give a charter to the Jews which would enable their return. He even recruited Turkey's ally, the German Kaiser, to his cause. Those attempts failed. But soon global circumstances would change.

4. JUDAISM REJECTS ZIONISM

When political Zionism came to the attention of world Jewry towards the end of the 19th century, Jews utterly rejected it.

The rejection came from various directions of Judaism: Secular Jews, assimilated Jews, religious Jews. But it was the rejection from the Jewish establishment that was the most potent.

That was logical. For centuries, Jews in Europe sought to obtain

---

6 – For more on Herzl, see Georges Yitzhak Weisz: "Theodor Herzl: A New Reading". For Herzl's German Nationalism years, see Jacques Kornberg: "Theodor Herzl – From Assimilation to Zionism". For a biographical background and analysis, see Shlomo Avineri: "Herzl's Vision: Theodor Herzl and the Foundation of the Jewish State". For my articles about Herzl's vision in *The Jerusalem Post*, visit the book's website.

rights and were turned down. Now finally they were on the right track and obtained certain liberties, including the right to vote and the right to live freely.

They finally accomplished what they believed at the time was their acceptance by the world nations. Acceptance at last! Jews finally gained the right to be French, to be German, to be Austrian, to be English.

Shortly after those astonishing inroads were accomplished, here comes Herzl and Zionism, and in the view of those Jews, proclaiming exactly what the anti-Semites were saying: "You are not French, you are Jews; you are not German, you are Jews; you are not Austrian, you are Jews; you are not British, you are Jews. Moreover, you should go to Palestine. Go back to where you came from."

The anti-Semites said, "Jews get out!" And establishment Jews falsely perceived Herzl to be calling for the same. As a result, the Jewish establishment – champions of assimilation within the Jewish world – rapidly became the primary adversary of Zionism.

It was neither the Arabs in Palestine nor the Europeans that served as the most potent opposition to Zionism. It was the Jews.

In fact, when the German Kaiser Wilhelm II reversed course and withdrew his initial enthusiastic support for Zionism, including his agreeing to lobby the Turkish Sultan for the advocacy of a Jewish charter in Palestine, it reportedly had to do with the Jews. The German prime minister explained years later that the reversal of the Kaiser's view was due to consultations with the leaders of the Jewish community who encouraged him to reject Zionism.

Similarly, when the British were ready to move forward with the Balfour Declaration, it was the establishment Jews who were the primary opponents. Moreover, Jewish minister Edwin Montagu was leading the opposition to Zionism from within the government.

In the United States, the establishment Jews of the early 20th century were adamantly anti-Zionist. American Jewish Committee President Jacob Schiff declared: "One cannot be both a real American and a supporter of the Zionist movement."

The Reform movement in the United States, growing in size and influence, adopted a similar anti-Zionist attitude and then went even further. It officially rejected Zionism in a resolution it passed in 1895, known as *The Pittsburgh Platform:*

> "We consider ourselves no longer a nation, but a religious community, and therefore expect neither a return to Palestine, nor a sacrificial worship under the sons of Aaron, nor the restoration of any of the laws concerning the Jewish state."

The opposition of establishment Jews to Zionism was so strong that French Prime Minister Georges Clemenceau, who knew Herzl, and along with US President Wilson and British Prime Minister Lloyd George, presided over the preceding of the 1919 Paris Peace Conference that ended World War I – compared the Jewish opposition to Herzl to that of Jacob in the Bible: "[Herzl] fought Israel," he told a reporter, comparing Herzl's struggle to that of Jacob's, depicted by the Delacroix painting at St. Sulpice. "Jacob seems more concerned with holding the angel near him on earth than resisting him ... You sense there is infinite love between those two, despite the struggle ... No longer Jacob, but Israel, and Israel blessed by the contact!" [7]

Jewish opposition to Zionism was so widespread right from the outset, that coming into the first Zionist Congress in 1897, Herzl recognized that he would face opposition even amongst those who would attend the Congress.

On the eve of the first Congress, he wrote: "Taken as a whole, the direction of these proceedings will, I believe, amount to a singular performance that will have no other spectator than the performer himself ... an egg-dance – with the eggs invisible." Among those eggs that Herzl listed as needing to be juggled through: The Egg of the Orthodox, Egg of the Modernists, Egg of Edmond de Rothschild, Egg of the Chovevei Zion in Russia and Egg of the Palestine settlers.

Herzl faced rejection from the Jews, and then objection from within the Zionist camp.

(i) Recall: Judaism 1.0 rejected Judaism 2.0

The initial rejection of Zionism was reminiscent of the rejection that occurred nearly two millennia earlier, when Judaism transformed from Biblical Judaism (Judaism 1.0) to Rabbinic Judaism (Judaism 2.0).

The Pharisees, over time, took over Judaism from the Sadducees. Judaism 1.0 was dominated by the Sadducees faction, associated with the priest and the Temple worship. The changes and innovations introduced by the Pharisees were utterly rejected by the establishment Jews of that time – the Sadducees. Despite the fierce objection, Judaism transformed from Biblical Judaism (Judaism 1.0) to Rabbinic Judaism (Judaism 2.0). The Judaism we know today – Judaism 2.0 – is the Pharisees' Judaism. The Pharisees indeed received Judaism in their hands.

And that was the Judaism that produced the strong objections to Herzl's Zionism.

---

7 - "Clemenceau Remembers Herzl", in "Theodor Herzl – a Memorial" (1929).

(ii) Zionism goes into a lull (1904-1914)

When Herzl passed away in 1904, Zionism was a defeated movement. It failed to get the support of the establishment Jews in Europe and in the United States. It failed to get the support of the world's nations in spite of sparks of hope along the way. Zionism, as Chaim Weizmann later described, stood before a "blank wall" in regard to the future of the movement.

(iii) Zionism in a lull: Rays of hope in Palestine – Practical Zionism

There were various rays of hope that broke that lull. One was the 20,000 Jews living in Palestine in 1905. While a minority of them lived there for generations, most came in two waves: in the early 19th century ("The Old Yishuv"), and in the 1880s and 1890s (First Aliya). Those Jews in Palestine, with small exceptions, were religious Orthodox Jews.

While much of the religious Orthodox establishment in Europe rejected Zionism, the Orthodox Jews in Palestine were naturally sympathetic to it. This was despite the dire personal risks that the introduction of this national Jewish philosophy posed to those settlers who were at the mercy of the Turkish rulers. Israel's early settlers were Orthodox Jews, and they were to leave a profound impression on Herzl.

When Herzl launched political Zionism in 1897, those Orthodox Jewish settlers were already on the ground.

At first, Herzl did not attribute too much weight to the Jewish settlements. He argued that the land should first be obtained diplomatically and secured in international law, and only then be settled. And yet, when visiting Palestine in 1898 in order to meet the German Kaiser, Herzl made a point to go see the Jewish colonies, and was shaken to his core by the young settlers. They were the evidence he needed that Jews can indeed be strong, proud and brave.

These were independent Jews who took control of their destiny. They served as inspiration to Herzl. As he wrote in his diaries, his eyes were filled with tears at the sight of the brave and skillful Jewish horsemen who he saw during his visit to Palestine – cheering, singing Hebrew songs and performing an impressive act on their horses, which reminded Herzl of the Wild West. The first night Herzl spent back in the homeland in the Land of Israel was amongst those settlers in Rishon Lezion.

Herzl's objection to Jewish immigration

Herzl strenuously objected to the "infiltration" of Jews to Palestine and to the creation of new Jewish settlements. He thought it would interfere with his efforts to obtain a Jewish state through political and diplomatic means, grounded in international law and with the blessing of the world's nations. He also understood that the immigration of Jews to Palestine before it had been granted to the Jews, would increase land prices, making it more difficult for Zionists to purchase it.

But by the time of his passing in 1904, the objective of securing a state through diplomatic and political means seemed to have failed. It failed primarily due to the Ottoman Empire's refusal to neither permit wide scale purchase of land nor to award a charter.

Jewish immigration after Herzl's death (1904-1914)

Given the lack of political progress and Herzl no longer being there to object, groups of immigrants from Russia and Poland, who admired Herzl, immigrated to Palestine starting in 1905, shortly after Herzl's death (the Second Aliya).

These were different Jews than the ones who came before them: They were inflamed with Herzl's ideology and the inspiration of the Zionist movement that had been building up in the previous 10 years.

They were mostly young Jews, many of them in their early 20s. Unlike the ones who came before them, many were not religious and did not want to depend on either the Jewish Diaspora or the feudal-like support of Rothschild.

While there were various narratives in the Second Aliya, the ones who took prominent leadership positions and were the most organized were the socialist factions. Those young Jews abandoned the Jewish religion, rebelled against the past, and were ready to begin a new future in Palestine. They were rejecting the old Jew, and creating the new Jew in Palestine. Amongst their leaders was David Ben-Gurion, who arrived in 1905 at the age of 20.

There lies the contrast that would accompany Israel for the next century. The farmers of the First Aliya who inspired Herzl were religious, somewhat older, and strong. Those of the Second Aliya, who were inspired by Herzl, were young, secular and initially perceived as substandard workers.

Ben-Gurion and his friends developed resentment towards the farmers of the First Aliya, who preferred Arab workers due to their higher skills, and Arab security due to their higher training.

They ushered in a new fashion not seen much in the Land of Israel until then – secularism. [8] Right there in the early 20th century, the contrast between the Second Aliya and First Aliya was the emergence of Israel's secular narrative. While the seculars were a small minority of Jews in Palestine, even after the Second Aliya, and were even a smaller minority of Jews in the Diaspora, they were instrumental in the growth of the Zionist movement in years to come, which in turn contributed to Israel adopting a secular ethos.

But there was another stunning contrast between those secular immigrants of the Second Aliya and the Jews who came before them: those immigrants did not come as "cowboys to the Wild West." Unlike the two waves of immigration that proceeded them, they came with the help of the Zionist institutions that assisted in the purchase of land and facilitated the process of immigration.

A subtle, yet meaningful shift occurred: Instead of rich individual Jews and Jewish communities that were supporting the 19th century immigrants, now it was official Zionist institutions that were funding and supporting the 20th century immigrants.

Political development in the Ottoman Empire – "The sick man of Europe" – and the 1908 Young Turks Revolution, provided greater degrees of "autonomy" to those living in Turkish-controlled areas. To some extent, Palestine became an "absentee landlord" environment, and that enabled additional land purchases, the establishment of Kibbutz Degania in 1909, and of other settlements in the Palestinian wilderness.

With the support of the Zionist institutions, the cornerstone to a Hebrew city was put in place in 1909 – Tel Aviv, named after the Hebrew title of Herzl's Utopian novel.

Herzl outlined his ideas in 1896 in *The Jewish State*, but he was able to demonstrate his vision in a more pictorial way through a 1902 novel he wrote, showing how it would all look once the Jewish state was in place. That novel was called *AltNeuLand* – Old-New-Land – or in its Hebrew translation – Tel Aviv.

Indeed, Tel Aviv quickly grew to be a symbol of what Jewish life in Palestine would look like. By the time World War I broke in 1914, the Yishuv – the Jewish community in Palestine, was well-established. It was small and represented a fraction of a percentage of world Jewry, but much due to the accomplishment of the Second Aliya, it provided an undeniable reality.

---

8 – There was one prominent group – Bilu – in the First Aliya who were secular, as well as secular individuals, but they were a small minority.

Zionism went into World War I not only with a network of settlements in Palestine, but also with the globally accepted notion that Jews settling in Palestine was not merely a hypothetical political idea, but already a practical reality.

(iv) Zionism in a lull: Rays of hope in the Diaspora – American Zionism (1904-1914)

While political Zionism was relatively dormant in its second decade (1904-1914) compared to the flurry of activities it had during Herzl's tenure (1897-1904), the movement continued to convene its Zionist congresses and the Zionist institutions were operating. By 1914, a shift began to emerge: In Eastern Europe, one could not ignore the rising populism of the Zionist movement amongst the Jews, despite its lack of political progress.

In the United States, Eastern European Jewish immigration was in full swing. Those immigrants, in turn, brought Zionism with them to America, right into the heart of New York and other Jewish centers.

This was done much to the dismay of the "veteran" German establishment Jewish leadership. The German Jewish establishment in New York, just like the German Jewish establishment in Europe, opposed Zionism. But given the rapidly changing composition of American Jewry, the Eastern European immigrants had planted the roots for American Jewry's Zionism for decades to come.

Zionism was in a lull for a decade after Herzl's death. Some minor progress in Palestine amongst practical Zionists moving in, and growing support amongst American Jews for Zionism served as rays of hope. But Zionism's seismic shift was about to occur, as a result of external global developments.

5. Zionism recognized By The Non-Jewish World

Herzl's ultimate failure came about with the Turkish Sultan's refusal to give Palestine to the Jews; Palestine was simply not available. He was well aware that sooner or later the Ottoman Empire would collapse, but this did not come during his lifetime. It occurred as a result of the Great War that broke out in 1914, and Turkey's surprising decision to enter it.

(i) Revolution of the Balfour Declaration – Political Zionism's Vindication (1914-1917)

As the war progressed, it became evident that the British might conquer Palestine. It was in this context that the British awakened the

Zionist movement and injected life to Zionism.

A process began in the British government in early 1917 to draft a statement of support for Zionism. On November 2, 1917, the British issued the Balfour Declaration, which viewed with favor the establishment of a Jewish homeland in Palestine. With it, global support for Zionism became a reality.

The support was broad, as resolutions similar to the Balfour Declaration were prepared by various other governments and bodies in Germany, Japan and the United States.

That crazy notion of a dreamer in Vienna, merely two decades prior, was suddenly supported not just by the British, but by virtually the entire world, including the Arabs.

(ii) Official Recognition by the Outside World

"Palestine for the Jews!" That was the headline of The London Times on November 9, 1917, the week after the British government issued the Balfour Declaration.

A year later, the Paris Peace Conference that convened in early 1919 to deal with the consequences of the end of World War I, recognized Zionism as a party of interest in the conference. Perhaps there lies early evidence of the transformation of Judaism 2.0 to Judaism 3.0. It was not a council of rabbis, some form of Sanhedrin, or Jewish community leaders who were called to represent the Jewish interest to the world powers. It was Zionism. Indeed, the world powers in the Paris Peace Conference reaffirmed the Balfour Declaration to view with favor the establishment of a Jewish homeland in Palestine.

The underlying concept of Zionism was not new. France, as early as 1799, issued a decree (by Napoleon) calling for an establishment of a Jewish homeland in Palestine. The Arab world was supportive of Zionism. Arab Emir Faisal stated that publicly and presented this view in front of the committee at the Paris conference.

He stated through an agreement he signed with Zionist leader Chaim Weizmann, that "all necessary measures shall be taken to encourage and stimulate immigration of Jews into Palestine on a large scale."

T.E. Lawrence (a.k.a. "Lawrence of Arabia") wrote in a letter that the "Arab attitude shall remain sympathetic." Spending time with Arab leaders, he assured his superiors in Britain of Arab support for the Balfour Declaration. [9]

Such broad world recognition of Zionism was further rooted in

9 – Malcolm Brown: "Letters of T.E. Lawrence".

international law via the San Remo treaty, and eventually by the League of Nations Mandate for Palestine, which incorporated the Balfour Declaration into it. With such ubiquitous international support for Zionism, the movement was no longer a fringe within Judaism, and establishment Jews had no choice but to recognize it.

(iii) Recognition by the establishment Jews in the US and Europe

Following the near universal global acceptance of Zionism in 1919-1920, European Jewish leaders finally accepted Zionism themselves. This was no doubt aided by the recognition that their rights as British, French and Germans were not infringed in the aftermath of the Balfour Declaration and enactment of the British Mandate.

In the 1920s Jews flourished in France (a Jew became prime minister), in Germany (a Jew became foreign minister), and throughout Europe. The fear that Jewish nationalism would hurt their local patriotism subsided.

In the United States, the largest Jewish movement, the Reform movement, that demonstratively rejected Zionism in 1895, had reversed course and de facto recognized it in its 1935 *Columbus Platform*:

> "In the rehabilitation of Palestine, the land hallowed by memories and hopes, we behold the promise of renewed life for many of our brethren. We affirm the obligation of all Jewry to aid in its up-building as a Jewish homeland by endeavoring to make it not only a haven of refuge for the oppressed but also a center of Jewish culture and spiritual life."

(iv) Shifts in Zionist leadership from West to East

Western Europeans were the first generation of Zionist leaders. Herzl was from Vienna, his right-hand man, Max Bodenheimer was from Germany, Jacob De-Haas was from England, Max Nordau, who was born in Hungary, lived for decades in Paris, and Otto Warburg was an assimilated German from Hamburg.

They deployed western thinking into Zionism. Herzl's Zionist ideas were drawn from his early exposure to German nationalism, his study of western liberal political philosophers and his acute observation of French politics and the French parliament. In fact, for the early Zionist leaders, the Jewish state would be the best expression of Western European liberal values.

While the first generation were Western Europeans, the next generation was raised in Eastern Europe, and they were more greatly exposed to the Eastern view of Judaism. Amongst them were Chaim Weizmann, David Wolffsohn and Nachum Sokolov, who were the instrumental Zionist figures in the decades following Herzl's death.

Notwithstanding the shift, Zionism remained a staunchly European movement. Even after the British took over and the mandate for Palestine was approved in 1923, the Zionist leadership, institutions and congresses remained in Europe.

6. ISRAELI TAKEOVER OF ZIONISM

During World War I, the Zionist movement was officially neutral, but that was only on paper. Chaim Weizmann, one of the key Zionist leaders, was working with the British military on ammunition technology while Ze'ev Jabotinsky and Joseph Trumpeldor, also Zionist leaders, formed a Jewish brigade within the British army, composed of Jewish volunteers from around Europe.

On the ground in Palestine, a Jewish underground was formed to help the British as they were getting closer to conquering Palestine.

The Turks, understanding where the Jews' hearts laid, deported Jews from Jaffa and Tel Aviv and imposed restrictions on Jewish movement as well as transfer of capital and goods to Palestine. Those harsh measures led to a monumental shift within the Jewish community in Palestine. The Old Yishuv was dependent on Diaspora Jewish money for their livelihood. Given the war, this was no longer available. The new Yishuv on the other hand (First and Second Aliya) produced their own food and catered to their own needs.

The Jewish Yishuv in Palestine got even more of the Jewish world's attention, as fear of a massacre of the Jews in Palestine by the Turks loomed. As news spread to the West about the magnitude of the Turkish atrocities in Armenia, the Jews took notice of the lack of a global outcry to the Armenian massacre. The Yishuv feared a similar fate. But the United States launched a separate peace negotiation with Turkey in 1915, and that might have saved the Yishuv. America made it clear to the Turks that what they did in Armenia would not be tolerated in Palestine, and in doing so, possibly saved the Jews and Zionism.

(i) Yishuv – from fringe of Zionism to the mechanism of its fulfillment

While Herzl's political Zionism was a prerequisite to the success of Zionism, it is likely that so was having Jews on the ground in Palestine ("practical Zionism").

This led to the so-called "synthetic Zionism" that was adopted as policy after Herzl's 1904 death. It blended Herzl's political Zionism with the immigrants' practical Zionism.

The 20,000 Jews that immigrated between Herzl's death and World War I (Second Aliya) not only provided more numbers to the existing Old Yishuv on top of the First Aliya, but created infrastructure that could be viewed as sufficient seeds for "state-building."

In a sense, they provided a prototype or an "advance team," which arguably gave the British and the world some comfort as they started the process of giving Palestine to the Jews. As Diaspora Jews recognized this, the importance of those settlers within the Zionist narrative was elevated.

The massive Arab immigration to Palestine in the late 19th and early 20th centuries also put more gravity on the local Jewish population. If there was a European Zionist myth of Palestine being "a land with no people, given to a people with no land," the myth was shattered as the magnitude of the Arab immigration became clear.

(ii) Jews were reluctant to come

Contrary to the hope and promises, the carte blanche environment to come to Palestine did not translate into Jews immigrating. To the dismay of those in the British government who supported the idea of giving Palestine to the Jews, the Jews did not come. This was in contrast to the thesis that the European Jewish population would come, bloom the Palestine wilderness, and bring their wealth too.

Chaim Weizmann issued a desperate plea to European Jews: "*Am Yisrael, Ayecka*? – The People of Israel – where are you?"

But Weizmann himself, like many of the successful, established and wealthy Jews, chose to stay behind. Herzl predicted this would happen – that the Jews would be reluctant to abandon Europe and its "fleshpots," as he called them. It was not simple to downgrade to the under-developed Palestine wilderness. Yet, some Jews did come.

(iii) Hierarchy emerges that favors the veterans (Ben-Gurion)

Each immigration wave that came after World War I consisted of Jewish populations from different places in Europe, and each wave held its own ethos. The immigration wave of 1919-1924 (Third Aliya) brought with it about 35,000 people – mostly from Russia and Poland, but also from other Eastern European countries. In addition to being driven by ideology, the dire economic conditions in Europe and the Russian civil war drove many of those immigrants to Palestine. Like the immigration waves that preceded it, this wave consisted of young Jews. Palestine was still not a suitable place for families, the logic went, and the prevailing notion for such Zionist families was of "wait and see."

Indeed, like the previous waves of immigrations, about 40% of the Third Aliya immigrants were single. This contributed to the atmosphere that existed even before the war: romanticism, country-building, newness, fun and high energy, despite the difficulties.

When economic conditions in Europe improved, the immigration dwindled, but soon a new crisis loomed that brought more Jews to Palestine. Taxes imposed in Poland, and adverse conditions for Jews, combined with America closing its gates for immigration in 1924 through the Johnson-Reed act, resulted in 70,000 new immigrants coming to Palestine, mostly from Poland (Fourth Aliya). This was a more wealthy and older immigration wave, which this time included families. "The homeowners" immigration, they were mocked by the Jews on the ground, due to their wealth.

Similarly, the immigration wave that followed in the early 1930s (Fifth Aliya) – the one resulting from Nazis taking power in Germany and the rise of anti-Semitism in Europe – was wealthy and older.

The elevation of the profile of the Zionist immigrants, combined with the diverse source-countries within Europe, further shifted the balance of power within Zionism towards the Palestine Jews.

Each wave of immigration tended to be snobbish to the one that followed. A "veteran" Yishuv person, or veteran Tel Avivi, was defined as someone who was there for merely five years, though sometimes less. An ethos began to develop that the longer you were in Palestine, the higher your social status.

Indeed, every wave of immigration was molded in the realm of the previous ones. In that context, the status of Ben-Gurion and his socialist colleagues, who came around 1905 (Second Aliya), was further solidified. He soon became the "elder statesman" of the local Palestine Jews, even though he was only in his early 40s.

A line in the sand was drawn between Ben-Gurion on the one hand, as an image of a Yishuv Jew in Palestine in khaki shirt and shorts – abrupt, direct, informal, and Weizmann on the other hand, as an image of the gentleman from the salons of Europe – formally dressed in a suit and tie, well-spoken, polite, hedged and proper.

Weizmann, serving as the head of Zionism (President of the Zionist Congress) became more of a problem for the Palestine Jews. It was disturbing to them that the persons representing Zionism were foreigners in the Land of Zion. That needed to change.

(iv) Impact of geopolitical destabilization (1917-1935)

The aftermath of World War I produced a relatively simple political reality in the Middle East, supported by Arabs and Jews alike: the establishment of a pending Jewish homeland in Palestine, next to a Hashemite Arab kingdom in Syria. The Hashemite Emir Faisal and Zionist leader Weizmann lobbied to formalize such an arrangement jointly.

But the prospect of a peaceful Middle East was quickly shattered by competing European interests: France invaded Syria, staking claim to the area based on prior French-British understandings including the Sykes-Picot Agreement. This led to a debilitating sequence of events. The pro-Zionist Hashemite Arab king Faisal was overthrown by France, ending the brief period of Arab independence in Syria. The British gave Iraq to the Hashemites as compensation, and later carved out Palestine and gave the eastern portion of it to Faisal's brother Abdullah.

Even though some claimed this was in violation of prior resolutions and declarations relating to establishing a Jewish homeland in Palestine (the San Remo Conference, Balfour Declaration), the Zionist leadership did not object and "gave their blessing" to the redrawing of the map.

This was based in part on the good relationship with the Hashemites and their earlier strong support of Zionism. But mostly, it was out of a general Zionist policy at the time to have "no daylight" between the Zionists and the British.

(v) Early signs of an armed struggle further support the importance of the Yishuv

The French invasion of Syria and its war against the Hashemite Arabs also triggered the first casualties of what would later become known as the Arab-Israeli conflict, as French-Arab warfare trickled into the Jewish village of Tel Hai in March 1920. [10] Shortly thereafter, a few Arab clans turned against the Jews and the following year a mob attacked Jews during the May Day parade. Local British military commanders contributed their share, deploying their well-tested colonialist strategy of divide-and-rule. They perceived the nurturing of the Jewish-Arab conflict to be in their interest.

Distrust and fear started to be built by the Arabs towards Jews. What was mostly a collaborative relationship began to turn into a suspicious and distant one. The distrust was solidified by the fear of displacement by

---

10 – Eight Jews, six men and two women, among them Commander Joseph Trumpeldor, died in this battle.

intra-Arab fighting as well as the sheer size of the Jewish immigration.

Regional history of population displacement and massacres, as well as specific incitement about Jewish and Christian takeover of the Temple Mount, eventually culminated in the first round of mass violence against the Jews, which occurred in 1929. The 1929 violence played a key role in the Yishuv's takeover of Zionism. The Yishuv was attacked and horrific atrocities were committed. It became clear to Jews around the world who was paying the price for Zionism, and who were the guardians and defenders of Zionism. It was no longer the people in suits in Europe, enjoying the golden age of the roaring 20s. It was the Jews on the ground in the Land of Israel who were paying with their lives.

The other way in which the 1929 riots affected Zionism was that it planted the seeds of an Arab national movement. Zionism was no longer about diplomatic negotiations with the Europeans – it was about a military struggle with the Arabs. The arena for this was clearly in Palestine, not in Europe.

(vi) European Zionists snub the Yishuv

Despite their heavy contribution to Zionism, to the British war effort in World War I and creating facts on the ground in settling the land, the Palestine Jews were frustrated that they did not get an adequate voice in the Zionist movement and its institutions.

Even at the 1919 Paris Peace conference that came after World War I, it was only European Zionists and not the Yishuv Zionists who participated. The Yishuv wanted its representative, Meir Dizengoff (mayor of Tel Aviv) to be included in the presentation to US President Wilson and the "Group of Ten." He even went to Paris, but he was rejected by Weizmann and the European Zionists.

Weizmann visited Israel in the aftermath of the violence that occurred in the spring of 1920. The British role in inciting it was alarming, and so was the high number of casualties. Weizmann then headed to Italy when the San Remo conference was taking place. He reported that he was "shocked" that Zionist leader Sokolov and British Zionist Herbert Samuel "were just sitting there in the lobby and not horrified from what was happening in Eretz Israel." [11]

Shortly thereafter, Samuel was appointed as high commissioner, further shifting the center of gravity to the Yishuv, given that a Zionist, a Jew, was now in command of Palestine.

But Samuel disappointed his fellow Zionists. Samuel reacted to

---

11 – Nathan Michael Galber: "Balfour Declaration and its origin" (Hebrew), 1938.

the 1921 Arab violence by succumbing to the Arab attackers. He not only limited Jewish immigration, but also supported the rioters' leader, Amin al-Husseini's quest to become the Mufti of Jerusalem. In doing so, Samuel was essentially taking sides between intra-Arab rivalries and gave power in Jerusalem to the more radical elements within the local Arabs.

European Zionist leadership decided not to overreact to the British appeasement actions, which further irritated the Yishuv. Shortly thereafter, the responsibility of Palestine was transferred to the Colony Office and a year later the first of the White Papers was issued, curtailing Jewish immigration. This was the beginning of a long process of the British reversal from the Balfour Declaration. This reversal only escalated after the riots of 1929. Again the European Zionist leadership decided to contain it and opted to maintain its cozy relationship with the British.

(vii) British reversal of policy further elevates Yishuv Zionists (1917-1935)

The British eventually reversed course completely. They ignored their League of Nations mandate, forgot about the Jewish homeland and all but stopped Jewish immigration to Palestine.

This was not due to anti-Jewish sentiment, it was simply due to British interests. The riots of 1936-1939 took a toll on the British, who needed to invest significant resources in an overseas territory that was not even an official colony, and was not as "profitable" as India, known as the Crown Jewel of the British colonies.

Oil became important, and as Arab nationalism rose, and Arab and Jews seemed to begin being at odds with each other, the British perceived Arab nationalism as more important to the British interest.

As another World War loomed, the British, recalling the tremendous contribution of Arabs in World War I, recognized they needed Arab support. Zionism was "thrown under the bus."

This came at the worst time for Jews, as the killing machines of the Nazis and their collaborators were in full force. By the British denying entry to Palestine, Jewish refugees from Europe seeking to escape persecution were doomed to their deaths.

Tragically, after all the support Great Britain lent to the Jews and to the Zionist cause till then, the British reversal of policy and refusal to let Jews into Palestine when they most needed it, was the second most important contributor to the fulfillment of the genocide of the European Jews, second only to the Nazis' decision to enact it.

The reaction of the Yishuv to the British reversal split the Yishuv.

A splinter group began to attack the British, at the same time that the mainstream was joining the British in their war effort against the Germans.

This chasm that was seeded then governs much of Israeli politics till today. David Ben-Gurion (mainstream Hagana – later Israel's Labor party and the left) vs. Menachem Begin and Yitzhak Shamir (splinter Etzel and Lehi – later Israel's Likud party and the right).

What became crystal clear early in the 1940s, as the Holocaust was taking place in Europe, was that Zionism was headed towards a military conflict. This, along with the disappointment in European Zionist leadership, made the Yishuv takeover of Zionism nearly inevitable.

(viii) Takeover of Zionism by the Ben-Gurion stream (1935)

Zionism was now led from Palestine, but that was just part of the story. The stream that took over in 1935 and held power until the late 1970s was a particular one. This stream, led by Ben-Gurion, was adamantly secular. To some extent, it was rebelling against the Jewish religion. It was also socialist and it was rigid, instituting the mechanism of adherence to the ethos that it itself instilled.

Ben-Gurion and his party led Zionism through nearly impossible challenges on multiple fronts: The now hostile British rulers, the new armed struggles with Arabs in Palestine, the tension with powerful Arab rulers outside of Palestine, the war in Europe and the Holocaust. Their ability to navigate Zionism through those challenges was proven successful: Thirteen years after they took over Zionism, the Jewish state was established.

Ben-Gurion and his colleagues were successful in part because they took complete control of Zionist institutions. The party had nearly absolute control and power of Zionism, and then of Israel. Controlling its government institutions, the media, the education system, economy and even business, allowed Ben-Gurion and his party to adjust the Zionist narrative retroactively, as they saw fit for what was needed for the survival for the fledgling state.

Zionism was secularized retroactively: Herzl became overly secular retroactively and even the First Aliya became secular retroactively.

Indeed, Zionism was now artificially overly associated with secularism.

7. AN ALTERNATE JEWISH CIVILIZATION CREATED IN ZION

Zionism was no longer a Utopia, it was real. Zionism was on the ground. It became abundantly clear that life back in the ancestral land represented a new form of Jewish life that was different from, and even in contrast to, the Jewish life of previous centuries.

(i) Negation of the Jewish religiosity

While many of the Zionists, even Weizmann, viewed this at a minimum, with an aspect of a religious and even a Messianic context (Weizmann wrote to his wife in 1919: "Messianic days upon us"), the Ben-Gurion stream of Zionism that was by then in firm control of the Zionist political structure, had another take.

Ben-Gurion's revolutionary movement rebelled against the past: The miserable Jew, the unproductive Jew, and indeed the religious Jew. Ben-Gurion's rejection of Jewish religiosity became Zionism's rejection of Jewish religiosity, and Israel was established in that realm.

Only after Israel's 1948 establishment did Ben-Gurion make a substantial correction and developed a strong interest in the Bible. [12] This interest served the Zionist agenda well, as it linked the current Jewish sovereignty to the historical one. While the Bible became a cornerstone of the Zionist narrative and continues to be so today, Zionism under Ben-Gurion was still perceived to be rejective of Jewish religiosity, following the mantra of "From the Tanach to the Palmach" – from the Bible to the elite units of 1940s Yishuv – skipping Rabbinic Judaism in the middle.

(ii) Negation of the Jewish Diaspora

The rejection of Zionism by the world's establishment Jews, as well as by significant portions of the Rabbinic establishment, had its "payday" in the 1930s.

With the rejection of Jewish religiosity came the outright rejection of the Diaspora. Zionism evolving as a revolutionary movement meant a rejection of the past, and the building of a new Jew in Palestine.

"With a shovel in hand, and rifle on his shoulders," as Zionist leader Yitzhak Tabenkin labeled it, that Jew looked, acted and lived very differently than his father in the Diaspora. [13]

To validate it further, those Jews who stayed back in the Diaspora were looked down upon. Their way of life was negated. This was somewhat akin to the American ethos, where those who moved to America were viewed as "exceptional," and those who stayed behind were viewed as non-daring people who simply stayed behind. But in Israel's case, it was

---

12 – Anita Shapira: "The Bible and Israeli identity," AJS Review, Vol. 28, No. 1, April 2004.
13 – See Anita Shapira: "Where did the negation of the Diaspora go?" Alpayim 25, 2003.

more extreme.

Such attitudes were a departure from Herzl's vision of Zionism. Herzl never negated the existence of a Jewish Diaspora, but Israeli Zionism as shaped by Ben-Gurion very much did, both geographically and culturally.

Geographically, negation of the Diaspora

From the beginning of Israel's existence, the call for world Jewry to make Aliya, to physically live in Israel, was loud and universal. There were no Israeli leaders who disagreed with the notion that Aliya was a top priority. Drawing from Weizmann's early call, "The people of Israel, where are you?", the call for Aliya, and the dissonance towards the masses who did not answer the call was core to Israel's developing ethos.

This was reflected in directing the Jewish Agency to act to accomplish this objective. Funded by millions of dollars and hiring thousands of envoys, the Jewish Agency converged upon Jewish communities in America and around the world with the clear message: "We need every Jew in Israel!"

Exerting a guilt feeling on those who did not make Aliya amounted to a geographical expression of the Zionist concept of negation of the Diaspora. But the negation was not only for those who refused to come. In fact, it was primarily directed at those who indeed came.

Cultural negation of the Diaspora

Negation of the Diaspora was not only rejection of Diaspora life outside of Israel, but also of rejection of Diaspora life in Israel. The Zionist narrative was about making sure that those who came to Israel were indeed "Israelized." This made a lot of sense, since the Israeli was being "invented" and a start-up culture was being composed. The success of the melting pot experience was dependent on people adhering to one culture, narrative, set of icons and in particular, language.

Volunteers, organized as the Hebrew Language Brigades, walked around the main boulevards and cafes of Tel Aviv and when they heard someone speaking in another language, they jumped at him with a reprimand: "*Daber Evrit*! – Speak Hebrew!"

The Jewish icons of Shalom Aleichem and other shtetl-era characters of Hershele, *Fiddler on the Roof*, of weak Yiddish Jews were replaced by Srulik, an Israeli with khakis and tembel hat.

The old weak Jew with the beard and kipa was replaced with the young, tall, good-looking pioneer – guys of handsome stature and forelocks, and girls with pony-tails and jumper dresses, as depicted in Israeli songs. The weak Jews stayed in the Diaspora and were negated by the new, strong and proud Jews.

The cultural negation of the Diaspora was also a byproduct of the shift in Zionist power from Western European Jews like Herzl to Eastern European leaders like Ben-Gurion. The Jewish Diaspora in Herzl's environment was of well-educated cosmopolitan Jewish gentlemen. The Jewish Diaspora in Ben-Gurion's environment was of the poor, weak shtetl Jews, and there was no room for them in the new ethos of the strong Israeli Zionists. As they were negated so was the entire idea of a cultural Diaspora.

(iii) Zionism conceived abroad, developed at home

It is important to note two points:

–While there were Jews in Palestine throughout the centuries, Zionism was conceived and developed outside of Palestine by European Jews who had never been to Palestine. The 19th century formation of Zionism was all done from the outside.

–The cultural ethos of today's Israel, however, was developed in Palestine in the early part of the 20th century by new "Israelis" who had moved there. The Israeli ethos was all done from the inside.

The negation of the Diaspora was in a sense a cruel rejection of "your maker," but deemed a necessity as the new Israel was being formed.

(iv) Israelis vs. Jews (1935-2020)

Indeed, this rejection of the Diaspora continued as Israeli society was taking shape and tuning-in its collective voice. The Palestinian Jew vs. the European Jew that had its early expression in the Ben-Gurion vs. Weizmann contrast, trickled to the next generations.

Intergenerational tensions were prevalent in the formative years of the late 1960s through the 1980s, where the ruling class in government and business were still the first-generation Jews, who were born in Europe, while the up-and-comers were "Israeli," who had never been to a shtetl. The under-50 crowd did not want to be like their parents. They spoke in a different dialect, a different accent, they thought differently and they had different preferences.

As they began to take over some positions of power, the rift was amplified. Prime Ministers Ben-Gurion, Levi Eshkol, Golda Meir and the establishment that ruled Israel through the 1970s indeed felt and sounded like Diaspora Jews (Golda Meir was an American Jew after all). Yitzhak Rabin, and later the Israeli "baby boomers" that took over such as Benjamin Netanyahu, Ehud Barak and Ehud Olmert, were not. They were Israeli.

The Israelis vs. Jews rift was present inside the Israeli government. Rabin and his colleagues in the military central command of the 1960s were reportedly mocking the politicians behind their backs as "The Jews". This was in particular in the lead up to the 1967 Six Day War as the "Israeli" generals became frustrated with the "Jewish" politicians, who they perceived were too hesitant in giving the order to go to war. [14] Ben-Gurion's colleagues who negated the Diaspora were then negated themselves as being "too Diaspora."

8. SYNTHESIS OF JUDAISM: JEWS RECOGNIZE ZIONISM AND ZIONISM RECOGNIZES DIASPORA JEWS (2020 –)

Establishment Jews in the Diaspora had rejected the fringe movement called Zionism. Once the fringe movement rose, it rejected Diaspora Judaism. That dance of rejections came to an end as the 20th century progressed. A synthesis emerged.

Diaspora Judaism has played an integral role in building Israel. In particular, the establishment Jews – those same Jews that just a few decades prior had led the global campaign against Zionism – were now fulfilling Zionism.

The establishment Jews demonstrated their support primarily through generous financial giving. Diaspora Judaism built Israel's hospitals, museums, concert halls, cultural centers, ambulance fleet, fire departments, universities, schools and youth centers. They turned into the primary sponsor of Israeli charities. Diaspora Jews also provided much-needed political backbone and a gateway to America's capital markets, social circles and corridors of power.

Israel eventually accepted that there is legitimate Jewish life outside of Israel. While the narrative till this day remains that "we need every Jew in Israel" (the narrative repeated by Israel leaders when meeting young Diaspora Jews), the volume and intensity of that narrative has radically decreased.

Israel's acceptance that Jews are staying outside and not coming "home" to Israel is in part due to the fact that it is no longer true that "we need every Jew here in Israel." The numbers game works differently now, and there is broad recognition and appreciation of the contribution of Diaspora Jews from the outside.

---

14 – Ami Gluska: "Eshkol, give the order!: Israel's Army command and political leadership on the road to the Six Day War, 1963-1967" (Hebrew).

Tactical differences remain and issues rise up once in a while, mostly with elements of American Jewish leadership. Yet, the situation today is light years away from the situation a century ago. Notwithstanding political disagreements, it is now clear that Diaspora Jews not only broadly accept, but also warmly embrace Zionism, while Israel and Israelis not only broadly accept, but also warmly embrace the Jewish Diaspora – a tribe of brothers and sisters.

9. THE BINARY JEWISH WORLD EMERGES

The Holocaust had all but eliminated European Jewry. A few years later, nearly the entire Jewish population of the Arab Middle East was forced out of their homes and nearly all of them immigrated to the newly established State of Israel. Towards the end of the 20th century, Soviet Jews, held behind the Iron Curtain for so long, were finally allowed to leave and immigrated en masse in the 1990s, mostly to Israel and the United States.

Consequently, by the early 21st century, a binary Jewish world emerged: About 85% of today's Jews are spread between North America and Israel. In other words, about 80% of Diaspora Jews are now in North America. [15] Therefore, the Israel-Diaspora relationship has turned in practice to be one of relations between Israel and American Jews.

This binary structure of the Jewish world allows an analysis of the state of Judaism to be done in the context of those two core centers. As is shown in the following sections, trends in those two core centers are indicative that Judaism is indeed transforming to Judaism 3.0.

---

15 – Jewish Virtual Library – Jewish population of the world, 2018.

IV

The Nature Of Transformations

Transformations are not typically recognized in real-time, nor are they linear.

1. RECOGNIZED IN RETROSPECT

There is no "announcement" of a transformation. Indeed, transformations are typically recognized in retrospect by historians and thinkers. It is hard to say at a specific moment that one form has switched to another, just like it is hard to say that one era ended and another began. Only after ample time has elapsed can people pick an event or inflection point and, in retrospect, anoint it as the point of transformation.

This was the case with the transformation from Judaism 1.0 (Biblical Judaism) to Judaism 2.0 (Rabbinic Judaism). Today, it is accepted that this inflection point was the 1st century exile that was forced by the Romans after the Temple was destroyed and the Jewish nation was deported from the Land of Israel.

In reality, the process took centuries, with trial-and-error, hurdles to transformations that sprung up, and changing global circumstances that funneled the transformation to Judaism 2.0 into the shape it ended up taking.

Similarly, it is likely that in the future, the inflection point of the transformation to Judaism 3.0 will be anointed to be the 1948 establishment of the State of Israel. But in reality, in Israel's first 70 years, there has not been a recognition that Judaism has transformed. Zionism has been viewed until now as a feature of Judaism, but not its core. As discussed in this book, multiple hurdles existed in Israel and in the Diaspora that delayed the fulfillment of the transformation.

Indeed, it is hard to diagnose transformations right at their inflection point, also because what seems to be in real-time a momentous event, turns out to be more or less "business as usual," like Year 2K. On the other hand, what seems to be just another "routine event" turns out to be, in retrospect, a major transformation like events in the summer of 1914 in Europe which were perceived to be "routine tensions" between the nations, or a virus in China in late 2019. Today, some believe that the Coronavirus pandemic will transform the way humans interact, socialize and work, while others view it as a pandemic that will pass.

Similarly, some believe that the 2020 UK divorce from the European Union (Brexit) marks the inflection point in Europe to which people in the future will look back and designate as the point of transformation. It is too soon to tell. This is a live example that transformations are not "announced," but pinpointed later. Indeed, it is typically the recognition of a transformation that serves as its fulfillment!

2. NOT LINEAR – CHANGE IN CONSCIOUSNESS

What starts as a movement can turn into a religion or even a nation. Such was the case with Christianity. If during Jesus' time somebody would have told Jesus or anybody else that a new religion was being born, that person would have likely been ridiculed. Theologians, historians and clergy concur that Christianity in its early days was primarily a social and reform movement within Judaism. It was similar with Islam, too. What was started by Mohammad as a social and political movement within the Arabian tribes rapidly morphed into a religion.

By the same token, a transformation can occur in the other directions – religions turning into nations. In Europe, a split in Christianity between Catholic and Protestant churches dictated borders and later defined empires and nations. National movements were born out of religious differences (for example: Ireland, Bosnia).

Similarly, the Arab world went through a transformation from tribes and clans as its organizing principle, into political entities (states) being the organizing principle. In the Middle East a century ago, nobody thought of themselves as "Jordanians" or "Palestinians" or "Saudi Arabians." Yet, there was a successful transformation from the clan, sect and tribe system (at least successful as of now).

The intra-Arab wars of the past were driven by the organizing principle of the past (for example, Qays and Yaman rivalry), while the wars of the present are driven by realities that were not even dreamed of a century ago, such as the intra-Sunni war on terrorism. Changes in form dictate new realities and relationships.

(i) Similar for Corporations and Ideas

This is also true in the corporate world. Until 1997, it was clear that a company was either a bank or an insurance company. In fact, it was illegal for one to own the other. When the merger of Citibank and Travelers Insurance was announced in 1998, it was met with wonder – a bank merging with an insurance company? These are two separate structures. How could it be? On top of this, it was illegal. Yet, the laws were changed, frames of mind were adjusted, and the merger went through, creating Citigroup.

Similarly, can one imagine a merger between a bank with Starbucks? Can coffee chains turn from a place to purchase coffee, to a banking delivery point, where the sale of coffee is merely an ancillary stream of revenues?

Various other transformations occurred by breaking with a past notion of what was familiar. Indeed, a few decades ago, who could have imagined a bank, not being a physical branch, but rather a website or a machine on a wall? Who could have imagined a bookstore without a store? Or even a bookstore without books to sell (as in bookstore cafes)? Barnes and Noble bookstores once had a side-business of selling books online. Within a few years, barnesandnoble.com became the Crown Jewel, and significantly more valuable, [1] as the physical bookstores became a declining business.

Similarly, who could have thought of a restaurant without a kitchen, redefining the definition of a restaurant from being primarily a place to consume food to being a social experience with the food consumed outsourced?

In Israel, grocery stores in recent years have taken over the role previously played by the post office, and cars are soon turning from a means of transportation to a captive venue for advertisement and data-collection as they turn autonomous.

When the idea of trains came to the world in the mid-19th century, there was a lot of resistance and mockery that so much money was spent on something that had very limited demand. Very few people traveled from Vienna to Moscow, for example.

Many thinkers rose to oppose the laughable, wasteful investment in something that was not needed. Herzl voiced his opinion on such thinkers: "In the earliest period of the European railway construction some 'practical' people were of the opinion that it was foolish to build certain lines because there were not even sufficient passengers to fill the mail coaches. They did not realize the truth – which now seems obvious to us – that travelers do not produce railways, but, conversely, railways produce travelers. The latent demand, of course, is taken for granted."

How could a seemingly religious concept (Judaism) be possibly transformed into a seemingly national concept (Zionism)? Because that is the essence of transformations. When a multi-discipline organism

---

1 – Barnes and Noble unlocked this value in an initial public offering for barnesandnoble.com in May 1999.

transforms, an element that was once secondary can become its primary organizing principle.

(ii) Transformation from Judaism 1.0 to Judaism 2.0 was not linear either

When did Judaism 1.0 (Biblical Judaism) transform to Judaism 2.0 (Rabbinic Judaism)? As mentioned, a simplified retroactive point of transformation would be the destruction of the second Temple in 70 CE, but in reality, the transformation occurred over a period of time.

The primary method of worship in Judaism 1.0 was anchored in the Temple and the sacrificial service, and in Judaism 2.0, the prayers. But even 1,000 years prior, in the Biblical story of Chana described in the book of Samuel, she introduced the concepts of prayers at the Tabernacle in Shiloh. Similarly, while the primary venue of worship in Judaism 1.0 was through the Temple, we know of the existence of synagogues centuries prior to the Temple's destruction.

Same can be said to the transformation from Judaism 2.0 to Judaism 3.0. Perhaps in the future people will point to the 1948 establishment of the Jewish state as the point when Judaism transformed and Zionism became its organizing principle, but as discussed in this book, the transformation to Judaism 3.0 occurred over a period of time and did not take full effect until well into the second decade of the 21st century.

3. RESTRUCTURING VS. TRANSFORMATION

A corporate restructuring can be a tactical one, for example, when a division or line of business is reorganized or eliminated, or it could be transformative. For example, Netflix moved from being all about receiving physical videos by mail to being about streaming of content.

Similarly, countries can restructure tactically – merging into one and breaking apart (Soviet Union, Yugoslavia), inter-company and inter-country relations can restructure (EU, OPEC, PPT). Scotland can be at certain times in unison with England and at other times, not. Similarly, with ideas – they evolve, they change tactically. But restructuring of companies, concepts, countries, entities and ideas can also be transformative.

Corn has been radically transformed. What is corn? In 1990, the answer would have been: "Corn is food." But by 2018, the answer would already be: "Corn is a source of energy." Only a small fraction of today's corn production is used for food. Its biggest use is energy and animal feed – collectively about 70%. Less than 20% of today's corn is used for food.

That has significant implications on the "corn community" – the farmers growing it, the cultivation decisions they make – their self-perception. [2]

Much of the consumer world is not aware of corn's transformation, since they only come in contact with corn through its original primary use as food. But the lack of awareness of an individual corn consumer, who always thought of corn as food, does not affect the fact that corn has transformed.

Similarly with technological innovations and the industrial revolution. Similarly with governments, too. Government restructuring could be linear – moving a particular unit to another department, but it could also be radical, such as from monarchy to republic.

Same with concepts. For example, marriage. Who would have thought a century ago that marriage would be anything other than a union between a man and a woman? The developments over the last decades show that concepts can also transform over time.

4. Organizing Principle of Judaism

There are over seven billion people in the world. They are grouped in one form or another, such as through countries, cultures and religions. Each of those seven billion people has his own hierarchy of identities associated with such groupings.

The sustainability of each of those groupings – be it Catholics, Belgians, Arabs, Harvard alumni – is a function of how strongly its members identify with the group – where it is in their individual hierarchy of identities.

In order for a group to remain as a viable entity, it must have a relevant organizing principle, something that unites its members. The organizing principle serves as an architecture that binds together the loose group of individuals who have conflicting interests, views and practices through a central reference point that is clear both to members and outsiders. For Jews, it is the Jewish nation; it is Zionism.

As explained in this book, Zionism is now the primary way in which Jews connect to their Judaism, and by which the outside world perceives the Jews. Israel is the geographical expression of Zionism, but Zionism is much broader than just its geographical expression. Zionism is the national expression of Judaism. A transformation of Judaism, whereby the Jewish national aspect is becoming its organizing principle and Israel once again becomes the primary Jewish point of orientation, is both

---

2 – United States Department of Agriculture, Economic Research Service, Aug 1, 2019.

natural and simple. It is on the one hand, a return to the natural state of being, and on the other, merely a shift from one aspect of the Jewish nation-religion to the other.

The transformation to Judaism 3.0 is less radical than other transformations discussed earlier; less radical than Christianity, Islam, Citigroup, corn and the emergence of Middle East nationalism.

Other groups have other organizing principles, too. As discussed, for much of the Arab world it has historically been the clan. While the West likes to view the Arabs in a national context, whether pan-Arab or through "line in the sand" states, for most Arabs themselves, the clan and the blood-relations are the relevant grouping. Loyalty runs within the clans, marriages traditionally occur within the clans. Different clans have different narratives, ethos and business practices. Clans can transcend countries, dialects, religious observance levels, and in some isolated cases even religion (there are mixed Muslim-Christian clans). They are united by a degree of mutual responsibility that each member of the clan has to the other.

(i) Reverse-merger of Zionism into Rabbinic Judaism

Taking it a step further, the transformation can be viewed as a "reverse-merger" of Zionism into Rabbinic Judaism. The once small nascent movement which was born fairly recently, is inheriting the infrastructure, awareness, membership and consciousness that the "parent" has.

Yet, one thing should be made clear: No aspect of Rabbinic Judaism is compromised as a result of the transformation. The Jewish laws, traditions, rituals – they are unaffected and as will be discussed, even strengthened. Zionism is succeeding Rabbinic Judaism as the organizing principle of Judaism by incorporating it into itself. Judaism 3.0 strengthens Rabbinic Judaism through all its streams.

Indeed, the debates, discussions and disputes about religious aspects can be both more genuine and more civil, once it is accepted that the organizing principle of Judaism is no longer the religious aspect, but the national aspect.

(ii) Organizing principle is not just a point of orientation

Early Zionist thinkers, including Ahad Ha'Am (Asher Zvi Hirsch Ginsberg), viewed the Jewish state as a spiritual center. The Jews would stay in their respective communities, and Israel would be there as a point of orientation.

Even before Ahad Ha'Am, Herzl delved into this relationship between people (which he called the subjective element) and land (objective). He argued that the people are the more important of the two, claiming that sovereignty can be accepted even without land: "One sovereignty, for example, which has no objective basis at all, is perhaps the most respected one in the world. I refer to the sovereignty of the Pope."

Zionism's relation to Israel could in theory have evolved to resemble that of the Catholic Church to the Vatican. The Vatican is a spiritual center for Catholics, as well as the provider of the religious infrastructure. Yet, only a tiny fraction of Catholics reside in the Vatican. The Vatican is a religious point-of-orientation for Catholics, but certainly not the organizing principle of Catholics. A practicing Catholic in America or in France is not expressing his Christianity through Vatican culture. Moreover, a non-practicing Catholic has no relationship with the Vatican.

The circumstances with Zionism turned out to be very different. It went far beyond the Jewish state being merely a point of orientation of Judaism. Not only have the "Israelis" taken over Zionism, but to a large extent, so has Israeli culture, achievements and contributions to humanity "taken over" Judaism. Unlike the Vatican, Israel remains relevant in the life of both the practicing and non-practicing Jews alike – both in the positive and the negative. Hence, Zionism has turned into the organizing principle of Judaism. Yet, one needs to understand the confinement of an "organizing principle."

(iii) Organizing principle is not absolute order

Organizing principle is "a core assumption from which everything else by proximity can derive a classification or a value. It is like a central reference point that allows all other objects to be located, often used in a conceptual framework." [3]

An organizing principle is not a hierarchical concept. It is a reference point, an architecture. Indeed, Zionism is the architecture which binds Judaism together.

During the first phase of Judaism, Biblical Judaism (Judaism 1.0) was the organizing principle of Judaism and the architecture that bound together Judaism: The Temple, the sacrifices, the centrality of Jerusalem and the Land of Israel.

There were Jews who lived outside of Israel; there were Jews who likely had never been to the Temple or participated in the ritual of sacrifices. But their Judaism was intertwined with the principles of Biblical Judaism. It is through those principles by which Jews connected to their Judaism.

3 – Wikipedia.

Similarly, during the second phase of Judaism, Rabbinic Judaism (Judaism 2.0) was the organizing principle of Judaism and the architecture that bound together Judaism: the prayers, Jewish law, rituals, canonization of the Oral Torah, and the yearning to return to the ancestral homeland. There were Jews who were detached from those elements, but their Judaism was still based on the principles of Rabbinic Judaism. It was through those principles by which Jews connected to their Judaism; similarly with the third phase of Judaism.

As is shown in the following sections, Zionism (Judaism 3.0) is becoming the architecture not only through which Jews connect to their Judaism but also by which the outside world perceives the Jews. As mentioned, we are at a unique time in which the vast majority of Jews (85%) live in only two centers: Israel and North America. Therefore, to assess the transformation, one must delve into changing realities and analyze undercurrents in those two arenas.

V

The Transformation Of Judaism – Israel

N
o one can think of Israel without Judaism or of Judaism without Israel. Israel and Judaism are intuitively intertwined. But this by itself does not suggest that we are in Judaism 3.0. In fact, in Israel's first 70 years, hurdles existed that made the transformation of Judaism outright impossible.

1. 20TH CENTURY: ZIONISM'S SUCCESS, BUT HURDLES DELAY THE TRANSFORMATION

When Herzl launched political Zionism in 1897 in Basel, he wrote: "Were I to sum up the Basel Congress in a word – which I shall guard against pronouncing publicly – it would be this: At Basel I founded the Jewish state. If I said this out loud today, I would be greeted with universal laughter. In five years perhaps, and certainly in fifty years, everyone will perceive it."

Indeed, precisely 50 years and a little over 8 months after Herzl wrote those words, the Jewish state was founded.

Zionism not only accomplished its practical objective in creating a Jewish state, but it also exceeded all external expectations – persevering and then prospering.

It was considered foolish to declare statehood in May 1948, as Arab armies were set to invade and obliterate the nascent state. Ben-Gurion insisted and Israel prevailed against all odds.

It was also considered by some to be unsustainable to allow the massive immigration into the nascent struggling state in the years that followed – Israel's population doubled in its first two years. [1]

Yet Israel was able to absorb the massive immigration, build institutions, a government, a state, a military, an economy and to survive.

Zionism became the salvation of Jewish life. In the same decade that much of Judaism was eradicated, Zionism led the revival and fulfilled the core Jewish tenet of the return – return at last, after 2,000 years of exile and misery.

The success was also with respect to social integration. The melting pot in Israel was working. European Jews, Middle Eastern Jews,

---

1 – From 650,000 in 1948 to 1,300,000 in 1950. Israel Central Bureau of Statistics.

Holocaust survivors, pioneers, religious, seculars, old and young, were all able to unite behind one flag, one national anthem, one language and one dream that was becoming a reality with their own making. The manifestation of Zionism in the State of Israel was working.

Normally, one would expect that the story of the nation coming back home after 2,000 years of exile would coincide with a transformation of this nation. It is no longer about life in exile, it is about life at home. But this was not the case with the Jewish nation and the establishment of the Jewish state. Through the 2010s, Zionism was merely viewed as an important part of Judaism, but not its anchor. Insurmountable hurdles in the first 70 years of Israel's independence prevented the transformation from materializing:

– *Zionism's secular nature:* Until the second decade of the 21st century, Zionism was perceived to be a staunchly secular movement that even rejected Jewish religiosity. Therefore, it could not possibly be the organizing principle of Judaism.

– *Haredi objection:* A large portion of the Jewish world and of Israel's citizens were anti-Zionist. The fierce ultra-Orthodox objections made the notion of Zionism being the organizing principle of Judaism laughable. It could not be the anchor of Judaism if those Jews who are the most observant utterly reject it.

– *Socialism:* Zionism evolved to be a socialist movement. This was at the time when a significant degree of the world Jewish population was capitalist and outright rejected socialism. Such identification precluded Zionism from taking center-stage in Judaism.

– *Poor and fragile:* Through the early 21st century, Israel remained poor, relatively isolated and vulnerable. It was perceived by Jews and non-Jews alike as a "charity case," that needed to be supported – not as the engine of Judaism.

– *Status quo driven:* Given its daunting challenges in the early years, Israel put a halt on the topic of Israel's religiosity by locking-in a status quo that deferred such discussion to an unspecified later date. This notion precluded the possibility of a radical transformation of Judaism.

Hurdles Now Removed – Transformation Occurring

Significant shifts in Israeli society over the last few years has led to the removal of those hurdles. The path to the transformation of Judaism has been paved.

2. ZIONISM ABANDONING ITS SECULAR ETHOS – RETURN TO JUDAISM

Zionism is no longer associated with secularism. This is due to two developments: further democratization of Israel, leading to a shift of power from the secular minority to the religious/traditional majority, and a religious rapprochement amongst Israeli seculars themselves, while staying secular.

(i) The artificial over-secularization of Zionism

The Ben-Gurion stream that took over Zionism in the 1930s shaped Israel in its mold. This included strong secular motifs. Moreover, the secular way of life was idealized. Israel's political leaders, business leaders, military leaders and the elite – they were seculars. If someone in that group wore a kipa, it would be highly noticeable.

Srulik, the icon representing the Israeli of the 1950s (the Israeli "Uncle Sam") was certainly secular. Same goes for the ethos of 20th-century Zionism: The kibbutz, farming, settling the land, building a Hebrew city – these were all associated with secularism and even to one extent or another, with the rejection of religiosity.

From neutral to secular

This overt secularism and rejection of religion was not in the early design of Zionism. It evolved to be this way. It was certainly not reflected in the 1897 Basel Program, which launched political Zionism nor in early resolutions of the Zionist Congresses. Indeed, during the first Zionist Congress, Herzl went out of his way to assure that Zionism would not do anything that would hurt the religious aspects of Judaism.

Moreover, right from the start of the first Congress, Zionism was launched with a blessing. Before any resolution could be passed, any speech heard, or any action taken, Herzl and his colleagues placed Zionism in its religious context. The Congress, and Zionism, was conceived with a blessing of *Shehehiyanu* – thanking God for bringing the Jews to this moment.

After Herzl's death in 1904, political Zionism faded into hibernation. With the lack of political progress, the balance of power had shifted from Europe, where the political attempts were made, to Palestine, where practical Zionism was practiced – purchasing land and settling.

Consequently the young settlers (The Israeli "Mayflower" generation), even though a small minority of all Zionists at the time – less than 1% of Zionist Congress delegates – had set much of the ethos of the rising Zionist movement. This was particularly in its cultural aspects, given the absence of political progress.

The masses who came to Palestine in the next few decades took their tone from the "Mayflowers." As discussed previously, for many of the "Mayflowers," Zionism was a revolutionary movement, consistent with other revolutionary movements of the time: creating a new Jew that had not much to do with his predecessor. Part of the rebellion was against religiosity, against Rabbinic Judaism.

While there were various other streams of Zionism at the time, including a religious one, the tone and ethos was shaped by those young secular settlers such as David Ben-Gurion who accentuated the revolutionary aspects of Zionism and left little room for religiosity in their Zionism.

Secular takeover

This exceedingly secular group took over the political institutions of Zionism in the 1930s through elections and shaped Israel's narrative for years to come. Therefore, their secular narrative stayed through Israel's 1948 establishment and until today. This is despite the fact that by Israel's early years, seculars were already a minority of Israel's population.

As mentioned, two years after Israel was founded, the country's population doubled. More than half of the incoming immigrants of the "mass migration" were religious and traditional Jews from the Middle East.

Just like in Europe today, there was a strong effort to integrate those new immigrants from the Middle East and North Africa. Iraqi, Persian, Moroccan, Yemenite and other Middle Eastern Jews were encouraged to "Israelize" into the melting pot ethos, which was secular. Perhaps some even hoped that those immigrants would abandon their "primitive" religious behavior and embrace the enlightened secular themes of the founders; that they would be "Europeanized."

Yet, the effort to secularize, what soon became half of Israel's population, was only partially successful. Most of those immigrants from the Middle East chose to keep elements of their religious faith – this gave birth to the "traditional" sector.

(ii) Jewish resurgence amongst seculars and the de-sectorization of Israel

About 43% of Israelis classify themselves as seculars. [2] No doubt seculars remain the dominant group in Israeli society. Yet unlike in the early decades, Israeli seculars are now increasingly incorporating elements of the Jewish religion into their lives.

As will be discussed, this is a product of a number of long-term processes occurring in Israel, including the blurring of the sector lines which in turn allows an Israeli in one sector to consume experiences previously only available in another sector; the emergence of the secular Datlaf ("sometimes religious") as the predominant stream within Israeli secularism, and the admiration Israelis have for the National-Religious sector, especially due to their leadership in military service and country-building. All of this dramatically alters the relationship between Zionism and the Jewish religion. Zionism is no longer rejective of the Jewish religion, it is intertwined with it.

De-sectorization allows seculars to somewhat de-secularize

In Israel's first few decades, anyone who was not part of the secular mainstream was considered being in a sector: the religious sector, the ultra-Orthodox sector, the Arab sector, the Sephardi traditional sector (Jewish immigrants from the Middle East and North Africa).

Placing the anomalies on the side as "sectors" gave room for the mainstream secular narrative to further flourish. The pronounced exception gave more validity to the rule and the exaggerated association of Zionism with secularism.

Ben-Gurion's Labor party ruled Israel in an *L'etat c'est nous* (the state is us) type of way, and therefore effectively elevated the secular Israeli to be the "Israeli icon." The end of their reign in 1977 marked the decline of the "party voice" and a shift towards a more pluralistic and diverse Israel that no longer aspired to one particular "Israeli icon." Indeed, by the second decade of the 21st century, Israel has been going through a slow process of de-sectorization.

The blending of the sector lines enables secular Israelis to engage in experiences that were previously limited to the religious sector, as sectors now consume experiences once unavailable to them. For example, an Ashkenazi Israeli can today enjoy Sephardi music such as Eyal Golan and Sarit Hadad – a taboo till the mid-1980s where such music was not

2 – Israel Central Bureau of Statistics.

even allowed on Israeli radio and television. Similarly, until the 2010s, mainstream radio stations played secular Israeli music, such as that of Shlomo Artzi and Berry Sakharof, while religious radio stations played religious Israeli music, such as that of Ishay Ribo and Yonatan Razel. But today, Israeli seculars enjoy religious music played on mainstream stations.

One of the most popular songs of the late 2010s was a duet by Shlomo Artzi and Ishay Ribo. In 2020, one of the more popular songs was a duet by Berry Sakharof and Yonatan Razel. In early 2021, one of the most popular songs was a duet by Aviv Geffen, an icon of the Israeli secular left, and Avraham Fried, a popular Haredi singer. The song had over 1,000,000 YouTube views within three weeks of its release.

More broadly, the blurring of the sector lines is evident when it comes to religious practices. The commonly accepted religious continuum in Israel runs from "secular" to "traditional" to "religious" to "Haredi." Increasingly, these divisions are getting blurred.

On the right side of the continuum, many Haredis are no longer as isolated as they were in past decades. Some are adopting behavior patterns more common to the National-Religious movement: Employment, military service, living in settlements, believing in the centrality of the Land of Israel. This is especially the case among Sephardi-Haredis, Chabad, parts of the Breslov Hasidic group, and so-called unaffiliated Haredis.

Meanwhile, the blurring of lines is occurring on the National-Religious end as well. Many individuals in that community are adopting religious patterns similar to those of the Haredis, while maintaining National-Religious social and behavioral patterns. Those are known as Hardal, an acronym for "Haredi National-Religious." This is partly a result of the 1970s and 1980s, when much of the National-Religious leadership took a turn towards stricter religious tones.

Such a turn has also contributed to a counter-reaction, with the rise of the so-called dati-lite (religious-lite). Many of the religious-lites are now finding more in common with those to their left of the religious continuum – the traditional and secular communities – than with the Hardals to their right. This is evident in their social networks, voting patterns and even who they opt to date and marry.

In addition, those who have left the religious community – the datlash, which stands for dati l'she'avar, or formerly religious – bring a religious flavor to their new secular communities, since many of them keep elements of their previous lifestyle, even after taking off their kipas.

The secular Israeli, who previously did not have much interaction with religious people, now has religious-lite friends, now has datlash friends and he himself is at greater social liberty to consume religious experiences.

The de-sectorization of Israel has broader implications. Political parties started mixing in the 2010s. For example, the large Yesh-Atid party which was perceived to carry the secular flag, had a rabbi as its #2 person. Its successor in 2019, the Blue and White party, had a Haredi woman as one of its leaders. Similarly, the National-Religious party had a secular person as its party leader and chairwoman. The secular Yesh-Atid party attracts religious voters and actively courts them, while the National-Religious party attracts secular voters and actively courts them. In the April 2019 election, former leaders of the National-Religious party formed a party that is officially half-secular, half-religious. In June 2021, the former leader of the National-Religious party, Naftali Bennett, became Israel's prime minister, much thanks to support from Israeli seculars.

The de-sectorization also has demographic effects. A mere fifty years ago Israelis almost universally married along Sephardi-Ashkenazi divide, yet today many of the secular newlyweds are of mixed heritage. According to one research study, 25% of Israeli babies today are born to such mixed couples, compared with only 5% of babies born in the 1950s. [3] That by itself contributes to Jewish revival. Given that the previous generation of Ashkenazis were predominantly secular and the previous generation of Sephardic were predominantly traditional/ religious, mixed couples bring a stronger Jewish exposure to the current generation. A child born to such mixed couples is more likely to be exposed to a grandparent who regularly goes to synagogue or otherwise displays religious practices central to his life.

THE MYTH OF THE ISRAELI TRIBES

In recent years, a framework has been gaining popularity, suggesting that there are four insular tribes in Israel, and that they are getting more and more polarized. Those are the seculars, religious, Haredis and Arabs.

This framework was put forward by Israeli President Reuven Rivlin and supported in various forms by academics and thinkers such as Amnon Rubinstein, so much that it became dogmatic and universally accepted in Israel.

The motivation behind suggesting this framework varies. Some claim that President Rivlin and others put forward the framework to dispel

---

3 – Okun, B. S., and Khait-Marelly, O. "Demographic behaviour of adults of mixed ethnic ancestry: Jews in Israel", 2008. This number has likely gone up.

the misperception that the seculars are the predominant "tribe" – that the framework is meant to point out that seculars, who in the days of the Labor party l'etat c'est nous regime, indeed controlled the ethos and narrative of Zionism, are in fact just one of the four "tribes." The other "tribes," which the secular "ruling class" is less familiar with, should also have a say.

Others approach this from the reverse. Not as a way to demonstrate that Israel should democratize and accept the end of secular rule, but that Israel is a fractured society and in decline due to internal strife. This view is heavily promoted by much of the Israeli media and has entered the mainstream conscience of Israelis. Israel's 71st Independence Day theme song, "a tribe of brothers and sisters", was mocked by the satire TV show *Eretz Nehederet* who redid the song as "a country of tribes and camps."

Contrary to the misperception of the tribes, Israeli Jewish society is one of the most homogenous in the Western world. Every country has divisions and "tribes." A gay playwright in Los Angeles is very different from a rancher in Texas. An African American living in subsidized housing in Harlem is very different from a white investment banker living on Park Avenue in New York, just a few minutes' walk away.

Same with European societies and other countries. The lines between Israeli seculars, religious, and the Haredis are clearly there, but they draw on a rock-solid commonality. As discussed, those sector lines are softening, not hardening.

Rebelling against the rebels

In addition to the blurring of the inter-sector lines, intra-sector trends within the seculars lead to a greater embrace of the Jewish religion by seculars relative to the early days. In a sense, Israeli seculars are rebelling against the rebels:

ROUND 1: THE REBELS (EARLY 20TH CENTURY)

Ben-Gurion and his generation rebelled against the previous generations of Jews. In their eyes, those were exiled Diaspora Jews, weak Jews, defeatist Jews and indeed religious Jews. Hence, the "Ben-Gurions" were implicitly rebelling against Jewish religiosity.

Since Israel was shaped in the image of the "Ben-Gurions," Israeli seculars growing up in the 20th century felt that part of their strong expression of Zionism and patriotism was a latent suppression of their own religiosity.

The Israeli religiosity was certainly there, alongside strong Jewish identity. It was expressed through various "non-intrusive" manners such as believing in God, observing major Jewish holidays and having life-changing events marked through religious ceremonies. However, it was done with some degree of apologetics.

Religious-tendency amongst seculars were disparaged. Nobody wanted to be suspected of turning religious. A secular person walking to a Bar Mitzvah in a synagogue on Shabbat would wait until the very last minute to put a kipa on his head, not to be seen and be suspected of having turned religious.

The strong secular narrative was reflected through various derivatives of the "party voice:" the youth movement, the social structure, the military social hierarchy, the business hierarchy. While the secular elite did not reject religious people, it certainly condemned secular people turning religious.

The ultimate family tragedy would be if a secular's child would be "Hozer B'tshuva" (become religious, akin to "born again") – a term that till this day sends shivers through Israeli seculars. This was associated with abandonment of everything the parent believed in, leaving one's family, clan, tribe, a departure, a one-way ticket out of society, a defection. This was somewhat akin to that era's stories of Americans who defected to Russia.

High-profile "defections," such as of actors Uri Zohar, Pupik Arnon and the wife of singer Arik Einstein created the ethos of "Hazara B'tshuva" as something for which parents needed to be on guard. This was along the lines of not assuming your child will not be tempted to do drugs or join a gang. There was a sense that those woes could happen in any family. [4]

It was clear that while there was fierce objection to a secular turning religious, there was not at all rejection of the religious sector. On the contrary, they were strongly respected. They were clearly not as "cool" as the seculars, but they did not bother the seculars either, and were viewed with some degree of reverence.

National-Religious people (the non-Haredi religious), were at peace with that image and their inferior status in the Israeli Zionist hierarchy. This was depicted by author Amos Oz, who reportedly labeled the National-Religious as the kosher inspector of the Cafeteria car on the Zionist train.

---

4 – This is captured in Einstein's melancholic song "Hu Hazar B'tshuva" (He became religious). It is one of the saddest of Israeli songs, with lines such as "I lost you my friend". It is played on memorial days and other sad occasions.

ROUND 2: REBELLING AGAINST THE REBELS (EARLY 21ST CENTURY)

Ben-Gurion and his generation's rebelling against the Jewish religion shaped Israeli Zionism in the 20th century, but today the new generation of Israelis are rebelling against the rebels.

Many in the current generation of Israeli seculars feel they were stripped of religious content, experiences and spirituality. While not becoming religious, Israeli seculars are finding new ways to re-engage with religiosity.

The emergence of the Datlaf ("sometimes religious")

Unlike secular Europeans, most secular Israelis do not reject religion, which, after all, is intertwined with their national identity. The vast majority of Israeli seculars are also not agnostic, and certainly not atheist.

Arguably, secular Israelis are more similar to American religious Christians than they are to their European secular counterparts. Many of the self-identified religious Christians in America view their religion as a central part of their identity, even though some of them may not engage in the full gamut of Christian practices on a regular basis. In this sense, the so-called religious "Cafeteria Christians," are similar to the Israeli seculars.

An increasing number of secular Israelis are engaging in ad hoc religious experiences while keeping their secular lifestyles. They are selectively choosing religious practices that suit them – whether related to Shabbat, halacha (Jewish law), rituals, learning or philosophy. These people can be categorized as seculars who consume religious experiences a la carte – they are sometimes religious, at their own discretion – hence, the term Datlaf, which is the Hebrew acronym for "sometimes religious" (dati lifamim).

This search for Jewish content and spirituality has contributed to the evolution of a "Jewish fashion" in secular Israel. It is reflected in secular attendance alongside religious participants in religious study groups and Bible-reading programs such as 929, the daily study of the Bible's 929 chapters (hundreds of such groups have been created throughout the country in recent years); selective observance of Jewish laws and rituals; participation in holiday programs such as Shavuot evening Torah study sessions and a general reverence to religion, religiosity and faith. It is also demonstrated in the popularity among the seculars of religious singers singing songs of faith – such as Yonatan Razel and Ishay Ribo. More broadly, it includes a change in the perception of religiosity itself.

Part of this rebellion might also include a latent insurgency against idealizing secularism and suppressing religiosity. But unlike in the past, the secular Israeli can incorporate such religious experiences without being perceived as becoming observant, a Hozer B'tshuva.

Unshackled from the pressure to adhere to the old guard's norms, there is no longer a need to be "religious at home and secular on the street;" now, one can openly be sometimes religious and sometimes secular.

Importantly, Datlaf behavior is a subset of secular behavior; it is not an extension of religious-lite. A person who genuinely states that he observes religious fast-days such as Yom Kippur and Tisha b'Av by refraining from having snacks between meals is not considered fasting, yet his statement indicates that he has some degree of consciousness regarding the Jewish law that requires him to do so. The Datlaf cannot be considered "religious between the meals." He is still secular, but he sometimes consumes religious experiences.

The Datlaf phenomenon brings with it an ancillary question of finding Datlaf-friendly rabbis – or perhaps it marks an erosion of the role of rabbis. Notwithstanding that "every mitzvah counts" (every element of observance), the concept of "sometimes observant" is fundamentally contradictory to the core of Jewish law. This is an issue that has emerged in the last two decades among the traditional and religious-lite sectors as well, given the non-existence of traditional and religious-lite rabbis in Orthodoxy.

What does seem clear is that secular Israelis choose to stay within the realm of Israeli Judaism with which they are familiar – Orthodoxy. They do not gravitate toward the Reform or Conservative streams, which comprise the vast majority of affiliated American Jews. They instead choose a point in the "sometimes" Orthodox continuum, as opposed to abandoning the continuum and going elsewhere. This rapprochement of secular Israelis with the Jewish religion removes a primary hurdle that stood in the way of a Jewish transformation until now, but moreover, it showcases the interconnection of being Israeli and being Jewish – of the Jewish national expression (Zionism) and the Jewish religion.

BROAD RANGE OF DATLAFS

There is no doubt that the range of "sometimes" observers is broad. As the Datlaf trend progresses, one might see variations such as the "Datlaf-lite" and "Hardalaf" (sometimes Haredi/National-Religious).

The Datlaf-lite might mark Shabbat by watching a TV program about the weekly Torah portion, with selective practices such as saying Kiddush or refraining from checking his emails.

For the Hardalaf, religiosity would be a more central part of life.

Whatever practices he chooses to adhere to, he would execute them with greater zeal. He might go to off-site religious seminars or join a Maimonides study group. While not wearing outwardly religious garb and choosing to stay secular, the Hardalaf would have a much higher religious consciousness and maybe even view religiosity as a Utopian value, a point of orientation (analogous to a vehement American Zionist who chooses to stay in the US).

Regardless of where on the "sometimes" continuum a secular Israeli chooses to park, it is becoming increasingly evident that the "never" attitude and anti-religious sentiments of the past are fading.

THE DATLAF'S CONTRIBUTION TO RELIGIOSITY

Surprisingly, the Datlaf brings to the religious practice of Judaism depth and vigor. If for a religious person, going to synagogue is to one degree or another a "routine," for the Datlaf, going to synagogue and consuming other religious experiences is organic and arguably done with stronger meaning.

For example, in Kohav Hatsafon, a secular neighborhood in Tel Aviv, where it is rare to see a person wearing a kipa on the street, a synagogue opened for the first time in 2015. The synagogue is not just well attended on Shabbat and holidays, but the worshipers (seculars/Datlafs), tend to participate in the full service, from start to finish, and seem to do so with great interest.

In other synagogues in Tel Aviv, composed of religious worshipers, one often witnesses people going in and out, as well as chatting during the service. There is a particular mundane "routine of worship." This, of course, is understandable since the religious person goes to synagogue every day — even a few times a day — while for the secular this is a unique experience. Yet, it highlights the contribution of the secular to religiosity in Israel — here is a synagogue full of seculars who attend less often, but once there, they often have a deeper experience than the religious worshipers.

Same with Bible study group: Seculars bring different perspectives, being less aware, and therefore less prejudicial of the views of Biblical interpreters and notable rabbis. A secular person would offer a point of view that a religious person may not have been aware of. In this way, seculars contribute to the renewal of the Jewish religion, and are doing so in an Orthodox way, compatible with Jewish law.

Another example is the large attendance for Selihot (prayers to God for forgiveness) that have occurred in public spaces, such as at the port of Tel Aviv before Yom Kippur. The port, epicenter of secular life with bars and clubs, hosts hundreds of people for this annual event – by observation very few of them wear kipas. This was not entertainment, but judging by the intensity of the participants, it was a meaningful religious experience for the hundreds of Tel Aviv seculars who were taking part in this religious ceremony.

Through such experiences, seculars are not just "students" learning about religion, but actual contributors who help lead to religious growth.

Seculars' admiration of religious people

One cannot ignore a soft trend in Israel that has developed over the last years. Israeli seculars tend to "look up" to religious people – a complete reversal from the looking down at the religious as the "Kosher inspector in the Zionist train" in the early years. This is driven in part by the characteristics of the National-Religious community: Greater giving, volunteering and civic service. Nowhere does this come to bear more strongly than in the changing composition of the country's military command.

In the 20th century, the admired commanders and war heroes were typically secular people from the kibbutz and the moshav. Today there is a high number of religious senior officers and heroes. The commander, as a role model, shapes much of the narrative of a 19-year-old soldier; hence, a commander with a kipa tends to contribute to the destigmatization of religious Judaism.

(iii) Democratization of Israel – Shift of power from the secular minority to the traditional / religious majority

Like the United States (and unlike Europe), the Israeli population is predominantly religious. About 57% of Israel's Jewish population classify themselves either as Haredi, National-Religious or traditional. [5]

Yet, as discussed, the Zionist ethos and political power has until recently been held by the secular minority. This painted Zionism with secular themes. While Israel's secularism was not as "sacred" as in France or pre-Erdogan Turkey, it was clearly the fashion and code of its mainstream. This was true not only in the early days, but through the turn of the 21st century, when seculars were already a shrinking minority.

But in recent years, the traditional and religious majority has been taking more and more leadership roles in Israeli culture, community, politics, industry and academia.

---

5 – Israel Central Bureau of Statistics.

Politically, there has been both an increase in Knesset members from religious parties as well as religious members in secular parties. In June 2021, a religious person, Naftali Bennett, became the prime minister of Israel. The other main challenger to Prime Minister Netanyahu in that election was also a Shabbat-observing Traditional (per his own definition), Gideon Saar. In the media, more and more religious reporters are seen on-screen and incorporated into the mainstream news organizations. For example, the chief political correspondent at Channel 11's News happens to be Haredi, and the chief political correspondent at Channel 12's News is National-Religious. In the military, within one decade, the senior military officers have turned from adamantly secular (Kibbutz/Moshav dominant) to religious-heavy (kipa-wearing generals). Similarly, the elite units of the army are more and more religious, and combat units across the military in general attract a higher proportion of religious soldiers.

Therefore, not only are the seculars consuming more religious experiences and having a closer relationship with their Jewish faith, but a shift of power is occurring away from the secular minority towards the religious and traditional majority. This impacts the essence of Zionism – no longer over-associated with secularism.

(iv) Changing dynamics within the religious communities contributes to the Zionification of Judaism

Intra-sector developments within the religious community contribute to such a trend and to a closer association of Zionism with Judaism.

Religious-lites penetrate secular society

The emergence of the religious-lites mentioned earlier, and their presence in Israeli secular circles sprinkles the Israeli experience with more of a Jewish feel. The ubiquity of the religious-lites makes Israel look a bit more Jewish – in its bars, cafes, workplaces, concerts and beaches. More kipas are seen, more blessings are heard, more of Judaism is felt.

Equally importantly, it transplants a much-needed boost of ideology and of optimism into the broader Israeli society. The National-Religious community is today a leader in military service, community volunteering and Zionist education. To a large degree, it is holding the baton of ideology and optimism that was held in the early days by the socialist "Mayflowers." The National-Religious community can help spread such values into the broader Israeli society, given the increased integration and latent demand for the elevation of such values.

US Modern Orthodox connect to religious-lites, hence, to Israel

The growth of the religious-lites also has implications for American Jewry and its view of Zionism. Arguably, religious-lites are more similar in their behavior (if not theology and customs) to their Modern Orthodox "cousins" across the ocean in America than they are to their Hardal "brothers" in Israel. This presents an opportunity for the American Modern Orthodox to adopt or perhaps blend with the Israeli religious-lites.

In addition, with the broad immigration of religious Americans to Israel, there are mixed couples and more mixed socializing between the Israeli religious-lites and the American Modern Orthodox. At the same time, there is less and less coupling between Israeli Hardals and Israeli religious-lites.

There is also the blurring of visible boundaries between the American Modern Orthodox and the Israeli religious-lites, particularly in dress. American Modern Orthodox often wear an "Israeli" knitted kipa, and Israeli National-Religious often wear an "American" leather kipa.

Emergence of a pan-religious experience

More broadly, much of the religious experience in Israel is turning into "open-architecture:" a morning class with a Litvak rabbi, afternoon class with an American Modern Orthodox teacher, evening service with a National-Religious congregation.

It used to be that an Iraqi Jew would go to an Iraqi synagogue and a Chabad Jew would study with a Chabad rabbi. Now it is mixed. The blurring of intra-sub-sector lines within the religious community creates a more unified version of Judaism in Israel. Such a pan-Orthodox experience is an Israeli experience. In other words, even the religious aspect of Judaism in Israel is turning into a Zionist experience. Unlike in the past, this is increasingly the case for the ultra-Orthodox as well.

Non-Zionist Haredi turning Zionist and rising

EARLY REJECTION OF ZIONISM BY THE HAREDIS

Early on, much of the Haredi establishment rejected Zionism. While some accepted the notion of a return to Palestine as a tactical method to save the lives of Jews in Europe, many others fiercely rejected it, believing that the return of the Jews to Israel could only be accomplished as part of a Messianic process. Zionism, in their view, violated the sacred Three

Oaths by attempting to accelerate the arrival of the Messiah, and hence, it was blasphemy. (According to the Jewish faith, the Three Oaths were a commitment made during Talmudic times, which included the oath not to rise from the exile prior to the arrival of the Messiah.)

With such an unequivocal rejection of Zionism from a significant group within Judaism, it was clear that it could not be the organizing principle of Judaism. But this is changing.

GROWING ACCEPTABILITY OF ZIONISM BY THE HAREDIS

Today, the majority of the global Haredi population resides in Israel. While most may not be Zionists by self-classification, arguably to a large extent Haredis are Zionists in practice.

A closed community, the Haredis are gradually becoming more core to Israeli life, this while staying religious, staying Haredi and staying in insular communities. This dynamic is possible, thanks to the emerging Israeli model of symbiotic particularity – accepting insular communities that can contribute to and flourish in Israeli society, such as the Druze, as opposed to the European model of aggressive homogenous integration.

In addition, while early in the process, there is a growing propensity of Haredis to work and participate in Israel's economic success. The Coronavirus crisis led to greater acceptability of flexible work conditions, such as working from home and at unconventional hours. This could enable greater Haredi employment without the fear of being exposed to unsuitable outside culture, nor at the expense of studying Torah in religious institutions. Greater Haredi participation in the workforce would create even more touch-points between Haredi and non-Haredi Israelis.

The Haredis' historic objection to Zionism is still reflected today in disdain for Zionism's father figures – Herzl and Ben-Gurion, who in the Haredi narrative led to mass-secularization of observant Jews. The anger is, in particular, at Ben-Gurion who, as discussed, instilled an aggressive secular narrative in the Jewish state early on.

When Haredis speak of Ben-Gurion, they often cite the mass-migration of religious Jews who came from the Middle East, and account for nearly half of today's Israeli population. Haredis accuse Ben-Gurion of "brainwashing" those religious Jews through school curriculum, youth movements, emissaries and secular propaganda. Their Israelization was intertwined with their secularization. Hence, in the popular Haredi narrative, Ben-Gurion robbed Jews of their faith, and did so in the name of Zionism.

But this type of Haredi disdain for Zionism is likely to also dissipate as well. As discussed, secular Israelis themselves are rebelling against this aspect of Ben-Gurion's legacy stripping them of Jewish content. Those secular Israelis are certainly Zionists. A disagreement with one of Zionism's icons should certainly not make someone not a Zionist.

This will also rectify the "guilt by association" Haredis place on Herzl, who died decades before Ben-Gurion's secular policies were enacted. In fact, as mentioned, Herzl, right at his opening speech in the first Zionist Congress, made assurances that Zionism would not do anything that might hurt the Jewish religion.

One of the primary expressions of the Haredis not being Zionists is through their refusal to participate in Israeli governments. But such refusal has eroded over the years. Haredis, in fact, did not participate in most Israeli governments during Israel's first 30 years. But since 1977, Haredi parties have participated repeatedly in coalitions formed by Israeli governments and held key ministerial portfolios in Israel's cabinet. Technically, the portfolios awarded to the Haredis are held by a deputy-minister, as opposed to a minister. However, this deputy-minister has the full authority of a minister. Eventually, in 2016, the hypocrisy of such arrangement was acknowledged, even by the Haredis and they began serving in the Zionist government as ministers (Haredi Ya'acov Litzman upgraded from deputy health minister to health minister). Through these measures, Haredi parties have been a strong and integral part of the Zionist story for the past 40 years.

The composition of the Haredi population itself has evolved. During Israel's early years, Haredis were primarily Ashkenazi descendants of communities in Eastern Europe (as well as of Jerusalemite communities). By the 1980s, more and more Middle Eastern Sephardic Jews joined the ranks of the Haredis. These Sephardi-Haredis tend to have strong Zionist ties (many are military veterans and often self-defined Zionists). While not a direct reflection of population, in the 21st century the electoral division between Sephardi-Haredis and Ashkenazi-Haredis has roughly averaged 65% Sephardic (pro-Zionist) and 35% Ashkenazi – though it should be noted the Sephardi-Haredi parties receive votes from non-Haredis as well. [6]

Even amongst the Ashkenazi Haredis, significant factions have demonstrated a strong display of Zionism. The Chabad faction, part of the Breslov faction, as well as significant elements of the Litvak faction have practiced Zionism through participation in land-settlement, increasing integration into the workforce, social ties with non-Haredi

6 – For more information, see Israel Democratic Institute, Dr. Gilad Malach, "Haredi Parties of Israel – What does the future hold", July 15, 2019.

Israelis and for some, even service in the military.

The hardcore non-Zionists are not as hard core as perceived. Beyond voting and getting elected to Zionist institutions such as the Knesset, and the World Zionist Organization, the Haredi hardcore has also participated along the gamut of Zionist activities in Israel. The 2003 election for mayor of Jerusalem of a hardcore Haredi was a strong demonstration of such participation. Haredi mayor Uri Lupolianski pursued similar Zionist policies as his secular predecessors and successors: Urban developments, housing, institutions, etc. Lupolianski was a Haredi builder of Zion who got the support of nearly 100% of the Haredi community.

Hence, the assertion that Haredis are non-Zionist is primarily a definitional matter. Notwithstanding fringe movements (less than 5%), most Haredis are de facto Zionists while others are even "Zionists in the closet."[7]

More importantly, as Zionism itself becomes more pluralistic, it can incorporate under its umbrella even those who choose to label themselves as non-Zionist Jews. (Just like it embraces as equal the non-Zionist Muslim citizens of Israel, and just like non-believer Jews today are still considered Jewish.)

Whether a closed Haredi community, closed Anglo community, or closed artist community, such communities today are an integral and important part of Zionist pluralism – symbiotic particularity.

New entrants to the periphery of Haredi circles such as Haredi-National-Religious (Hardal) as well as the increasing "open-architecture" of religion in Israel mentioned earlier, contribute to the increasing de facto Zionification of the Haredis.

In addition, the residual Haredi objection to Zionism has less of an impact today than it did in the early days of Zionism. Back then, Haredis served as the exclusive religious Jewish conscience. By now, National-Religious institutions and rabbis have emerged, broadening such religious Jewish consciousness.

GROWING ACCEPTABILITY OF HAREDIS BY ISRAELIS

While Haredis and non-Haredis get along, key issues continue to engulf the Haredis from the broader Israeli population. Perhaps the most polarizing one is the exemption from mandatory military service.

---

7 – For expansion on Haredi issues, see my *Foreign Policy* and *Jerusalem Post* articles available on the book's website (www.judaism-zionism.com): "The Ultra-Orthodox Will Determine Israel's Political Future," *Foreign Policy*, April 17, 2018, "Celebration of Zionism in Sha'arei Hessed", *The Jerusalem Post* August 6, 2016.

On this issue, Haredis feel that it is a two-way street, that there is a tendency to crush the religious soldier's religiosity once in the army – not to let him be himself.

Haredis now realize that this is changing. The army is more understanding of religious needs and is keen to accept Haredi soldiers. Indeed, as Zionism has evolved, so has the military. The secular generals from the kibbutzim and moshavim are gradually giving way to religious ones from settlements and religious neighborhoods. Such dynamics could open doors to those Haredis who previously feared being secularized while in the army.

Moreover, the military created designated outfits and programs that provide a suitable environment for Haredi soldiers. Most notably, Netsah Yehuda – an elite combat unit composed of Haredi soldiers and commanders. This enables Haredis to serve in the military while keeping their Haredi lifestyle.

While military service has been one key issue alienating the wider Israeli society from the Haredi community, the other bone of contention is that of Haredi employment. Many Haredi males get subsidies for studying, and do not work. As a result, Haredis disproportionately receive welfare, leading many Israelis to regard Haredis as a double burden.

However, in affluent Haredi neighborhoods like Jerusalem's Sha'arei Hessed, many Haredi men do work. Some are successful high-tech entrepreneurs, real estate developers, lawyers and doctors – builders of the country and its economy. There is now a growing and recognized sub-segment in the Haredi community called the "working Haredi."

Certainly, as more Haredis participate in the workplace, Israelis have greater interaction with the community, which in turn mitigates the third issue that alienates Israeli society against Haredis: prejudice.

There is growing recognition of the Haredi contribution to the broader community. Long-serving former Health Minister Ya'acov Litzman, who is Haredi, garnered unprecedented support in the first nine years of his service (before getting embroiled in some controversies).

Similarly, Israelis feel a debt of gratitude to the hundreds of ultra-Orthodox medics on motorcycles who are often first to arrive at a scene of an emergency, saving thousands of lives. In addition, many Israelis have benefited from the services of Yad Sarah, a Haredi charity organization that provides subsidized wheelchairs and other rehabilitative home care equipment.

As Israelis increasingly appreciate the contributions of the Haredi community, prejudice will likely erode. Given that Haredi insularity is also a two-way street, the acceptance by the broader society of Haredi lifestyle as legitimate and not something that needs to be "cured" might enable a less defensive and more open posture in the Haredi community.

The changing composition of the Haredi population mentioned earlier also leads to more touch points between Haredis and non-Haredis. In the 1980s, Rabbi Ovadia Yosef created a mass Haredi movement amongst Sephardic Jews.

In a sense, this was going full circle and then some. Sephardic families who were predominantly religious in Iraq, Iran, Yemen, Syria and North Africa were subjected to an aggressive secularization campaign upon arrival in Israel in the 1950s. This was part of the melting pot and Israelization efforts led by Ben-Gurion, and resulted in once-observant Sephardic Jews reducing their religiosity. Just as the seculars are now rebelling against Ben-Gurion stripping Jewish religiosity out of Zionism, so do many children of religious Sephardic families, who went the full circle from being observant before moving to Israel, to secular upon arrival in Israel, back to being even more religious – to being Haredi.

While Ashkenazi Haredis tend to have mostly Haredi relatives, due to arranged marriages and closed communities, Sephardi-Haredi families are mixed. Most Sephardi-Haredi families include close relatives who are traditional and secular. This also contributes to the growing trend of greater mutual acceptability.

Another contributor to the rapprochement between the broader Israeli society and the Haredi society is a reaction to the extreme confrontations that occurred in the 2010s around Haredis. At its height, minor news stories were blown up as ammunition against Haredis – one action of one Haredi villainized the entire sector: Haredis throw stones, Haredis beat up little girls.

Some in the National-Religious community were at the forefront of the anti-Haredi wave during the early 2010s. This is in part due to their disproportionately carrying the burden of military service, and perhaps in part to emphasize to the broader Israeli community that they themselves are not Haredi, putting some distance between themselves and the Haredis. But in recent years, there have been moments of reflections throughout Israeli society, recognizing that the anti-Haredi incitement went too far.

This came to bear in 2020 during the Coronavirus pandemic. The Haredi community was hit hard and quickly accusations flared of Haredis being the spreaders of the virus – these voices by some in the media and even political leaders echoed classic anti-Semitic tones. [8] This was met

---

8 – Avi Shafram: "How Coronavirus Sparked an Open Season of Hate for Haredi Jews", HaAretz, April 29, 2020.

with a remarkable counter-reaction. Even those in the media who are adamant critics of Haredis came to their defense. Tel Aviv, the secular capital, colored its landmark municipal building with a heart that goes out to Bnei Brak (the neighboring Haredi city). The crisis underscored to Israeli seculars and religious alike that the Haredis are brothers – that we are one nation.

This brotherhood was evident again a year later in May 2021, when a stampede during a religious festival on Lag BaOmer killed 45 Haredi worshipers. The mourning was a national mourning. Israeli seculars, Traditionals, National-Religious and Haredis mourned as one, and so did Israeli Arabs and Druze citizens.

The following day, on Shabbat, secular Israelis lined up in Rabin Square to donate blood and that evening to light candles in memory of the victims.

Israel declared a national mourning day, and cafes throughout the country played sad music akin to the feel on Memorial Day. This again dispelled how exaggerated the myths about tribes and rifts are.

GETTING CLOSER

Indeed, rapprochement increasingly occurs on personal levels – in one-to-one relationships. As more Israelis visit Jerusalem, they encounter Haredis, and when Haredis are on vacation, they head to secular Tel Aviv Port and surrounding parks. As the Haredi population grows and expands into previously secular neighborhoods, it is inevitable that Haredis and non-Haredis will have interactions. Once such interactions occur, prejudice gets reduced.

Such Haredi-secular unity was strongly demonstrated in the aftermath of the murder of Shira Banki, who was stabbed by a Haredi man while marching in the gay pride parade in Jerusalem in 2015. What followed was a broad Haredi-gay dialogue. Most notably, in weekly gatherings in Jerusalem's Zion Square for discussion-circles comprised of gays and Haredis. For many in those circles, this was the first time they spoke to a Haredi.

Starting in the early winter of 2017, Haredis from a particular court ("The Jerusalem wing") blocked the main roads of Jerusalem and paralyzed its light rail in retaliation for the arrest of their colleagues for draft-dodging. Haredis are still required to register for the draft, even if later getting an exemption. Most do, but the rabbis of the Jerusalem wing instructed their students to disobey the law, in part for fear that while there for just a few hours registering for the draft, the Israeli secular authorities would try to "secularize" the students and expose them to inappropriate influences.

Blocking traffic for hours led many religious and seculars to express their frustration openly and bluntly. Arguments and dialogue ensued, but what was interesting was the degree of "understanding" by the Israeli public – on both sides of those affected by the demonstration and in general, including the media.

There was no sympathy for their actions blocking the streets or for their refusal to register for the draft, but there was no hostility as there was in previous episodes. This happened around the same time that people in wheelchairs were protesting and doing the same – blocking roads and paralyzing traffic.

Perhaps the natural sympathy to Israel's handicapped protesters projected to lack of hostility towards the Haredi protesters. This led to the "humanization" of the Haredis, allowing seculars to see people beneath the black coats and black hats.

Another step closer was taken during the Coronavirus crisis. Haredi communities, by and large, followed the confining instructions of the "Zionist government," including when it came to lockdown, prohibition to go to synagogues and to the yeshivas. There were exceptions that grew as the crisis prolonged, but both health officials and the prime minister made a point to commend the Haredi community for their cooperation. Public message posters posted in Haredi neighborhoods (pashkevils) stressed the rabbis' order to follow the Israeli government's instructions, and that failure to do so was a violation of Jewish law. It was only symbolic that the Israeli army took command of the Haredi city of Bnei Brak, hit the hardest, and uniformed soldiers delivered food and supplies to the Haredi residents in lockdown.

Another symbolic gesture of getting closer lies in the affiliation of the Haredi health minister who managed the crisis. Rabbi Ya'acov Litzman is a member of the strict Gur Hasidic group. When he himself got sick with the Coronavirus, seculars, religious and Haredis alike prayed for his rapid recovery.

The images of Israeli soldiers supporting the Haredi city of Bnei Brak and a Haredi rabbi directing the national health system of the Zionist state all symbolize how old dogmas about Haredi attitudes towards Zionism are now eroding.

HAREDI-SPRING AND HAREDIS AS FLAG-CARRIERS OF ZIONISM

As a result of growing acceptability of Haredis on the one hand, and the greater propensity of Haredis to work on the other, it is possible that Israel is on the verge of attaining its next engine of economic growth, planted in the high entrepreneurial and studious excellence of the Haredi community.

Every society and every country has a lower social-economic class. In most countries, this class is characterized by a lower education level, high crime rate, propensity for gangs and drug consumption, teen pregnancy and stagnation.

The Haredis are the predominant population composing the Israeli poor. But unlike in other countries, the Haredi lower social-economic class has a high education level, negligible crime rates, no gangs, nor widespread drugs or teen pregnancy. Hence, this lower socioeconomic class is more ripe than any other country's lower social economic class to be the next engine of growth for the nation.

Financially poor Haredis are very learned in religious studies: halacha, Mishna, etc. The discipline, structure and conviction all make the arrival of a Haredi-Spring nearly inevitable, and with it no doubt, an Israeli-Spring!

Just like with the immigration from the former Soviet Union in the 1990s that gave Israel chemists, engineers, and other high-level brains, and contributed to the high-tech boom and Israeli economic miracle of the 21st century, a Haredi Spring of the 2020s can provide a radical boost to Israel's economy.

The Haredi Spring is a Zionist Spring, not just because of the boost it gives the State of Israel and its people, but also because it symbolizes the degree to which Haredi life pivots around Zionism.

The meaningful objections to Zionism amongst Haredis is being reduced to small nuances. For example, not reciting prayers that other religious Jews recite for the success of the state of Israel and its leaders or prayers associated with Israel's Independence Day. In other words, the objection to Zionism is reduced to less than 1% of the content of weekly prayers.

Haredis consume, breathe and promote Zionism in their daily interaction: on the bus, in the bank, in the workplace, in the charity they give, in their service to the benefit of the broader Israeli society, in dialogue, in walking to the Kotel (Wailing Wall), in being protected by Israeli soldiers and police, in being proud to be part of the Jewish nation.

Perhaps, the most profound expression is the migration of the Haredi language over the last decades from Yiddish to Hebrew. Indeed, the vast majority of Haredis today speak Hebrew as their primary language.

3. ZIONISM ABANDONING ITS SOCIALIST ETHOS

(i) Zionism's evolution to socialism

Zionism has been affiliated with socialism, not by design, but as a result of the shift of power mentioned earlier, from European Zionists to the settlers on the ground in Palestine, who eventually took control of Zionism. The predominant settler parties were composed of Polish and Russian immigrants, inspired by socialism and the revolutionary ideologies of the time (David Ben-Gurion admired Lenin and viewed him as a role model).

They won elections to Zionist institutions in the early 1930s. Consequently, going into 1948, Israel was founded by socialist leaders. The internal political debate was mostly between competing socialist factions. Moreover, both during the pre-Israel years and its first few decades of independence, the ruling socialist party, through its vehicles, controlled or strongly influenced the major resources of the country.

Given that nearly half of the Jews at that time lived in the United States and the capitalist West, there was a need for Judaism to stay separate from Zionism. This was especially important since at the same time as the socialists in Israel consolidated power and took over Zionism, the American rejection of socialism became more pronounced. The Cold War that emerged between the United States and the Soviet Union was viewed as that between capitalism and communism, and by extension socialism. American Jews needed to keep an arm's length from a movement that carried the same underlying philosophy as their adversary.

(ii) Zionism as a model global capitalist economy

By the second decade of the 21st century, Israel has abandoned socialism and turned into a model of a successful liberal economy. Israelis are conducting business all over the world, building companies, investing in opportunities, and turning ideas into multi-million-dollar ventures.

Along with the rejection of the exaggerated secular past, there has been an outright rejection of the exaggerated socialist past.

Capitalism, free-market and wealth-creation are core to the current Israeli narrative. No doubt, this came at a price, with growing income inequality, and there is a robust debate about aspects of the capitalist society in Israel. But the shift from socialism to capitalism removed a hurdle that stood in the way of the Jewish transformation. Zionism being in line with the West and consistent with the economic views of the majority of the Diaspora Jews clears the path for it to be the anchor of Judaism.

4. ISRAEL: FROM THE CHARITY CASE OF JUDAISM, TO THE SUCCESS STORY OF JUDAISM

(i) Israeli economic miracle

Israeli economic success is remarkable. The Israeli economy has experienced a high growth rate (about 3.5% in both 2018 and 2019). A developing country a mere decade ago, Israel's per capita GDP (gross domestic product) has mushroomed from $21,000 in 2000 to $43,500 in 2019, placing Israel in the world's top twenty wealthiest economies.

The global shift to technology-driven economies provided Israel with great fortunes, given a significant portion of its GDP is in the tech sector. This reality also places Israel in an advantageous position to sustain the Coronavirus crisis relative to other countries. In addition, the discovery of natural gas off Israel's shores and its successful defense conversions have contributed to Israel rapidly shifting from a country that was perceived to depend on charity and mercy, to an economic miracle. In doing so, a hurdle that existed for Jewish transformation has been removed.

(ii) Israeli wealth and prosperity

The opening of the Israeli economy created Israeli wealth, prosperity and a radical increase in the quality of living. As a whole, Israelis have not only stopped being the "charity case" of the Jewish world, but are gradually turning to be "the rich Israeli uncle" of the Jewish world.

For example, this became evident during the 2020 Coronavirus pandemic when Diaspora Jews made it clear to Israeli charities that their support levels would be dramatically reduced, while at the same time, Israeli-related sources, such as the Jewish Agency, announced that they would give more money to support Diaspora Judaism. Even before the crisis, the Israeli Ministry of Diaspora Affairs had created programs to support Diaspora Judaism in the United States and elsewhere. [9]

This by itself paves a path to a transformation as an organizing principle associated with success is much more relevant than one that is associated with pity. An early indication of this reality was seen in 1967.

---

9 – On July 5, 2020, the Israeli government enacted the "Government framework to assure the future of the Jewish people in the Diaspora."

The first 20 years of Israel's independence was marked by fear of destruction – of a second Holocaust caused by the military might of the Arab armies. The surprise victory of Israel in the 1967 war – more than doubling its territory in just six days, changed this dynamic overnight.

Many secular Jews in America and around the world suddenly discovered their Judaism. Indeed, the post-1967 time period is one of great Jewish revival – of a return to Judaism. This return was an outcome of Israel's success.

Today, once again, Israel is astonishingly successful and generates Jewish pride through its technological advances, its medical breakthroughs and its thriving economy. This paves the path for Jews to look at Israel as a conduit to their Judaism, and like in 1967, to experience a great Jewish revival through Israel – underscoring the reality of the transformation.

5. A CULTURE OF CHANGE REPLACES THE STATUS QUO

(i) Early perpetuation of the status quo

Israel was invaded the day it was established. Given the external threats and the survival difficulties of the fledgling nascent state, Israel decided to defer issues relating to religious-secular relations to an unspecified "further date." Until that date, it had been broadly agreed that the status quo had to be maintained. Hence, for the next 70 years, religious-secular tensions have been tested relative to the status quo (do they break the status quo or are they consistent with the status quo?), not based on their merits. As a result, there is essentially a freeze of the situation that existed in 1948. This freeze however reflects a distorted picture. This is because following Israel's establishment, a broad immigration of religious and traditional Middle Eastern Jews occurred. In the early 1950s (post the abstract status quo), Israel's population doubled and in subsequent years doubled again. Therefore, the status quo reflects the dictation of the now secular minority (the founders) at the expense of the traditional/religious majority.

(ii) Breaking of the status quo

The third decade of the 21st century presents a unique opportunity in Israel. One of the previous decade's key themes was the concept of change. The value of change now far trumps the value of status quo.

Change was the theme of Barack Obama's 2008 campaign and carried into the Israeli ethos. This was reflected in Israel's 2011 summer protests, a confederacy of multiple and often competing agendas, uniting under the broad, amorphous call for "change in national priorities." This grassroots rise against the old guard coincided with the political ascent of post-ideological parties over the last two decades, which came at the expense of the traditional large parties. In June 2021, the theme of change was further elevated when a new government was formed that was even called "the change government", composed of parties with opposing ideologies from right and left, united in the quest to change the current government of long-serving Prime Minister Benjamin Netanyahu.

The Coronavirus crisis of 2020 put a final blow to the concept of the status quo. What was before, is no longer now. The Coronavirus pandemic has been a catalyst for the concept of change. Indeed, even in its early stages, Israelis were quick to adapt to realities of the lockdown. They were also quick to internalize that the post-Coronavirus world will be different from the one before, and hence, have been spending time in Zoom calls, online lectures and through their own research figuring out the path to prosper in the post-Coronavirus world.

The value of change is also expressed through a shift away from idealization of a homogenous "Israeli icon" (needed in the early days when the concept of the "Israeli" was developed), to a wider embrace of diversity and pluralistic Israel.

Indeed, the call for change is across the board, including in secular-religious relations and in Zionism's previous over-association with secularism. There is a sense that anything and everything is on the table, and a rejection of doing things just because we are accustomed to doing so that way. Such an ecosystem of change is fertile ground for the fulfillment of the Jewish transformation in Israel.

(iii) Dynamic society quick to change

The Israeli "herd mentality" and single market enables changing circumstances to result in immediate acute adjustments. Israel is a one-nation market. A person in its most northern city of Kiryat Shmona listens to the same radio stations and reads the same newspapers as a person in Tel Aviv. This allows for changes to happen fast.

In the early 21st century, Facebook penetration in Israel was amongst the lowest, but within a year or two, Israel became amongst the world's highest.

Whether adapting to an app-based world, changing traffic patterns, social media trends, war, routine of rockets, social-distancing life, delivery-based food consumption, or digital socialization that came about in 2020, the Israelis adjust. This is not just the young and the "opinion leaders" – this occurs throughout the country and across ages and sectors.

This harks back to a motto of Israel's early days during the fight for survival – "we will win with whatever we have." Israelis needed to be adaptable in order to survive.

This Israeli adaptability is a key enabler of the transformation to Judaism 3.0.

Israeli pluralism

The blurring of the sector lines and of the sub-sector lines, as well as the rejection of the arcane status quo and even the idea that a status quo should exist, are also indicative of a unique model of Israeli pluralism.

The broad acceptance of Zionism as a common denominator contributes to an authentic "be who you are" society. There is a bedrock ideology that unites Israeli Jews, and therefore there is a wider confidence bandwidth for pluralism. There are strong uniting values such as the military, Jewish holidays, memorial days and the Israeli ethos. Thanks to those uniting values, an Israeli can feel comfortable enough in his own skin and his own behaviors – religious or secular, straight or gay. It also allows communities that choose to self-segregate to do so, while still participating in the Israeli experience. This includes Haredis, and as will be discussed, also Israeli Arabs and Druze. For them, the model of Israeli pluralism goes even a step further – symbiotic particularity. This suggests that the group's maintaining its unique insular particularity is not just "tolerable" by the overall society, but actually beneficial to it. This is since being who you are is more conducive than being forced to be who you are not.

This is a complete reversal from the melting pot ethos of Israel's early years. The melting pot was important back then, when the Israeli character was being formed. Now the Israeli is alive and well, as well as self-confident, and hence, there is room for some de-melting. Indeed, Israeli society now being so grounded and deeply rooted enables greater Israeli pluralism and social experiments.

(iv) Bottom-up society

The British rebelled against their government in the spring of 2016 through the Brexit process, Americans in November 2016 by electing Donald Trump. Israelis rebelled against their government back in 1977 – 40 years earlier.

Until that time, dating back to the day Israel was founded, a consensus was formed around the government's actions and its leaders. Israelis in 1977 decided that they had enough of "being told what to do," and in a stunning act of breaking of the status quo, voted out the Labor party that had been in power for 40 years, founded the country and shaped the course of Zionism since the 1930s.

Israelis continued to defy the authorities through tactical movements, such as bypassing traditional media, and creating in the 1980s an alternative channel for popular Sephardi music that the establishment-controlled radio refused to play.

Israel is a country where prime ministers, presidents, and military commanders are referred to by their nicknames: Bibi, Buji, Bugi. It is highly informal and flat, and the ultimate demonstration of what other nations strive to be: "We the People."

This means that Israelis do not accept dictations from outside, but from their own path, which further demonstrates the reality of a Jewish transformation in Israel. Israel is at Judaism 3.0, not by some order of the government or dictation by a Jewish planning committee or an elite. Israel is at Judaism 3.0 because Israelis are at Judaism 3.0.

Hurdles to transformation removed

Indeed, by the beginning of the third decade of the 21st century, the huddles that stood in the way of a Jewish transformation in Israel's first 70 years have been removed.

With Jewish resurgence amongst the seculars, and a secular's ability to stay secular while still consuming religious experiences a la carte as well as with the blurring of the sector lines in Israel, including between the religious and the seculars, Zionism has disassociated itself from secularism.

Democratization of Israel allowed a shift of the Israeli Zionist narrative and power from the secular minority towards the religious and traditional majority. This is reflected in the military, in Israel's economy, in the booming technology industry and even in the media.

The objections that the Haredi population previously had to Zionism are gone. To an increasing degree, Haredis are becoming the poster-child of Zionism. The prospect for a "Haredi-Spring" is high, which would provide Israel with a new engine of economic growth and for the Haredi population, a greater buy-in into the Zionist narrative.

Israel's socialist characteristics had faded by the end of the 20th century, and Israel has turned into a model for a liberal free-market capitalistic society. Israel is no longer viewed as poor and fragile, and indeed as a thriving center of Jewish wealth.

The artificial lock that has been placed on the secular nature of Israel through the so-called status quo, has also been removed. Religious-secular relations can now turn to be a reflection of the current Israeli population and not that of 1948 Israel, prior to the mass immigration of religious and traditional Jews from the Middle East.

Not just that the road to a Jewish transformation is now paved, it is becoming increasingly evident that Israelis view Judaism as a Zionist experience and not the other way around.

Israelis connect to Judaism through Zionism

Israeli Jews connect to their Judaism through Zionism in two ways. One is in a passive way: The most Jewish-related experience for an Israeli, religious and secular alike, is his life in Israel. Unlike the Diaspora Jew, the Israeli Jew is reminded every day and every hour of his Jewish affiliation through his interactions – from buying groceries in Hebrew, through having shops closed on Shabbat. He operates in an environment filled with Jewish symbols and experiences that are delivered through Zionism. For example, the Star of David on ambulances and on Israeli flags he sees on the street.

But there is also a more consciousness connection to Judaism. Secular Israelis are passionate Jews not because they attend synagogue, observe religious laws or regularly engage in Jewish practices. They are passionate Jews due to their connection through the Jewish state – due to Zionism. National-Religious Israelis took this connection a step further and incorporated it into their theology and religious practice, under the teachings of 20th century Rabbis Avraham Yitzchak Kook, and his son Zvi Yehuda Kook. [10] For Haredi Israelis, as discussed, there is a bifurcation between de jure stance and de facto behavior. The connection to Judaism through Zionism is evident as soon as the Haredi Jew steps out of his synagogue. His prayers for the return of Jews to Israel have a particular context when he sees with his own eyes Jews in the streets of Israel. His prayers for the building of Jerusalem have a different context when he sees the numerous cranes around the city that are deployed to do exactly that. The miracles are fulfilled through Zionism. Therefore, for a deeply believing Haredi Jew, it is impossible to disassociate Zionism from faith.

As hurdles are removed and Israeli Jews of all strides connect to Judaism through Zionism, a transformation of Judaism is occurring in Israel. Moreover, shifts in the Israeli ecosystem provide strong support for Judaism 3.0.

---

10 – For more on Rav Kook and his influence on Zionism, see Ari Ze'ev Schwartz: "The Spiritual Revolution of Rav Kook", Hagi Ben-Artzi: "New shall be sacred: Rav Kook as an innovative posek" (Hebrew).

Israeli Societal Shifts Facilitate The Transformation

6. SHIFT FROM TEL AVIV TO ZION

During 2,000 years of exile, the longing was to Zion – a name for Jerusalem. This while Jaffa, from which Tel Aviv developed, was known primarily as the port of Jerusalem.

When British General Edmund Allenby conquered Tel Aviv from the Ottoman Turks, he wrote: "On 16th of November [1917], Jaffa, the seaport of Jerusalem, was taken by advance troops of the British."

Over the next century, Tel Aviv grew from being a seaport of Jerusalem into the epicenter of Israel. Indeed, Tel Aviv is the city that most people associate with Zionism. After all, it is known as "the first Hebrew city" and named after Herzl's novel, *AltNeuLand* (translated to Hebrew as Tel Aviv).

Yet, in the last few years there has been the beginning of a reversal: a shift of power and narrative from Tel Aviv back to Jerusalem – back to Zion.

(i) 20th century shift to Tel Aviv

When the Zionist movement was launched in 1897, the Land of Israel was home to about 50,000 Jewish residents. The vast majority of them were religious and some of them rejected Zionism, especially the ultra-Orthodox living in Jerusalem.

Rather rapidly it became clear that Jaffa, and not Jerusalem, would need to be the informal "capital" of the new expanding Jewish community in Palestine. This was also consistent with the relatively diminishing importance Jerusalem had played in the Ottoman Empire. Palestine had not been a distinct political entity for most of the Ottoman era. Much of the administration that governed the city was managed from Damascus and other cities.

For the incoming Jews, the lack of an existing infrastructure in Jerusalem due to centuries of neglect, the antagonism towards Jerusalem's poor religious population, as well as the distance from the port and inconvenient access roads, made Jaffa a natural choice. Tel Aviv grew out of Jaffa in 1908 as the "first Hebrew city," having the first Hebrew school (Gymnasia Herzlia) and a strong Zionist culture. Over the years, as Israel developed, Tel Aviv became more and more central in the Zionist narrative (even though the word Zionism is derived from Zion – a name for Jerusalem).

Tel Aviv became the center for business, art, commerce, diplomacy and culture. Tel Aviv is the city to which young Israelis aspired to live. Even the nascent Israeli government established in 1948 set much of its operations in Tel Aviv, taking advantage of existing British infrastructure. Till today, the headquarters of the Department of Defense is in Tel Aviv and so are various other units of government, even if nominally headquartered in Jerusalem.

The refusal of foreign governments to recognize Jerusalem as the capital of Israel and base their embassies there further contributed to the elevation of Tel Aviv. Even as late as 2017 when US Senator Lindsey Graham asked then US Secretary of Defense nominee James Mattis, "what is the capital of Israel?" General Mattis answered: "For me, the capital is Tel Aviv."

Politically, from 1968 to 1999, all the prime ministers from the Labor party were from Tel Aviv, and they were all from the Ramat Aviv neighborhood, considered to be the elite of Tel Aviv.

But such dynamics are changing.

(ii) 21st century shift back to Jerusalem

As Israel democratizes, power previously concentrated with the old elites is being decentralized. There is a shift from left-wing-Tel Aviv, who ruled the country until 1977, to right-wing-Jerusalem which has ruled the country since, with brief interruptions. [11]

The shift from Tel Aviv to Jerusalem is also a reflection of the overall decline of the disproportionate power of the seculars (Tel Aviv), and the Ashkenazis (Tel Aviv), and the rising power of Haredis (Jerusalem), National-Religious (Jerusalem), and Sephardis (Jerusalem).

Perhaps as a reflection of this shift, from 2001 to 2021, two out of three of Israel's prime ministers were from Jerusalem, and none from Tel Aviv.

A new train line that was inaugurated in 2018 connects Jerusalem to the rest of Israel. Jerusalem is now only 20 minutes away from the airport, 33 minutes away from Tel Aviv. A new massive complex of office buildings and entertainment centers is being built close to the Jerusalem train station.

The shift from Tel Aviv to Jerusalem symbolizes a closer association

---

11 – This was reflected in the March 2021 election when right-wing parties won 72 of the 120 seats in the Knesset (60%). The rest was split between centrist, left-wing and Arab parties. The government that was subsequently formed by right-wing Prime Minister Bennett included left-wing parties under the banner of a "change government", formed to unseat long-serving Prime Minister Benjamin Netanyahu.

of Zionism with Zion and with the heart of Judaism.

Israel was established in 1948 and Jerusalem came under Israeli control in 1967, but it is only in the 2020s, as Israeli ethos and power shifts to Jerusalem, that one of humanity's most meaningful cycles has been completed.

The arc that started 2,000 years ago when Judaism was deported from Jerusalem has reached its destination. Judaism is coming back home to Zion. It is not just the intercity shift that provides tailwind to the transformation of Judaism, it is also the developments within those two cities.

(iii) Shifts within Tel Aviv

Tel Aviv has changed significantly over the last decade, starting with the end of the second Palestinian Intifada in 2006. Up until then, the endless wave of suicide bombings led to outright fear to go to cafes, bars, restaurants, public places and buses. Tel Aviv was not Tel Aviv when people stayed at home. The end of the Intifada has opened Tel Aviv up.

Young Israelis began moving to Tel Aviv en masse. Tel Aviv always attracted the young coming out of military service or completing university studies, but as Tel Aviv became safe and then prospered economically, a massive migration of Israelis to Tel Aviv occurred.

Today, most Tel Avivians that one encounters in cafes, bars and on the streets of Tel Aviv only moved to Tel Aviv during the last 15 years!

Young people wishing to move to the country's big metropolis are not unique to Israel. But unlike in other countries, in Israel, this is completely possible. A young man from Mississippi wishing to move to New York might find it unfeasible: The long distance, finding housing, the cost of living and "making it there" might make his dream just a dream. Same with a villager from Provence who possibly had never been to Paris or a young chap from the English Midland, who fantasizes to move to London.

But Tel Aviv is accessible. Family connections, childhood friends, and military connections provide a network in Tel Aviv for most Israelis. In addition, the short distance and the easy reversibility of the move makes the proposition of moving to Tel Aviv a viable option for every young Israeli, despite the high cost of living.

In addition, the relative availability of shared apartments, the culture of living with roommates, innovative housing models, the cafe and outdoor culture, the popularity of the chic "starving artist" culture, as well as Israeli camaraderie and Israeli creative ways to get by, makes moving to Tel Aviv even more realistic.

As a result, young Israelis not only dream of living in Tel Aviv, they actually move to Tel Aviv, yet most are temporary migrants. Those domestic migrants experience Tel Aviv for a few years, and then once they get married and their family begins to grow, they tend to settle elsewhere – both due to lifestyle, social protocol and affordability (wife and kids can't live in a small room with roommates).

The mass domestic migration into vibrant Tel Aviv in the last decade yielded an exaggerated image of the "Tel Avivian" – when it comes to cynicism, aggressiveness, promiscuity, alcohol, and indeed religion. Some sought to be more Tel Avivian than the Tel Avivians. The insecurity of the young migrants who felt a need to prove that they are "real Tel Avivians" manifested itself in a dual face: "Be yourself at home and a Tel Avivian outside."

The insecure young migrant from the periphery seems to feel the need to prove to the real Tel Avivians that he is cool and can be accepted as "one of us."

This was manifested, amongst other examples, by such migrants mistakenly perceiving anti-religious behavior as posh. It also manifested itself in other "Tel Aviv checklist items" which included artificial rejection of ideology and cynicism towards Zionism.

By the early 2010s, Tel Aviv became an exaggerated image of itself. In fact, one way to still recognize an original Tel Avivian is seeing that the person is *not* engaging in such exaggerated behavior.

The domestic migrant to Tel Aviv becomes the local

Once the migrant became comfortable, and indeed became the local, there was no longer a need to prove such exaggerated Tel Aviv "credentials." When everyone in Tel Aviv is a migrant, there is no longer a need to "prove yourself." Confidence levels have been going up and therefore natural behavior patterns resume. This in turn has yielded a broader counter-trend against what was previously viewed as the "State of Tel Aviv" and its exaggerated relation to the anti-religious culture. Also, a growing percentage of the migrants to Tel Aviv are religious-lites, as well as people from Jerusalem, Haifa and other cities where the culture is more moderate and polite. This has contributed to softening the image of the new Tel Avivians. (This process continues.)

Tel Aviv is moving away from the exaggerated image it had in the early 2010s towards a genuine and authentic reflection of who its residents really are, including an overt embrace of Zionism. Tel Aviv is coming home to the roots of its true soul.

Tel Aviv population replacement

The "adulting" of the 21st century migrants to Tel Aviv is occurring as the older population of Tel Aviv is dying or moving to assisted living facilities. The first and second generation Tel Avivians, especially those who settled in its northern neighborhoods in the 1950s-1970s have left. The ones who replaced them are not their children, but rather those migrants to Tel Aviv. Hence, a narrative shift.

In residential buildings throughout Tel Aviv, it is now uncommon to see an elderly neighbor or one who has been living there for decades. Similarly, a noticeable trend in the upscale neighborhood of Ramat Aviv is the gradual move of its original residents to the two upscale assisted-living centers located in the neighborhood, while renting or selling their homes to wealthy newcomers to the neighborhood. This completes the process of a pollution replacement in Tel Aviv: From Foreign-borns bringing Europe and the Middle East to Tel Aviv, to domestic-borns bringing the rest of Israel to Tel Aviv.

If in the 20th century the ruling monarchs of the Tel Aviv kingdom were "The house of Berlin and Warsaw," it is now "the house of Tiberius and Netanya."

Once the new rulers recognize their rule, and that the young are now the ones prevalent in the streets and cafes of Tel Aviv, the behavior of the ruling class stops being reactionary – trying to prove that they are compliant with the messages of the previous "ruling house" – and instead, begins to be organic and true to their own personas and inner-truth. This is manifested amongst other things in the dramatic rise of synagogue attendance in Tel Aviv.

Synagogue attendance and Shabbat

Synagogues that were empty for years and even operating part-time have now revived. A primary contributor to this revival is the French immigration to Tel Aviv.

With worsening conditions in France and the shift in French Jews from vacationing in Southern France to vacationing in Tel Aviv, more and more French have moved, bought vacation homes and spend ample time in Israel.

The French Jews, especially of North-African descent, are an anomaly in the choice between Tel Aviv and Jerusalem – even though they are traditional or religious, they tend to choose Tel Aviv over Jerusalem. The beach is of higher importance to the French than it is to other religious groups of immigrants. Hence, Tel Aviv, Netanya and Ashdod have become destinations of choice for the French.

Given their religiosity, they go to synagogue. This paves the way for the domestic migrants to "come out" and do the same and contributes to a growing Tel Aviv trend: young traditional Israelis who used to go to synagogue in Tiberias or Jerusalem, and were too insecure to do so once in Tel Aviv, now are comfortable to do that. The more such traditional Israelis see young people attending synagogue services (including attractive singles, male and female), the more they are comfortable breaking through their adopted artificial "Tel Aviv persona."

Similarly, secular Israelis who never attended synagogues are exposed to synagogues in Tel Aviv since their friends are doing a Bar Mitzvah, Sheva Brachot or Shabbat Kiddush, and since some of their friends are indeed those French or traditionals. Hence, a revival of synagogue and Shabbat culture is taking place in Tel Aviv.

Reflected demonstration of overt Zionism

Not only has a Jewish fashion emerged in Tel Aviv, such as religious classes, seminars and synagogue attendance, a Zionist fashion has emerged as well – there are more salons and discussion groups, in part thanks to the contribution of young American and European secular Jews who are now living in Israel. [12]

While in the 2010s much of the ideological, religious and Zionist tendencies of Tel Avivians was closeted, towards the end of the second decade of the 21st century it became much more overt.

Aggressive behavior, such as the ubiquity of smoking in non-smoking bars and cafes, has subsided. The police and municipality, with the support of residents, have begun enforcing rules against motorcycles storming Tel Aviv sidewalks, and other antisocial behavior. The "broken windows theory" seems to have worked in Tel Aviv on a social level. The theory, deployed in New York City in the 1990s, suggests that when one sees broken windows on the street, he is more likely to litter himself, yet when the streets are clean, he is more likely to keep them clean. In Tel Aviv, when motorcycles are no longer riding on the sidewalks, a person is less likely to do so himself; same with smoking in non-smoking areas. The gradual shift towards Tel Aviv becoming a cycling city, based on shared resources such as shared bicycles and scooters, also contributes to the softer, cleaner environment.

---

12 - For example: TLV International Salon, The Sanhedrin, Parasha and Herzl and Tribe Tel Aviv are forums established in recent years in Tel Aviv composed of young, mostly secular people.

In a sense, if the stereotype of a Tel Avivian was that of an aggressive, cynical person and that of a Jerusalemite of a good boy, then it is fair to say that the Tel Avivian is inching towards becoming more like the Jerusalemite.

Tel Aviv as AltNeuLand

Tel Aviv has been elevated not only in the eyes of Israelis but also in the eyes of international travelers. It has become a destination city for Europeans seeking a weekend getaway, and for tourists from all over the world looking for the combination of beach, party, art, entertainment and innovative culture. It has also turned into a destination for high-level international conferences such as CyberTech and the DLD Technology Festival.

Tel Aviv is not just a travel destination alternative to Barcelona or Berlin, it is a Utopia coming true. In its outdoor cafes, startups are being created; in its bars and clubs, the joy of life is celebrated, and in its street urban innovations are practiced, such as the systems of shared bikes, scooters and cars. Tel Aviv is a sports city, where every evening joggers take to the parks and beach boardwalk. It is a city with ample yoga classes of all sorts and free outdoor fitness centers. Tel Aviv is a city with a strong passion – Tel Aviv is a celebration of life.

The informality and directness of its residents and the *je ne sais quoi* has made Tel Aviv a unique global phenomena. The balance of power shifting from Tel Aviv to Jerusalem does not detract from the magic of Tel Aviv, nor from it being the fulfillment of Herzl's Utopian novel that it is named after. Indeed, Tel Aviv embodies the vision of his dream. Tel Aviv is a powerful postcard of Judaism 3.0.

Tel Aviv as Uganda

Given the temporary migration to the city, Tel Aviv is perceived by many of its young residents, not as an ideal, but as a "night-shelter."

In this regard, Tel Aviv is Uganda – the area in Africa which Herzl considered to protect the Jews from harm in Europe until the Land of Israel would become available.

Ultimately, the Israeli seeks to arrive at the "Promised Land" – get married, build a family and move out of Tel Aviv. Tel Aviv is for "when you are young and single," hence, even if there are problematic aspects with the narrative it projects, such as the image of "The State of Tel Aviv" being detached from "real Israel," it needs to be put in perspective.

Not only that as described, there are undercurrents within Tel Aviv that support a greater embrace of Zionism, but any perspective that Tel Aviv stands in the way of the strong embrace of Zionism is mitigated by the fact that, just like Uganda, it represents for many young Israelis a "phase," not an "ideal."

(iv) Shifts within Jerusalem

The dichotomy in the Israeli's frame of mind is that "Tel Aviv is for playing and Jerusalem is for praying."

If Tel Aviv is perceived as a playground, Jerusalem is perceived as reality. Tel Aviv is a place that one goes to when young to explore, date, play and enjoy. Jerusalem is revered and feared. Jerusalem is loved, but it is loved from a distance.

Indeed, most Israelis maintain arms-length relations to Zion. They would rarely visit Jerusalem, and associate Jerusalem with terrorism, overt religiosity, the old, conflict and poverty.

But things are changing in Jerusalem.

The 3,000-year evolution of Jerusalem

For its first 1,000 years, Jerusalem, known as the City of Peace, was the nexus of Judaism and home to the Temple. But in the first century CE, the Second Temple was destroyed and the city burned. In exile, Jews continued to focus much of their identity around Jerusalem – facing the city and praying three times a day to return, wishing one another "next year in Jerusalem" and more.

During the 2,000 years of exile, Jerusalem inched away from the regional spotlight. During Ottoman rule, which started in the 16th century, Jerusalem was no longer a primary political center.

While in the 18th and 19th century many Jews and Arabs who moved to the then-desolate Palestine chose to settle in Jerusalem, the mass immigration that followed later in the 19th century and early 20th century was focused on other parts of the land. Jaffa and then Tel Aviv, became the primary hub zone of the new Jewish settlement, leading to a further shift away from Jerusalem.

The military siege imposed on Jerusalem during the 1947-1948 War of Independence, and the daring effort to rescue Jerusalem's Jewish population from starvation and destruction, shaped the image of Jerusalem for many of today's Israelis.

The fall of the Old City of Jerusalem and the expulsion of its Jewish residents as refugees had devastating psychological consequences. Centuries of continuous Jewish life there had come to an end in 1948. It was the first time since the Crusades that the Old City was Jew-free

– this contributed to an image of a highly revered, yet pitiful Jerusalem.

Even after it was reunited in 1967, Jerusalem, for many Israelis, continued to be associated with terrorism, poverty, religiosity and the past. It was somewhat inconsistent with Tel Aviv-centric Zionist themes, as depicted by authors such as Jerusalem native Amos Oz, who said in the 1990s: "In the war between Jerusalem and Tel Aviv, I am all on the side of Tel Aviv – sanity, secularity, the present."

But Jerusalem has gradually evolved. The expansion of institutions such as the Hebrew University and Bezalel Academy of Arts and Design attracted a younger population. The development of top-notch museums, sold-out annual international art shows and wine festivals, the massive investment in infrastructure and urban renewal such as the light rail and the new 33-minute fast train to Tel Aviv, as well as the wealth brought in with the rising number of vacation homeowners and tourists, all have contributed to the gradual turning of Jerusalem into an elegant destination city.

Indeed, Jerusalem of the 2020s is more accommodating to Israelis, young and old, than that of prior decades. For example, the stunning vibrancy of Machaneh Yehuda market with its restaurants, cafes and bars dents the old paradigm that "Jerusalem is where to pray and Tel Aviv is where to play."

Shifting more of the Israeli narrative to Jerusalem (Zion) places a greater emphasis on the return to Zionism – the return to Judaism.

(v) Half empty vs. Half full

The Jerusalem vs. Tel Aviv debate is often a debate between the half-full and half-empty glass of Zionism. Hence, the shift to Jerusalem gives more vibrancy to the Zionist narrative. This is demonstrated anecdotally by new immigrants (Olim) coming to Israel. Repeatedly, they report different reactions to their decisions to immigrate to Israel in Tel Aviv than they do in Jerusalem. In Tel Aviv the reaction is often *Frier* (fool) or "why did you come here" or "If I had a green card." In Jerusalem, the reaction is often a hug, a warm welcome, and a display of gratitude.

Jerusalem is the symbol of the half-full, while Tel Aviv tends to be perceived as the half-empty – complaints, cynicism, even negativity. As the Israeli motto goes: "A protest – not really important about what – *Hafgana lo hashuv al ma.*" Complain first, think second.

The half-full supports the transformation of Judaism because optimism is at the core of Zionism. Herzl put it this way in a speech he delivered in London 1899 (in English): "Each and every one of us will carry with him the memory of enthusiasm, as a precious souvenir that we will safeguard in our hearts. This enthusiasm gives us the strength to move forward."

Enthusiasm is essential for Zionism to move forward and for the transformation to take effect. Hence, the shift from Tel Aviv to Jerusalem supports it.

Herzl also identified the malaise of cynicism. He describes his conversation with a Parisian Jewish Professor: "He trotted out that satirical anecdote about what things would be like in the Jewish state. Two Jews meet: What do you do here? I sell opera glasses. And you? I sell opera glasses, too." But Herzl was not deterred by such cynicism: "To this masterly argument I replied quite calmly: 'Sir, neither you nor I sell opera glasses.'"

The particular need to focus on the half-empty seems to carry from the salons of Paris of 1895 to the cafes and bars of Tel Aviv in 2020. Hence, the shift to Jerusalem is a shift away from cynicism. This was also demonstrated in the wide popularity of the 2011 summer protest in Tel Aviv, and the lackluster reaction to it in Jerusalem.

Figures of cost-of-living showing that the cost-of-living in Israel is higher than in other western countries are often skewed, because they ignore the fact that a disproportionate number of young Israelis live in Tel Aviv and Jerusalem – percentages that are nearly unheard of in the United States and most European countries.

The more appropriate measure is comparing the cost-of-living in Tel Aviv to that in New York or London – not to the country at large, not comparing Tel Aviv to rural America.

The financial ability of a young person to get to Tel Aviv, stay in Tel Aviv and live in Tel Aviv is a great testament to the success of the Israeli story. But in the "half-empty" narrative such statistics are ignored.

In Jerusalem, the equation is different. In poor neighborhoods, smiles are abundant and the poor are happy. For example, the Jerusalem neighborhood of Nachlaot has Sephardi religious Jews living in small dilapidated old homes next to foreign workers and secular students living in shared apartments. Next to them are wealthy Americans and Europeans who bought and renovated. The sense of camaraderie, optimism, appreciation and indeed love is strongly felt through the narrow alleys of the neighborhood. "We love our soldiers" reads one sign from a balcony; "This land is very very good" [13] reads another one, carved in stone on one of the homes. The "half full" is fully celebrated in Jerusalem.

---

13 – Biblical quote of Caleb (Kalev Ben Yefune), Numbers 14:7.

(vi) Supporting shift from Tel Aviv to the periphery

The Israeli experience has been Tel Aviv-centric. This is not unusual. For example, the French experience is very much Paris-centric. As mentioned earlier, this is reflected in young people moving there en masse after the army or their university studies.

Tel Aviv dictated much of the Israeli narrative, and its only "competitor" at doing so has been Jerusalem. But in recent years the periphery has been rising. This is driven by a number of factors including the massive investment in infrastructure over the last decades. For example, Carmiel, once a faraway city in the far north is now 90 minutes from Tel Aviv, thanks to a new train line. Same with Nahariya near the border with Lebanon. It is also supported by soaring real estate prices in Tel Aviv and its suburbs, and the "One Israel" reality that exists in part thanks to the army, family connections and small geographies.

In fact, the periphery is disappearing as a periphery, and rising as thriving communities. From high-tech industry to universities, more and more of Israeli trends are set far away from Tel Aviv. More power and more and more people are moving away from the center. This provides further strength for the Jewish transformation because people in the periphery tend to be more idealistic, less susceptible to artificial anti-ideological fashion that exists in certain circles in Tel Aviv, and indeed tend to display their Zionism more overtly (similar to the situation in other places such as in the United States).

(vii) Arab-philia

The increased exposure Israelis have to Jerusalem and the rise of the periphery also leads to a greater exposure to Arabs and the shedding of myths. In Jerusalem, Jews and Arabs interact in the Shuk, in the light rail, in the malls, in the hospitals – this interaction is very different from what can be perceived from the news, and it contributes to a rising trend of Arab-philia amongst Israel Jews.

What started with the passion Israelis have for Arab hummus has grown in recent years to admiration and consumption of Arab culture, including in music, art, language and cuisine.

A century of conflict has clouded the natural affinity toward Arabs that existed when Jews resided amongst them and exists now. Even in the TV show *Fauda*, where an elite Israeli military unit operates in the West Bank and Gaza, the show's main characters seem to exhibit Arab-philia and a degree of sympathy to the culture of their adversaries.

Israeli Arab-philia was on display starting in late 2020 as Israelis began flocking to Dubai and Abu-Dhabi following the Abraham Accords. Israelis were actively seeking to consume Arab culture and experiences.

Arab-philia is an indication of the confidence bandwidth of Israeli society. But it is also notable that there is no substantial "Yiddish-philia" in the Israeli general society – quite the opposite. This is a further indication that a transformation is taking place – the Israeli Jew's conduit to his Jewish identity is through his national realities in the State of Israel, which naturally includes an element of Arab culture and not Eastern Europe culture.

7. Israel's non-Jews' engagement with Zionism

Zionism is the lowest common denominator in Israel's Jewish society. The notion of Israel as the homeland of the Jewish people is accepted nearly universally amongst the Jewish population. But what might be surprising is that this narrative is more and more being accepted by the non-Jewish population of Israel as well, which comprises about 25% of the country's population.

(i) Israeli Arabs

Over 20% of Israel's population is Arab. The Israeli Arabs are certainly not Zionists, but they very much interact within the constructs of the Zionist narrative and are contributors to it. Unlike the Haredi for whom being part of the Jewish nation is core to their identity, the Israeli Arabs' connection to Judaism is external, and it is clearly channeled through the Jewish nation and not the Jewish religion.

In the early years of Israel, Israeli Arabs were closer in narrative, culture and language to their Palestinian brethren across the "Green Line." But in the 70 years that have ensued, Israeli Arabs have developed a narrative that is distinct and different from that of the Palestinians.

Israeli Arabs are by now closer culturally to Israeli-Jews than they are to Palestinian Arabs living in the West Bank, Gaza or Jordan. While Israeli Arabs are neither Zionist nor Palestinian (if defining Palestinians politically as those beyond the Green Line), if one had to map their day-to-day life against those two bookends, the vast majority of them would arguably be much closer to Zionism than to "Palestinianism."

This is evident in Jerusalem, where there are two separate Arab populations: One is the East Jerusalem Palestinian (and along with them other Palestinians from the West Bank), the other is the Israeli Arab from Yaffo, Haifa and northern Israel – most of whom are in Jerusalem to study or to work, many in government.

There are very few points-of-interaction between East Jerusalem Palestinians and Israeli Arabs, and it is clear that Israeli Arabs tend to socialize with Israeli-Jews much more than they do with East Jerusalem Palestinians. This is seen in Jerusalem's cafes, bars and campuses.

Israeli Arabs typically do not reside in Palestinian areas of Jerusalem. Some religious Muslim women from northern Israel who come to Jerusalem to study at the Hebrew University and naturally want to reside in Muslim environments, still opt to live amongst the Jews rather than in the Palestinian environment.

Similarly, residents of the Arab village of Abu Gosh lobbied for more housing permits in order for the next generations to be able to stay in the village. But after a few years, the village came together to lobby against granting the building permits and village extension they so desired previously. This is because they began recognizing that Palestinians from East Jerusalem would be buying apartments in their village.

The Arabic that is spoken by Israeli Arabs has Hebrew words incorporated into it – a new dialect developed of "Israeli Arabic." Some Arabs speak Hebrew as their first language and Arabic only as second, and a minority of younger Arabs do not even speak Arabic fluently.

The Israeli Arab leadership is by far more extreme than the Arab population, but even that needs to be put into context. The most extreme elements in the Israeli Arab leadership, the Umm al-Fahm-based "northern wing" of the Muslim Brotherhood, initiated protests when the idea came to move their towns to a future state of Palestine as part of a potential peace agreement. They simply do not want to be Palestinians. In other words, the most extreme elements in the Israeli Arab society want to stay Israeli!

This played out again a decade later when President Trump's peace plan called for the possibility of moving Arab towns to a future Palestinian state. The rejection to that aspect of the plan was nearly universal in the Israeli Arab community – by its political leaders, religious leaders, and mostly by Israeli Arabs themselves.

This was also reflected in the 2021 elections with the success of the political party of the "southern wing" of the Muslim Brotherhood, led by Mansour Abbas, who was openly sympathetic to the Zionist government of right-wing Prime Minister Benjamin Netanyahu, and later joined the government led by right-wing Prime Minister Naftali Bennett.

More so, in May 2021, when incited Arab mobs attacked Jews and Jewish-owned properties in mixed Jewish-Arab cities, there was condemnation by Arabs for such violence. Yet, the condemnations were not about downplaying Israel's policies in Gaza and in Jerusalem, nor about support for Zionism. It was in the context of the core tenet that we live together, succeed together, and thrive in our own particularity.

Indeed, while Israeli Arab society is completely different from the Palestinian society in the West Bank or Gaza, there is a related theme: The ability to disconnect or suppress politics. Israeli Arabs (as well as a growing number of Palestinians) being able to put politics aside, paves the way for the wealth of opportunity that Israeli society offers – from high-tech to science.

The old narrative of "Jews go back to Europe" is gone. There is no acceptance of Zionism as an ideology (such as by the Druze minority), but there is interaction with it, as Arabs are increasingly becoming a cornerstone of Israeli Zionist society. This is done in non-political ways. For example, a large percentage of the Jewish state's doctors, nurses and pharmacists are Arabs.

Arab medical professionals were at the forefront of the successful Jewish state's battle against the Coronavirus, and when Israeli Jews of all political and social backgrounds took to their balconies to clap for those professionals, they were clapping and displaying great gratitude to Israeli Arabs.

Rejection of externally forced identity

There is an absolute rejection amongst Israeli Arabs for colonialist-like dictations coming from Europe that attempts to group all people with Arab ethnicity into one and force a narrative of victimhood and distress upon them.

Israeli Arabs are often forced into their Palestinian identity when going to Europe and having questions about their identity posed. Even a simple question such as "where are you from?" could turn a casual conversation into an unwanted political situation. In some paradoxical manner, it incepts the previously non-existent Zionist element in the Israeli Arab's complex mix of identities. When forced into the casual question, the Israeli Arab clearly feel less being from "the Palestinian Authority" and more "from Israel."

Indeed, in cafes in Haifa populated by young people, one cannot tell who is Jewish and who is Arab. Israeli Arabs and Jews in the cafes dress the same, look the same, and talk with the same accent. Short of name or discussion of military service, it would be impossible to tell.

Israeli Arabs are a sector within Zionist Israel, and by being so, accepting the narrative of being Israelis. The narrative is not Zionist by definition, but it is implicitly a de facto acceptance of Zionism.

The 2018 Nation-State Bill that reaffirmed that Israel is the nation-state of the Jewish people was met with far more objection in the Israeli Jewish society than it did in the Arab society, which fiercely rejected it, but for the most part, viewed it as yet another episode of intra-Israeli politics. This was reflected in voting turnout.

The Israeli left and Arab political leaders expected the Arab population, which normally has a relatively low turnout, to vote en masse in the April 2019 election due to their objection to the Nation-State Bill that was enacted shortly before that. This was not the case. In fact, while the overall Israeli population had a high turnout of 69%, Israeli Arabs had one of their lowest, estimated to be at 49%.

In March 2020, the issue was no longer the Nation-State Bill, and the Arab turnout mushroomed. A new political issue surfaced – the Trump plan that was introduced shortly before the election and called for the redrawing of borders in such a way that Israeli Arab towns would become part of the future state of Palestine. This angered Israeli Arabs who are generally opposed to such ideas. But perhaps even a bigger contributor to the high Arab turnout was the refocus of the leaders of the Arab party – the Joint List – away from Israeli-Palestinian conflict issues to social-economic issues that affect the Israeli Arab society. In this election the Arab population had one of the highest turnouts of 59% – a full 10% higher than a year prior, where the issue was the nation-state law. This while the overall population's turnout was roughly the same at 70%. [14] This is telling of the sentiment of Israeli Arabs – they are Israeli, not Palestinians (in the political definition of Palestinians). They certainly care about Palestinians, but naturally care more about what is happening at home, than what is happening in Ramallah.

In addition to the higher turnout in the 2020 elections, another intra-Arab trend was a shift of votes from the Jewish parties, such as Meretz and Labor to the Arab Joint List, leading to an increase of power from 10 seats in the April 2019 election to 15 seats in March 2020. This is despite the fact that the Joint List was a combination of various Arab parties with diverging views. This underscored the obvious – the Israeli Arab is a distinct group with a distinct narrative. But it also underscored that this group is an integral part of the Israeli political process – indeed, of Israel.

Such realities strengthen the Zionist narrative in Israel – it negates the alternative approach of universalism – that we are all the same. At the same time, the high participation underscores the active Arab participation in the Jewish state.

---

14 – Israel Democratic Institute, Israel's Central Election Committee.

Symbiotic Particularity

Most Arabs want to stay Arab. Some choose to self-define themselves as Israeli Arabs, others as Palestinians, but it is rare that an Israeli Arab will feel a lack of Arab particularity and not feel any sense of Arab identity. Israeli Arabs are not a homogenous group, but there are enough connecting points that makes them different from other Arabs – including those living in the Palestinian Authority.

The clear trend of Israelization amongst Israeli Arabs is not an indication of their desire to stop being Arabs. This is just like the fashion of Arab-philia within Israeli Jews does not mean they want to stop being Jewish.

Neither suggests a merger, it is a celebration of the other group's particularity. Jews celebrate Arab particularity through their actions when they listen to Arabic hip-hop bands, and Arabs celebrate Jewish particularity through their action when they converse with one another in Hebrew. And what is the particularity of the Jewish group that Israeli Arabs celebrate? It is not the Jewish religion – it is not studying Mishna or Kabalah. There is no Judaization of Israeli Arabs, there is Israelization. The interaction of Israeli Arabs is with the Jewish nation, not the Jewish religion.

Symbiotic particularity is not unique to Arabs in Israel. There are similar trends in other countries where Arabs reside. Over half of the citizens of the Hashemite Kingdom of Jordan are not Hashemites – many of them self-describe themselves as Palestinians. The Hashemites, a Bedouin tribe that came from the Arabian Peninsula during the 20th century, set the national ethos of Jordan. It is even in the country's name.

Palestinians not only accept the Hashemite narrative of Jordan, they celebrate it. It is not in conflict with their own Arab identity – in fact it augments it.

Let's be clear – Israeli Arabs are not Zionists, just like Jordanian Palestinians are not Hashemites. Not being Zionist, however, does not preclude Arabs from being a cornerstone of Israeli society in non-political ways, such as Arab leadership in medical professions.

No doubt, there are ample issues and challenges, but not the European-type negation. Arab women dressed in Muslim garb are common on the beaches of Tel Aviv, and are absolutely safe. The Israeli model of symbiotic particularity is indeed in sharp contrast to the European model of multiculturalism – parallel societies with no synergies and in competition with one another. But it is also different from the American model of cultural pluralism, where multiple cultural branches are anchored in a strong common trunk – Americanism, as Israeli Arabs are not Zionists.

The election of the first hijab-wearing member of the Israeli Parliament in the March 2020 election was welcomed with a degree of pride by many Israeli Jews, including on the right. This is despite the fact that most Israeli Jews oppose MK Iman Khatib-Yasin's political views and reject her affiliation with a Muslim Brotherhood-linked organization. Her anti-Zionist political views have nothing to do with her hijab. Indeed, her wearing a hijab in the Israeli Zionist Knesset is a great symbol of Israeli symbiotic particularity – a form of implicit recognition of Zionism.

The Israeli Arabs' compatibility with Zionism was envisioned by Herzl in his novel, *AltNeuLand*, where Muslims were not "integrated" nor forced to accept the "Jewish way of life" as they do today in Europe. They lived in their villages by their own values, as they in fact do today in Israel. In Herzl's book, Muslims were staunch Zionists – so much that a Muslim is one of the leaders of the Jewish state. This has yet to happen today with Israeli Arabs, but it is happening with Israeli Druze.

(ii) Israeli Druze

Druze are icons of Zionism. They serve in the military, in the police, in the justice system, foreign service, and throughout Israeli government. Some of the top commanders in Israel's military and police are Druze, and indeed the Druze are an elite within Israeli Zionist society.

In addition, for many Druze, Hebrew has become their first language and Arabic their second. For example, in the popular Druze website carmel.co.il, users can write in either Arabic or Hebrew, and most comments are in Hebrew.

Attempts to recruit Druze to the opposition to the 2018 Nation-State Bill mostly failed. That is because for most Druze it is obvious that Israel is the national homeland of the Jewish people, just as it is obvious that they have full rights and are full partners in its endeavors.

Druze pride is not at all inconsistent with Zionism. Most Druze live in Druze villages, marry other Druze and are proud of their particularity. When Prime Minister Benjamin Netanyahu delivered his victory speech after the March 2020 election, right in front of him, a Druze flag was waved next to an Israeli flag. Such depiction of Druze attitudes towards the Jewish state supports the reality of a Jewish transformation, as it is clear that the Druze relate to Judaism through Zionism.

(iii) Russian non-Jews

The Russian immigration of the 1990s brought with it many non-Jews to Israel. This was done through family members and otherwise. Most of the Russian Jews themselves tend to be not religious and some of them all but abandoned Jewish religiosity.

But that is certainly not the case when it comes to Jewish nationalism. Indeed, what connects Israeli Russians, Jews and non-Jews alike, to Israel is not the Jewish religion (Judaism 2.0) – it is Zionism (Judaism 3.0).

Russian non-Jews serve in the military, join elite forces, get involved with Zionist thinking, in country-building and indeed are at the forefront of Zionism. This is reflected through voting patterns. The party who is associated with representing Russian-speaking Israelis, Yisrael Beiteinu led by Avigdor Lieberman, is adamantly secular, and at the same time adamantly nationalistic and Zionist.

(iv) Foreign workers

The first Palestinian Intifada in the late 1980s and early 1990s presented a challenge to Israeli-Palestinian relations. Until then Palestinians from the West Bank and Gaza Strip would come to Israel and work.

The wave of terrorism and the subsequent intense intervention of European and multinational organizations led to a separation of Palestinians from the Israelis. It also led to a more violent Second Intifada in the early 2000s that followed the Oslo Accords, which has kept Palestinians out of Israel. This had a devastating effect on the Palestinian economy and job prospects, but it also created severe labor shortages in Israel.

The Russian immigration provided temporary relief – and images of professors and scientists cleaning the streets were common. But as the Russian immigration settled and the Israeli high-tech industry mushroomed (in part due to these immigrants), even temporary relief evaporated.

Israel began to import labor from Africa and Asia. While those were meant to be temporary guest workers, a lot of them overstayed the visas and built families in Israel. In the 2000s, Bedouin smugglers helped another wave of African migrants enter Israel via the Egyptian border in seeking refuge and/or work (this was stopped when Israel built a wall along its Egyptian border). The net result was the establishment of a migrant community in Israel, similar to the ones that exist in Europe.

Those neighborhoods are mostly in Tel Aviv – where much of the labor was needed. Neighborhoods that were once poor Jewish neighborhoods, such as Neve Shaanan and Shapira, are now populated by African migrant workers. But unlike the African migrant to Europe, in Israel there is a degree of integration that occurs through the children.

The children go to Israeli schools, speak Hebrew, are often given Hebrew names, and within a few years, a proud and even patriotic generation of African migrants has risen in Israel. They are not Jewish, nor want to become Jewish. They do not seek to join the Jewish religion.

Their life in Israel pivots around Zionism – not around Rabbinic Judaism. As some of them begin to reach 18, they serve in the army, and some in combat and elite units. Like the Druze and other non-Jews in Israel, the foreign-workers' community accepts and adopts Zionism as the organizing principle for their life in Israel (Judaism 3.0).

8. SHIFT FROM EUROPEAN INFLUENCES TO AMERICAN INFLUENCES

(i) Early opinion leaders: Europhiles, Socialists

A contributing factor to the transformation is the general shift in Israeli cultural influence from Europe to America. This is in part due to a shift of power away from the Ashkenazi elite, who were very much aligned with Europe – from where they came. Another factor is the shift from socialism that drew to a large extent on European social democrats and socialist philosophies.

And yet another factor is just the passing of time. Israel's early immigrants were raised in Europe; their children were born in Israel. As European influence recedes in Israel, so is the glorification of secularism. Today's European "secular religion" is missionary, aggressive, and exclusive, e.g. "mono-atheistic," adapting the concept of the exclusive jealous Lord (El Kanay) to European secularism and even atheism.

The receding European influence makes Israeli secularism less radical and more open to other ideas. Hence, it allows Zionist seculars to embrace religious content and for the secular Israelis to stay the "people of faith." This in turn supports a Jewish transformation that is centered around Zionism – no longer perceived as an ultra-secular movement.

(ii) Current generations: American-influenced

Today's Israeli generation grew up with a large American influence. There are Israelis who speak English in a nearly impeccable American accent, simply by watching American television shows.

The American way of thinking, American pop-culture and American capitalism all have had a significant influence on the current generations of Israelis. The young Israeli's pursuit to join Israel's thriving high-tech sector is also a contributor to such a shift from European influences to American influences.

If in the previous generation the Israeli elite would draw an imaginary bridge in their minds to the libraries of Berlin and the concert halls of Vienna, today's Israelis draw a not-so-imaginary bridge to Silicon Valley.

Through America, the Israeli gets exposed to religiosity. Unlike in Europe, where religiosity is looked down upon, in America one can be a successful high-tech entrepreneur and be religious – the same goes for being an actor, lawyer or hedge-fund manager.

The shift from Europe to America is also a shift from extreme secular influences to religious-friendly influences, hence, supporting the transformation to Judaism 3.0.

(iii) The Israelis' rejection of universalism and embrace of particularity

For a long time, some Jews just wanted to be like everybody else, but they were denied this dream – first by the outside, and then by Zionism which affiliates them with an ethnological nationality – the opposite of universalism.

Brought from Europe – "be like everybody else"

Tracing back to the Biblical quest for a king "like the other nations," many Jews wanted to be like the other nations. This was very much prevalent in 19th-century Europe, and through the establishment of Israel. Most notably, Ben-Gurion shared his dream of having in Israel a Jewish thief, a Jewish prostitute – this would be an indication of having a normal regular country, he argued.

This also manifests itself in the desire to be loved, at times measuring happiness by how many points European countries give Israel in the Eurovision song contest. The UN and world organizations who are chronically critical of Israel just amplified this desire to be accepted. But in recent years, the desire to be "like everybody else" was put in perspective. In the end, Israelis want to be Israeli.

Israelis choose to be Israeli

This is demonstrated by the strong Israeli ethos that has developed outside of Israel. Israelis living in the US and throughout Europe choose to stay Israeli: They consume Israeli culture, keep Israeli friends and go back to Israel frequently.

Similarly, with the emergence of American and Anglo enclaves in Jerusalem such as in the German Colony, and French enclaves in Tel Aviv, such as in Neve Tzedek, Israelis have an opportunity to consume non-Israeli experiences. And yet, most Israelis in those neighborhoods consistently prefer to socialize with veteran Israelis ("Sabras") rather than with the Americans/Anglos. This is not just "snubbing the newcomers" – it is a preference for Israeli particularity – in music, culture, army folklore, and Israeli pop culture.

Indeed, some people from Tel Aviv say they are not happy in Jerusalem because it is "too American." Israelis of all political and social strides take increased pride in what it means to be Israeli, and are not at all apologetic about it.

Israelis on the far-left are turning into defenders of Israel when in Europe or on college campuses in the US. This is especially evident since the most extreme elements of European Israel-bashing exist in far-left circles such as the arts and academia. A far-left Israeli in London or Paris is bound to encounter hostility, which turns him or her even more Israeli, even more Zionist.

Israelis do not get "swallowed-up" by the local Jewish community as one would expect, nor in their non-Jewish environment. They keep their distinct Israeli ethos: in music, in food, in Hebrew, in news, in frame of mind, in dress, in names of their children, in behavior patterns.

Quite simply, Israelis reject universalism and embrace particularity – Israeli particularity. This was evident in the mass return of Israelis during the Coronavirus crisis. It went far beyond a natural "flight to safety," it was a "flight to Israeli particularity." During times of crisis, one wanted to be in Israel, in Israeli togetherness, in Hebrew, in Israeli culture.

Such realities provide a powerful demonstration that the universalist notion that Israel is just a place where its citizens live is outright rejected by most Israelis.

Israelis choose to return home

Israelis have a high exit rate – many leave Israel after their military service or university studies. But Israel is not a nation of forever emigrants. Israelis have high repatriation relative to other countries.

After traveling, pursuing a career, chasing dreams, even building lives, Israelis tend to come back home. Just like young Israelis tend to spend a few years in Tel Aviv, many choose to spend a few years or even a few decades abroad.

This notion of eventual return is deeply rooted in the Israeli ethos, expressed in its cultural heritage assets, like its music. For example, in Arik Einstein's popular song, "Sitting in San Francisco by the water", which portrays the longing for Israel, or in Yehonatan Geffen's "Yehonatan, go back home", written in London, or in reverse in Chava Alberstein's "London does not await me".

This desire to return and recognition that at the end of the day there is no place like Israel, is not some youth movement propaganda or getting intoxicated off some government-provided Kool-aid. This is a consensus value that is present in all sectors of Israeli society, including in the Bohemian left. As Einstein states in his San Francisco song: "I love to fall in love with the Land of Israel – little, warm and wonderful." In spite of all the problems, many complaints, economic hardship and wars, the romantic notion of return remains a core element of the Israeli ethos – as depicted in Geffen's song, to simply "grab a backpack and a cane, and head back to the Land of Israel."

9. CONCLUSION: FOR ISRAELIS, ZIONISM IS THE RETURN TO JUDAISM

Israelis are in Judaism 3.0. Hurdles to the transformation of Judaism that existed in Israel's early years have been removed. This includes Israel's previous over-association with secularism and socialism, the Haredi objection, Israeli poverty, the uncertain security situation, and the lock on the status quo.

Indeed, when Herzl planted the seeds for the transformation of Judaism, one could have expected that it would be fulfilled upon the establishment of the Jewish state. It did not, due to the hurdles mentioned, but now that those hurdles have been removed, it is indeed occurring.

The ecosystem in Israel is very much supportive of the transformation: There is a shift of the Zionist ethos from Tel Aviv to Jerusalem – back to Zion, while at the same time an elevation of the international stature of those two cities, both a manifestation of Zionism. Similarly, Israel's astonishing economic and high-tech success – the start-up nation – is very much a manifestation of the success of Zionism (Judaism 3.0), as opposed to a manifestation of the success of Rabbinic Judaism (Judaism 2.0). It is a product of Jewish nationalism, not of Jewish religiosity.

Unlike in the early decades, non-Jews are increasingly becoming part of the mainstream of Israel: Druze generals, Arab doctors, non-Jewish

Russian artists and entrepreneurs. The path those non-Jews relate to the Jewish state is not through the religious aspects of Judaism, but through the national aspects.

Most Israeli Arabs utterly reject universalism and embrace the notion of symbiotic particularity – they celebrate their own particular Arab identity – not negate it – and hence, implicitly provide backing to the particularity of Zionism. Most Israeli Arabs recognize that the Israeli mosaic works better for them if each piece is secure and cherished on its own merits.

There is a small minority in the Israeli fringe whose association with the word "Zionism" is with kitsch, something from the history classes and from the past. There is even a smaller minority who, like many in Europe, would associate Zionism with occupation, colonialism, military, war, violence. For the vast majority of Israeli Jews, Zionism is a relatable manifestation of their Judaism, and of their core being.

For the National-Religious, it is reflected through service in the army, the volunteering, the yeshivas, the redemptive theology expressed by Rav Kook, the Kotel, the building of the society, the deep appreciation to be back in the Land of Israel and to settle it. For the Haredis, it is the orientation of life around Zionist realities in Israel, the connection of the Diaspora through Israel and the centrality of the Jewish nation in Haredi religious practices and theology.

For the seculars, it is not just that Zionism is core to their identity, it is also the primary vehicle to connect to their Judaism. In addition, part of the reason Israeli secular non-observant Jews choose to remain in the Orthodox camp and to reject the continuous effort of Reform Judaism to court them, is driven by the perception (false as it may be) that the Reform movement lacks a sufficiently enthusiastic support of Zionism and of Israel. Zionism is what unifies the various fragments of Israeli Judaism. The debate on various aspects of Judaism continues, but it continues within the Zionist tent.

As Israeli Jews connect to their Judaism through Zionism, the transformation of Judaism is turning into a reality. It is not based on a decision or a resolution. Indeed, Israel is already in Judaism 3.0.

VI

The Transformation Of Judaism – American Jews

American Jewry has completed an epic journey over the last century. Arriving in America as an insular nation-religion, American Jews denationalized, reducing American Judaism to a religion, and then secularized. While an estimated 20% of American Jewry keeps the Jewish flame in America – the Orthodox and other engaged Jews, the core of the American Jewish community is on a trajectory towards evaporation.

This is where Zionism comes in. Zionism too has made an epic journey in America over the last century. American Jews initially rejected Zionism. When Israel was founded, Zionism became an important part of the American Jewish ethos, but certainly not its core. But now, as old connectors to Judaism are eroding, Zionism is turning into the most relevant (or the least irrelevant) aspect of Judaism for the American Jew. This is occurring through both positive and negative connections. Israel's astonishing success on the one hand, and its lightning rod controversies on the other, turns Zionism into the meeting point of the American Jew with his Judaism. Indeed, the Jewish transformation in America to Judaism 3.0 is not only an existential necessity but also a growing reality.

1. 20TH CENTURY: SUCCESS OF JUDAISM 2.0 IN AMERICA – NO NEED FOR ZIONISM

The history of American Jews is a recent one. In 1880, there were only 73,000 Jews in America. In 1900, 400,000, and by 1940, one million Jews. The rise of Jewish life in America coincided with the rise of Zionism. But that by itself did not suggest an embrace of Zionism by American Jews. On the contrary, American Jews were on a different path and Zionism was not particularly relevant to their journey.

(i) Zionism: rescue of the Jews – built on their misery

Political Zionism was perceived to address the misery of the Jews. Herzl identified anti-Semitism in Europe as a propelling force that would draw the Jews into Zionism. But American Jews were free. They simply did not need Zionism.

Moreover, Zionism was the "Jewish Answer" to the "Jewish Question" that was looming in Europe at the end of the 19th century. As he launched it, Theodor Herzl knew that the Zionist movement's success would not be due to its historic justice nor due to the world nations' moral obligation to create a Jewish homeland. Herzl recognized that Zionism would succeed only if it would be needed – by the Jews, and by the world's nations.

Indeed, that is how Zionism rose from a fringe movement to being the anchor of Judaism. It was needed!

First and foremost, Zionism was needed by the Jews. Starting in 1905, Jews began coming to Palestine in the immigration wave of 1905-1914 (the Second Aliya), due to problems in Russia. In later immigrations in the 1920s and 1930s, in response to problems in Poland, then in response to problems in Germany and other areas of Europe.

Immigration from countries where the Jews prospered was significantly smaller. Hence, the founding generation of Israel tended to be Polish, Russian and German Jews and not French, British, American and Middle Eastern Jews.

But as Herzl calculated, Zionism was not only a solution to a need of the Jews. It was also a solution to a need of the world. Indeed, the world's nations needed Zionism and benefited from it. The British used it to serve their interests in Palestine, including to curtail French aspirations for the Holy Land.

Similarly, Arabs needed Zionism and used it to promote their own interests. As discussed, Emir Faisal supported Jewish nationalism and Zionism in part to solidify support for the nascent concept of Arab nationalism expressed through his own kingdom. Even earlier, engagement of the world's nations with Zionism was driven by a need. Turkey entertained the idea of Zionism based on Jewish banking contacts that could help relieve it of its mounting debt problems. Germany engaged with Zionism as a way to rid from its society the undesirable elements, including socialists, anarchists, and the poor Jewish immigrants from the East. Russia had a similar idea and hence was ready to lobby the Turkish Sultan for a Jewish charter. In sum, Zionism offered Europe what Europe had yearned for centuries: To get rid of its Jews.

And so, Zionism only succeeded with audiences for which it was needed: needed by European Jews, needed by European nations, needed by Arabs. But for American Jews, Zionism was simply not needed.

American Jews were doing fine in America without Zionism. Moreover, Zionism presented a problem. It raised issues of dual loyalty and interfered with the trajectory of Americanization. Hence, Zionism was met with a chilled reaction by the American Jewish community in general and the establishment Jewish leadership in particular.

Moreover, Zionism was on a collision course with a historic process the Jewish nation-religion was beginning to go through as Jews moved to America.

(ii) America – the first widespread experiment of Jewish denationalization

When Jews came to America, they were part of the Jewish nation-religion. That is how Jews viewed themselves, and how they were perceived by others since the beginning of Judaism and through the early days of Jewish life in America.

This package was challenged in the 19th century in Western Europe by the Enlightenment, Emancipation, the French Revolution and Napoleon's conquests. There was an attempt to denationalize Judaism and reduce it to a "religion." But this experiment only affected a small percentage of world Jewry prior to the immigration of Jews to America – a subset of those living in the West. The vast majority of Jews lived in closed communities in Eastern Europe and the Middle East. Yet, with the mass Jewish immigration to America such denationalization went "viral." It became a dominant theme of 20th century American Judaism. With the prevailing homogenous "Mayflower narrative" in America, it was only logical for Jews to reduce their nation-religion to the "Jewish Church."

Exit from the Ghetto was the exit from the Jewish nation

Like other groups who arrived in America around that time, the Jews stayed a close-knit group in the early years. Like the Irish and Italians, the Jews tended to socialize and marry within their Jewish circles. They worked in particular professions that were "Jewish professions," just like the Irish worked in "Irish professions." Similarly, just as the Irish maintained a strong Irish identity, and the Italians maintained a strong Italian identity, the Jews maintained a strong Jewish identity during the first part of the 20th century.

Our crowd vs. new immigrants

The pioneers of Jewish denationalization were German Jews who arrived in America in the late 19th century. They came already as assimilated Jews. While there were Jews in America before them, it is those German Jews who set up much of the ethos for American Jews (somewhat akin to Ben-Gurion's group and the Second Aliya in Israel).

With the massive immigration of poor Jews from Eastern Europe in the early 20th century, the veteran German Jews who had been in America since the 19th century were suddenly faced with a crisis.

The German American Jews were part of a massive wave of attempted assimilation that engulfed German Jews of the late 19th century. Their attempt to assimilate in Germany failed due to the utter rejection by German society. But in the United States, the attempt was successful. This was for two reasons: First, there was no "legacy society" that needed to defend itself from "the influence of the Jews," such as the case of Germany (America itself was a "start-up nation"), and second, due to the ideals of the American Revolution and American ethos. German Jews were welcomed in America. German Jews lived in freedom in America – freedom at last! This included the freedom to assimilate out of Judaism.

But the successful assimilation of German Jews in America was suddenly challenged when the masses of Jewish immigrants arrived from Eastern Europe. These Jews were poor, religious and very Jewish. Quickly a bifurcation was forming between "establishment Jews" (also known as "representative Jews"), and Yiddish-speaking immigrants who would reside in New York's Lower East Side and similar Jewish "ghettos." [1]

The establishment Jews felt they needed to "educate" the masses, both for altruistic reasons, and so that those Jews would not reflect badly upon them. In doing so, they instilled their own values on the new Jewish immigrants. Part of this re-education was to effectively denationalize the new immigrants, who at their entry point felt very much a part of the Jewish nation.

The tension between veteran immigrants and new immigrants to America was not unique to the Jews. Every immigrant group had the veteran immigrants take care of the new immigrants, but typically in doing so, also they created social hierarchies. For example, in the American-Chinese community, the American-born Chinese have completely different social circles, organizations and behavior patterns than new Chinese immigrants. Such was the case in the early 20th century between the "establishment Jews" ("Our Crowd") and the new Jewish immigrants.

One can draw parallels to the process discussed that occurred in Israel where the Labor party and the Ashkenazi elite re-educated the religious Jewish masses from the Middle East. (Indeed, the Labor elite referred to one another as *Anshei Shlomeinu*, roughly translated as "Our Crowd".)

---

1 – For expansion, see: Stephen Birmingham: "Our Crowd: The Great Jewish Families of New York".

The establishment Jews in America played an important role in helping the new immigrants exit from the ghetto and shaped them in their image. As Jews got out of the ghetto, they were able, at least for a while, to remain Jewish due to their religious practices (the "Jewish Church").

This was complemented by the longing for the old country (the Jewish shtetl), and soon thereafter by the memory of the Holocaust. These were sufficient to hold Jews together, even if they no longer felt part of the Jewish nation, and even if they no longer felt religious.

Attitude towards Zionism – "Our crowd" vs. new immigrants

The Eastern European new immigrants came from areas where Zionism was popular, and they were not part of the American Jewish establishment that had long rejected Zionism.

Also, they did not enjoy the success and integration into the American elite that the establishment Jews had, and to which Zionism represented a threat. But the reality remained that the Jews "who mattered" were opponents of Zionism. The German Jews rejected Zionism, and being the only voice of Judaism in America that counted, it became evident that American Jewry rejected Zionism. However, this reality changed right on time. In 1915, Zionism recruited a star – Louis Brandeis.

Brandeis was a powerful lawyer who became a political powerhouse in the Progressive movement and later a close confidant of US President Wilson. He eventually became a US Supreme Court Justice.

Brandeis grew up in a secular assimilated Jewish environment. He was indeed part of the "establishment Jews." His family immigrated from German-speaking Prague in the mid-19th century, and became a family of influence, dwelling in circles of wealthy Jews, professionals and academics. But his legal career took him to become the "people's lawyer." In that capacity he was called in 1910 to arbitrate between striking garment workers and their factory owners. Those workers were Jews that Brandeis had limited exposure to before – Eastern European Yiddish-speaking immigrant Jews, who would be the base for the Zionist movement in America.

Later, through a series of meetings with Jacob De-Haas, a confidant of the late Herzl, Brandeis was recruited to the Zionist cause. [2]

Like Max Nordau and Israel Zangwill in Herzl's time, the ability to

---

2 – Peter Grose, "Louis Brandeis, Arthur Balfour and the declaration that made history", *Moment Magazine*, November 2013.

recruit a known star to the Zionist movement had enormous effect. It showed that it was not just a movement of young delusional dreamers.

The establishment Jews, led by American Jewish Committee President Jacob Schiff, continued to resist Zionism, but they became more and more marginalized, as the preponderance of the American Jewish community became no longer only German Jews, but also Jewish immigrants from Eastern Europe, who were the passionate Zionists.

Interestingly, those Eastern European Jews did not rebel against the establishment and accepted their leadership and structures on general issues pertaining to Jewish life in America, but when it came to Zionism, they did not hesitate to voice their views.

The exit from ghetto life that occurred in the 1920s and 1930s, the success of those previously new immigrants, the wealth generated by the new immigrants alongside the wealth erosion and dispersal by establishment Jews, as well as the mixing through marriage, all resulted in today's composition of American Jewry.

Today's American Jew is a hybrid of all of those legacy experiences and ancestries. Hence, on the one hand, the early affinity to Zionism that Eastern European immigrants brought to America trickled to today's American Jewry, yet on the other hand, as Jews abandoned the ghetto, Zionism was pushed to the back burner along with other Jewish aspects of the American Jew.

(iii) Israel established – American Jews still did not need Zionism

When Israel was established, American Jews were jubilant. But this did not change the basic reality that neither Zionism, nor Israel was needed by American Jews.

Concerns of dual loyalty were even more pronounced now that there was a Jewish state. Those concerns were heightened in the 1980s with the Jonathan Pollard affair – an American Jew with high security clearance who was convicted of spying for Israel.

American Jews thrived in 20th-century America. In particular, the last two decades of the 20th century were a Golden Age, not just for American Jews, but for Jews around the world. The existential threats were removed. European Jews were safe, Russian Jews were no longer held behind the Iron Curtain, and Jews in Israel, while facing tactical threats, were no longer viewed as under imminent threat of extinction as they were in Israel's first two decades, no longer under the mentality of "the last person out, turn off the lights."

American Jews enjoyed unlimited freedom, were assured that their fellow Jews around the world were now safe, and felt secure in their Jewish identity. But that was about to change.

21st Century: Failure of Judaism 2.0 in America – The Need for Zionism

2. FAILURE OF DENATIONALIZATION OF JUDAISM

With no preparation or advance planning, a new radical form of Judaism emerged in America – a Judaism without Judea. Or at a minimum, Judaism that was now based on the checkered past ("we came from Judea") as opposed to a hopeful future ("return to Judea").

Yet, even after stripping Judea from Judaism, American Jews were able to stay as a distinct community. Indeed, in the 1920s, the majority of American Jews were living in a "Jewish ghetto" to one degree or another (physically on the Lower East Side, or culturally through social circles). Many Jews still spoke Yiddish as their primary language, and 60% of them were born outside the United States. But as the 20th century progressed, American Jews rapidly left the ghetto. American Jews successfully integrated into the overall American society – they turned family businesses into national enterprises, became bankers, lawyers, politicians and staples of 20th century America. After 1,800 years of suppression, the exit from the ghetto was a great Jewish success story, but it came at a heavy price.

(i) End of new religion – Judaism without Judea

The idea of Judaism without Judea was revolutionary. Judaism, since its inception, was anchored in Judea – whether by physical presence (during Judaism 1.0), or in the yearning to return (during Judaism 2.0).

But it was only the first of three unprecedented processes American Jewry went through. Soon thereafter, it was followed by an even more revolutionary idea: the denationalization of the Jewish nation-religion.

Those two revolutionary processes – disassociating Judaism from the Land of Israel and reduction of Judaism to a mere religion – could have worked, as long as what remained of Judaism – the religious aspect – would stay strong.

But the first two steps of stripping Judea from Judaism and then narrowing Judaism to the "Jewish Church," was soon followed by a third one: Secularization.

American Jews abandoned the "Jewish Church" and in doing so left American Judaism without a substantial anchor.

(ii) End of temporary glues of American Jewry

To address the void, American Jews over the last 80 years connected to their Judaism primarily through two new substitute glues:

1. *Memory of the Holocaust:* The Holocaust has been the most significant Jewish issue that united the Jews in the second half of the 20th century through today. The Holocaust, along with its lessons and memories, drives Jewish organizational policy and has dominated much of the Jewish community ethos. The most Jewish topic depicted by Hollywood is the Holocaust (there are more movies about the Holocaust than about all other Jewish issues combined). Similarly, the most common theme of Jewish museums is the Holocaust.

2. *Nostalgia for Ashkenazi/Eastern European roots:* The second American Jewish glue was the culture of Yiddish, the shtetl, Jewish food (gefilte fish, bagel and lox) and Eastern European Jewish heritage. With the "grandmothers generation" alive, the American Jews united around the cultural symbols of their old country.

Not surprisingly, the American Jew looked at the ancestral "Old Jew" through a lens similar to that of the American Italian, who looked at its ancestral "Old Italian," or the American Irish who looked at those from Ireland. They looked at their ancestors in terms of home-country, in terms of "where we came from." They looked at their previous geography of domicile with nostalgia and even pride. There was never a divorce from the past. While an early theme of the Israeli Jewish immigrant was negation of the Diaspora, the American Jewish immigrant embraced the Diaspora. While the Israeli Jews rebelled and created a "new Jew," the American Jews brought the shtetl with them to America.

The good news for the American Jewish community is that in the last 80 years, the memory of the Holocaust and the nostalgia for the Eastern European past successfully replaced the fading glues of religion, insularity and discrimination. Those replacement glues kept American Judaism intact through the early 21st century.

The bad news is that these glues are rapidly fading: The memories of the Holocaust will not be as acute when the survivors die out, and nostalgia for the old Jewish life will diminish once the Jewish grandmothers pass away.

There are no natural successors for these replacement glues – they were one-time fixes. Therefore, a large vacuum is already emerging and is likely to grow. This vacuum represents an existential threat for survival of non-Orthodox American Jewry. [3] Given that, two options are possible: Either the vacuum will immediately be replaced by something else, or non-Orthodox American Judaism will evaporate within a few decades.

(iii) Judaism low in hierarchy of identities

To be clear, Judaism is important for most American Jews. It plays a role in their life, but this role tends to be subordinate to the role of other elements in their life.

In the middle of the 20th century, an American Jew's Jewish affiliation was high on his hierarchy of identities. When asked what he is, he would probably answer a Jew, or perhaps an American Jew. Being Jewish was core to his identity. But by the 2010s such Jewish affiliation has gone down the hierarchy of identities. That is in part due to the reasons described: The exit from the Jewish ghetto, the fading of religiosity and the passing of the immigrant generations. Yet, it is also due to new identities and memberships that have climbed up the hierarchy of identities.

Membership in synagogue and sending children to Jewish day-schools are there some place on the hierarchy, but often it would be below other memberships such as college alumni affiliation, country club membership, professional group affiliation, or sending children to a particular music school.

If a Jew in the early 20th century would bring up his synagogue or Jewish school early in a conversation, today he is more likely to discuss being a Harvard alum, West Point graduate, a particular country club member, Rotary Club member, Goldman Sachs banker, etc. Similarly, he is less likely to discuss the weekly Torah portion or rabbinical gossip, and more likely the latest restaurant that opened or recent movie he watched.

Just like other groups, such as Irish Americans and Italian Americans, the ethnological national affiliation still exists for Jews as well, but it is low on their hierarchy of identities.

---

3 – As discussed through the book, non-Orthodox Jews consist of about 90% of American Jewry. The analysis in the book pertains to the non-Orthodox majority.

(iv) Orthodox and engaged Jews are only a small minority

There are American Jews for whom Judaism remains high on the hierarchy of identities. This includes two groups:

Orthodox Jews – those indeed connect to their Jewish identity through its religious aspect – observing Shabbat, keeping a kosher home, attending synagogue. For them, connection to the religious aspect and the national aspect of Judaism is one and the same. Also, this is the one group of Jews who are living in a distinct community. The children tend to go to Jewish day-schools and yeshivas, and much of the day-to-day life revolves around Jewish community institutions. It is hard to assess how big this group is. Research ranges from 5 to 15%, but those figures also include secular Jews who are members of an Orthodox synagogue. For example, for those who once a year attend synagogue on Yom Kippur in an Orthodox synagogue. This is a substantial group since Chabad has synagogues in places where no other synagogues exist, of any stream. [4] It is often pointed out that Orthodoxy is the fastest-growing group in American Jewry. That is true due to its high birthrate and low intermarriage rate, but mostly due to the evaporation of non-Orthodox American Jewry.

Engaged Jews – these are Jews who are actively involved with Jewish causes, go regularly to Jewish events, and "wear their Judaism on their sleeves." Some call them Super-Jews, a term of endearment given to such people by their friends – Jews and non-Jews alike – who often view them as "their Jewish friends." For example, a single Jewish woman living in New York's Upper West Side and regularly going to benefits and singles parties hosted by Jewish organizations, a young Jewish couple who holds leadership roles in their Reform or Conservative synagogue, or Jews that when you come into their house, you know right away that you have entered a Jewish home.

Some of the so-called Super-Jews are observant Reform and Conservative Jews. While the degree of observance in Orthodox Judaism is by definition, very high, the vast majority of Reform Jews tend not to be observant Jews, by their own definition. Those who are observant (in whichever form they choose), are not on a path of evaporation. Judaism is high on their hierarchy of identities, just as it is for observing Orthodox Jews. But the size of this group is small.

---

4 – Chabad, an Orthodox organization known for outreach to Jews, has 3,500 centers and institutions, in 100 countries. Source: chabad.org.

Naturally, it is impossible to assess what percentage of American Jews belong to this amorphous loose collection of engaged Jews. It obviously depends on the exactness of definitions. But through interpretation of various research and surveys, as well as consultation with researchers and Jewish leaders, it is safe to say that it is not more than 10% of non-Orthodox Jews. If one includes the Orthodox – who are engaged Jews by default – then the totality of Jews for whom Judaism is high on the hierarchy of identities and are not at risk of evaporation is somewhere in the range of 15-20% of American Jews. [5]

Percentages can certainly be debated, but what is indisputable is that Orthodox and engaged Jews are a minority of American Jewry. And yet, most research about Jews is done in the context of this minority. Jewish engagement is often measured through them, which leads to an illusion about the viability of the American Jewish community as a whole.

If one would want to study the life of Catholics in America, it would be irrelevant to analyze the institutions of the Church or the Vatican – what does a hipster in Brooklyn or a lawyer in Chicago have to do with the institutions of the Church? Same with the Jews.

Thirty percent of American Jews self-classify themselves as unaffiliated, but in reality, most of the Reform and many of the Conservative Jews are under-affiliated to a point that the lines between them and unaffiliated Jews become blurry. Synagogue membership is not the same as engagement with Judaism, just like having a library card does not mean you read books regularly. Indeed, probably most holders of library cards have not been to their library in years.

3. FAILURE OF PREVIOUS TRANSITION ATTEMPTS

There have been various attempts to address the fading connection of American Jews to their Judaism. Those attempts failed and American Jewry continues its trajectory towards evaporation.

(i) Failure to change history: switch of Jewish old country

As they arrived in America, Jews adopted the basket of local narratives, concepts and terminologies. Such was the case for all immigrants. For the Irish Americans, their old country was Ireland, for the Italian

---

5 – For example, the 2021 Pew Research Center's survey indicated that 80% of Jews report low or medium "traditional religious observance". For this group, the primary Jewish cultural activity is sometimes or often cooking Jewish food (75% of respondents). There is no data if this group also often or sometimes cooks Asian or Italian food.

Americans, it was Italy. That was their home before coming to America; that is what they left behind.

But when the mass of Jewish immigrants arrived, it was not from Judea. Rather, it was mostly from the Pale of Settlement of Poland and Russia – from the Jewish towns, from the shtetls.

Suddenly, Jews were "Polish" or "Russians" – something they never were – not by their own definition, nor by the Polish/Russian definition. Nobody in the outside world would think of Jews living in Poland in the early 20th century as "Polish." In their old country, they were Jews.

In America, staying in tune with the overall notion and terminology, the Jews adopted a false retroactive old country – Eastern Europe. This came along with the customs, language, culture and rituals of the old country: Yiddish, gefilte fish, *Fiddler on the Roof.*

Polish Jews were never Polish

Astonishingly, nostalgia to the old country became nostalgia to values and elements of life which the Jews utterly detested while they were there. The ghetto life in Poland that was considered miserable in real time, became idolized in America. First and foremost, Yiddish and its associated culture became the symbol of nostalgia for the old country.

This is the same Yiddish that Herzl refers to as "ghetto language… which used to be the stealthy tongue of prisoners." The retroactive glorification of Yiddish and Polish/Russian old country was done since there was no tangible connection to the real old country – to Zion.

That, however, dramatically changed once Israel was established. The real old country became real again. Yet American Judaism stayed stuck in the old false narrative; stuck in Judaism 2.0.

(ii) Failure to retain Jews through Community Judaism

The attempt to reduce American Judaism to a community context has also failed. This is primarily since America and global society in general has become less community-driven. The community affiliation is not physical, and non-exclusive, and indeed the Jew is a member of various other communities.

The Jewish community certainly exists for Orthodox Jews as well as other engaged Jews, but as discussed, they are only a small minority of the Jews (estimated to be about 20%) and are not at a risk of evaporation. For the majority, being part of the Jewish community is a non-committal value, low on one's hierarchy of identities and priorities.

Even if a Jew belongs to a synagogue or a Jewish community center which he occasionally visits; even if he sends his children to Jewish Sunday school, camps or trips to Israel, the abstract Jewish community is insufficient to serve as a solid connection to his Judaism. The makeshift of such an abstract community does not create dependency on the community, nor does it sufficiently elevate Judaism to a meaningful place in the Jew's hierarchy of identities. The sense of Jewish community for today's American Jew is a far cry from his grandparents' sense of Jewish community: living in a Jewish neighborhood, having predominantly Jewish neighbors, being part of a Jewish circle of friends, speaking Yiddish and working in a Jewish profession.

(iii) Failure to retain Jews through cultural Judaism

Researchers point out that the American Jew's connection to Judaism is predominantly a cultural one. [6] Indeed, there was a time where Jewish culture was integral to the life of the American Jew, but this is no longer the case. Indeed, today, the culture of the American Jew is American culture. Except for those 20% of Jews for which Judaism is high on the hierarchy of identities, an American Jew might state that Jewish culture is important to him and point to various aspects of it such as eating bagel and lox, but in reality, it is not distinct, and he does not really consume it regularly. After all, how many times a month does an American Jew really eat bagel and lox? In this regard, Jewish culture is important to an American Jew just as Irish culture is important to the American Jew (indeed, the American Jew drinks Guinness), and just as Indian culture is important to the American Jew (indeed, the American Jew does yoga). Same with Japanese culture (Shiatsu, Sushi) and Chinese culture (Chinese medicine).

As discussed, there are various inputs into the American Jew's identity and day-to-day life, such as his profession, political views, sexual orientation, and gender. Jewish culture is just one of those many components. Hence, the attempt to form a sustainable connection to Judaism through Jewish culture is weak and not particularly relevant to the contemporary life of the American Jew.

(iv) Failure of the Reform attempt

The mass of Jewish immigrants who came to America in the late 19th century and early 20th century were religious Jews, strictly observing

---

6 – According to the American Jewish Committee survey, 59% of American Jews say that being Jewish is mostly a matter of ethnicity and culture. AJC 2019 Survey of American Jewish Opinion, June 2, 2019.

religious law. The German Jewish immigrants who preceded them a bit earlier in the 19th century were mostly secular. Those German Jews no longer observed the halacha, rituals and customs. Those German Jews also brought with them from Germany the Reform movement.

The reformation of Orthodox Jewish immigrants

As new Jewish immigrants arrived from Eastern Europe through the early 20th century, German Jews quickly became a minority of American Judaism. Yet, as discussed, their early influence not only left a strong mark, but it also shaped the American Jewish narrative for years to come.

Over the next few decades, as the Eastern European Jewish immigrants exited the Jewish ghetto, they changed their synagogue affiliation from Orthodox to either Reform or Conservative. According to the 2020 Pew Research Center's study, only 9% remained Orthodox. [7]

One can draw parallels between the reformation of Orthodox Jewish immigrants from Eastern Europe to America in the early 20th century, and the secularization of observant Orthodox Jewish immigrants from the Middle East to Israel in the 1950s. In Israel's case, it was Zionism that served as Judaism's firewall as immigrants became non-observant; in America, it was the Reform movement.

The Reform movement's Firewall saved American Jewry

The Reform movement was there at the right place at the right time to provide a safety net for those Jews who exited the ghetto en masse:

- It provided a "Jewish Church," which in turn translated to tangible Jewish affiliation.
- It allowed for those Jews who turned secular to consume Jewish experiences that were consistent with their lifestyle. It provided an experience that was both easy and non-committal.

The Reform movement was both a religious retention vehicle, and an affiliation (national) retention vehicle. In this regard, it is possible that had the Reform movement not been there, the evaporation of American Jewry would have happened much sooner – at that point American Jews stopped keeping Shabbat and observing the Jewish laws.

Not enough – loose connection

However, as mentioned, given the loose relationship of the Reform

---

7 – Down from 10% in the 2013 Pew Research survey, "A Portrait of Jewish Americans".

Jew with his religious expression of Judaism, the retention vehicle set up by Reform Judaism is fading.

Unlike the Orthodox stream, wherein 80-100% of Orthodox males go to synagogue on Shabbat and/or mark Shabbat in some particular manner, most Reform Jews do not mark Shabbat in any manner. About 85% of Reform Jews do not attend synagogue regularly. [8]

Reform Jews are not a separate Jewish entity. They are non-Orthodox Jews who belong to a Reform synagogue or participate in Reform programs. This affiliation should not be overstated, given the low engagement and infrequent visits to such synagogues. For these under-engaged Jews, it is hard to point to the exact line between a Reform and Unaffiliated Jew. The secular American Jew's membership in a Reform congregation should be put in context. Just like having a Walmart credit card does not make you a "Walmart American" simply because you are part of that club. There are, however, efforts to draw an artificial wedge. For example, in Wikipedia, there is an attempt to make a distinction in one's religion – not "Jewish," but "Orthodox Jewish" or "Reform Jewish," in a similar manner that distinctions are made between "Catholic Christian" and "Greek Orthodox Christian."

That is a laughable distinction, since for both Reform congregants and for most of its leadership, the Reform affiliation is radically inferior to their Jewish affiliation. Just like a Jew would not define his Jewish identity by the specific synagogue he attends ("I am a Har Sinai Synagogue Jew"), his affiliation with which stream of Judaism needs to be taken into context – just like his Walmart credit card.

It is not only the low commitment of Reform congregants that leads to its failure to serve as an anchor to American Jewry, it is also the key narratives that the Reform movement has attempted to deploy. Most notable is the attempt to distinguish Judaism through an alternative glue – Tikun Olam – making the world a better place.

Failure of the Tikun Olam connector

The attempt to draw American Jews through Judaism's historical purpose as a "light to the nations" was bound to fail from the start. This is both due to conceptual reasons and contemporary realities. Historically, the concept of being a "light to the nations" was primarily about spreading the monotheistic religion to the world. The United States, however, has very much been a monotheistic culture since its founding.

8 – Analysis by Prof. Steven Cohen prepared for the purpose of this book, based on Pew Research and other data.

In its current iteration, Tikun Olam, which means repairing the world, is also about correcting the wrongs, doing good, engaging in charity and making the world a better place. But that is a very weak connector, since other groups engage in similar charitable actions.

If anything, it supports the notion of universalism – of Judaism not being any different than any other group, religious or otherwise. Since many groups engage in such charitable activities, all groups engage in Tikun Olam. Rabbis can write endless books about how Jewish Tikun Olam is different – this could be relevant to religious scholars, but completely irrelevant to the average Jew.

Moreover, a Jewish person engaging in such good-doing does not need to do it in a Jewish context. Indeed, the vast majority of American Jews engaging in charity are doing so through non-Jewish, community-wide organizations and activities.

Attempts to make Tikun Olam relevant to young Americans, by making it about the environment, human rights, or humanitarian aid – make it an even less relevant connection to Judaism, since an American Jew does not associate those values with Judaism. The Reform movement identified values that are relevant to the Jew, but those Jews who care about them do not do so under a "Jewish hat." The Reform pitch to engage in Tikun Olam is similar, if not subordinate to others who pitch the Jew about humanitarian aid and charity.

With lack of particularity in its message and with the bulk of its members only loosely connected, the Reform solution came short.

While there is enough substance to sustain a set of communities and messages, there is certainly not enough to sustain Judaism. The Reform attempt, just like the attempted switch of the old country, has failed to preserve the American Jewish community. Hence, it is continuing its trajectory towards evaporation.

(v) Failure of the Conservative attempt

The Conservative movement, which developed in the United States in the 20th century, and is simplistically viewed as "halfway" between Reform and Orthodox, has also failed in its attempt to keep American Jews engaged with Judaism.

Like the case with Reform Jews, the majority of Conservative Jews have a low engagement level with Judaism. Some Conservative leaders and researchers would point out that Conservative Jews typically have a more committed relationship with Judaism than Reform Jews do.

Indeed, the safety net that the Conservative movement offered to secularized Jews was situated higher in the free fall from the confines of insular religious Jewish life. Hence, just like the Orthodox stream, the Conservative structure theoretically provided an ability to preserve American Jewry through the conduit of the Jewish religion.

There was only one problem – lack of demand, both in terms of membership and in terms of engagement.

Only 17% of American Jews identify with the Conservative movement, [9] and many of them keep a loose relationship with the Conservative synagogue. So much so that many non-Orthodox Jews do not make a meaningful distinction between Reform and Conservative synagogues. The choice as to which one to join is often based on factors such as location, annual dues, programs and personal relationship – not on theological nuances or level of observance. [10]

The Conservative attempt to stop the evaporation of American Jewry has failed, and by now, much of the Conservative growth potential comes from the cannibalization of currently engaged Jews – those attending Orthodox synagogues. Some have even suggested merging the Conservative and Reform movements. This might yield operational synergies, and perhaps provide more clarity, offering a united Jewish-lite alternative for the under-engaged Jew, but it would not likely change the realities of the Jewish evaporation that is occurring amongst the members of both of those streams.

(vi) Failure of the Orthodox attempt

Another possible way for American Jews to remain as a distinct group would have been to take advantage of the one group of Jews for whom Judaism remains on the top of their hierarchy of identities – the small Orthodox minority. This could have been done by looking at Orthodox Jews as one's personal conduit to Judaism. Looking at that Jew in your environment who wears a kipa, as a reminder of one's own Jewish core, as a representative of a Jewish community, which represents some degree of an abstract home.

Just like an observant Jew is required to wear tzitzit – so he can look at it and be reminded of all of God's commandments – so can an under-engaged Jew look at an Orthodox Jew with a kipa and be reminded of his own Jewish identity. This is akin to non-practicing Mormons seeing a Mormon missionary on the street or in a train station and feeling Mormon

---

9 – Pew Research Center, May 11, 2021.
10 – For more on Conservative Judaism: Tikvah Fund podcasts, David Wolpe on the Future of Conservative Judaism, February 27, 2019, and David Wolpe on The Pandemic and the Future of Liberal Judaism, May 27, 2020.

pride, and an augmented sense of Mormon belongingness. It is possible that Herzl himself felt this type of connection to Judaism through seeing Orthodox Jews. In a few important intersections of his life, when he needed to make tough decisions, he found himself wandering around the religious Orthodox neighborhoods of Vienna. While such a Herzl-inspired connection could have worked for a few Jews, it is not strong enough or widespread enough to serve as that connector to Judaism. This is in part because Orthodox Jews tend to move in different circles than non-Orthodox Jews.

Unlike in Israel, where a secular and Orthodox religious Jew inevitably see each other in the cafe, bar, military, workplace, supermarket and on the street, in America, the Orthodox tend to live in different areas and have limited interaction with other Jews. The American Jew will not bump into Orthodox Jews in the restaurant (Orthodox Jews eat in kosher restaurants). Surely, most American Jews have far more non-Jewish friends and acquaintances than they have Orthodox Jewish friends.

The growing presence of the Chabad Orthodox stream on college campuses also provides an outlet and a door for more American Jews to connect to their Judaism through Orthodox religiosity. While the availability of Chabad might be viewed with favor by many non-practicing Jews, only a small percentage of non-Orthodox Jews on campus actually go to Chabad events.

In addition, in recent decades, a political rift has emerged between American Jews as a whole, and Orthodox Jews. In presidential elections, the Democratic candidate has garnered 70-80% of Jewish vote over the last three decades. But Orthodox Jews are now Republicans, and aligned with the Christian evangelicals. [11]

Donald Trump's administration served as a litmus test – highly admired by Orthodox Jews and disdained by many non-Orthodox Jews. Symbolic of this is the number of Orthodox Jews who have worked in his administration, including his daughter, son-in-law, and the ambassador to Israel. This while two non-Orthodox Jews led the process of his impeachment in 2020.

Such a political divide leads to the growing unlikelihood that the core of American Jewry will look at Orthodox Jews as a point of orientation for their own Jewish affiliation.

Some people point to the growing percentage of Orthodox Jews in American Jewry as an indication that the Orthodox attempt is actually a

11 – According to the 2021 Pew Research Center's study, 75% of Orthodox Jews identify as Republican, while 80% of Reform Jews, 70% of Conservative Jews and 75% of Jews of "no particular branch" identify as Democrats.

success. As discussed, this is the wrong way to look at the numbers. It is not that there is migration from Reform, Conservative and unaffiliated Jews towards Orthodoxy. This percentage growth is due to the natural birthrate of the Orthodox, and mostly the early stages of evaporation of non-Orthodox American Jewry.

The Reform, Conservative and Orthodox attempts have all failed to stop this evaporation – that is simply because the anchor of American Judaism is no longer the religious aspect of the Jewish nation-religion. There is a transformation of Judaism's anchor from its religious aspect to its national aspect. The failure of the transition attempts is further aggravated by the reduced significance of American Jewish leadership.

4. END OF POWERFUL JEWISH AMERICAN LEADERSHIP

American Jews are not hierarchical. They may or may not be aware of their Jewish leaders, but are certainly not "disciples" or "constituents." This is just like they may or may not be aware of their university alumni association leadership, or professional association leadership. For the most part, Jews are ambivalent to Jewish leadership.

This is true for both community leadership and religious leadership. Theological, political and spiritual debates between Orthodox, Conservative and Reform scholars are relevant to Judaism, but they are not of particular interest to the Jews. Those 80% or so of American Jews for whom Judaism is low on the hierarchy of identities may not even be aware of those types of debates, and if they are, it is ancillary. The leaders can fight it out, but without the masses.

(i) Passing of the Jewish leaders' generation and the end of Jewish leadership

The 20th century produced great Jewish leaders who helped shape the American Jewish community and were recognized and looked up to by many American Jews. They wielded influence way beyond America's borders – both in Israel and in global politics. International leaders would meet regularly with those Jewish leaders who had the ears of American presidents. But such Jewish leadership gravitas did not transcend to the next generation.

By the 2010s, many of the leaders of prominent Jewish organizations were in their 70s and 80s. Some of the legendary American Jewish leaders passed away in recent years, and with them the era of the great Jewish leadership. For example, Ace Greenberg, who led the infamous UJA Wall Street Dinner roll call, where members of the audience announced their generous donations to that Jewish organization, and Kenneth

Bialkin who served as Chairman of the Conference of Presidents of Major American Jewish Organizations, Chairman of the America-Israel Friendship League, Chairman to the Anti-Defamation League and President of the Jewish Community Relations Council. The anticipated retirement of Malcolm Hoenlein of the Conference of Presidents of Major Jewish Organizations after 35 years of service also symbolizes the end of that era. Hoenlein has been perceived as the closest thing to the dean of American Jews – in White House ceremonies or in meeting with global leaders.

There is certainly strong American Jewish leadership in place today. The dedication and sacrifice of so many competent Jews who choose to dedicate their time and talent to Jewish leadership is admirable. But just like in the case of the Reform movement, the organization they lead only has a loose connection with American Jews. Jews who are involved may know or care about their leaders, but in the digital age, most American Jews do not need "Jewish leaders."

An American Jew can access his own tailor-made basket of leaders that suits his own evolving preferences: A rabbi, a teacher, a blogger, a progressive Jewish thinker, a comedian, a tour-guide he had in Israel or an Israeli political leader. Hence, the Jew can now turn away from Jewish Federations, the UJA and other Jewish structures as the point of orientation for Jewish leadership, and instead turn towards Israel.

The inevitable end of the era of American Jewish leadership supports and perhaps even necessities a transformation to Judaism 3.0. This is somewhat akin to a Protestant reformation, from having the institutions of the Church intermediate and control having a direct relationship with God, with Jesus and indeed with Christianity. But the American Jewish "reformation" goes further than that. Instead of having top-down messaging that is forced on the American Jew and hence ignored, the American Jew now chooses his own customized set of conduits to his Judaism. As a result, the Jewish experience becomes more relevant. This in turn allows the American Jew to feel more connected to ALL aspects of his Judaism. This certainly includes a connection to Judaism through existing conduits, including religion. But just like with general Jewish leadership, an inevitable disconnect emerged between religious leadership and the Jews. This is in particular the case in the Reform movement.

(ii) Wedge between Reform leadership and Reform Jews

The decentralized nature of the Reform movement leads to two nearly distinct sets of Reform Jews: The Reform leadership and the Reform Jews.

Reform leaders are part of the 20% of American Jews who are highly engaged with Judaism. Reform Jews, on the other hand, are not. Most of them are amongst the 80% for whom Judaism is low on the hierarchy of identities. This has led to an imbalanced relationship and a set of inevitable conflicts. It also suggests that Reform Jews might need new themes outside the assortment of themes coming out of "Central Command." Such themes could be found in the sphere of Zionism.

The Reform Jew can continue to look up to his local Reform rabbi, who is the American Jew's leader in that particular Reform "franchise." But as far as "national leaders," and icons that Reform Jews can look up to, they are not necessarily going to be found in New York or in Washington – they will be found in Israel.

Postmodern society enables a Reform congregant to draw from Orthodox rabbis, Conservative rabbis, professors, scholars and political leaders. There is no need for a redundant layer between a Reform Jew and his subject of worship. There is no need for a redundant layer between a Reform Jew and his primary Jewish point of orientation – Israel. The lockdown realities in the early stages of the 2020 Coronavirus crisis elevated this. It made Israel equidistant to the local synagogue – both were now on a computer screen. It therefore contributed to the process of American Jewry's disintermediation – power to the people.

(iii) Attempted hijacking of Reform Judaism by elements of Reform leadership

Politics dominates much of the life of a nation. Religion, beliefs, human rights principles and other values are all recruited to promote one's political agenda. That is legitimate. For example, "The Emergency Committee for Israel" recruited (or some say "hijacked") the value of protecting Israel to promote Republican candidates in recent US elections. Similarly, on various other topics, there were those who seized the value of Reform Judaism to promote liberal agendas, and in some cases anti-Israel agendas.

One is the value of Tikun Olam – repairing the world. Parts of the Reform leadership seem to have commandeered this abstract value to shape the world in those leaders' own image.

Another example is of elements within the Reform movement laying claim to the value of freedom and arguing that Israel is an oppressor of human rights. Some Reform Jews joined forces with pro-Palestinian Europeans around the centennial of the Balfour Declaration to support the notion that recognizing Judaism as a nation was "an innocent mistake" the British made, misunderstanding Judaism to be a nation and not merely a religion. Moreover, that this British "mistake" was driven by anti-Semitism.

Perhaps one of the most prominent examples of hijacking values by elements of the Reform movement was the bizarre battle over the women's section at the Wailing Wall. That battle was escalated in 2016 by leaders associated with the Reform movement, including Reform rabbis.

The argument was that the Israeli Orthodox arrangements of separation between men and women created a wedge between Israel and the American Jewish community, which is overwhelmingly non-Orthodox.

American Jews love Israel, the narrative goes, and then one day they come to the Kotel, and get turned off by Israel. Seeing that the Israeli government officially endorses such gender separation is inconsistent with their values. The argument goes further to claim that American Jews come all the way to Israel and then they cannot pray with their spouse. Shame!

The charge that the Kotel arrangements puts a rift between Israel and American Jews quickly became the consensus view in Israel itself, based on the claims of those American leaders. It became accepted that maintaining the status quo at the Kotel creates a significant divide between Israeli and American Jews, and the question is balancing the interest of American Jews and of Israeli Jews, who are Orthodox – whether religious or secular. But such a view of the dreaded Kotel visit is detached from reality.

The majority of American Jews have never visited the Kotel! This is because the majority of American Jews have never been to Israel (only 41% of American Jews are estimated to have ever visited Israel). [12] That by itself defuses the argument of American Jews being "turned off" to Israel as a result of their Kotel experience.

Just as important, the majority of American Jews who do visit the Kotel, including the vast majority of Reform Jews, are enamored by the experience, and take the gender separation arrangements as a given – as part of the "experience set" that is delivered to them.

No doubt that some are indeed bothered or disappointed by the gender separation, but not to a degree that would compromise their experience. A negligible tiny minority of Reform Jews, concentrated in its leadership, do feel that this is a serious problem that severely compromises their Kotel visit experience.

---

12 – AJC 2019 Survey of American Jewish opinion, June 2, 2019.

But even for them, do they really remember this "trauma" an hour later when they visit the Museum of Yad Vashem? Does it really rise to the level that elements in the Reform movement leadership have made it to be: A seismic rift between American Jews and Israel?

A view of significantly less than 1% of Reform Jews, a negligible percentage, became a top headline for months in Israel as a "wedge between American Jews and Israel." [13]

Such messages have nothing to do with Reform Jews or Reform Judaism. It has to do with agendas. Agendas of elements amongst the leadership of the Reform movement, agendas of individual Reform rabbis, or of an individual's political aspiration. This is symptomatic of the growing disconnect that exists between American Jewish leadership and American Jews.

(iv) End of Jewish icons

With the fading of the Jewish community glues, cultural glues and the influence of Jewish leadership, also came an end of the old Jewish icons. The American Jewish stereotype is no longer reflective of a contemporary American Jew, but of a historic Jew.

Jackie Mason, Jerry Seinfeld, Barbara Streisand and Jon Stewart are not personifications of today's Judaism, just as J.R. Ewing and his family are not personifications of today's Dallas. Neither has much to do with contemporary realities.

In today's Dallas, cowboy hats are sparse and J.R. Ewing-looking oil men are not often seen. Similarly, Jews today do not look, act or even relate to the icons that American Judaism still holds. Perhaps the retirement of some of the earlier-mentioned icons over the last few years is symbolic of the end of Jewish icons.

More broadly, the image of an American Jew as a Yid is disconnected from the way young American Jews look, act and feel. That image associated with Judaism 2.0 of a weakling, along the lines of the Jewish stereotypes depicted in Woody Allen movies is historic, not contemporary.

More importantly, such stereotypes are certainly no longer viewed as a source of inspiration for the young Jew, as they were in the past. On the other hand, the Israeli Jew does inspire young American Jews.

Those Jewish icons, just as other Jewish symbols such as Yiddish and the pastrami sandwich, are not as relevant to the Jewish American in

---

13 – Reform leadership is a small percentage of Reform Jews, and those in Reform leadership who took up this issue are a minority within Reform leadership.

his capacity as a Jew, as much as they are relevant to Americans of all backgrounds, as a Jewish reference point.

5. American Judaism turning into a Pan-American brand

Indeed, the Jewish brand is now one of a number of ethnic American brands that are available for consumption by all Americans: Irish, Italian, Jewish. Those American brands can be consumed by all Americans, regardless of their ancestral affiliation, and are certainly not limited to consumption within a distinct community.

The Jewish glues have faded, but just like with other American communal experiences that turned into pan-American brands, the brand value of Judaism remains strong and ripe for consumption by the broad American public.

This is just like the Irish American brand, once consumed exclusively by the Irish community, is now consumed by all Americans. St. Patrick's Day parades are broadly attended and Irish beer and culture are broadly consumed by Americans of all backgrounds. Moreover, it is safe to say that by today the majority of consumers of the Irish brand in America are non-Irish.

Similarly, a growing number of Jews now skip Passover Seders and Rosh Hashana dinners while there is more and more interest from the broader American population – friends of Jews who were always curious, as well as others seeking a "Jewish experience." This is just like most customers in Italian restaurants are not Italian and most of those ordering Chinese takeout are not Chinese. Indeed, only a minority of Katz Deli customers are likely to be Jewish.

Groups that came to America in the late 19th century and early 20th century have experienced evaporation. They no longer "dominate" the set of experiences that are associated with their own group. The collection of American brands, from Italian pizza, through Irish beer, to the Jewish pastrami sandwich, are now here to the benefit of all Americans.

Some groups have stronger dominance with their own brand and some weaker, but the relations of American ethic groups to their set of brands, has turned from a linear function to a matrix function.

Same for the Jews.

Default path: Evaporation of American Judaism

The fading of the glues that held Judaism together, as well as American Jews perceiving Judaism as low on their individual hierarchy of identities, combined with the lack of significant leadership and failure of previous transition attempts all lead to an inevitable process of evaporation of American Jewry. The evaporation of American Jewry and the turning of American Judaism into an "American brand" is consistent with trajectories of other ethnic groups that came to America around the same time.

In the early days, the immigrant groups' prominent identity association was their ethnological national origin. (An Irish American would say: "I'm Irish.") A few generations later, the American identity became much stronger than legacy heritage identity. (An Irish American would more likely say: "I'm American" or "I'm a New Yorker.")

The associations, such as for Irish with the Boston Police and Fire Departments, are weak and not sufficient to maintain the group as a whole as distinct. This is the likely path of American Judaism as well.

6. EVAPORATION OR TRANSFORMATION?

Evaporation of a group is a legitimate and natural process. Yet, it seems clear that given their past and current behavior, American Jews do not want to evaporate. Therefore, American Jews now need Zionism to keep them as a distinct group. Zionism is turning into the relevant conduit to their Judaism.

This completes the full circle from American Jews rejecting Zionism and not needing it, to American Jews depending on Zionism for their survival as a distinct group.

Paradoxically, if American Judaism evaporates, then by definition the transformation takes effect, since in such a scenario, nearly the entire Jewish world would be in Israel.

One thing seems fairly clear: American Judaism as it existed in the 20th century is not coming back. Thus, the question is, what follows? Will it be an evaporation or a transformation? While evaporation is the more natural path, new circumstances have emerged in America that can facilitate a transformation, assuring American Judaism's survivability. Indeed, the transformation from Judaism 2.0 to Judaism 3.0 is evident already.

The Israelization of the American Jewish Experience

7. NEW VEHICLE FOR CONNECTION TO JUDAISM: ISRAEL

As old glues, experiences, products and values through which an American Jew connected to his Judaism have faded, a new set of connectors has emerged. There is a gradual cultural Israelization of the American Jewish experience alongside its gradual de-Yiddishization.

Today's American Jew has been rejecting the legacy Jewish products available to him. From Seinfeld through Pastrami sandwiches to Jewish literature and magazines. For Orthodox and other engaged Jews, bagel and lox-type connections to Judaism are certainly relevant, but as a whole (the 80% majority), American Jews no longer find such connectors relevant to their contemporary lifestyle, and therefore face a structural disconnect to their American Jewish identity. But thanks to the expanding array of relatable Israeli products and experiences, Judaism, through Zionism, is becoming increasingly relevant for the young American Jew. This is not by duty, but by choice.

Whether it is emotional criticism of Israel's policies or pride in its technological achievements, the Israeli connector is an organic one that originates on the American Jew's end. For example, during the May 2021 Israeli-Hamas conflict, numerous social media posts harshly criticizing Israel began with "As a Jew..." Many of those American Jews do not write other posts "as a Jew," and are not engaged with other aspects of their Judaism. In such instances, the American Jew chooses to initiate a connection to Judaism through Israel. It is done actively through his own volition. Same with positive connections through Israel.

This active willing engagement with Israel is relatively new. Until recently Israel was viewed through a prism of charity: The blue box, planting trees, helping our poor brethren in Israel. For many American Jews, "Israel was shoved down your throat." It was not something one sought, but a call one felt obligated to answer. Now that has changed.

Indeed, with the relevancy of Israel, not only the connection to Judaism switched from "duty" to "want," but it also switched from a top-down process to bottom-up. If one were to examine the confluence of transactions an American Jew has with Judaism, he would find that more and more of those are now Israel-related.

(i) Wide array of Israeli products to connect around

Israel's innovative breakthroughs, its entrepreneurial spirit, its flourishing art and culture scene, the Israeli wine industry, Israel's academic centers, think tanks, these all have suddenly made Israel the repository of an array of attractive products and experiences that are second to no other culture.

The more items there are in a supermarket, the more likely a consumer will be to purchase at least one product. The Israeli supermarket of Jewish experiences has a wide array of connections to choose from, while the old Jewish supermarket (Judaism 2.0) is more limited.

An American Jew who is a wine lover can connect to his Judaism through award-winning Israeli wines. An American Jew who is gay can connect to his Judaism through the Israeli gay culture. An American Jew who is into yoga can connect to his Judaism through Israeli-themed Zoom yoga classes.

Indeed, to the American Jew, Israeli products are now something that he desires and seeks, while the Jewish American products are the ones that are "shoved down his throat." Given the choices a young Jewish American has, such continuous shoving of Jewish products would likely result in retching. But consumption of attractive Israeli products would result in digestion, buy-in and Jewish pride.

(ii) Non-political connection

The array of appealing Israeli products enables American Jews to more easily embrace Israel, even if they disagree with its policies. Since this is now a connection through want, as opposed to duty, it will take a lot for consumers to deny themselves the experiences they seek. When France refused to join the United States-led coalition in Iraq, anti-French sentiments in America ran high, but there was no drop in consumption of French wine. Clearly, French wine is not purchased as a political endorsement of France's policies – it is purchased because people like to drink it. Similarly, being against a particular action Israel might take in Gaza is not likely to stop an American Jew from continuing to watch an Israeli TV series on Netflix that he enjoys. Equally, it does not get in the way of celebrating Tel Aviv's gay pride parade or feeling a sense of appreciation when consuming award-winning Israeli wine.

Coincidently, this is related to trends in the Palestinian society. The ability to disconnect or suppress politics paved the way for Palestinians in the West Bank to seek employment and mentorship by Israelis, and to even get funding for Palestinian start-ups from Israelis. This underscores how audiences can connect to Israel's success and desirability without endorsing or having a particular opinion on political issues.

Attempts by Israel-bashers to label Israel's gay-friendly culture in the context of "pink-washing" and Israeli employment of Palestinians in the context of "collaborators" makes occasional headway within the Israel-bashing community, but for the most part, these kinds of attempts have failed to have an impact. Gay people from around the world come to Israel to celebrate gay pride, regardless of their own political positions, and Palestinians continue to be employed and mentored by Israeli companies, regardless of their personal political views.

The rapid rise in Israeli female combat soldiers over the last decade also contributes to the American Jew's ability to relate through Israel in a non-political way. For example, a twenty-year-old American female who might be critical of Israeli politics and military actions is likely to look differently at an Israeli female officer her age with a machine-gun than she would of an Israeli male soldier that symbolizes the occupation in her mind. After all, the Israeli female soldier has the same issues on her mind that she does, and might even hold similar political views. She too goes to bars, parties and the beaches, sometimes toting her M16. This makes the Israeli female in uniform – a symbol of Zionism – relatable to those who might be avid critics of Zionism.

Arguably, the Israeli female combat soldier (Judaism 3.0) passes the "I am just like you" test – more than the equivalent image associated with legacy American Judaism, such as one of a Jewish camp counselor (Judaism 2.0).

(iii) Israelization of American Jewish culture

Not surprisingly, for a secular Jew, connecting to secular themes is much easier than connecting to religious themes. Similarly, connecting to the present (high-tech, innovation) is easier than connecting to the past (Yiddish), and connecting to happiness (art, wine) is easier than connecting to tragedy (Holocaust).

Hence, there is a growing connection of secular American Jews through Israel: through the present, through happiness, through success. The political criticism by some American Jews of Israel is a form of connection, especially since most of those American Jews who are critical of Israel politically, still have Israeli friends or colleagues (on the left). Some of them have a view of "curing Israel" or "fixing Israel" as opposed to outright bashing Israel.

The Israelization of the American Jewish community is not a political one, but a cultural one. This is reflected in the shift in the type of Jewish-related entertainment that American Jews consume. Popular TV shows include *Fauda, Shtisel, Mossad 101* and *Tehran*. The Israeli characters in those shows are the Jewish icons to which an American Jew is exposed. This is a shift from previous years where Jewish-related shows were mostly about the Holocaust and Yiddish culture.

The Israelization of the American Jewish community is also a product of the American Jew's complete integration into the broader American society. Non-Jewish Americans have a more natural connection with Jewish culture via Israeli culture than through legacy Jewish culture. Given the contemporary integration of American Jewish and non-

Jewish society, the more non-Jews embrace Jewish themes – e.g. Israeli innovations, Israeli art, Israeli wine, Israeli TV shows – the easier it is for the American Jew to do so himself. The non-Jew consuming Israeli experiences gives additional credibility for the Jew to connect to his Judaism through them.

Memory of the Holocaust itself is getting "Israelized"

As mentioned, with the fading of the religious and national connectors to Judaism, the Holocaust served as a replacement glue that held American Jewry together in the second half of the 20th century. But even that is now getting "Israelized."

The American Jewish and Israeli societies have had two different narratives related to the Holocaust. In America, there has been a greater emphasis on victimhood. In Israel, the emphasis has been on heroism and revival – the Warsaw Ghetto Uprising is a key aspect of Israeli Holocaust remembrance. Moreover, in the early years, there was an accentuation of the Holocaust in America ("Haven't the Jewish people suffered enough"), while there was a degree of suppression in Israel – it interfered with the Zionist narrative. Similarly, in America there were those who would not buy German cars or visit Germany, while in Israel there was a greater focus on rebuilding.

Even when it came to applying the lessons, there was a rift – for American Jews it translated into fear of neo-Nazis and right-wing ultra-nationalists, while in Israel into threats from Iran and those seeking to annihilate the Jewish state.

But in recent years in America, as the generations transition, there is a shift. There are fewer and fewer American Jews who would categorically refuse to visit Germany or buy German products. There is a move away from victimhood.

The Coronavirus crisis augmented the fear of a doomsday scenario. This contributes to the shift in the Holocaust perception in American Jewry from that of victimhood, to internalizing that the response to the Holocaust is a strong and safe Jewish state. This is further enhanced by the rise of lethal anti-Semitic incidents in America in 2017-2019, such as the ones in Pittsburgh, San Diego and Virginia.

It might be in the dungeon of one's consciousness, but the reassuring knowledge that there is a Jewish state to "run home to in case of" gives the American Jew reassurance. The American Jew recognizes that Zionism is the relevant response to the Holocaust, and increasingly links the memory of the Holocaust with it. This too is in line with a shift from past-driven connections – the Holocaust – to contemporary and relevant ones – Israel.

8. Removal of the Aliya burden facilitates the connection through Zionism

Zionism can now become the anchor of Judaism, given the growing understanding that Zionism goes well beyond immigration to Israel. Zionism was perceived to be about the establishment of the State of Israel and making Aliya. Indeed, Aliya was essential in the early years of Israel, and for decades Israeli leaders urged American Jews to make Aliya. A Jew choosing to stay in the Diaspora was viewed with disappointment by Israelis, exerting some degree of guilt feeling – someone who is not fulfilling his "duty" as a Jew.

(i) Zionism was not designed to be just about Aliya

From its inception, Zionism had both practical and ideological aspects, but over the last century, the focus tended to the practical side, since it was so successful – the Jewish state was established and is now thriving. It is exactly this success that paves the way to unleashing the ideological aspect of Zionism that has been suppressed. Herzl was aware of the danger in misunderstanding the ideological aspects of his Zionism. He stressed that the Zionist objective is not just the return to the land, but that "Our ideal is the great eternal truth." Herzl underscored that Zionism will continue being an ideal after the establishment of the Jewish state because Zionism embeds "not only the aspiration to the Promised Land...but also the aspiration to moral and spiritual completion."

The shift in the perception of Zionism from focusing on its practical to ideological side would enable Zionism to turn into that eternal truth Herzl talked about and be the conduit through which Jews connect to their Judaism.

(ii) Judaism 3.0 redefines the Diaspora-Israel Relationship

With the recognition of the Jewish transformation to Judaism 3.0, the relationship of American Jews with Israel, marked with decades of brotherly tension and mutual-rejection, is now ready to reach a Nirvana.

American Jews' historic rejection Zionism

Herzl understood that Jew-hatred in Europe was not going away, even if the governments would attempt to fight it. He wrote to Otto von Bismarck, Germany's first Chancellor: "There is no use in suddenly announcing in the newspaper that starting tomorrow all people are equal." But unlike in Europe, Jews in America were indeed free and not subjected to the dangers of European anti-Semitism – the ground was prepared.

When political Zionism was launched in the late 1890s, Jews utterly rejected it. That included rejection by the nascent American Jewish community. American Jews finally lived in emancipation, in equality and were climbing up American society. Zionism, however, was getting in the way. The rise of the national aspect of the Jewish nation-religion was the exact opposite direction of the path set by the American Jewish leadership.

The US Reform movement officially rejected Zionism before it was even launched, stating that Judaism is no longer nation-connected in its 1895 Pittsburgh Platform.

When Herzl launched political Zionism the following year, American establishment Jews, just like their European counterparts, misunderstood and escalated their opposition. American Jewish Committee President Schiff said in 1907: "One cannot be both a real American and a supporter of the Zionist movement."

CHANGING WINDS

But that all changed after 1917. Within a period of three years, the Zionist movement rose from the fringe to the basis on which the British mandate was awarded. The Balfour Declaration, the Paris Conference, the San Remo Conference, the League of Nations mandate, and the appointment of a Zionist Jewish High commissioner to Palestine, all marginalized the initial Jewish opposition to Zionism.

Other events followed. There was a reversal of the Reform movement's 1895 rejection of Zionism as expressed in its Pittsburgh Platform and de facto recognition of Zionism in its 1935 Columbus Platform. Louis Brandeis, the face of American Zionism, became a Supreme Court justice, further invalidating the previous claim of establishment Jews that one cannot be both American and Zionist. And so, by the 1940s Zionism was broadly recognized by American Jews.

A few years later, the Holocaust reaffirmed the need for a Jewish homeland, and support of Zionism became nearly universal amongst the Jews. By the early years of Israel's existence, it is fair to say that the vast majority of American Jews and European Jews were strong supporters of Zionism, even if they chose to stay in the Diaspora.

Zionism's negation of American Judaism – Aliya and Israelization only

HISTORICALLY: ALIYA ONLY – GEOGRAPHICALLY

In Israel's first 70 years, the promotion of Aliya was central to its relations with the Jewish Diaspora. The clear message Israel sent was "we need every Jew in Israel." This was exemplified by the army of Jewish Agency delegates, paid by the State of Israel, who converged on the various Jewish Diasporas to convince local Jews to move to Israel.

It was reflected in speeches of Israeli politicians, including its prime minister, to Jewish communities around the world. Whether it was opening the Maccabiah games with a call to the participants to make Aliya, or speaking in synagogues in North America and Europe, Israeli leadership gave a clear message: "Come!"

Therefore, on the receiving end there was built-in discomfort with the relationship of an individual Diaspora Jew with Israel. Structurally, there was an "unfulfilled ask" – an official request by Israel that you as an American Jew failed to fulfill, and could not fulfill. An "original sin" of sorts, which led to inevitable distance, in the same way, one would avoid a Chabad Tefillin stand or a Greenpeace activist on the street – "I hear you, I care for you, but I will make a detour in order to avoid your ask."

HISTORICALLY: ISRAELIZATION ONLY – CULTURALLY

Not only did Israel want every Jew in Israel, it also sought to "Israelize" the Jews as soon as they arrived – the Israeli demand was that the Jew, turned-Israeli had to abandon the Diaspora way of life and accept the Israeli culture. There was, and still is today, an expectation that the person who makes Aliya will learn Hebrew and speak it. This is why new arrivals get subsidies to attend *Ulpan* – Hebrew language classes.

The Hebrew Language Brigades that patrolled the main streets of Tel Aviv in the 1920s would socially reprimand anybody not speaking Hebrew to each other. The idea of speaking Hebrew was so extreme that merely 30 years prior to the Hebrew Brigades, Herzl himself ridiculed the idea to converse in Hebrew: "Who amongst us has a sufficient acquaintance with Hebrew to ask for a railway ticket in that language?" Indeed, only a small percentage of Jews in Israel in the 1920s and 1930s spoke Hebrew as their native language. The only way for Hebrew to catch on was if the immigrants arriving in the Land would speak it. It was not just Hebrew, it was the newly created Israeli culture. If you came to Israel, you had to Israelize. [14] (In a somewhat similar manner, France today has been attempting, unsuccessfully, to do the same with its own immigrants, forcing on them the French version and mechanism of the "French Brigades.")

(iii) Zionism's ask redefined and expanded – be a Zionist as you are

Now there is a change in attitude. The Jewish Agency, the same semi-government organization that invested millions of dollars and hundreds of personnel to go around Diaspora Jewish communities to convince Jews to move to Israel, no longer aggressively advocates for Aliya. Instead the pitch to the Diaspora Jew is to maintain strong connections with the Jewish state.

In addition, Israel's improved security situation, relative economic prosperity and programs such as Birthright, allow many Jews to come to Israel anyway, and to be exposed organically to the country. This is without being on some path towards Aliya. If in the past, any visiting Jew would be bombarded upon his arrival with pitches to make Aliya – by the government, by friends, by random customers in a cafe he happened to be sitting in – it is now fully acceptable to Israelis if the Jew does not make Aliya. This is somehow analogous to the Datlaf phenomenon described earlier – just as one can stay secular and consume religious experiences a la carte, one can stay in America and consume Israeli experiences a la carte.

Paradoxically, the removal of the "Aliya requirement" as a perceived condition for admission as a full member of the Zionist club paves the path to greater connections of an American Jew to his Judaism through Israel.

Choose from a range of alternative relationships with Israel that suits you

Now that Zionism is not just about Aliya, an American Jew can choose not only from a diverse array of Israeli products and experiences through which he can connect to his Judaism, but also from a wide

---

14 – Reestablishing Hebrew as the national language was also a major goal of Ezra and Nechemiah when they returned from the first exile in the 5th century BCE. They found a high level of assimilation amongst the remaining Jews in the Land. "And half of their children spoke the language of Ashdod, and they could not speak the language of Judah, but spoke the language of various peoples." Nehemiah 13:23-24.

range of alternative relationships with the Jewish state: He can stay at home and consume Israeli experiences through his laptop or phone, he can be a serial visitor, he can own a vacation home in Israel or he can indeed make Aliya. Not only that, he can now choose whichever point on this continuum that is suitable for him, but also all those points are much more accessible today than before. Hence, the connection to one's Judaism through Israel is much more feasible in the 2020s than it was just a few years ago.

9. CLOUD-ZIONISM ENABLES INFINITE CONNECTIONS TO JUDAISM THROUGH ISRAEL

An American Jew no longer needs to visit Israel in order to experience Israel. The digital revolution, social media and mental shift to the cloud makes this possible. Hence, through Zionism, Judaism is more accessible than ever. The Jew can surgically connect to exactly the point that is suitable to him, whether it is news, social engagement or culture. For example, *The Jerusalem Post* readership had historically been mostly in Israel (print), and is now overwhelmingly abroad (online).

All of a sudden, Zionism is not about the physical and difficult task of making Aliya; Zionism is now on a cloud – a cloud that is accessible and easy.

The Coronavirus crisis amplified this reality. An American could have access to a lecture or a concert in Israel with the same ease as he did in his own neighborhood. The lockdown period and its aftermath turned out to be a contributor to the mental shift to Cloud-Zionism.

Israel at your fingertips

Indeed, Israel is now at the fingertips of an American Jew. He can access Israeli music exactly as an Israeli does – since neither do that via the local radio station anymore. He can access Israeli TV shows and tune into Israeli webinars. He can watch Netta win the Eurovision and an Israeli sports team compete in a tournament. He can do it in the same manner as an Israeli does, since most no longer consume such content via television. An American Jew can even tour Tel Aviv and Jerusalem from his living room, and engage in various workshops about Israeli archaeology, history or Israeli wine. He can enter a Houseparty chat of Israelis online. He can go to the Kotel through its webcams (and can do that next to his wife, if he chooses to). This was symbolized by the annual Passover Priestly Blessing in 2020. The Coronavirus restrictions prevented the tens of thousands of Israelis from coming to the Kotel for it. Instead, there were 10 Priests (Kohanim) who prayed at the Kotel and delivered the blessing to the public via YouTube. Amongst those Priests was the American ambassador to Israel, David Friedman. An American could access this blessing just as easily as an Israeli, and the fact that it is conveyed by an American government official, only highlights this.

For those Americans who do want to visit Israel in person – this too has become much easier.

Easier to visit Israel

The Coronavirus crisis that on the one hand contributed to a Jew's ability to connect through Israel from his living room, also put a freeze on the more powerful connection to Israel through visiting. Yet, it underscored how many Americans long to visit Israel.

Indeed, a community of American Jews and other Diaspora Jews has emerged over the last few years who come to Israel very often. This too was enabled by recent realities – Airbnb has changed the affordability of staying in Israel, the reduction in airline prices, greater ease of travel, and the increase in the number of daily flights to Israel from more destinations have all contributed to making Israel more accessible.

Similarly, the fast train connection from Ben-Gurion airport to both Tel Aviv (10 minutes) and Jerusalem (20 minutes), makes short-term travel more feasible since getting to and from the airport is more predictable. A virtual bridge has emerged – so much so that its suspension during the Coronavirus pandemic created a secondary crisis for Americans and other Diaspora Jews, feeling in "exile" by denial of their ability to be serial visitors. These are not just religious Jews, but also young millennials – some of whom were first exposed to Israel through Birthright – as well as secular American Jews of all ages and backgrounds.

The serial visitors to Israel are in line with global trends, such as the NyLon, who travel frequently from New York to London and maintain similar lifestyles and social circles in each city. NyLons would encounter the same people in restaurants, clubs and events in each city – walking into the SoHo House in London, they would see familiar faces from the New York branch. When dining in Cipriani in London they would notice people they might see in Cipriani in New York.

The same dynamic exists today with the DiasporaSraeli. Many American serial visitors would encounter the same people in parties, lectures and festivals in Jerusalem or Tel Aviv that they would see in New York or Los Angeles.

But there is an important distinction – NyLons are both New Yorkers and Londoners – there is parity. In the DiasporaSraeli case, those are

Diaspora Jews connecting through their visits to Israel and not the other way around.

Vacation homeowners – the new Aliya

The serial visitor, along with the new realities of Cloud-Zionism, enables the virtual bridges from Israel into the various centers of Diaspora Judaism, and the removal of the Aliya requirement makes it "legitimate" to be on the other side of those bridges. Yet, in recent years, some have taken their connection through Israel a step further and instead of just being a serial visitor, they decided to purchase a vacation home in Israel. Instead of having a more accessible home in the Hamptons, Maine or the Bahamas, more and more American Jews are choosing to purchase their second home in the place that is more accessible to their heart and to their Judaism – Israel.

The recent ascension of Jerusalem and Tel Aviv has led to a sharp rise in purchases of such homes by American, French and other Diaspora Jews in those two cities. The choice of Israel for a vacation home has adverse effects on real estate availability and prices, but vacation home ownership also fuels the Israeli economy, creates jobs, infuses capital, generates population diversity, globalizes the city and boosts tourism. It also creates a long-term trickle down effect: The vacation home owner's children, relatives and friends are much more likely to visit Israel, spend money in restaurants and stores, invest in local businesses, direct funds to Israeli charities and maybe even make Aliya.

Beyond the economic benefit to the cities and its residents, Diaspora Jews visiting their Israeli vacation homes regularly contribute to the development of Israel's society across various spectrums. Greater day-to-day interaction of foreigners and Israelis exposes Israelis to global business opportunities, and fosters innovation, idea-generation and international business standards.

Such an affluent demographic brings more of the outside world into the heart of Israeli cities. Israeli society is strong enough to allow a higher degree of pluralism and sustain a more diverse range of residential preferences. Israel is only at the beginning of understanding the concept of vacation home ownership and has yet to embrace it. Indeed, as of now, it discourages it.

The current debate is reminiscent of a debate that occurred in Israel in the 1920s. Just like now, much of the local Israeli public and many Israeli leaders were critical of a wave of affluent Diaspora Jews coming in, boosting real estate prices and bringing with them Diaspora European behavior patterns: "The homeowners have arrived," they were mocked.

These are not country-builders!

It is true that the 1920s Fourth Aliya boosted housing prices (over 100 percent) and contributed to the economic hardship of the late 1920s. But those same immigrants also transformed Tel Aviv from a collection of neighborhoods into a metropolitan city. They created an industrial infrastructure in Israel, and brought with them technology, art, capital and innovation. Their arrival was highly beneficial to Israel's development – economically, socially and politically. Contrary to some perceptions at that time, they were indeed builders of Israel. In a similar manner, American and other vacation homeowners today are builders of Israel.

But still – despite the ease of connecting to Israel through the cloud, to visit regularly and even own a vacation home, there is no better way of connecting through Israel than to make Aliya. The removal of the "Aliya requirement" does not mean that it is not still the aspiration – Zionism's preferred course of action. Indeed, Aliya is easier today than ever before.

The Ease Of Aliya

Not only is the aggressive "ask" to make Aliya eliminated, and therefore is now "voluntary" and more organic, so is the aggressive ask to "culturally Israelize" once the new Israeli settles in the Land.

Until recently, an American Jew who wished to make Aliya faced the dual burden of leaving his geographical, professional and business life on the one hand, and leaving his cultural life on the other. An American moving to Israel was expected to stop being culturally an American, and to now become an Israeli. But that is no longer the case. The negation of Diaspora life in Israel has itself been negated.

Strong Israeli culture

The Israeli who needed to be created in the early decades of the 20th century is now alive and well. There is no pressing need for the mass Israelization that existed back then. Therefore, for an immigrant to speak English, have American friends, live in a Jewish American community, such as in the German Colony or Baka neighborhoods of Jerusalem, does not conflict with Israelization.

This makes it an easier task to make Aliya, just as it makes it easier to be a serial visitor, and even to relate to Israel remotely as a point of orientation. Now Israelis speak your language and understand your culture. Israelis are now coming to you, as opposed to you coming to Israel. One is no longer faced with the immediate challenge of learning Hebrew or culturally turning into an Israeli. One can be himself and just come. There are synagogues such as HaNasi and The Great Synagogue in Jerusalem, as well as 121 Ben Yehuda in Tel Aviv where English is spoken. There are American rabbis, thinkers, lectures and community activity. This is all possible and welcomed due to the strength of the dominant Israeli culture.

SECOND GENERATION AUTO-ISRAELIZATION

Unlike immigrants to France and Germany, the children of immigrants to Israel will speak Hebrew as their mother language in an Israeli accent, and will be part of the Israeli culture.

The Israeli education system generally discourages opportunities to go to specialty "international schools," and unlike in other places, very few immigrants choose to send their children to such schools.

Moreover, the children's upbringing ecosystem, the culture of curiosity and engagement with others, all lead to a unique reality in Israel – children of immigrants are as culturally Israeli as those of Israeli parents. For the most part, by the time the child is 18, the mandatory military service serves as the egalitarian mechanism and fully Israelizes the immigrant.

Therefore, the second generation of immigrants are fully Israeli. This further reduces the need of an immigrant to Israelize, and hence makes it easier to make Aliya and through it embrace Zionism.

Proto-Cloud-Zionism: Ahad Ha'Am vs. Herzl

An opportunity has emerged for an American Jew to center his identity around Israel, whether by purchasing a vacation home, by visiting regularly, or without leaving the United States, by staying in touch with Israel via the cloud. To a large extent this is reopening the late 19th century debate between the two Zionist leaders at the inception of the movement – Ahad Ha'Am and Herzl.

Just like the feud a few decades later between American Zionist leader Brandeis and London-based Weizmann, the debate between Ahad Ha'Am and Herzl was much about personal issues, having Herzl the outsider show up on the Jewish stage from nowhere, with no background or knowledge of Jewish life, and without the sufficient reverence that was reserved for the "dean" of Eastern European Jews, Ahad Ha'Am.

The substantial disagreements may not have been that large, but they can be viewed in the realm of proto-Cloud-Zionism.

Ahad Ha'Am viewed the establishment of a Jewish state as a "point of orientation." This was developed by Weizmann who said: "Zionism is about Judaizing the Jewish communities." But this was in fact very similar to Herzl who said in the first Congress and then in a subsequent article that Zionism, before it is anything else, is the return to Judaism.

The transformation to Judaism 3.0 is exactly that – a connection around Israel enabling a Jew to return to Judaism. It allows him to not only stay Jewish but also deepen his Jewish identity.

Less than a week after publishing *The Jewish State*, Herzl attended a meeting of the student union Kadima in Vienna. Struck by the extreme enthusiasm of the students, Herzl calmed them down and shared a profound aspect of his plan to re-establish the Jewish state: "Maybe we will never get to Zion, so we need to aspire to the Zion that is in our hearts." After 120 years, for those Jews who haven't got to Zion, the conditions are ripe to aspire to that Zion that is in their hearts.

This is much easier now, since this Zion is no longer an abstract concept, it is no longer a fable, it is no longer a charity case. It is no longer something that is "shoved down your throat" nor that is demanding. Indeed, today Zionism is the Judaization of the Jewish communities. And thanks to Cloud-Zionism, this can be done while the Jews in those communities stay there. It took 50 years as Herzl predicted in Basel for the Jewish state to become a reality. It took 120 years for Cloud-Zionism to become a reality.

10. THE NEW AMERICAN JEW: CONTRIBUTION OF THE ISRAELI AMERICAN

The core of American Jews came from Eastern Europe. The narrative that they instilled was defined by the Yiddish culture, with which came a particular stereotype of a Jew often viewed as "nebishi" – Jerry Seinfeld, Woody Allen, Jon Stewart. But over the last few decades a new type of Jew has entered the American-Jewish scene: The Israeli American.

The arrival of Israeli Americans and their growing relevance has profound implications on the American Jewish narrative and is a key contributor to the transformation of Judaism to Judaism 3.0. This is both since the term "American Jew" is shifting – it is gradually becoming something else than what it was until now – and in particular since it underscores the Israelization of the American Jewish experience.

(i) Emergence of the Israeli American

While Israelis have been immigrating to the United States since Israel was founded, they have tended to be on the fringe of American Jewish life. Their demographic ("taxi drivers/movers"), combined with the negative image they had in Israel as *Yordim* – descenders, distanced them from American Jewish circles.

Our crowd vs. Taxi driver

In the last two decades, an abundance of Israelis have earned their MBA degrees in top US schools, as well as advanced Law degrees and PhDs. Many Israelis are getting senior positions in American high-tech companies, founding their own companies and are represented across the American business, academia and art spectrum. Israeli society no longer views Israelis living abroad as a negative. The American Jewish community has found it easier to embrace an "Israeli MBA" than an "Israeli taxi driver."

Prominent Israeli Americans are entering key positions not only in business and academia, but also in politics and community. Rahm Emanuel, an Israeli American was the mayor of Chicago and White House Chief of Staff. At the time he was even mentioned as a potential candidate for President of the United States.

Safra Catz, an Israeli American who is the CEO of Oracle, was frequently mentioned as a potential Cabinet member of the Trump administration. Similarly, out of all the Jewish organizations that President Trump could address in 2019, he chose an Israeli one – the Israeli-American Council. Clearly, the Israeli American is no longer on the fringe – he is now front and center of American Jewry.

The Israeli American brings Israel to the American Jew's home

The growing prominence of Israeli Americans has had a profound effect on the Jewish American community and its ability to relate to Zionism: It presents an alternative role model for young American Jews and an alternative Jewish experience in America.

It also brings Israel into the hearts of American Jewish communities in a similar way that the fundraisers system did in the 19th century. Back then, when Jews in Israel were dependent on donations from Diaspora Jewish communities, representatives of Jewish communities in Palestine, known as Shadars, would make reverse-pilgrimages to the communities of Europe to collect money. In doing so, they would report about conditions in Palestine and give European Jewry a tangible taste of contemporary life in Jerusalem, Tzfat (Safed) and throughout the Land of Israel. With advances in banking and technology, those Shadars were no longer needed, and thus life in the Land of Israel became more abstract. The updates of the goings-on in the Land were learned through newspaper articles, indirect stories and letters. Not having scheduled visits by the Shadars from the Land of Israel made it farther away, and in doing so, allowed people like Herzl to rely more heavily on imagination, including idealizations.

Until recently, many American Jews rarely saw an Israeli (59% of American Jews have never been to Israel), and hence relied on over-stereotyping. This made Israel and Israelis distant and imaginative – whether idealized ("people dancing Hora in the streets"), or villainized ("ruthless Israeli soldiers"). But now, with Israeli Americans in their midst, American Jews can see Israelis in a more realistic realm – it brings Israel alive, and into the Jewish American's home. It also migrates Israel from the newspaper story into routine conversation. It makes Israel more relatable, and it is hence easier to have as one's primary Jewish point of orientation. Similarly, it de-stereotypes the Israeli. The film *Don't mess with the Zohan* underscored the cliche of Israelis in the eyes of Americans.

Having continuous, routine, multi-layered interaction with actual Israelis in one's own social circles leads to a more appealing delivery of Israel to the American Jew. It also inevitably softens the criticism of Israel by the American Jews who are avid critics. This is due to the ability to have dialogue with Israelis on the current hot topics, and about being a soldier in the Israeli Defense Forces. It is much easier to harshly criticize an abstraction (the hypothetical "ruthless Israeli soldier") as opposed to a real person ("my friend Avi was an Israeli soldier"). Ultimately, the presence of the Israeli American represents a catalyst of the Israelization of the American Jewish experience.

(ii) Emergence of Middle Eastern, Persian and Russian Jews

The Israeli Jew is not the only relatively new arrival to the American Jewish scene. There are more Persian Jews and Sephardi Jews. They not only tend to have stronger ties to Israel, but also have more of their Jewish identity intertwined with Zionism. For example, Beverly Hills – staple of the old American liberal Jewish elite – had a Persian Jewish mayor elected in 2007. Similarly, there are more Russian Jews and more Jews from Latin America – not just in numbers, but also in positions of influence within American Jewry.

The legacy character of the pan-American Jew – depicted through Jewish stereotypes, through Jewish icons and in Jewish leadership – has shifted. The previous American Jew associated with Eastern Europe and Judaism 2.0 is giving way to a more heterogeneous American Jew who is far more connected to Israel and associated with Judaism 3.0.

American Jewish Societal Shifts Facilitate The Transformation

11. AMERICAN JEWS IN SEARCH OF AN IDEAL

With secularization, people of all backgrounds searched for another ideal to replace that of religion. For example: socialism, and later during the 21st century: Intersectionality, the environment, human rights. For American Jews, the search for a Jewish ideal meets Zionism.

(i) Popularity of heritage – Identity reflected through Israel not Eastern Europe

There is a rising trend amongst young Americans to reconnect with their heritage. More Irish Americans are seeking to consume some limited degree of Irish culture. This is similar with Italians and other Americans – young Americans of German heritage who did not necessarily have much connection to Germany through their grandparents, given the political reality at that time, are now also connecting to their German heritage. This is not recentering one's identity, but identifying a source of pride and belongingness.

For the Jews, the re-establishment of Israel, its success and the availability of Cloud-Zionism enables such heritage identity to be reflected through Israel. The American Jew's real heritage is Judea (Israel), not Eastern Europe. This is just as the Italian American's heritage is Italy, not Ellis Island.

The American trend of heritage-identity allows a correction of the previous attempt to label the Jewish "home-country" as Eastern Europe. One reflection of this trend is the anemic response to the attempt to revive the Yiddish language and culture, alongside the robust response to Israel-like activities.

The 2019 off-Broadway staging of *Fiddler on the Roof* in Yiddish drew large audiences, but those were still a drop in the bucket, relative to those who attended during the same time period concerts of Israeli musicians, watched Israeli TV shows like *Fauda* and *Shtisel* or consumed other Israeli-related entertainment experiences. The American Jew's search for an ideal meets Zionism not only due to demand but also since Israel triggers his Judaism.

(ii) Jews defined by relations to Israel – de facto

The American Jew is increasingly defined by his relationship to Israel whether he chooses to or not – in both negative and positive. An 18-year-old Jewish college student quickly realizes that he has an involuntary passive affiliation with Israel just by virtue of being Jewish. This often forces him to make a decision about his relationship to the Jewish state.

As a Jew, he is inevitably a target of anti-Israeli discussions and sometimes protests. He has an immediate choice to make: "Fight or flight." He can choose to defend Israel, or, alternatively, he can choose to actively put daylight between himself and Israel. He can even choose to join many other Jewish students in criticizing Israel. But there is one thing the Jewish student cannot do: He cannot stay agnostic.

Same with American Jews in the workplace, on social media and throughout the public space. People generally associate Jews with Israel, whether Jews like it or not. This negative decision-juncture is similar to a positive decision-juncture that faces a young Jew:

Birthright forces a Jew (or his parents) to take a position about his engagement with Israel: to exercise that birth-right for a free trip, or to decline. That choice is stemmed exclusively by that person's Judaism. Once again, even by making such an active decision, and even if declining, the young Jew is forced to be defined by Israel.

Birthright is the primary Jewish experience for most young Jews

Having the right to go on Birthright, whether one goes or not, is an affirmation of one's "club membership." Birthright is not just a trip to Europe or summer vacation and goes well beyond the actual visit. It provides folklore and connection to other Birthrighters – whether in Israel at the same time as the young Jew's own group, or in the context of "alumni."

Birthright creates a narrative, and it is a Judaism 3.0 experience. It is this kind of experience that typically shapes movements and religions (for example, the Exodus from Egypt as a key theme in Judaism).

The decision if to go, when to go and with what group, occupies the mind of these young Jews more than any other Jewish-related issue. By extension, the same goes for their parents. The preparation, excitement and concern leading up to the trip, and of course the trip itself – all make Birthright akin to the Bar Mitzvah – an initiation ritual into Judaism.

But unlike the Bar Mitzvah, done at a much younger age of 13, which is a Jewish religious experience (Judaism 2.0), Birthright is a Jewish national experience (Judaism 3.0). Hence, the most potent Jewish experience of a young American Jew is turning out to be a national one.

Well beyond the content acquired, the experiences on the trip and the friends the young Jew makes on the trip, Birthright first and foremost solidifies the Jewish person's sense of belonging. It radically elevates Judaism on the hierarchy of identities and that is because it is a Zionist experience, not a religious experience.

12. AMERICAN JEWS IN SEARCH OF THE NON-COMMITTAL AFFILIATION

Judaism is clearly not the defining characteristic of most American Jews. As discussed, for only a small minority, Judaism is high on the hierarchy of identities (Orthodox Jews and those involved with Jewish causes), but for the majority of American Jews, Judaism is one of the many identities that comprise them.

Clearly, for Judaism to be relevant, it needs to be attractive and desirable. Absent an outside wall like in the past, and without internal group commitment (such as with Orthodox Jews), American Judaism needs to thrive in a non-committal environment. This is especially since in a postmodern world, the concept of commitment is no longer necessary.

Products and experiences that require commitments are under-consumed. "Can cancel at any time" is on the rise, and "long-term contract" is dreaded. This is reflected in consumer products, services, personal relationships and career choices.

(i) Non-committal Judaism 2.0 – impossible

An American Jew increasingly seeks the non-committal component for his various experiences, including for his affiliation with Judaism. But such non-committal affiliation is not possible under Judaism 2.0. The "ask" for the American Jew is to commit more: join and come to synagogue more often, send your children to Hebrew school, donate to the UJA, be a member of the Jewish community center and the other community Jewish organizations.

The Israeli Jew can be a Datlaf – sometimes religious, because the religious affiliation is only secondary in his Jewish identity. His day-to-day experiences in Israel shape his Jewish identity. Regardless of the Israeli Jew's attitude towards Jewish religiosity, he is committed and fully affiliated with Judaism.

On the other hand, for the American Jew who has been connecting to his Judaism through Judaism 2.0, it is the Jewish religious affiliation that serves as a primary barometer of the depth of his connection to Judaism. Whether reflected through synagogue attendance or community activities, the American Jew is under built-in constant pressure to change, to do more, to commit – the exact opposite of non-committal Judaism.

(ii) Non-committal Judaism 3.0 – be who you are

American Jews can consume Israeli products and experiences a la carte. Moreover, by its nature, the connection of an American Jew to his Judaism through Cloud-Zionism is a non-committal connection – it is abstract. It is exactly this non-committal aspect that makes this connection a solid and sustainable connection. It is by choice.

An American Jew can go see a performance of Israeli singer Idan Raichel and only three years later go see a performance of Israeli singer Netta. His Jewish affiliation drew him to those performances, but as a choice, not as a chore. The lack of commitment – having skipped three years of Israeli live music – does not detract from the fact that his participation in those experiences was a reflection of his Jewish affiliation. This while in between those events, his Jewish pride generated through such experiences has not wavered.

Same with consuming Israeli wine, following Israeli news, watching an Israeli TV show on Netflix, admiring Israeli technology and even visiting Israel. By design, the American Jew does it when he chooses to, not due to commitment. Same with connection through the negative – when it comes to being exposed periodically to criticism of Israel or his own organic reaction to developments in Israel.

Under Judaism 3.0, the American Jew is not required to "change" in order to be affiliated. He is drawn to the Jewish affiliation while staying exactly who he is.

(iii) Judaism 3.0 suitable for various points on the evaporation track

Different Jews are on different points along the evaporation track. An estimated 20% of American Jewry is still in the safe zone, comprising the Orthodox and the strongly committed. But the majority are some place along this track beyond the safe zone.

Some are far along and have already disaffiliated. For them, the transformation to Judaism 3.0 may not be the answer that brings them back to Judaism, but it provides new tools and therefore offers new connection points. For some, the transformation will stop further deterioration and change the trajectory point. For others, the transformation will serve as a catalyst to connect.

Recognizing the transformation will allow each individual Jew to relate to Judaism given his or her own circumstances.

(iv) Renewed focus on Anti-Semitism forces Jews to their Jewish identity

In recent years there has been a sharp increase in anti-Semitic attacks against Jews in America: The Pittsburgh synagogue attack in 2018, the San-Diego synagogue attack in 2019, the Monsey synagogue attack in 2019, as well as the 2017 Charlottesville rally where right-wing ultra-nationalists yelled "Jews will not replace us." Indeed, a 2020 survey by the Anti-Defamation League showed that 63% of Jews feel less safe today than they did ten years ago. [15]

This forces the unaffiliated and under-engaged Jew right back into his Jewish identity. But what is this identity? What is the point of Judaism that such a "Jew in abstention" passively seeks to "go back to?" It is not the synagogue which he has not frequented, nor the Holocaust that he does not think much about. The rise of such "Jewish existential thinking" leads the Jew into Israel as his identity benchmark – this is the relevant association with his Jewish affiliation – this is where he hears or thinks about Judaism. This reality is exactly what Herzl envisioned when he said that anti-Semitism is a propelling force into Zionism. It is turning bad circumstances into a positive outcome: making Aniline out of coal tars – producing vibrant colors out of waste, as Herzl described in his short story, *The Aniline Inn.* [16]

13. THE REFORM MOVEMENT CAN SAVE AMERICAN JEWRY AGAIN

The strongest Jewish infrastructure in place in America is that of the Reform movement. Outside the Orthodox community, which is insular, the network of Reform synagogues is the closest thing to a grassroots "branch of Judaism" connector. Same goes for other aspects of the Reform movement's infrastructure – its summer camps and its educational programs. Indeed, one of the biggest enablers of the transformation to Judaism 3.0 could be the Reform movement.

15 – The Anti-Defamation League survey on Jewish encounters with anti-Semitism in the United States, April 21, 2020.

16 - A similar process can be said about the inadvertent contribution of Richard Wagner to Zionism. Wagner, the anti-Semite opera composer, sought to harm the Jews, but it was through his operas that Herzl received unexplained inspiration for the Jewish State, and for Zionism. "Only on the evenings when there was no opera did I have doubts about the correctness of my ideas," Herzl wrote. Herzl even arranged to have an adaptation of the overture of Wagner's 1845 opera, *Tannhauser* played in the Zionist Congress.

The Reform movement can add to its flagship theme of Tikun Olam, another flagship theme – Zionism. This way the Reform movement could become a primary enabler of Jewish continuity and at the same time ensure its own survivability. This is a golden opportunity to take advantage of the natural leadership vacuum of American Jewry mentioned and fill it with the relevant content of Judaism 3.0. The transition from Judaism 2.0 to Judaism 3.0 need NOT occur outside the Reform movement, but rather serve as a concurrent transformation of the Reform movement itself!

Zionism is a relevant, provocative and distinct theme that is already embraced by the Reform movement – it would not be revolutionary. Indeed, adding Zionism as an organizing principle of the Reform movement is reflective of the preferences of Reform Jews themselves – affiliated and unaffiliated, supporters and critics of Israel alike.

(i) Reform infrastructure not relevant for Reform Jews in Judaism 2.0 but perfect for Judaism 3.0

What does it mean for Jews to be affiliated with the Reform movement? Go to synagogue regularly? No, because they do not do that. Surveys indicate that less than 15% of Reform Jews regularly attend. Observe Jewish laws and perform rituals? No, because most state that they do not. Communal Jewish connection? To a very limited extent, as previously discussed.

Tikun Olam? No, because Reform Jews who are engaging in Tikun Olam are mostly doing so outside the structure of the Reform movement in different frameworks: charity organizations, volunteering, perhaps even a soup kitchen in the local church.

So what does it really mean for Jews to be affiliated with the Reform movement/synagogue? To be affiliated with Israel!

This is not by statement, but by actions. Take a young Jew going on a Birthright trip through the Reform movement – the majority of his lifetime engagement with the Reform movement has likely to have occurred on this trip – not just in terms of hour-count, but also in terms of memories. Same with a synagogue trip to Israel. Only secondary to that are anomalous religious events such as Bar or Bat Mitzvahs, and only after this are the routine Reform touch-points (going once a year to High Holiday services, and Tikun Olam).

It is safe to say that the number of Jews engaging with Israel through the Reform movement is significantly higher than the number of Jews engaging with Tikun Olam through the Reform movement. On an individual level, the broadest common denominator of Reform-affiliated

Jews is their engagement with Judaism through Israel – not engagement with Judaism through Reform programs.

Even more important than engagement through action is engagement through narrative.

True that the Jew under Judaism 3.0 does not need the Reform movement or the synagogue to be connected to his Judaism through Israel – it is not an organization or hierarchical connection. This is just like the liberal voter does not need the Democratic party affiliation to affirm his liberal values, and that the conservative voter does not need the Republican party affiliation to feel conservative.

But from the point of view of the Reform movement, having Israel as a point of orientation could be an enabler of its own survivability. Jumping on the inescapable conclusion of a Jewish transformation, the Reform movement would survive, and hence, American Jewry survives. The Reform infrastructure can be viewed as akin to what used to be the Jewish Agency structure – the Reform rabbis and presidents akin to Jewish Agency representatives, *shlihim*.

Conversely, failure of the Reform movement could trigger a spiral trajectory towards evaporation of American Judaism. Such a shift in the Reform movement is easy to accomplish and arguably already happening, given the franchise nature of the movement.

A Reform congregation rabbi and synagogue president have a lot of discretion about how to run their community. It is, of course, in line with the demands of the congregants. The rabbi and president serve the members "below," not the central leadership "above."

Hence, having Israel as the connecting thread makes sense – it will bring congregants in, provide content, provide direction, provide passion. Arguably that is already what is happening in many Reform communities. All that is required by Reform leadership is to "own" what is happening on the ground, and give its blessing.

Zionism as the anchor of Judaism is not only consistent with Reform Judaism, but can also be celebrated through the infrastructure of the Reform movement, given its decentralized structure.

Hence, the Reform movement can be a key enabler of the Jewish transformation to Judaism 3.0.

(ii) "Hostile takeover" of the Reform movement?

If the Reform movement fails to recognize the will of its congregants and instead insists on continuing to push down messages of limited relevance, including about the Wailing Wall and confrontation with Israel, then there is a solution: Hostile takeover!

The Reform members can replace its management through the movement's political process. They can even further "Protestantize" Reform Judaism and marginalize the leadership into having limited coordination and support roles.

This has happened before and is highly attainable. Also, let's not forget that the Reform movement changed its staunchly anti-Zionism stance to pro-Zionism already. This was done in part to reflect the views of its members at the time.

Zionism itself was born out of a similar process. At first, Herzl went to the Jewish leadership that he deemed relevant, including Baron Hirsch and Baron Rothschild. Once he saw the reluctance of the leadership, he took his messages directly to the Jewish masses, who essentially engaged in a "hostile takeover" of Judaism!

The Jewish shareholders started a long process to replace their leadership – this process is now culminating with the recognition of the Jewish transformation – to Judaism 3.0!

14. CRITICISM OF ISRAEL IS INDICATIVE OF A JEWISH TRANSFORMATION

One of the clear realities in American Jewry is that a significant portion of it is critical of Israel. Whether it is the settlements, the peace-process, the religious-secular relations or the nature of the prime minister or government, American Jews are vocal critics of Israel.

This too is a demonstration of a Jewish transformation. Such criticism is not against issues related to Judaism 2.0, but against issues associated with Judaism 3.0.

In fact, if one wishes to stay engaged with the Jewish religion and does not like his rabbi, synagogue, or other aspects of Rabbinic Judaism, he can switch – switch from Conservative to Reform, or between Reform synagogues or practice in a different manner. Such switching is not indicative that the person has disengaged – on the contrary, such action demonstrates his engagement in Judaism.

Similarly, the more an American Jew engages with the issues of Israel's policies, the stronger his connection to Judaism. More so, such criticism is a celebration of the transformation, since it is an increased engagement with one's Judaism through Israel.

Much of the criticism is coming from "unaffiliated Jews" who are on an inevitable path of evaporation anyway. Paradoxically, the "coincidental" engagement with Israel of this group helps keep them Jewish.

Another part of the criticism is coming from Reform leadership and liberal Jewish organizations. For them as well, such might be indicative that the transformation is already occurring.

A third part of the criticism comes from those who use Israel as a proxy to put distance between themselves and their Judaism. Such motivation for criticism is indicative that one cannot divorce Zionism out of Judaism.

(i) Criticism of Israel from unaffiliated Jews

The American Jew is increasingly defined by his relationship to Israel whether he chooses to or not, particularly in progressive circles where intersectionality runs high. There is an expectation that if one supports human-rights, gay-rights, women-rights and the environment, he will also be, at a minimum, critical of Israel's policies.

A young Jewish person – especially with a Jewish name – can feel no connection to Judaism, but being part of such progressive circles evokes his Judaism. Unlike non-Jews, a young Jew in such circles faces the "are you with us or are you against us" question simply due to his Jewish last name or ancestry. In other words, it is through Zionism where the young Jew meets his Judaism.

For many young liberal and progressive Jews, Zionism has become the primary arena in which they engage with their Judaism.

This will not go away. As discussed in the upcoming section about "Israel-bashing," a Jew cannot escape from his Israel affiliation. Even the progressive Jew who criticizes Israel, supports BDS and engages in Israel-bashing, would always be a "suspect" – or at a minimum, he would always feel an insecurity that would make him need to prove his anti-Israel credentials. This keeps him Jewish, and possibly even leads to an emotional connection, maybe even to marrying another Jewish "suspect" from the same circle. In such a case, it is the "suspect" status, as opposed to "Jewish tradition" that serves as the Jewish commonality. This is indicative of the far-reaching power of Zionism and its centrality for these American Jews. It cannot be ignored. Even those Jews who are critical about an element of their Jewish affiliation choose it to be Zionism (Judaism 3.0).

(ii) Criticism of Israel from liberal Jewish leadership

Much of the criticisms of Israel in America come from the organized Jewish liberal leadership. Many of them state that Israel's policies are making it difficult to be Jewish. Israel is drawing a wedge between the Jewish person and his Judaism.

Such Jews would argue – "how can Zionism be the organizing

principle of Judaism, and Israel its point of orientation, if I despise Israel's policies, reject Israeli behavior and repeatedly state that Israel does not represent my values?" But such attitudes are actually supportive of the transformation:

First, most Jews in this grouping tend not to criticize Israel as a whole, but rather a political party, or its prime minister. For many of them, a change in government could change the tone and intensity of their criticism. Some are even active in attempting to convince Israelis to change their government. This by itself supports the reality of the transformation. Such people are engaged in trying to change Israel for the better as they see, and they do so, as a manifestation of their Judaism. They are not trying to change Rabbinic Judaism as a manifestation of their Judaism (such as Halachic laws and rituals). They choose Judaism 3.0 as their Jewish arena, not Judaism 2.0. Second, most of those people are amongst the minority of Jews who are NOT on a trajectory of evaporation. They are part of the 10-20% of American Jews for whom Judaism is high on the hierarchy of identities. Like their Orthodox brethren, this group of engaged Jews, who are involved with Jewish activity, is, anyway, likely to remain Jewish. Unlike the unaffiliated Jew who stumbles into his Judaism through Zionism, this group chooses to consciously engage with their Judaism through Zionism. There is an active choice to be Jewish. Even if Israel's policies run to the extreme, it would not sway them out of Judaism.

For this group of liberal Jewish leadership, the threat that they would seek "divorce" from Judaism and even from "Israel" is akin to the threat that they would move to Canada, whenever a Republican gets elected to President of the United States (like in 2000 with Bush and 2016 with Trump). While there was news of a "wide phenomenon", there was negligible change in the number of applications the Canadian government received from Americans for long-term visas or immigration after those elections.

Hence, the criticism of Israel from this group does not represent a risk of exiting Judaism – it actually represents a stronger connection to their Judaism through Zionism (Judaism 3.0).

(iii) Criticism of Israel as a proxy for distance from Judaism

There is a national Jewish trauma that stems from the Holocaust. For some American Jews, the notion that their relatives or parents' relatives paid with their lives due to an association with Judaism is deeply rooted. Many of the Jews who perished in the Holocaust did not choose to be associated with Judaism. Some had long left Judaism and were completely detached. Yet, anybody who was even passively associated with Judaism was to be killed – the Nazi criteria for the murder was having just one Jewish grandparent.

Judaism was a cause of their death back then, therefore per this trauma, Judaism is perceived to be a threat to their life today.

Catering to this fear, some Jews feel that their interest and safety is served by a weak Jewish state, and maybe even its elimination. This is from where the perceived risk to their lives comes. Zionism (Judaism 3.0) perpetuates Judaism. Only 80 years ago, we were killed for having a passive association with Judaism – let us therefore mitigate (or eradicate) the source of the threat to our survival today, the logic goes. This leads to an instinctive obsessive criticism of Israel that is chronic and at times irrational. For example, in June 2021, some American Jews helped promote the libel that a court-mandated eviction of eight Arab families from Jewish-owned properties amounted to Israel committing ethnic-cleansing.

By itself, the perception that it is now Zionism which is the source of danger for this trauma is indicative of Jewish transformation, but Zionism is also the remedy for the trauma.

Facing intense Jewish opposition to Zionism and combating a different national Jewish trauma in his time, Herzl came up with the concept of Mauschel – an anti-Zionist Jew. Mauschel, he claimed, "is a recurring character throughout the times, a companion to the Jews. He is so attached to the Jews that people interchange Mauschel and Jews … Mauschel even spread a poisonous slogan against the Zionists: They are anti-Semites." But Herzl also understood the Mauschels. One cannot expect newly freed people to act free, he argued. One cannot tell the Jews: "You are emancipated, and expect a metamorphosis to a free, proud, liberated Jew."

The concept of the "prisoner refusing to leave prison" is rooted in the Jewish nation-religion. The Israelis coming out of Egypt were not free enough to accept God's will and went astray, even wishing to go back to slavery in Egypt.

In Herzl's time, the doors to the Jewish ghetto, locked for centuries, had been opened due to emancipation, but Jews chose to stay in what Herzl called *The New Ghetto*.

Arguably, today as well, some American Jews to one extent or another refuse to leave the ghetto of the Holocaust. These are not the survivors – this is American Jewry – young and old.

The Holocaust has served as the substitute glue to American Jewry after the national and then religious connections faded. Hence, many

American Jews, especially the survivors and their families, (Judaism 2.0) grew up with the Holocaust narrative ingrained in their psyche. Israeli Jews (Judaism 3.0) grew up in defiance of the Holocaust narrative.

Now, as time passes and as the Holocaust generation passes away, two parallel processes are occurring – on the one hand, as discussed, the fading of the memory of the Holocaust could lead to American Jewry losing a substitute glue that was vital to their connection to Judaism. Yet, on the other hand, it also mitigates the Jewish national trauma and removes a hurdle to the transformation to Judaism 3.0 – it opens the door to embracing one's Jewish affiliation with no fear.

This process is similar to another American Jewish woe, which can turn from a perceived liability to an asset.

15. INTERMARRIAGE DEFINES AMERICAN JEWRY AND NECESSITATES TRANSFORMATION

A surprising boost to the transformation from Judaism 2.0 to Judaism 3.0 comes from the widespread phenomenon of intermarriage amongst American Jewry.

(i) Intermarriage – the flagship of American Jewry

Intermarriage is a reality of American Judaism. In fact, if one had to list the leading attributes of American Judaism, marrying a non-Jew would be on the top of the list.

Intermarriage is higher than any other commonality that characterizes American Jews. It is the flagship attribute of American Jewry. The intermarriage rate is estimated to be as high as 72% for non-Orthodox newlyweds. [17] This rate is radically higher than synagogue attendance, radically higher than Hebrew School enrollment, religious observance or any other measurable statistics of American Jewry characteristics. In other words, intermarriage is a key staple of American Judaism.

(ii) Judaism 2.0 "Remedies" to intermarriage failed

Judaism 2.0 is not suitable to address the "intermarriage epidemic." Its primary tool has been conversion. Through various versions, degrees and debates on type of conversions, Judaism 2.0 has offered the conversion solution at the top of its toolbox. The Reform movement took it a step further, with basically enacting "forced conversions."

The Reform movement put in place "patrilineal descent" – reversing

---

17 – Analysis by Prof. Steven Cohen prepared for the purpose of this book, based on Pew Research and other data.

its own century-old religious practice, and that of all other streams of Judaism – that in order for a child to be considered Jewish, his mother had to be Jewish. Now, as long as one of the child's parents is Jewish, the child is considered Jewish (essentially automatic conversion, whether the person wants to convert or not). That solution failed.

Most children of a non-Jewish mother identify themselves as "half-Jewish" or "of Jewish heritage." Indeed, to a large degree, that is how those children are viewed by the Jewish world across its streams – Reform, Conservative and Orthodox. In addition, research shows that such children of only one Jewish parent have significantly lower connections to Judaism than those of two parents. [18]

Whether converted or not, the non-Jewish spouse of a secular Jew typically does not feel fully accepted under the Jewish tent, and neither do the children.

The "ask" is too big. Even if the ask has technically been fulfilled and the spouse converted, the retention is low, while the resentment to Judaism that is generated by the process is high. The box was checked, but the price for "checking that box" is detrimental.

The ask of the non-Jewish spouse to have a "siddur in your library" is simply unrealistic, especially since the secular Jewish spouse does not have this Jewish prayer book either. This leads to antagonism and rejection.

Given the strong united families that characterized the Jewish spouse, such rejection typically affects the Jewish spouse and then filters down to the children. The result is that the Jewish spouse often becomes even less connected to Judaism than before the conversion marriage. Thus, the mechanism that is offered under Judaism 2.0 is not only unhelpful, but it also produced adverse results.

(iii) Judaism 3.0 turns intermarriage from foe to friend

Now, with Judaism 3.0, the intermarriage spouse has a home. That is because the affiliation ask is no longer a "siddur in your library," but it is an "Israeli flag in your heart."

In many cases, the pro-Israel aptitude amongst non-Jews who intermarry "in" is higher than it is amongst under-engaged Jews who intermarry "out." It connects to the intermarried spouse's past and tradition, since the predominance of the intermarriage "in" pool in the United States is Christian. Many of them have religious Christian parents or grandparents from where they acquired a strong emotional affinity to Israel.

---

18 – Stephen M. Cohen: "Which of our Grandchildren will be Jewish in this Age of Intermarriage", *The Forward*, October 14, 2016.

Paradoxically, since the general American population tends to be more enthusiastic about Israel than the non-Orthodox Jewish population, recognizing the transformation to Judaism 3.0 would make intermarriage accretive to the Jewish family's Jewish connection. By marrying a non-Jew, the under-engaged Jew increases his chance, as well as his children's chance, to remain in Judaism – because he can remain in Judaism by remaining in Judaism 3.0 (Zionism).

This is not about changes to the Halacha

As mentioned, the transformation has no effect on religious practice, the halacha (Jewish law), Jewish traditions and rituals. Just as Herzl reassured in the first Zionist Congress, when he planted the seed to the Jewish transformation, Zionism does not do anything that hurts the religious aspect of Judaism.

The transformation is neutral to ongoing debates about the halacha, including the conversion issues. This is similar to kosher practices in restaurants. A restaurant can be "kosher," but a person might not eat there because the certification is not according to his standard. Some would be satisfied by a standard kosher certificate, others would require Glatt kosher, while others would require a certificate from a particular agency.

Under Judaism 3.0, a child of intermarried parents, whose mother was converted by a Reform rabbi could still be viewed as part of the Jewish nation, even though an Orthodox rabbi would not accept the conversion. When that child grows up and is about to marry someone Jewish, there could be repercussions from his mother's Reform conversion. Same goes for the child of intermarried parents whose mother did not convert at all. Those are individual choices.

To reiterate, Judaism 3.0 is not about making a halachic determination if the child of an intermarried couple is Jewish or not. It is about recognizing the inevitable inclusion of this child in the Jewish nation because the organizing principle of Judaism is now its national aspect (Zionism), and not its religious aspect (Rabbinic Judaism). Rabbis and dayans (rabbinic judges) maintain their full authority to determine a child's religious designation in such cases. (For expansion, see "New risks as a result of the transformation" in the chapter, Judaism 3.0.)

This is not about Immigration to Israel

Judaism 3.0 is not about making legal changes to the Law of Return or qualifications about immigrating to Israel. Israel's Law of Return currently states that as long as an applicant has one Jewish grandparent (e.g. he is a "quarter Jew"), then the applicant qualifies for immigration to the State of Israel.

The transformation to Judaism 3.0 is about the state of Judaism – not about the question of "who is a Jew?" The question of "who is a Jew" has different answers, depending on who is asking and in what context:
 – Halachic point of view.
 – Legal point of view.
 – Individual point of view.

There need not be a unified answer to such a difficult question. Judaism 3.0 suggests that Zionism is the anchor of Judaism and the conduit through which Jews connect to their Judaism. The religious, legal, institutional and individual choices are beyond the scope of this discussion of a transformation to Judaism 3.0.

Just like in Judaism 3.0, it is the rabbis and rabbinic judges who will continue to determine "who is a Jew" from a halachic point of view, the State of Israel would continue to determine "who is a Jew" for the purpose of Law of Return and immigration to Israel.

(iv) Intermarriage is not assimilation

In the Jewish discourse and public discussion, intermarriage is viewed as synonymous with assimilation. Yet, while intermarriage may be a cause for assimilation, intermarriage does not necessarily lead to assimilation. In fact, intermarriage may not be the threat it is commonly perceived to be. One can intermarry and stay Jewish, as described, just as one can intra-marry and assimilate out. In assessing Jewish continuity, it is important to understand the various paths to assimilating out of Judaism.

Assimilation through Intermarriage

Intermarriage is indeed a path to end a family's Jewish lineage, such as when the Jewish spouse adopts the culture of the non-Jewish spouse and/or the children do so. Intermarriage has been viewed as the superhighway to assimilation and evaporation of American Jewry. But is intermarriage really the primary contributor to assimilation?

Group assimilation

When one examines the history of nations and groups that have disappeared, the question needs to be addressed: Did they vanish through intermarriages?

Unlikely.

The majority of ancient nations have vanished. Most likely, such large-scale evaporations were not a result of a person by person exit, but rather of the entire group stopping to be a distinct entity.

Nations began looking more and more like their neighbors. In the case of today's American Jews, a Jewish couple from the Upper East Side looks, acts and behaves in a very similar manner to a non-Jewish couple from the Upper East Side.

Arguably, the Moabites, Assyrians and similar historical nations, just blurred into a more dominant culture that was around them. Or in reverse, it is said by the sages that the Hebrews in Egypt stayed as a distinct group since they kept their distinct names, clothes and language. The reason they stayed together and did not disappear was because they kept their arsenal of national identities. It was not due to lack of intermarriage. In fact, it is evident through the Biblical narrative that intermarriage was common, and yet the Jews stayed as Jews.

For the same reason, there have been Jewish groups that assimilated out of Judaism as a group, not due to intermarriage, such as the Kaifeng Jews in China. They stopped being Jewish as a group. To support that, research shows that even after they converted, they continued to marry one another.

Similar patterns occurred with Jews who converted to Christianity in the 19th century. For example, in the case of Col. Albert Goldsmid, one of the early Zionist leaders – both he and his wife were children of Jews who converted to Christianity. An indication of converts marrying other converts is widespread. They are part of a group of former Jews. But a few generations later the memory of being descendants of converts fades, and those former Jews are simply Christians.

By extension, a similar thing could be said for unaffiliated Jews marrying other unaffiliated Jews. Both of the spouses are clearly Jewish according to Jewish law, but are such unaffiliated Jewish couples really likely to keep the distinct Jewish characteristics into the next generation or are they part of a group assimilation, as was the case with the Kaifeng Jews and 19th century converts?

Herzl addressed this in his play, *The New Ghetto*. He showed that even though liberal Jewish society was no longer in a physical ghetto, it was still operating in a ghetto – just with different rules and different malaise.

Today, a Jew marrying another Jew and staying in the "New Ghetto" is simply creating the groundwork for group assimilation down the line.

In Herzl's time the danger of group assimilation was prevented by the rejection of European society, but that is not the case in America. Now that they are welcome and free, intra-marriage assimilation could be the more potent threat than intermarriage assimilation. As discussed, such group-wide assimilations are likely the more common ways nations disappeared, historically. They simply assimilated out as a group.

And yet today under Judaism 2.0, an unaffiliated Jew marrying another unaffiliated Jew is not considered being part of the intermarriage crisis (it is considered a "good marriage"). However, absent a transformation of Judaism, such marriages are indeed a strong component of the assimilation crisis. On the other hand, intermarried couples (a Jewish reality), with a recognition of the transformation to Judaism 3.0, and having Zionism to cling to, could be enablers of Jewish survivability.

Individual assimilation

No doubt, throughout history individuals chose to leave groups and nations. They did so as individuals, couples or families, sometimes due to mundane reasons, such as relocation. A Texas family living in New York is likely to have such an experience. By the next generation, their children will no longer speak with a Texas accent, or necessarily marry Texas natives.

The question really is what the "outbound" individual is assimilating to. Assimilating to Americanism is very much consistent with the Zionist narrative, and hence, through the assimilation, the Jew can actually become more closely connected to his Judaism. That is as long as there is a recognition that Judaism is transforming and that Zionism is becoming its organizing principle.

Staying Jewish won't work if it is merely to please grandparents. Similarly, staying Jewish won't work if it is in order to be loosely affiliated with a synagogue.

Under Judaism 3.0, for the intermarried spouse, joining Judaism is not a forced response or a "negotiation point" to please others. The intermarried spouse would join Judaism 3.0 because it is cool and relevant. This intermarried spouse would *want* to be part of the Jewish nation (Zionism).

Being a part of Judaism 3.0 makes the person more of everything that they are currently. For example, it makes them more American and could make them more liberal too (this would please their liberal circles).

Mostly, it allows the person to be more Jewish and through that, Judaism is strengthened. Indeed, recognizing the transformation to Judaism 3.0 would turn one of Judaism's biggest woes into an enabler of its survivability, and ultimately lead to the thriving of American Jewry.

16. The Experience of other Jewish communities contributes to the transformation of American Jewry

The American Jewish community is going through a transformation, but other Diaspora Jewish communities have long been in Judaism 3.0. While 85% of Jews live in Israel and North America, the connection to Judaism through Zionism in smaller Jewish communities, from Europe to Latin America to Russia (the remaining 15%), provides support for the transformation of American Jewry.

(i) Israel has long been a primary point of orientation

European and Latin American Jews are more connected through Israel than Jews in North America. While only 41% of American Jews have visited Israel, the majority of European Jews have. For example, 65% of French Jews have visited Israel. [19] European Jews in closer geographical proximity and more comprehensive family connections contribute to such closer ties. This is aided by the general European population's higher propensity to travel. In addition, higher religiosity levels and affiliation levels makes the connection more natural and organized.

Same can be said in Russia and Ukraine, where religiosity is low. Those Jews who are connected to their Judaism are typically connected not through religion, but through family, emotional sentiments of belongingness with Israel – in other words through Judaism 3.0 and not through Judaism 2.0. In addition, with the Russian Federation being a mix of various nationalities, it is accepted, agreed and understood by non-Jews and Jews alike, that Judaism is a nationality. It is even stated so on one's ID card.

(ii) Dynamics and narrative of the local population facilitates the transformation

Jews in smaller Jewish centers are more likely to look at the case of other ethnic groups and nations that live close to them. Such "case studies" as well support the transformation to Judaism 3.0.

For example, from early on, Herzl looked at Irish leader Charles Stewart Parnell for inspiration. He wrote in his diary: "I shall be the Parnell of the Jews."

A century later, Ireland was a big geopolitical issue in the 1990s. Hence, much of the world has looked at the successful Irish peace process as inspiration for possibilities within the Israeli-Palestinian

19 – AJC 2019 Survey of French Jewish Opinion, June 2, 2019.

peace framework. And by extension, parallels were drawn between Israel and Ireland.

In Ireland, the political question was reformatted and a well-supported narrative emerged: One can be both Irish and British. It is not an issue of Catholic vs. Protestant. Yet, until the peace process and indeed still today, when people around the world are asked about the Irish conflict, the likely response will be issues relating to Catholics vs. Protestants. The fact is Ireland is more of an issue of Republicanism vs. Monarchy.

Studying the evolution of the Irish issue is just one example of how Jewish communities can apply local experiences towards the recognition of a transformation from Judaism 2.0 to Judaism 3.0. Just as one can be both Irish and British, one can be both a European Jew and a proud Zionist!

(iii) Inspiration for Jews in America

Smaller Jewish communities outside of Israel and North America already being in Judaism 3.0, is not only relevant because it supports the inescapable conclusion that Judaism is transforming, but also because it provides an example to American Jews of Jewish communities whose primary Jewish anchor is indeed Israel and Zionism.

Just like it was easier for the British to issue the Balfour Declaration when there was a Jewish beachhead in Palestine, and just like it was easier for political Zionism to conceptualize the dream, given the Jewish settlements in Palestine, so it is easier for American Jews to comprehend the transformation, thanks to smaller Diaspora Jewish communities already being in Judaism 3.0.

17. CONCLUSION: FOR AMERICAN JEWS, TRANSFORMATION IS BOTH NECESSARY AND A REALITY

Trends in American Jewry lead to an inevitable transformation of Judaism. Just like with Israeli Jews, American Jews are transforming to Judaism 3.0, not through a decision or a resolution, but through the realities of their daily life. American Jewry is on an evaporation track. The combination of denationalization and secularization have doomed a growing percentage of American Jews. Various attempts to hold American Jewry through alternative glues such as memory of the Holocaust, nostalgia to their Eastern European past, community activities and abstract and non-particular themes such as Tikun Olam have all failed. The evaporation is reflected through the high intermarriage rate and the under-engagement and disaffiliation from Judaism of even those who marry other Jews.

A Jewish transformation is an alternative to evaporation. The transformation to Judaism 3.0 in America is not only a necessity, but it is also a growing reality. There has been a gradual cultural Israelization of the American Jewish experience. American Jews connecting to their Judaism through Israel is much easier today than in the past due to the success and vibrancy of the State of Israel and the array of Israeli products and experiences that one can connect through: Israeli innovations, culture, art, wine, life, etc. This is also the case when it comes to criticism of Israel in Jewish circles – that too is a connection to one's Judaism through Israel, and hence, a demonstration of a transformation. The ease of connection through Cloud-Zionism, allows American Jews to center their Jewish identity around Israel without ever leaving the United States or even their own homes. The changing composition of American Jews and the rise of the Israeli American demystifies the connection to Israel. Existing structures such as the Reform movement and existing realities such as intermarriage can turn into enablers of the transformation.

Recognizing the transformation would even provide a remedy for those far along on the evaporation track. With Judaism being low on the hierarchy of identities, it is easier to connect to Judaism through the country you never visit than through the synagogue you never visit.

Zionism gives American Judaism meaning, vibrancy and relevancy that is in line with current American realities – generational and behavioral. Indeed, Zionism not only provides a uniting Jewish issue but also a relevant topic for discussion and debate.

After all, how many of American Jews today are having passionate conversations about Halachic issues around the dinner table or in the bars? ("Should rice be kosher for Passover?") But Zionism provides a natural lightning rod that sparks conversations that are natural and relevant to the American Jew. It is very likely that if one had to measure what is the number one Jewish topic that American Jews argue about, debate and discuss – it is safe to say that it is Zionism, not Rabbinic Judaism. This serves as another indication that American Jews are in the midst of a Jewish transformation.

Indeed, recognition of the transformation would fuel energy into all aspects of American Judaism: Tikun Olam is more credible knowing that Judaism is closely associated with Israel – the Tikun Olam state that exports technologies making the world a better place. Similarly, memory of the Holocaust is more fortified when recognizing the revival that came after it, and nostalgia to the Eastern European past (such as bagel and lox) is more relevant when associated with a contemporary conduit to Judaism. Having a stronger sense of Jewish pride will also augment connections through Jewish learning, tradition and faith.

Indeed, recognizing the transformation would inject vibrancy into the full spectrum of American Jewry. Moreover, once recognizing the transformation to Judaism 3.0, American Jewry would be more in line with trends in the broader American society.

VII

The External Environment – America

American Jews are integrated into the overall American society. Therefore, developments in America impact the state of American Judaism just as much as trends within American Jewry itself. Such developments are very much supportive of the Jewish transformation.

"America is an idea!" These were the first words that Joe Biden said when announcing his run for US President in 2019. This idea is intertwined with Zionism. The United States was founded as New Zion. It is rooted in an ideological bedrock – Americanism, just like Israel is rooted in an ideological bedrock – Zionism.

Arguably, the predominant American ethos is more compatible with Judaism 3.0 than with Judaism 2.0. Indeed, while Americanism is closely associated with Zionism, it is not closely associated with secularism.

1. US AND ISRAEL ARE RELIGIOUS SOCIETIES; AMERICAN JUDAISM IS NOT

The United States and Israel are both deeply religious countries, contrary to many misperceptions. Research shows that over a third of Americans attend a place of worship nearly once a week, and that an overwhelming 75% of Americans attend at least once a year. This is significantly higher than in most other western countries. [1]

As pointed out earlier, the majority of Israeli Jews are also predominantly religious or traditional, engaging in religious activities to one extent or another. For example, 63% of Israeli Jews fast on Yom Kippur and 93% attend a Passover Seder. [2]

Even those Israelis who self-classify themselves as secular tend to consume a broad array of religious experiences, and display faith characteristics that are similar to those of the American religious community. For example, the vast majority of secular Israelis have a Mezuza on their door, which contains key Biblical verses.

---

1 – https://news.gallup.com/poll/1690/religion.aspx
2 – Data based on Israel's Central Bureau of Statistics, The Guttman Center for Public Opinion and Policy Research, Israeli Democratic Institute, and Pew Research Center's survey, 2016, indicating that 87% of Israeli seculars attend a Passover Seder.

While Israeli Jews are religious, American Jews are not. In fact, American Jews are often viewed as leaders of the secular minority in America, and those who are at the forefront of a push for increased secularism of America. The campaign for a more secular America gets ample attention in American media and at times labeled as "war on religion" or "war on Christmas." Not only that, American Jews are on the counter-path of religiosity trends prevalent in the rest of America, as well as in Israel.

(i) Increased religiosity in America – Counter-trend of American Judaism (Judaism 2.0)

Most Jews, upon arrival in America were religiously observant, but over the years the majority has gradually turned secular. The percentage of Jews today who follow the various religious laws is low.

On the other hand, throughout the United States, more and more American Christians are increasingly incorporating religious elements into their lives. That is expressed through the resurgence in church attendance, amongst other measurements. During the spring of 2020, as the Coronavirus pandemic was raging, 49% of Christian Americans stated that they attended a virtual prayer service, while only 17% of American Jews said they did the same.[3]

Moreover, immigration patterns to the United States fortify the religious character of America as more and more religious Christians arrive, in particular from Latin America. As such, there continues to be a fundamental disconnect between American Jews under Judaism 2.0 – increasingly secular and even rejective of religion, and the American public at large – increasingly religious. This is reflected not only in observance but also in culture and speech.

Therefore, there is a structural misalignment between much of the American public and American Jewry (Judaism 2.0). Once the transformation of Judaism is recognized and the public will increasingly look at American Jewry through the prism of Israel and Zionism (Judaism 3.0), there will be greater unison between American Jewry and the overall American public.

Zionism is a more relatable point of Jewish reference for Americans than the legacy state of American Jewry (secular Rabbinic Judaism). It correlates better with the religiosity levels of the general American public and eliminates the built-in tension within both narrative and practice that exists under Judaism 2.0

3 – Pew Research Center, August 7, 2020.

(ii) Inherent rejection of religious America by American Jewry (Judaism 2.0)

It is not only the secular nature of American Jews that generates a disconnect with the predominantly American religious ethos; it is also the Jews' perceived interest as a religious minority for America to be secular.

America was established as "One Nation Under God." From various prisms, the establishment of America was a religious event. Notwithstanding the sacred separation of church and state, the citizens of America at its onset and still today are predominantly believers, and the American narrative they broadly embrace is a religious narrative at its core.

Jews immigrating to the United States quickly embraced the American narrative, but a disconnect emerged. The Jews are a small religious minority in America. A view quickly developed that the more secular America would become, the greater room there would be for such religious minorities. This was in particular the case, since a Jewish denationalization occurred shortly after the Jews arrived in America. Jews stopped viewing themselves as one of the many ethnological national groups making America (Irish, Italian), but rather as members of the Jewish religion. This further elevated their sense of being a religious community, hence, a religious minority.

Had the Jews stayed a nation-religion, as they were throughout history, and as they have been perceived by the general American public, then the religious nature of America would be less of a concern to them. But as a religious minority, some Jews began to draw discomfort from religious symbols such as churches, crosses, Biblical references and nativity scenes.

If one were to take this to an extreme, there is a political continuum: Theocracy on one end and the purely secular state on the other. On one extreme, theocracy is defined by religion. Therefore, a religious minority in a theocracy, even if it enjoys full civil rights, is by definition a "lower class" in that theocracy. But on the other extreme, a purely secular state is completely neutral to its citizens' religion, and therefore all religions are on equal footing.

Jews self-defined themselves as a religious minority, therefore they perceived it to be in their interest to promote gravitation towards the bookend of the purely secular state. But that was outright inconsistent with the American narrative. America is not a theocracy, but it is far from being a purely secular state: "One nation under God" is recited by millions of American children in the "Pledge of Allegiance". On the

American currency it is clearly stated: "In God We Trust".

As a result of those realities, American Jews who metamorphosed from an ethnological group to a self-proclaimed religious minority turned to be in a perceived continuous tension with Americanism, a religious-inspired concept.

(iii) For American seculars – Judaism 3.0 offers a more natural secular connection to Judaism

Zionism is a more relevant connecting-point to the Jew. This is both for religious Americans, and even more so for secular Americans.

For a secular Catholic in New York, it is not intuitive to relate to his secular Jewish friend through the Jewish religion. This is because neither practice their religion.

The Jewish friend is not a flag-carrier for the Jewish religion in the Catholic friend's mind. But his affiliation with Israel, even if loose or latent and even if he has never been to Israel, is something that is much more relatable for the Catholic friend.

The Catholic friend is more likely to speak to the Jewish friend about news from Israel such as elections in Israel, war, terrorism, peace initiatives or any other developments in Israel, than he is to speak to him about religious developments in Judaism. Whether spoken or unspoken, for the Catholic friend, the Jewish friend is a flag-carrier of Israel – the Jewish state.

And so, even for American seculars, Judaism is now more associated with the Jewish national affiliation (Judaism 3.0) than it is with the Jewish religious affiliation (Judaism 2.0).

(iv) Remedy for American Jews: Religious by association (Judaism 3.0)

There is a remedy American Jews can implement: they can stop defining themselves in terms of their religious practices (or lack of), and instead define themselves through their national affiliation – Zionism.

This would be the definition that is relevant to today's circumstances and accurate from a historical standpoint. Jewish Americans are not a religious minority. They are an ethnological group that is an integral part of the mosaic of America – just like Irish Americans, Italian Americans and Mexican Americans. Certainly, one's affiliation as an Italian American does not compromise his stance on religiosity or religious practices.

Zionism allows the American Jew to be associated with a religious society (Israel), even though he himself is not religious. Hence, once recognizing that Judaism has transformed to Judaism 3.0, the Jew would be more in line with the general American public and the predominant American narrative.

Trends In America Support Judaism 3.0

2. AGE OF CLARITY

America and the world have been moving away from gray and ambiguity into a world of clarity and unhedged communication.

The age of clarity, to a large extent, is a counter-reaction to the overreach of the previous attempts to gray everything. The politically correct revolution has produced crippling effects on sections of society and the economy. Over-hedging suppresses freedom and creativity. It curtails return on investment.

The culture of saying what you believe you are supposed to say, as opposed to what you believe, has been debilitating. But that is changing with a natural generational shift and advances in technology, as well as through mind-setting disrupters such as the Coronavirus pandemic. The shift from gray to clarity was on display in the 2020 social protests, where people who took to the streets spoke their truth – in a clear and direct way, not through hedging or through "saying the right thing."

The generational etiquette is changing. Millennials operate in a manner that is less driven by risk-aversion and fear, and this projects up to the broader population. The objective is no longer to mitigate risk and downside. Hence, there is less thought about hedging, and as a result, there is greater re-assertion of creativity and expression. This is demonstrated, for example, on Facebook, dating sites and even in writing a simple text or WhatsApp message without bearing the consequence of record retention. This is despite privacy issues. There is less suppression and more "out" and this has trickled up to the "adults" as well.

The success of the gay-rights movement contributed to others getting out of their own closets. It allowed one to be "out" of whatever closet one was in, allowing for more clarity.

For example, this is seen through a shift in *Saturday Night Live* skits pretending to be gray in the 1990s, such as the "ambiguously Gay Duo" or the gender-ambiguous character of Pat, to being outright bold by the 2010s, such as in an audacious skit addressing the sexual orientation of the Divine. [4]

Humans are more comfortable in black and white than they are in

4 – *Saturday Night Live*, April 16, 2016.

gray. That is especially true for Judeo-Christian societies that cherish the separation between pure and impure, between day and night.

The graying phenomena that intensified through the 20th century was to some extent influenced by Europe, where such aggressive graying was a reaction to the shock of the two world wars of the early 20th century, and the Cold War that followed. The cause of war was perceived to be the rise of nationalism, religion, ideology. Hence, if those can be sedated and suppressed, the world would be safer, the logic went – the world is safer in gray. But like with other forms of artificial suppression, human forces rebelled against graying in the second decade of the 21st century.

In multiple European elections, people sought leaders who express their views, as opposed to a melting pot of views which leads to neutrality and lack of differentiation.

The democratization that occurred in the 20th century and the political constraint facing world leaders simply forced politicians in most countries to be in gray in order to get elected and stay in power. There was a need to be able to please multiple constituents. Otherwise continuous changes in government would occur and lead to instability.

The rise of the "Third Way" in the 1990s is a reflection of the elevation of Gray. Bill Clinton, Tony Blair, Gerhard Schroder all promoted a centrist-oriented political doctrine that would be gray enough to allow it to attain power. This was accepted by the voters in their day.

But as the world has been inching towards clarity, some politicians realized that they can win through the polars – that elections are about getting your base out to vote, as opposed to convincing the other side to vote for you. Hence, there has been a built-in shift from seeking the gray center to doubling-down on the clear polars.

This understanding was reflected on the left with the rise of clear ideological candidates like Bernie Sanders in the United States, Jean-Luc Melenchon in France and Jeremy Corbyn in Britain, and the decline of gray-like candidates such as Hillary Clinton. It was reflected on the right with the rise of Donald Trump and runner-up Ted Cruz in 2016, at the expense of gray-like candidates like Jeb Bush, as well as with the success of Boris Johnson in Great Britain in 2019.

The victory of Trump in 2016 also reflects a clear choice between "talking points" vs. "tweet from the hip." Clarity allows a voter to focus on a decision to accept/reject based on content. Not based on the hedge/ trigger warning that precedes the content. While the debate on how far one goes away from gray towards clarity remains, this has a profound effect on the state of Judaism in America.

(i) De-graying as a catalyst for the transformation of Judaism

An attempt to reduce Judaism to the "Jewish Church" or to dissociate it with Israel, is an attempt of graying Judaism. It was tolerated during the age of Gray. In truth, to the outside world, the Jew is associated with Judea – with Israel. Certainly not the type of place of worship he chooses to attend once a year.

And hence, in the age of clarity, the Jew who claims he is of the Jewish religion but not of Jewish nation is increasingly perceived as a relic of the 20th century, a relic of the gray in an increasingly direct, honest, and clear American and global environment.

Official recognition

A Jew is clearly a member of the Jewish nation, bound by history and the present ties to Judea – to Zion. This reality received official recognition in December 2019 when President Trump issued an executive order acknowledging that Judaism is a nationality. Democrats and Republicans alike supported this and were in the process of drafting bipartisan bills in Congress to state the same.

This was prompted by Jews being targeted on campuses. If Judaism is merely a religion, then as long as the targeting is not religious-based, it is supposedly legitimate.

With the new Executive Order, those seeking to discriminate against Jews cannot hide behind the claim that Judaism is merely a religion and not a nation. The United States government made clear what is obvious to Americans in the age of clarity: The Jews are indeed a nation-religion.

3. MULTI-IDENTITY REALITY

Being in an age of clarity paves the way to embracing multiple identities an individual possesses. An individual can be American, New Yorker, gay, Yale alumnus, an investment banker, Goldman Sachs employee, member of a hard-to-get-into country club, sailor, part-owner of a bar, a poet. These affiliations mean different things to different people. For example, there are those who view their Goldman Sachs affiliation as a source of income, others as a social status, and others as a springboard to boards of charity organizations and into politics. There are bankers in Spain employed by Santander who would categorically not socialize with people working for the competing bank BBVA, while there are those who would separate work from pleasure.

There are those who would be an active Yale alumnus and feel it is part of their identity, while others would view such affiliation as nostalgic of their college days. In the age of gray there was suppression of identity – in the age of clarity there is an encouragement to access all aspects of one's identities and that includes national identities.

(i) Political nationalism, ethnological nationalism and economic nationalism

There are American citizens who choose to showcase an American flag in their front yard, while others do not. There are those for whom being an American is core to their identity, and others who view it more superficially of where they vote or where they live. There is no right or wrong. This is an individual choice. The latter is no less of an American than the former.

Even if an American citizen chooses to degrade his nation by speaking ill of America, this does not affect his membership status in the American nation. He is still allowed to vote. This is absolute and unquestionable.

This is also the case with ethnological national affiliation. There are those who feel that their Irish ancestry is a source of pride. This does not mean that they need to belong to a "community" – it could manifest itself in wearing a "Kiss me, I'm Irish," t-shirt, or wearing green on St. Patrick's Day. Others just view it as a lower identity factor – simply as the geographic place from where their ancestors came.

Similarly, there are those American Jews who feel strongly that they are a part of the Jewish nation and for whom Zionism plays a key role in their identity. On the other hand, there are others who view Judaism merely in an ancestral context – the affiliation of their grandparents. Just like in the case of political nationalism, all are acceptable and the latter is no less of a Zionist than the former. Under Judaism 3.0, they are all in the Zionist tent, no matter their attitude towards Zionism.

Economic nationalism

This is also the case when it comes to so-called economic nationalism. An individual can choose to buy American no matter what, can choose to buy American when the quality/price difference is reasonable, or can choose to be neutral and buy what is best for him regardless of where it is made.

Same with American corporations. An American company can choose to be "globalist" and make decisions, such as where to open a factory, based on worldwide considerations. The company can also choose to be an "economic nationalist" and factor in national considerations, such as how the decision will benefit American workers.

The US government can incentivize or disincentivize corporations based on economic nationalism. This is the choice of a government, just like any other policy matter, and it gets manifested through elections to the Executive and Legislative branches of government while in line with the Judicial branch.

Despite the political discussions in the last years, it remains clear that the "freedom to choose" is vested with the company. Even in the most extreme propositions of economic nationalism, there have been no credible suggestions to take that away. An employee, consumer or investor can make his own choices in response to that company's choices.

Such empowerment of the American individual is very much core to the existing American narrative.

It is not just freedom to choose, it is the liberty to be wherever one decides to be on any component of his identity compositions.

This is true for an American Jew, as it is true for any other American: He can be wherever he chooses to be on the continuum relationship to his political nationalism (his US citizenship), ethnological nationalism (Zionism) and economic nationalism.

(ii) Counter-Intersectionality

A failed attempt to rob individuals of choices is the so-called Intersectionality movement, which is associated with elements of the Progressive movement. Intersectionality suggests a binding package deal for one's identity. For example, if one is gay, he is an environmentalist, leftist, anti-Israel and has socialist leanings. This, of course, fails as many gays tend to be wealthy and capitalists, admirers of Israel, in part due to its gay rights record, and some vote and get elected as Republicans. Indeed, many now realize that intersectionality is a form of homophobia, just like it is a form of racism. It forces a person into a set of opinions purely based on one's sexual orientation or race.

The failure of intersectionality represents a further affirmation of America's multi-identity reality. Such dismissal of intersectionality strengthens the transformation to Judaism 3.0. An American Jew can be straight or gay, Reform or Orthodox, believer or atheist, rich or poor, and he can still center his Jewish identity around his Jewish ethnological national affiliation – Zionism (Judaism 3.0).

(iii) Disintermediation and breaking of the package deal

As discussed, the postmodern world allows people to pick and choose experiences a la carte. It used to be that a person had one bank where he managed his entire financial relationship. He would get his mortgage from that bank and use it to manage his money. Today, most Americans bank at one place, get their mortgage from another, and choose an external asset manager. Same with the breakdown of the mega-department stores and other package deals – both physically and socially.

The unbundling of the packaged basket of experiences is a celebration of one's freedom, and it goes hand-in-hand with the disintermediation of society. This is reflected in paying through Bitcoin, booking accommodation through Airbnb, working in a shared WeWorks office, commuting through shared rides/cars/scooters/bikes and moving to a cloud mentality. There is a general greater "Protestantization" of one's life – a direct relationship with whatever you choose to have a relationship with. This was further evident during the lockdown realities that occurred due to the Coronavirus outbreak – there were fewer intermediaries. Most of those who continued to work did so from home, making the path from input to output more direct – no buses, no traffic, no elevators.

The disintermediation trend also leads to a more direct and genuine relationship of a Jew with his Jewish identity, without artificial constraints. However, that has not always been the case.

4. FROM THE MAYFLOWER NARRATIVE TO CULTURAL PLURALISM

(i) From Judaism to Americanism

In the early days of Jewish immigration to the United States, America was very much defined by the "Mayflower narrative" – that of the homogeneous society.

This made sense. America was a start-up society – building something new that was different from, and in contrast to, the Europe that was left behind. (Similar to what Israel would experience a few centuries later.)

A melting pot of English, Scottish, French and later Italians, Irish, Russian and Jewish immigrants needed a strong unifying narrative. This narrative, at its core, included disavowing loyalty to one's previous country – such as to the King of England or the King of Prussia – and pledging loyalty to this new society.

Indeed, till today, when a new American citizen is sworn in, the person is required to pledge: "I hereby declare, on oath, that I absolutely and entirely renounce and abjure all allegiance and fidelity to any foreign prince, potentate, state, or sovereignty of whom or which I have heretofore been a subject or citizen." Before there is a pledge to fulfill any of the duties, one is required to perform as an American citizen (seven obligations such as supporting and defending the constitution and laws), there is the requirement to disavow one's past loyalties.

For the Jews, just like for any other new immigrants, it was utterly clear they needed to do exactly that in order to take part in America and Americanism. For most Jews, this was a powerful, yet inconsequential pledge. Historically, Jews were never allowed to have such allegiances to a foreign prince or state, since they had no rights in their origin countries. The debate over emancipation and the granting of partial rights was nascent and only affected a small minority of the Jews – those living in Western Europe.

The non-Jew who immigrated to America switched from one home to another, but the Jew who came to America switched from no home to finally having a home. For Jews, America was the first home they had since being exiled from Judea.

The degree of Jewish love and appreciation for America and what it represented was paramount and organic. This was not only on the individual level but also on a group level.

There was no requirement to disavow one's religious, ethnological or ethnic affiliation. This was not expected from the Catholic Italian Sicilian immigrant or the Protestant Swedish Nordic immigrant. Indeed, immigrants remained proud Italians, proud Sicilians, proud Catholics, all while no longer having a loyalty to their previous king.

Similarly, the Jew could have stayed a member of the Jewish nation-religion. Yet, the desire to succeed and be an integral part of America contributed to the astonishing phenomena of Jews shedding the national aspects of their nation-religion and trying to narrow Judaism to a religion.

Understandably, given their background and decades of persecution, once out of the ghettos, the Jews were overly concerned by "what would the neighbors think." As the years progressed, those neighbors ("the Smiths and Joneses") would indeed find it peculiar if their Jewish neighbor would have some sort of secondary national affiliation, particularly since such an affiliation did not involve a country, but an abstract idea, or a country that existed 2,000 year prior. For the Irish, it would be understandable, since he came from Ireland and his old country existed. But for the Jew...?

Hence, Jewish denationalization seemed not only logical, but natural for the new American Jews of the late 19th and early 20th centuries.

(ii) Flourishing of a new "substitute religion" – Americanism

As Jews abandoned their old ways of life, they became a member of a bigger "religion": Americanism.

As many Jews moved away from the rituals of their old religion (observing the Sabbath, wearing a kipa, keeping kosher, going to the synagogue), they felt very comfortable at the core of their new ideal – Americanism. That ideal was so strong that it effectively functioned as a neo-religion. It filled the void created by the abandonment of religious observance.

Jews no longer needed to convert in order to survive or to get a particular job, as was the case in Europe. They could now stay as Jews while being incorporated into Americanism. Indeed, Jews have played a crucial role in shaping the American narrative, particularly in post-World War II Americanism. If Americanism was the new religion, Jews served as some of the leading priests in its shrines.

Price of Americanism

The fear of perceived sacrosanct behavior and dual loyalty was dreaded. Centuries of persecution in Europe took its toll – it produced trauma. "The ghetto continues though its walls are broken down," Herzl commented, noting it takes time to abandon old behavior. In this context, the emergence of Zionism triggered old traumas for many American Jews. It was perceived not as a blessing, but as a threat. But in the last few decades America evolved.

(iii) American Cultural Pluralism

America's ethos is no longer shaped by the "Mayflower narrative," but instead by a strong embrace of cultural pluralism – incorporating broad input from the various branches of Americanism, as long as those are centered around the strong core trunk – America.

In contrast to Europe, where multiculturalism involves new immigrants with no connection to the local narrative, and at times even disdain for Europe, American cultural pluralism is predicated on support, love and an embedded commitment to promote the American narrative.

If the Jew who wants to be like his neighbors was concerned in the 20th century about "what would the Joneses say," the Jew who wants to be like his neighbors today needs to be concerned with "what would the Rubios say," or "what would the Rodriguezes say." Those neighbors, proud Americans, maintain strong relationships with their national affiliation, say Cuban or Mexican. In this context, a Jewish person maintaining contact with his Jewish national affiliation makes him now even more acceptable to the neighbors.

While such diverse neighbors are not just Latinos, but also Korean, Taiwanese, Indians and many others, there is no doubt that in the last few decades there has been a rise of a new center of power in America: Latino Americans.

The rise of the Latino constituents solidifies the cultural pluralism trend that contributes to Jews feeling more comfortable to center more of their identity around Israel and Zionism. The Latinos celebrate their national heritage proudly and do so in strong concert with their American patriotism. Two Cuban American candidates who ran for President in the 2016 elections repeatedly argued which one of them is more Cuban, not which one is more Christian. One of them (Marco Rubio) even accused the other (Ted Cruz) of not speaking Spanish.

Behavioral patterns of the Latino community are such that for most, despite the relatively high religiosity, the national characteristic is stronger than the religious one. Mexican Catholic churches differ from Puerto Rican Catholic churches, even though the theological nuances are small. This is because the national value is the dominant one.

Therefore, applying the Latino American model to the Jewish American community, identification around Zionism is much more consistent than identification around the synagogue. Or taking it one step further, the religious synagogue identity (Rabbinic Judaism) resides within the national identity (Zionism), just like for a Mexican American, the Mexican church is a byproduct of his Mexican heritage, and not the other way around. Not only that, a Jewish person maintaining contact with his Jewish national affiliation makes him more acceptable to the neighbors. This affiliation is no longer abstract or based on a historic national affiliation from 2,000 years ago. The re-establishment of the Jewish state allows the Jew to have a very clear point of orientation for his national-religious identity – The State of Israel.

Furthermore, just like neighbor Rubio would be frowned upon if he would engage in denial of his heritage, so would the Jewish neighbor in denying his Jewish national affiliation (Zionism). It might even turn him into a less credible person.

Diverse faces of America

Diversity is also reflected in America's choices: On the right, there is a full acceptance and even embrace of a first lady, Melania Trump, who was born in the former Soviet bloc, Slovenia, and speaks with a heavy Eastern-European accent. The acceptance is even by the so-called right-wing nativists. On the left, Hillary Clinton's top aide was Muslim and was raised in Saudi Arabia. While there were various criticisms and attacks on Huma Abedin, the fact that she was raised in Saudi Arabia was only a minor element of the criticisms. Similarly, Kamala Harris being the daughter of a Jamaican and of an Indian was not perceived as a liability, but as a great asset – same with her skin color; a complete reversal from just a few decades prior.

America has elected a black president and a black vice president. To the north, the representative of the Queen in Canada, the Governor General, was of Haitian descent.

The discourse that followed the May 2020 killing of George Floyd by a white police officer underscores the point that there is no longer a homogenous pan-American face or character. We are no longer in Mayflower America. Different groups have different narratives, challenges and fears. For example, there are different associations when seeing police officers. Beyond the violence, negativities and polarization, the events of the summer of 2020 also contributed to the recognition that America's cultural pluralism has shifted. There is a reality that the diverse faces of America no longer suppress their ethnological affiliations. Neither should the Jews.

(iv) Dual loyalty has shifted – Americanism is more consistent with Judaism 3.0

Theodor Herzl observed that patriotism is intrinsic to the Jewish character. This was even the case in areas where Jews had no rights and even if such patriotism was rejected. In *The Jewish State*, he wrote: "In vain are we loyal patriots, our loyalty in some places running to extremes; in vain do we make the same sacrifices of life and property as our fellow-citizens; in vain do we strive to increase the fame of our native land in science and art, or her wealth by trade and commerce."

Jewish patriotism in America runs into extremes as well, but this time it is not in vain. Indeed, American Jewish patriotism is broadly acknowledged and appreciated. If there is unfounded insecurity, it is for different reasons than before, such as American Judaism's perceived aggressive advocacy of secularism.

If such unfounded insecurity presents discomfort, then it can be easily rectified by Jews centering their Jewish identity around their Jewish national affiliation.

Indeed, Zionism (Judaism 3.0) is more in line with the American narrative also because it provides greater clarity to the American about who is a Jew, at a time when Americans increasingly embrace and expect clarity.

The question of Dual Loyalty is not new

One of the core objections Jews had to Zionism at the onset had to do with the fear of a perception of dual loyalty. Centuries of discrimination and denial of basic rights came to an end, and now a Jew could finally be French or German. Europeans broadly opposed giving Jews such rights, and there were increasing calls by the end of the 19th century to revoke the rights given earlier to Jews. Jewish opponents of Herzl were outraged at him: Jews finally had the rights as French and Germans, and here comes Herzl, and joins the anti-Semites' claim: "Jews are a nation."

Meeting with French Chief Rabbi Zadoc Kahn in Paris on November 16, 1895, in a long-shot attempt to recruit him to his cause, Herzl read to him his manifesto, later published as *The Jewish State*. After two hours of conversation, Herzl drew a daring confession from the rabbi: "I am a Zionist," the rabbi said. But then he clarified that his French patriotism also demands its right, and therefore, he felt he "must choose between Zion and France."

In the past, many Jewish Americans would think that over-embrace of Zionism would dent their own patriotism, and just like Rabbi Kahn of France, they too would need to make such a choice and in their case, choose between Zion and America. But as described earlier, this choice is the same. Choosing Zion *is* choosing America!

"He is one of those small Jews," Herzl belittled the French rabbi in his diaries after his rejection. But the rabbi was living amongst a society that held strong disdain for Jews, which was manifested in institutional hatred (such as through the Dreyfus Affair). American Jews, on the other hand, live in a secure and accepting environment, hence, they need not be small.

(v) Zionism (Judaism 3.0) as a better representation of today's Americanism

Given the earlier discussion, if early in the 20th century, over-embrace of Zionism could have been considered a loyalty reducing characteristic, raising concerns of dual loyalty, today such overt love of Zionism would be considered a positive loyalty-enhancing characteristic.

Given America's demographic trends, a second derivative of cultural pluralism has evolved in the 21st century. Not only has the hyphenated American been making a comeback, but he is now encouraged to maintain loyalty to all sides of those hyphens, without compromising one another.

Early in the 20th century, the philosopher Horace Kallen discussed the concept of the American symphony, with each heritage group essential to the success of the great symphony. In his time, the ethnological identity was far more dominant than the emerging "Americanism." The symphony was bottom-up. However, in the 21st century, Americanism is the dominating tune. Therefore, having the confidence and bandwidth encourages the individual instruments to play-up, to demonstrate the power of American cultural pluralism. [5]

Indeed, in the top-down American Symphony, each instrument now has even greater importance for the success of the symphony. A Cuban American strengthens the American Symphony by extending his Cuban national identity. Similarly, a Jewish American strengthens the American Symphony by extending his Jewish national identity – Zionism.

In a sense, there was a shift from American universalism (Adherence to a universal American type), to American particularity (Adherence to the particularity of one's own background).

(vi) American rejection of European Multiculturalism strengthens Judaism 3.0

There are two crucial distinctions that must be made when examining cultural pluralism in America:

Ethnological affiliation is not political affiliation

Cultural pluralism does not mean that an ethnological affiliation (such as being Cuban American or Jewish American), leads to a political affiliation (being a Cuban citizen or an Israeli citizen).

In addition, it does not mean that the hyphenated American needs to agree with his heritage nation's government and policies (Marco Rubio does not agree with the Cuban regime). Yet celebrating one's heritage nation's affiliation and caring about it is a profound manifestation of 21st century Americanism.

American Cultural Pluralism is not European Multiculturalism

America's version of cultural pluralism is not multiculturalism. It is not a collection of unrelated cultures in competition with one another, as the case is in Europe. Rather, American cultural pluralism is about groups who are components of a dominating core culture and idea – Americanism.

---

5 – For more on Horace Kallen, see Sarah Schmidt: "Horace M. Kallen: Prophet of American Zionism".

One's ethnological affiliation is a net-contributor to the perfection of America; not a net-user of it, as is the case in Europe.

Hence, a Cuban American celebrating his Cuban ethnological affiliation is by itself a celebration of Americanism. His exercise of his Cuban affiliation, heritage and culture is a net-contributor to the core narrative of Americanism.

By the same token, a Jewish American celebrating his Jewish ethnological affiliation (Zionism) is a celebration of Americanism. Arguably, even more so than in the case of the Cuban, since in addition, there are synergies between the American Jew's love to old Zion (Israel) and to new Zion (America).

Having such a network of strong national cultures (Cuban, Jewish/Zionist, Italian) as net-contributors to the American narrative must not be confused with attempts to undermine the American narrative itself.

European Multiculturalism is a simultaneous threat to both American Cultural Pluralism and Israeli Symbiotic Particularity

The threat to the American narrative comes from universalism, and from a misapplication of cultural pluralism. It is the argument of America as an arbitrary place of residence: "Live in America; you can be American, you can be anti-American; America is simply a home for all of its citizens."

America is not merely a place for its citizens to live. Americanism is an ideal in the same way that Zionism is an ideal.

Those who want to make America "like everybody else," those who deny American exceptionalism and the unique nature of the American narrative, dent the American ideal. In this realm, universalism is the negation of Americanism.

America is much closer to the Israeli model of particularity than it is to the European aspired model of universalism and its actual model of multiculturalism.

There are those in Israel who believe Israel should cease to be a Zionist state and become a "state for all its citizens." As discussed in the Threat chapter, this debate is essentially a battle for the survival of Israel and despite some political noise, the overwhelming majority of Israelis outright reject the universalism approach.

In Europe, on the other hand, the question is reversed: Can a third generation of immigrants living in Paris pursue their own narrative, which is independent of the French narrative? The narrative can be religious-related, such as wearing the burka, or cultural-related, such as speaking Arabic on radio stations.

More so, in the French example, some of those third-generation immigrants openly express disdain for the dominant French narrative and behave in contrast to it (opposition to French liberal values which are core to French society, such as gender equality and secularism). But it is not just France. The same disdain is directed to Europe as a whole and to European values. Is France ceasing to be French and turning into a "state of all its citizens" – a loose collection of parallel societies?

In contrast, Americanism accepts and encourages multiple cultures, as long as they are supportive of, and integral to, the dominant American narrative. Same with Israel and the dominant Zionist narrative.

Dual loyalty to America and to one's ethnological national affiliation is natural and built into Americanism. Just like dual loyalty to America and one's state or municipality is natural and built into Americanism. Dual loyalty is acceptable, but anti-loyalty is certainly not.

Indeed, anti-loyalty, similar to that expressed by some insular immigrant groups in France and throughout Europe is a negation of Americanism. So is an extremely absolutist expression of universalism philosophy that attempts to negate the American narrative at its core.

Cultural pluralism is strongly welcomed, but European multiculturalism is not – it is a threat to Americanism.

Similarly, in Israel, symbiotic particularity is welcomed, including celebrating the choice of Israeli Arabs to self-segregate and still contribute to society. Israeli Arabs are at the forefront of the medical and pharmaceutical industries in Israel. Their contribution is not in spite of their self-segregation, but thanks to being able to make their own lifestyle choices, which in turn optimizes their contribution. This is in contrast to the European multiculturalism model, which leads to chronic mutual-negation.

5. American Revolution – An Embrace Of Zionism (Not Of Judaism 2.0)

(i) American Revolution as abstract Zionism

Americans rebelled against prevailing European dogmas. They reinstated an old dream, a Utopia, a return. The American Revolution has been romanticized as a return to Zion. As a result, many towns and main streets in the United States were given Zionist names: New Canaan, new Jerusalem, Bethlehem, Bethel and Shiloh.

Choosing names from the old "Promised Land", as opposed to names that are religious, underscores that first and foremost, this was about a political philosophy more than about religion or theology.

America is a form of abstract Zionism. Indeed, the establishment of New Zion (America) is synergistic with the Jews' return to Old Zion. Both processes started around the same time in the 16th century. In Old Zion's case, as the Ottomans took control of Palestine from its previous rulers, they changed the narrative and encouraged Jewish return. In New Zion's case, as Europeans discovered America, they created a new narrative and began immigrating.

The same Church and institutions that had persecuted the Puritans and led Christians to seek religious freedom in America, had at various times persecuted the Jews.

The Church was an accomplice in the deportation of Jews from Spain, as well as from England and France.

In both cases, it was not religious differences as much as competition, envy, political consideration and national aversion that caused the actions of the Church, and led to deportation and expulsion. [6]

European Christians went to America; European Jews went to the Ottoman Empire, including to Palestine.

As Christians re-established Zion in a new land, Jews re-established Zion in their old land. Given that Christianity and Judaism are essentially sister monotheistic Judeo-Christian religions – these two Zionist movements can be viewed retroactively as two branches of the same creed.

Theodor Herzl said that "Zionism is the return to Judaism." In a similar manner, Americanism is the return to Christianity.

Today, as European countries turn secular and even atheist, Americanism is the primary ideology that preserves monotheistic Christianity. This leads to the sacred trinity of religion-Americanism-Zionism.

(ii) American exceptionalism and particularity as abstract Zionism

A key ethos that came out of the American Revolution is the notion of American exceptionalism. As America was taking shape, it became a society of risk-takers who dared to think big and come to the new world. When there was a famine in Ireland, the ambitious ones left, the less

6 – For more on the national aspect of the persecution of Spanish Jewry, see Benzion Netanyahu: "The Origins of the Inquisition in Fifteenth-Century Spain".

ambitious hesitated and stayed. When there were Jewish persecutions, the bold ones made a move, the less so lingered. Same with the Italians, Russians and English. Those who came to America came to upgrade – to build, to create, to dare. Hence, the American gene pool and the top-level narrative have generated a society marked by exceptionalism.

This exceptionalism is intertwined with the American notion of particularity. It means something to be American. It is an ideology; it is an ideal – it is not just a place where one lives.

While for many, it may no longer be President Kennedy's vision, "ask not what your country can do for you, ask what you can do for your country," the relationship between America and its citizens remains an emotional one – a relationship of love. Not of an arrangement (pay taxes in exchange for services).

American particularity is rooted in both its ideology and the nature of the people who immigrated to America. This includes French Huguenot Protestants who rebelled against France, demanding rights and freedom – many of them came to America. This also included Germans who, in the quest for human rights, did not remain passive, but took to the streets in the 1848 revolution demanding such rights, demanding nationalism, demanding republicanism. Many of those so-called 48'ers ended up in the United States. The ones who were more passive, forgiving, tolerant to the European monarchy – they stayed behind in Europe.

Such American particularity is similar to the particularity of Zionism. The establishment of the State of Israel is symbiotic with the idea of American exceptionalism and particularity.

Hence, the triumph of Zionism (Judaism 3.0) strengthens the American narrative in its philosophical debate against contemporary European universalism.

This is yet another example of how an American Jew's support of Zionism is also a support of Americanism. And yet, some vocal sections of American Jewry are champions of such European universalism that is on the other side. This is providing further evidence that Zionism (Judaism 3.0) is a better reflection of Americanism than the existing American Jewish narrative (Judaism 2.0).

(iii) 21st century divide: American particularity vs. European universalism

A counter-narrative to American exceptionalism developed in Europe. It is the same story about the immigrants, but in reverse. When the going got tough, the weak ones left for America and the strong ones stayed in Europe. Those who had convictions and were loyal, weathered the storm and kept Europe thriving. The riffraffs escaped.

Those two narratives are inevitably on a collision course: Move/ Immigrate/be active/fight/ascent ("Lech Lecha") vs. stay/let time pass/ be passive/accept/linger. [7]

This rift between the American narrative and the European narrative is not just a matter of history. It comes to the fore in contemporary debates – expanding from the question about exceptionalism or counter-exceptionalism to a broader question – Is America any different?

Americanism is under threat from universalism – the negation of particularity – the notion that "we are all the same," and hence, the negation of Americanism.

There are contemporary attempts to erode the American Revolution and its messages. Those attempts, not surprisingly, are coming from Europe. The once subtle philosophical disparagement between Americanism and Europe gets elevated with contemporary issues such as Brexit and the presidency of Donald Trump.

This disparity is likely to increase in coming years as election cycles in the United States and Europe put such core philosophical issues on the table even more. Whatever the outcomes of such elections might be, the issues will rise up, and there will be ripples and counter-actions as a result of the outcomes of those elections.

At its core, is the key question: Is America really an ideal? There lies the intensifying of a philosophical debate between Americanism and Europeanism. American particularity vs. European universalism. This might be turning into the philosophical global divide of the 21st century, akin to the late 20th century divide between capitalism (US) and communism (USSR) and the 19th century one between republicanism and monarchy.

For an American Jew, a connection to Judaism through Zionism (Judaism 3.0) is a profound demonstration of support of the American-led side of this philosophical debate, since Zionism at its core is about particularity and counter-universalism.

6. SECOND ACT OF THE AMERICAN REVOLUTION

There seems to be a "second phase" of the American Revolution against Europe, 250 years since first rebelling. Europe has long ceded control of its American colonies, but the European narrative is still very

---

7 – For comparison of Abraham's call of Lech Lecha to today's context, see my article: "The exodus from Babel continues", *The Jerusalem Post*, November 19, 2020, available on this book's website.

much present in the American discourse, and arguably increasing. Some Americans view the prospect of Europeanization of the American ideal as welcomed, while others feel it is a negation of the principles of the American Revolution, and in opposition to it. This gives rise to the second act of the American Revolution – the ideological phase.

(i) European narrative in America and American narrative in Europe

While this view of the second act of the American Revolution tends to be associated with the American-right, it has strong roots in the American-left as well.

This is not simply USA vs. Europe. There are those in America promoting the European narrative, and there are those in Europe promoting the American Revolution-inspired narratives.

Just like in the 18th century, the debate today also has to do with internal disagreements in both the US and in Europe. There are "Loyalists/Tories" in the United States who promote European values in America – a legitimate and welcomed part of the American democracy. There are Separatists/Exit'ers and others in Europe that promote American values in Europe – a legitimate part of the European democracy (this should be viewed as legitimate and welcomed, but regrettably not always is).

This became apparent in the Brexit vote and the debate that followed. In some way, a choice was presented between aligning more closely with Europe vs. aligning more closely with the US.

This debate continued in other European countries and was processed through elections: In Germany, Austria, Italy, Sweden, to the European Parliament. As evidence of that, Steve Bannon, who was an advisor to President Trump and an architect of his 2016 victory had been aggressively promoting the American ideal in Europe, as he saw it – advising European politicians and leaders that wanted to be less aligned with the EU and its values, and more with the United States and Americanism.

Too soon for the American experiment to settle

There is broad consensus in America – Republicans and Democrats alike – that America is not just a country where people live, but rather about an ideology: Americanism. The American Revolution was not just about the physical exodus from Europe – Europeans moving to America. It was also an ideological exodus from Europe and negation of centuries-old well-rooted European dogmas.

While it has been 250 years since the success of the American Revolution, revolutions of such magnitude and impact often take longer to settle. For example, the Christian Revolution against paganism took about the same amount of time just to have its first significant accomplishment and a few more centuries to settle.

Too soon for the European fall from grace to settle

For 2,000 years Europe dominated the global narrative and economy. As such, Europe has yet to come to terms with its sudden fall from grace that occurred in the early part of the 20th century. Europe was not "mentally" prepared for the unexpected loss of its colonial assets, nor to the swift shift of power to the United States.

As a result, while Europe physically decolonized, it has not done so mentally. This is reflected in its treatment of its own non-white residents, in its disruptive actions overseas (such as in the Israeli-Palestinian affairs), and indeed in its growing hostility towards the American narrative.

(ii) European Union as force of counter-Americanism

The European Union has been increasingly positioning itself in recent years as a global force to counter Americanism. Its messages highlight the divide: America is religious, Europe is increasingly atheist; America is capitalist, Europe is socially conscious; America is militaristic, Europe is pacifist.

In seeking to federalize Europe, create a European army (as opposed to American-led NATO) and in spreading European values to the world, Europe has positioned itself as the alternative power to America. For many Europeans, American rejection of universalism is interpreted as a rejection of Europeanism ("the colonies are rebelling"). "America first" is interpreted as "Europe last."

The election of Donald Trump as the US president in 2016 gave the European Union the ability to position itself as the "responsible adult." America needs the EU to protect itself from "rogue presidents and crazy policies," the thinking goes.

Indeed, there are voices in Europe that call for the "enlightening" of America with contemporary European values. This includes universalism, counter-particularity, counter-exceptionalism, counter-nationalism, counter-sovereignty, multilateralism, over-determent from use of force, appeasement, flavors of socialism, environmentalism, human-rights-driven approaches, aggressive secularism and even atheism.

These voices are certainly legitimate. A country or empire spreading its influence and promoting its values is a legitimate part of global politics.

But such intervention inevitably leads to a counter-reaction in America – and to the beginning of the second act of the American Revolution – the ideological phase. This has implications for the American Jewish community and about how Americans perceive the Jews.

Shared interests trump ideological/philosophical differences

America and Europe are strongly aligned when it comes to military cooperation, the war on terrorism, key policy issues such as non-proliferation of non-conventional weapons and to a lesser extent in the outdated West vs. East political conflict.

Given the urgencies of these issues, and the existence of common enemies and adversaries, the ideological and philosophical differences are being set aside. However, with Europe's attempt to spread its ideology to America, this might change.

(iii) Europe's sphere of influence in America – Judaism 2.0

The rise in power of the EU and its attempts to influence Americanism goes hand-in-hand with the domestic rise of universalist forces in America. Some connect the two and feel that there is an attempt to erode the value system of the American Revolution and to import values back from Europe – to "Hellenize" the American people and the American way, to instill in them "proper European values."

Who are these importers of European values to America? Who are these "Hellenizers?" They are the ones with the broadest set of touch-points with Europe: Those in banking, in academia, trade, journalism, and other such jetsetters – a group that is perceived to strongly correlate with American Jews. (Judaism 2.0). [8]

Exports From Europe to America: Israel-bashing and BDS

The export from Europe is not just of values such as universalism and secularism. In recent years, Europe has also exported to the United States a particular form of anti-Israel sentiment. The Israel-bashing movement that originated in Europe in the 2000s (most notably in the form of BDS – Boycott, Divestment and Sanctions), has amassed power in both the European white communities and in the European Muslim communities. It has now traveled to America as part of the overall basket

---

8 – During the Greeks' invasion of Judea and their aggressive campaign to Hellenize the Jews, the key message-carriers of the Greeks were Jews themselves – the Hellenized Jews.

of values imported from Europe.

The importers of Europeanism in general also inadvertently facilitate the introduction of the European form of Israel-bashing into America. Indeed, the anti-Israel movement resonates primarily with communities that are at the point-of-entry to European values: primarily within liberal and progressive, as well as in the Jewish communities, but less so with the American Muslim community.

The absence of broad aggressive anti-Israeli sentiment in America's Muslim communities is due in part to the reality that it has fewer touch-points with Europe, the birthplace of Israel-bashing.

On the other hand, there is a notable geographic fit between Europeanization and the anti-Israel movement – mostly in the Northeast and on the West Coast – areas with a significant Jewish population and influence.

There is a correlation between those communities exposed to Europeanization of America and those experiencing high Israel-bashing and BDS penetration. Both correlate with the American Jewish community (Judaism 2.0).

While Judaism 3.0 is a reflection of the American ideal and the values of the American Revolution, Judaism 2.0 is to a certain extent, a reflection of the European sphere-of-influence in America, including its perceived European counter-Americanism.

(iv) American Revolution: From Divine-right monarchy to Divine-right republic

The monarchs who ruled Europe for centuries claimed that their source of authority was from God. For centuries, there was stability in Europe under the system of Divine-right monarchy. The notion that God appoints the kings created both buy-in of the population into the ruling structure, as well as institutional knowledge that passed seemingly throughout the generations of monarchs.

Divine-right monarchy is consistent with the recurring Biblical concept, which is the cornerstone to both Christianity and Judaism: God is the sovereign of earth. (For example, Leviticus 25:23, "For the land is Mine; for you are strangers and settlers with Me.") God is the sovereign, the monarchs derive their right from Him.

American revolutionists never disavowed the notion that the Divine provides the right. It disavowed that such Divine-right is given to the monarchs. Instead, the American Revolution claimed that such Divine-right rests with the people.

This is very similar to the Zionist ideal (Judaism 3.0), stated by Herzl:

"God would not have preserved our nation for such a long time had there not been another purpose designated for us in the history of mankind."

(v) Europe reactionary: From Divine-right monarchy to no Divine

On the other hand, Europe is on its own long, multi-century, two-step process of replacing the Divine-right monarchies: First negation of the Divine-right and shift to a non-Divine republic, and then, to a growing extent, to non-Divine monarchy – the EU. [9]

Both America and Europe arrived at the same point: Rejection of Divine-right monarchy. America did it by rejecting the monarchy, Europe did it by rejecting the Divine.

As the European Union, which could be viewed as a neo-monarchy, has gained power and influence, it has sought to spread its philosophy into America. This has been consistent with European historic behavior. The Napoleonic wars were not just about the French invading European countries. It was about spreading a philosophy – the values of the French Revolution (successfully).

The same is happening today. The EU is attempting to spread the ideas of post-nationalism, post-religion and universalism, dedicating significant budgets and political capital to it. These ideas are in a head-to-head conflict with the ideas of the American Revolution.

More and more people in America feel that it is time to do away with that residual European narrative – to complement the physical decolonialization from Europe that occurred 250 years ago, with a philosophical one.

(vi) The European-American conflict as a catalyst for the Jewish transformation

A significant part of European influence in America involves American Jews – Judaism 2.0. As discussed, many Jews are "honorary ambassadors" of Europeanism in America. As America engages de facto in the second act of the American Revolution against Europe – an ideological one –

---

9 – The EU arguably displays both paganic-like elements and monarchy-like elements, such as sourcing power from itself through the European Commission. For expansion, see my articles available on the book's website www.judaism-zionism.com: "The Resurfacing of European Colonialism", *The Jerusalem Post*, January 19, 2019; "The Battle for Europe", *The Jerusalem Post*, April 6, 2019; "Time for a new European Peace Conference", *The Jerusalem Post,* January 1, 2020. More at www.europeandjerusalem.com .

inevitably, there is a subtle indirect rebellion against such ambassadors of Europeanism – against Judaism 2.0. Recognizing that Judaism has transformed and is now in Judaism 3.0 would allow Jews to disassociate from the European side of the European-American conflict, and be more closely aligned with Americanism through Zionism.

Jerusalem – an arena for Europe vs. American conflict

The European-American divide came to bear in European reactions to the American move of its embassy to Jerusalem. US President Donald Trump's announcement recognizing Jerusalem as Israel's capital was monumental. But perhaps just as fascinating were the European objections to the announcement. This contrasted with the relatively tame reaction among Palestinians and Arab states.

A common argument aggressively pursued by Europeans was that the US recognition of Jerusalem would spark violence of extreme proportions. This is perhaps symptomatic of a monolithic (and arguably Islamophobic) view some Europeans have of Palestinians – that they act in unison as a mob, rioting on command.

Europeans have ignored the centrality of Jerusalem in the core essence of Americanism. Indeed, presidential candidates from Bill Clinton to Barack Obama stated during their election campaigns that Jerusalem is the capital of Israel. The US Congress passed the Jerusalem Embassy Act in 1995 with an overwhelming majority of 95-3 in the Senate and 347-37 in the House of Representatives. Such broad bipartisan support is a testament that it is not politics but ideology that drives American attitudes about Jerusalem.

Unlike the American consensus, French President Emmanuel Macron argued that "the status of Jerusalem is a question of international security which concerns the entire international community." This European position is based on a 1949 UN resolution that designated Jerusalem and Bethlehem as a "corpus separatum" to be placed under an international legal regime – essentially a European colony.

This is another expression of the Europe vs. America divide: America recognizes Jerusalem as it is, Europe wants to take it away. Indeed, taking Jerusalem is a recurring theme in European history – though the methods have changed.

Even in this round, the methods are "flexible." While on the one hand, Macron claims that Jerusalem should be placed under an international regime, on the other, he seems to make an exception when it comes to the "colonial assets" of France – those of course must stay

French. This was implied in Macron's visit to Jerusalem in January 2020. As he was entering the Church of Saint Anne, Macron confronted his Israeli security detail. "Get out," he frantically yelled at them, invoking a dubious colonialist deal of the 1850s, when the Ottoman Empire gave the Church of Saint Anne to France as a reward for France's support in the Crimean War.

Macron went further to argue that kicking out the Israelis is based on "the rules that have been in place for centuries." This sets up the symbolism of the European-American conflict in Jerusalem: Cherishing the colonialist arrangement that has been in place for 170 years (Europe) vs. cherishing the origins of Judaism and Christianity which have been in place for 3,000 years (Israel and America).

Europe's aggressive stand towards Jerusalem

In 2016, European countries astonishingly supported or abstained from a UNESCO vote that suggested Jews and Christians do not have a historic connection to the Temple Mount, and by extension to the city of Jerusalem. [10]

The UNESCO vote can be seen as a watershed moment in Europe's relationship to Jerusalem. While for America, Jerusalem is the shining city on a hill – for Europe it is a Muslim city which, as implied in the UNESCO vote, has no historical Christian or Jewish ties.

Europe chose Jerusalem as an arena for its philosophical battle with the United States. Sadly some Jews in America sided with Europe. European opposition to Jerusalem epitomizes its opposition to Americanism.

Here lies the ultimate evidence of a Jewish transformation: Americanism and Zionism on one side, Europeanism and Judaism 2.0 on the other.

Israel Is The Most Relevant Aspect Of Judaism For Americans

7. AMERICANS' CONSUMPTION OF ISRAELI EXPERIENCES

The more non-Jewish Americans relate to Judaism through their own Israeli experiences, the easier it is for Jews to relate to Judaism through Israel. This view is strengthened by the dynamics mentioned earlier that the Jewish and non-Jewish communities in America are integrated.

---

10 – UNESCO Executive Board, Item 25: Occupied Palestine, October 12, 2016.

When a non-Jew has a positive Israel-related experience that he shares with his Jewish friend, it has a positive influence on the American Jew.

Therefore, a non-Jewish American who relates to Judaism through Israel contributes to the fulfillment of the transformation of Judaism in two ways. Both since it is evident that for him Judaism is associated with Israel, and since it makes it easier for the Jew to connect to his own Judaism through Israel.

After all, only 41% of American Jews have been to Israel. Hence, a visit by a non-Jew serves as a bridge. It also serves as a "legitimizer" – if the non-Jew admires Israel, then so can the Jew, without being nervous about being suspected of dual loyalty.

Case study – Israeli wine

The recent success of Israeli wineries in producing top quality wines and winning international wine-tasting competitions has resulted in growing attention from wine experts around the world.

Just as wine drinkers connect to France through French wine, they are now starting to connect to Judaism through Israeli wine. This is becoming a touch-point of the general public to Judaism. That is especially the case, since Israeli wines tell the story of Judaism and of the Jewish people – they allow wine-drinkers to connect to the romanticism of the Bible and to the ancient land – regardless of their religiosity.

Today, sipping Israeli wine uncovers the vibrancy of Israel. There are more female winemakers and winery owners in Israel relative to other countries, as well as winemakers who are gay, Arab, ultra-Orthodox and young – some under 30. The Israeli wine industry is a reflection of Israel's entrepreneurial, innovative spirit.

Incidentally, Israeli wine might have even had a role in the origin of Zionism. Herzl stated that he did not know where he got the idea for the Jewish state, but he speculated that it was planted in a bottle he received from Jewish wineries in Palestine – the first time he had Israeli wine (or Brandy in this particular case).

As is evident of just how much Israeli wines are associated with Judaism, they are typically displayed in wine stores across America under a section titled Kosher. There are Italian, French, Chilean sections, but for Israeli wine, it is a Jewish designation – not a regional one. This further emphasizes the connection to Judaism through Israel.

Case study – the Shuk

In Jerusalem's Machaneh Yehuda market, known as the "Shuk", one can see daily the astounding expressions of dozens of visitors, many of whom are not Jewish, who see, feel, smell, drink and consume the vibrancy of Israel.

The Shuk is not interpreted as a random sightseeing experience, but as a Jerusalem experience, an Israeli experience and therefore a Jewish experience.

This is reflected in the increased number of delegations coming to the Shuk. From US senators to hedge fund managers to technology entrepreneurs, the Shuk has become a beacon to the world.

For example, Forbes chose Israel for its Top 30 Women under 30 global summit, and the Shuk as the venue for the after-party. Up-and-coming leaders from all over the world converge on the Shuk and bring back home this Israeli experience – this Jewish experience.

Similarly, when Technology company OurCrowd hosted its annual conference in 2020, which included 18,000 people from 189 countries, those investors, technology entrepreneurs, journalists and innovators from all over the world headed to the Shuk after the conference for a traditional bar-hop.

Attorneys General from a dozen US states toasted in the New Year in 2020 in the Shuk as part of an America-Israel Friendship League (AIFL) delegation. Similarly, in an AIFL delegation of influential American women, Gina Louden, advisor to then President Trump, commented that "The Shuk is a reflection of what I love about Israel – about raw free markets, about freedom. All this magic is created from nothing." Louden, who later briefed President Trump about her visit, is just one of many whose visit to the Shuk has helped to shape their relation to Israel and to Judaism. [11]

Moreover, when visitors come home to America and share their experience with their Jewish friends and neighbors, those Jews are also led to increase their interaction with Judaism through these Israel experiences.

8. AMERICA'S STRATEGIC ALLIANCE WITH ISRAEL

For most Americans, Israel is a strategic partner, reliable ally and a friend – this includes those who are critical of Israel's policies, its prime minister or government. Indeed, Zionism evokes emotions also in the

---

11 – Interviewed in my article: "Jerusalem Shuk as Beacon the World", *The Jerusalem Post*, December 12, 2018.

negative. In progressive circles, there is no doubt that Israel is the most significant Jewish issue. A quick survey of the tweets of Congresswomen Alexandria Ocasio-Cortez and Rashida Tlaib shows that they tweet about Israel far more than they do about any other Jewish issue.

Israel's alliance with the United States is unshakable, spanning multiple touch-points, including military cooperation, war on terrorism, intelligence sharing, biomedical cooperation and defense-related job generation in the United States.

For liberals, Israel being a liberal democracy with strong gay rights and women rights is a source of core support, even if there are disagreements on policies. Congresswoman Ocasio-Cortez repeatedly refers to Israel as an ally even when she rebukes its policies.

For libertarians in particular, the notion of "sub-contracting" elements of Middle East defense needs to Israel allows less intervention of the United States overseas, and is consistent with the view that regional actors should deal with their own issues ("the United States is not the world's policeman"). Elements of such libertarian philosophy exist both on the right, on the left and even far-left.

For conservatives, the strategic alliance with Israel is an issue of moral clarity and is a core consensus issue.

While support for the Jewish state and what it represents is broad and solid, support for the American Jewish "religion" (Judaism 2.0) and what it represents (secularism) is certainly not.

Hence, America's strategic alliance with Israel is also an enabler of the transformation from Judaism 2.0 to Judaism 3.0.

9. AMERICA'S POLITICAL SHIFTS SUPPORT THE JEWISH TRANSFORMATION

Long-term shifts in American politics are also indicative of the transformation from Judaism 2.0 to Judaism 3.0.

(i) Shift in the Liberal Movement in the US

Rightly or wrongly, there is a strong association of American Judaism with American liberalism. According to surveys, 77% of American Jews voted for Joe Biden in 2020;[12] 78% voted for President Obama in 2008 and 70% in 2012.

For many in America, the impulsive association of a "Jew" is no longer that of a rabbi, but that of a reporter for *The New York Times*, Wall Street

---

12 – GBAO Strategies, based on exit polls. Some question the data since the survey was done on behalf of J-Street, which supported Biden.

investment banker, Hollywood producer or Washington lobbyist. This might sound anti-Semitic and politically incorrect, but it is rational and it is true.

Just like the impulsive stereotype association of an "Irish" is not of someone that goes to a particular church, but that of a policeman or a fireman, or of someone who enjoys drinking a good beer.

More and more, when people think of Jews, politically, they think of a liberal – hence, the term "liberal Jews." Therefore, one's view of the Liberal movement affects how one views Judaism. As those views change, so does the American perception of Judaism.

Irrelevancy of liberal Judaism in the eyes of liberals

Jews being associated with the Liberal movement does not necessarily mean that the Liberal movement is any longer associated with the Jews.

Jews did play a significant role in the Liberal movement and the Democratic party in the past: Over the last 40 years, about 20% of Democratic senators have been Jewish, 75% of Supreme Court judges appointed by Democratic presidents (and 80% of those nominated) have been Jewish. By the time he took office on January 20, 2021, President Biden had nominated no fewer than 12 Jews to top positions in his administration. Similarly, leaders of liberal organizations from the National Association for Women to the Civil Rights movement have had significant Jewish leadership. [13]

The Liberal movement and the Democratic party are shifting. New forces have emerged that are taking the movement in a different direction, and those no longer have strong Jewish associations. Not only do those new directions have only limited Jewish influence, but to a large extent, as will be discussed, some of those new liberal forces house scornful sentiments towards the old style liberalism that was associated with liberal Judaism.

A significant part of the base of the Democratic party and the Liberal movement is now made up of African Americans and Latino Americans. They are often the plurality of voters for a given Democratic candidate in a primary. Joe Biden's victory in the 2020 Democratic party presidential primaries was achieved, with much thanks to African American voters. For most African American Democrats, the old-style liberalism is not very relevant. Rather, the issues important to those constituents tend to be community issues, immigration, entitlements, health care and police relationships.

---

13 – For more, see Kenneth Wald: "The Foundations of American Jewish Liberalism".

This became apparent in the 2020 protests that followed the killing of George Floyd. The issue that dominated liberal political discussions had nothing to do with old-style liberalism or old-style liberal issues. Moreover, the civil rights cause, equality for African Americans and affirmative action, have all been staples of liberal Judaism. Suddenly, there is a new dialogue occurring around the African American community, with different language, concepts, currency and leaders. Old-style liberalism is now not part of it. The baton of civil rights advocacy has moved away from liberal Judaism. Indeed, the protests, in many respects, symbolizes the end of the old liberal ethos and a powerful display of a new one.

Core to this new ethos is the rise of the Progressive movement. If African Americans and Hispanic Americans are the numeric base of the Liberal movement, the Progressive movement is increasingly becoming the ideological base of the Liberal movement.

Progressives are at their core anti-establishment. Their rise represents a subtle rebellion against the old-style Liberal movement and Democratic party establishment, which is heavily associated with liberal Judaism (Judaism 2.0).

This was demonstrated by the decline of Congressman Elliot Engel. He was a staple of Jewish liberalism who won 16 consecutive elections to Congress until 2020 when he was defeated in the Democratic primary by a candidate who is part of the new cadre now carrying the baton. Yonkers school principal Jamaal Bowman defeated Engel decisively, winning 62% of the vote, compared to Engel's 35%.

The third group, loosely defined as Alt-Left, houses a consortium of anarchists, revolutionists, neo-Communists, rebelling teenagers of various ages and various others. They are not just anti-establishment; they are anti-system. This is a group that in general does not participate in the democratic process, but can be rallied behind a cause or a candidate (such as turning out to vote for Barack Obama in 2008 when he ran for president, and for Bernie Sanders in the 2020 primaries). For parts of this group, the Jew is "the Man." Whether it is disdain for the Jewish Wall Street financier or to the Jewish party bosses, there is an outright rejection of liberal Judaism. This group was on high display during the June 2020 protests and parts of it are blamed for hijacking an issue-based popular protest, in an attempt to turn it into all-out chaos.

Putting the forces of those three groups together, and their rising demographic power, it can be concluded that Judaism 2.0 is losing its hold on the American Liberal movement.

At the same time, Zionism (Judaism 3.0) is becoming the more relevant Jewish issue to those new forces of the Liberal movement, whether from a positive or negative point of view.

For the African American and Hispanic American base, strong religiosity translates into strong support of Zionism. Many in this group can be called the religious-left. For some of those constituents, liberalism is coated with Christianity. As mentioned earlier, American Christians are strongly affiliated with Zionism and that includes the African American and Hispanic communities (notwithstanding a few notables, though statistically small exceptions). Liberal Judaism (Judaism 2.0) may no longer be relevant for them, but Zionism (Judaism 3.0) very much is. [14]

Martin Luther King, an American icon who naturally continues to have great influence in the African American community, was an avid Zionist. For example, he said: "When people criticize Zionists, they mean Jews, you are talking anti-Semitism." Dr. King represents an early prototype of Judaism 3.0 – the inseparability of Judaism from Zionism. His legacy continues to shape views in America, and in particular the African American community.

For the Progressive, while being anti-establishment means anti-liberal Judaism, Zionism (Judaism 3.0) represents an issue that evokes passions and strong emotions – mostly, from a negative point of view. The Progressives are arguably the most Israel-skeptic group in United States politics, but they are not purely anti-Israel, and the vast majority are not anti-Zionist. It is policy issues, such as settlements, Israel's use of force and wars in Gaza that energizes the group. Those are issues relating to Judaism 3.0 which they want to engage with, and not issues relating to Judaism 2.0, which they simply tend to ignore. The group's primary relationship with Judaism is defined through Israel.

The Alt-Left provides perhaps the stronger evidence of a Jewish transformation, since they tend not to make much distinction between Jews and Israel. For many of them, there is no difference: "Jews control the world" is the same as "Israel controls America." (Depicted, for example, in Jon Stewart's January 2014 skit in the Daily Show: "The Senator from the Great State of Israel.")

Hence, whether from a positive or negative point of view, trends in the American Left and Liberal movement support the reality that there is a transformation of Judaism in America from Judaism 2.0 (liberal Judaism) to Judaism 3.0 (Zionism).

---

14 – Attachment of African Americans to Zionism has a long history and also draws on Martin Luther King's avid support for Zionism.

As for liberal Jews themselves, more and more of them are choosing, through their actions, to define their interaction with their Judaism through Israel (Judaism 3.0) as opposed to through legacy liberal Judaism (Judaism 2.0). Many of the leaders of the BDS movement are Jewish.

Same goes for the lower degree of anti-Israel activities. Perhaps most telling is that the most prominent lobbyist group in Washington that is set up to criticize Israel's policies is indeed a Jewish group! (J-Street).

Not only is J-Street leading the Israel criticism group in Washington, it is gaining more and more acceptability within liberal Judaism itself. More and more liberal Jews are willing to carry its flag. As discussed, increasing numbers of Jews manifest their liberal Judaism through criticism of Israel. Hence, even for the liberal Jews themselves, the issue of Zionism (Judaism 3.0) is more and more central in their Judaism, and hence, validating the reality of a transformation.

Disdain of liberal Judaism (Judaism 2.0) by Conservatives

For the Republicans and Conservatives, rejection of the liberal philosophy has become more and more vocal. The age of clarity, described earlier, also translated into louder tones. Hence, the move away from gray means that the disdain for liberalism is more amplified.

Given the strong association of Jews with the Liberal movement, the rejection of liberalism translates into an indirect implicit rejection of American Judaism (Judaism 2.0).

Indeed, some would even replace the term the "liberal elite" with the "Jewish elite." This is not new. That same reality existed in Europe in the late 19th century. Herzl recounted a conversation he had with a Viennese lawyer as he was shaping his Zionist thoughts. The lawyer argued that the right-wing outrage was not against the Jews, but simply against the liberals. It just so happens that Jews are liberals.

No doubt such attitudes exist today, and indeed it also has clear anti-Semitic trappings. For example, the 2019 impeachment of President Trump has been described by some far-right outlets, such as TruNews, as a "Jewish coup" (the two lead impeachment managers – Congressman Adam Schiff and Congressman Jerry Nadler are Jewish). But this is also reflected in non-anti-Semitic manners. Nobody suspects the popular comedy show *Saturday Night Live* of being anti-Semitic. This interchangeability of liberal elite and Jewish elite was depicted on *Saturday Night Live's* mockery of a 2016 Republican Presidential debate in which Senator Ted Cruz attacked Donald Trump for having "New York values." In the skit, Senator Cruz is asked to explain what he means by "New York values," and after initially dodging the question, he finally answers: "Believe me, if I could say liberal Jews, I would." [15]

The strongest disdain of liberal Judaism is expressed by Jews themselves. Unshackled from accusation of being anti-Semites, Orthodox Jews and politically conservative Jews are at the forefront of expressing disdain at liberal Jews and outlets associated with liberal Judaism such as *The New York Times*. Those conservative Jews can say what other conservatives cannot.

For this group, strong support of Israel is paramount. The liberal Jews' attack on Israel is loathed. To a large extent, this group is already in Judaism 3.0, having Israel as a key element in their Jewish identity. Some evidence already exists on how this is reflected on the ground in the political process. Jews have demonstrated multiple times that they would prefer the non-Jewish pro-Israel candidate than the Jewish candidate who shows a cold shoulder to Israel. This can be indicative that Jewish Americans would rather support a candidate who is more pro-Judaism 3.0 (pro-Zionism) than a candidate who is pro-Judaism 2.0 (simply being of Jewish heritage).

(ii) Shift in the Conservative movement

The support for Israel amongst the right is not only deep but also broad. Various groups that make up the conservative coalition in the United States support the State of Israel, each for its own set of reasons. For some conservatives, support for Israel is even a core issue on which they will decide which candidate to elect.

This is very different from conservative behavior patterns in past decades. Through the turn of the 21st century, supporting Israel in some mainstream conservative circles was viewed in the context of American oil interests in the Middle East (before that energy dynamic changed).

As the Republican party shifted, the groups that were wary about support for Israel ("old line establishment Republicans") got voted out of power and for the rising groups in the party, support for Israel is a core issue.

Christian Right

Ninety percent of Americans self-identify as believers. Hence, the religious influence of voters cannot be underestimated. Religiosity is broad and cuts across party, denominational and racial lines.

In particular, it is a core issue for the Christian Right. Many say a

---

15 – *Saturday Night Live*, January 16, 2016.

rock-solid support for Israel is a prerequisite when it comes to deciding for which candidate to vote. These dynamics played out in the 2016 Republican primaries. Candidates seeking Christians donors, supporters and voters in the South, had to prove their Pro-Israel credentials. It continued in the 2020 campaign when President Trump frequently showcased his support for Israel when speaking to Christian audiences.

Libertarians and Isolationists: Limited government

Rising groups in the Republican party are calling for less government intervention, including overseas engagements. For this group, support for Israel is also driven by the strong alliance and ability to rely on Israel in the war on terrorism and protection of American interests in the region, in lieu of sending American forces.

This came to bear in the 2018 announcement to withdraw US troops from Syria. President Trump said: "We give Israel $4.5 billion a year. And they're doing very well defending themselves."

Alt-Right

The Alt-Right is a diverse group, with diverging attitudes towards Israel and Judaism. Like the Alt-Left, this is a loosely defined group that is not unified nor hierarchical. Elements of Alt-Right are outright Jew-haters, racists, bigots, neo-Nazis and white-supremacists, while others are anti-establishment far-right Americans that include pro-Israeli Jews.

The images of mobs identified as Alt-Right yelling "Jews will not replace us" in Charlottesville is entrenched in the American mind. President Biden stated that this was an impetus for him to run for President. But there are also those identified as Alt-Right who express disdain at the establishment, but do not engage in such hateful activities.

Many in this part of the Alt-Right display strong passionate support for Israel, while at the same time they express outright passionate criticism of liberal Jews. This is manifested in Alt-Right websites that are owned or managed by Jews such as *Breitbart* and *DailyWire*. Given this dichotomy between outright dismay to liberal Jews on the one hand, and outright admiration for Israel on the other, the recognition of the transformation of Judaism would have a monumental effect on this group's perception of Judaism. From disdain (Judaism 2.0 – liberal Jews), to admiration (Judaism 3.0 – Israel).

Military families

Military families tend to be more national-security conscious and supportive of Israel as America's strong ally in the Middle East. These families tend to be more value-driven and, from an interest point of view, happy that Israel is a client of the US Defense industry.

Since military personnel tend to come less from Jewish-concentrated areas such as New York and Los Angeles, for many in the military, the primary interaction with Judaism is done through interaction with Israelis – be it Israeli soldiers they train with or Israeli defense officials they interact with. This supports the transformation to Judaism 3.0 as, for this group, there is a greater association of Judaism with Israel.

(iii) The Shift away from Liberal-Conservative divide and rise of the Unaffiliated

There is a bigger shift in American politics that has a far-reaching effect on American Judaism. There is a shift away from the Liberal-Conservative divide and the rise of anti-establishment forces on the left, right, and unaffiliated. This is especially the case with young Americans.

Anti-establishment and Zionism

A global wave of anti-establishment bears some resemblance to the revolutionary movement of 1848 and even the French Revolution. Establishment is out. One of the staples of the establishment in the US is the Jews (Judaism 2.0). For many, the symbol of such establishment power is AIPAC, the pro-Israel lobbying group which is perceived by many as "the Jewish lobby." One of the characteristics of the anti-establishment wave is that there is a tendency to prioritize anti-establishment sentiment above political opinion. Hence, in Italy a coalition formed from left-wing populism and right-wing populism. In the US, Trump attempted to court Bernie Sanders' voters in the 2016 match against Hillary Clinton. Those anti-establishment voters have a joint-interest: The transfer of power from AIPAC and other Washington special-interest and lobbying groups to the people.

The anti-establishment wave not only suggests that the old Jewish establishment and Judaism 2.0 is falling out of favor, it also insinuates that even those opposed to Zionism can empathize with a transformation of Judaism away from the establishment forces of the past (Judaism 2.0), to a more relevant expression of contemporary Judaism (Judaism 3.0). This was already reflected in the 2016 and 2020 presidential election cycle.

Trumpism and Bernieism

The rise of Donald Trump and Bernie Sanders in 2016, which carried through the 2020 campaign, also has a strong long-lasting effect on Judaism in America. In both movements, there is a subtle discomfort with American Judaism (Judaism 2.0).

Trumpism and Bernieism are to a large extent energized by the rejection of establishment power, as well as that of the millionaires and billionaires, the excessive power of Wall Street, of lobbyist, of "deep state" and of insiders. Indeed, while not intended as such, there might be a sub-talk (subliminal?) of rejection of what could be perceived as old "Jewish power." And yet, both of these groups like to engage on Israel. In the case of Trump voters, pro-Israel; in the case of Sanders' voters, many were energized by his criticism of Israel.

Indeed, for both crowds, Israel is THE Jewish issue. The Jewish issue is about Judaism 3.0 and not about Judaism 2.0.

Trump has showcased his support for the Jewish community through Israel-related actions, such as relocating the United States embassy to Jerusalem and recognizing Israeli sovereignty over the Golan Heights.

Bernie Sanders, interestingly, has distanced himself from Judaism. Debbie Wasserman Schultz, DNC Chair in 2016, distanced him even further when she reportedly suggested portraying him as a non-Jewish atheist. Yet, when it came to Israel, there was no such distancing – Sanders was proud and open to have lived on a kibbutz. His adversaries as well as journalists even suggested that he holds Israeli citizenship, which Sanders denied and took issue with, but not in a manner that suggests he rejects Israel.

Sanders seems to distance himself from his Judaism affiliation (Judaism 2.0), but not his Israel affiliation (Judaism 3.0).

10. Conclusion: America is already in Judaism 3.0

Changing dynamics in America support the transformation of Judaism. The broader American public relates to Judaism more naturally through Zionism and Israel (Judaism 3.0) than it does through the secular form of Rabbinic Judaism (Judaism 2.0). This is in part because America and Israel are both religious societies, while American Jews are not. The unshakable bond between Americanism and Zionism dates back to the founding principles of America. The success of Zionism strengthens the ideology of the American Revolution and contributes to its contemporary defense from attempts to erode it. On the other hand, American Jews are perceived to be importers of European values of universalism that are in conflict with key principles of the American Revolution. The embrace of cultural pluralism and popularity of heritage identity in America makes it more palatable for an American Jew to center his Jewish identity around Israel, and to be proud of his ethnological national affiliation.

Strong bipartisan political alliance with Israel, as well as the popularity of Israeli products and experience by the broader American public, makes Israel and Zionism the more relatable aspect of Judaism for Americans.

The American Jew increasingly relates to Zionism as a byproduct of being American, not just as a byproduct of being Jewish. America being in Judaism 3.0 does not just enable, but also makes it inevitable for American Jews to recognize the transformation to Judaism 3.0.

VIII

The External Environment – World

Judaism has historically been defined by the outside. That outside has persistently viewed Jews as a nation. This is evident today in the evolution of the age-old opposition to Judaism – now funneled through Zionism, and in the evolution of the embrace of Judaism – now directed towards the Jewish state. To understand these Judaism 3.0 realities, one must first place the world's perception of the Jews in its historical context.

1. History of the world's relations with Judaism

The world's relationship with the Jews can be divided into three distinct periods:
– Biblical period (from the inception of Judaism until the 1st century CE exile)
– Exile period (1st century CE until the 20th century)
– Jewish state period (1948 thereafter).

In each period there were different themes governing the world's engagement with Judaism, which ultimately defined the state of Judaism.

Biblical period – Judaism 1.0's relations with the outside world

The books of the Bible, as well as archeological and historical accounts, shed light on the 1,000 years' relationship between the Jews and the surrounding powers: the Egyptians, Philistines, Arameans, Assyrians, Babylonians and Persians.

Those accounts depict cooperation and conflict, peace and war. Yet, for the most part, the relationship between Israel and the ancient world was relatively cordial.

Even the relationship with Egypt as reported in the Bible was reasonable. Pharaoh engaged with Moses and with monotheism. He could have dismissed Moses and even executed him, but instead chose to engage. The Bible itself explains that this was through God's miracle. The Egyptians liked the Israelis.

Later conflicts with nations in the Middle East were also deliberated within reason. This is described in the Bible and supported by external sources.

For example, the Israelis' conflict with their arch-rival the Philistines, was a relatively reasonable one, as expressed in the Biblical account of the David vs. Goliath duel and later in David's own relationship with the Philistines (there needs to be a degree of trust to agree to settle a geopolitical conflict through a duel instead of war).

Non-Israeli soldiers even joined the Israeli army and reached top positions, like Uriah the Hittite. Even the first exile was only inflicted after ample warnings by the Babylonians and, according to Judaism's own account (per Jeremiah), a result of political miscalculation and internal lack of faith.

Periods of peace and cooperation are broadly reported in the Bible – especially during the time of King Solomon. As a whole, the relationship of Jews to their surrounding neighbors seemed "normal." Conflicts were not driven by hate, but by competing claims.

Today, all of this is of limited relevance because none of those nations with which the Jews lived in relative peace survived. All of those ancient nations were either destroyed or assimilated out of existence.

The only two surviving nations with which the Jews interacted during the latter part of the Biblical period are not from the region, but rather invaders to the region from Europe: the Greeks and the Romans.

In the European invaders' case, the rules of engagement were completely different than they were with the local nations. That is in part because the conflict was not about issues such as land, taxes or territory. It was about eradicating Judaism and coercing by force the European way of life.

In the second century BCE, Jews began their 2,300 years of interaction with Europe – a relationship that has defined today's Judaism. Even during the Biblical era, it was marked with ups and downs. The relations with the Greeks and then the Roman invaders were not monolithic, but the mission of the European invaders to negate the Jewish way of life led to bitter conflict. This conflict carried into the next phase of world relations with the Jews.

Exile period – Judaism 2.0's relations with Europe

When Jews were exiled from their land in the 1st and 2nd century CE by the Romans, most made their way into Europe, living as refugees for 1,800 years, migrating every few centuries from one European area to another in response to orders by the authorities and as a function of developments in the European-Jewish relationship. There were Jews in the Middle East and elsewhere, but as discussed, historians estimate that 80-90% of Jews were in Europe during these times.

Deportations from England, France and Spain forced the Jews further east in Europe. Subsequent deportations in the East eventually limited the Jews to a confined area – the Pale of Settlement – where, by the 18th century, the majority of Jews resided. They lived in small towns and cities, in today's Poland and Russia, akin to living in one gigantic Jewish ghetto.

Given the Jewish concentration in Europe, the relationship of the world with the Jews was essentially the relationship Europe had with the Jews. Europe, during this period, was the dominant world power and controlled world themes.

One such global theme was that Jews were not self-defined, but consistently defined by others – e.g. by Europeans.

A turning point in the Jewish-European relationship came in the 19th century in the aftermath of the Enlightenment, the French Revolution, and the spread of the revolution's ideas to the rest of Europe through the Napoleonic wars.

Jews began migrating back to Western Europe, especially to Germany and obtained rights through the process of emancipation. However, the Jews were not accepted by European society. Only a few decades after giving them rights, Europeans, led by the Germans, took those rights away from Jews and eventually murdered them.

Current period – Judaism 3.0

The 1948 re-establishment of the Jewish state revolutionized the relationship between Jews and the world. Yet many of the old themes remain, including defining Judaism from the outside and viewing Jews as a nation.

2. JEWS WERE ALWAYS DEFINED BY THE OUTSIDE, NOT BY THEMSELVES

Jews can have endless debates about who is in the Jewish tent and who is not – debates from the point of view of Jewish law, from family connection and from the legal status.

Yet throughout history, the only definition that really mattered was how others defined the Jews.

In their long years in exile, the monarchs and sovereigns were the ones to define the relationship with Jews – their status, where they could live, in what capacities they could work and even how many children they could have.

"We are what the ghetto made us," said Herzl, and that could be expanded to all sorts of old, new and virtual ghettos till today.

The bilateral European-Jewish relationship was unilaterally driven by Europe. The definition from the outside was both for the good and the bad.

Defined by outside: In good times, by friends

It was not just the European monarchs who dictated the relationship with the Jews and defined who they were. This is still very much the case today with modern-day politicians.

Friends of the Jews often define them in a way that makes no separation between Jews and Israel.

When US President John Kennedy met Israeli Prime Minister David Ben-Gurion in May 1961, a few months after taking office, Kennedy told Ben-Gurion: "I know I got elected thanks to the Jewish vote. I owe them my election."

Kennedy's way to reward his Jewish supporters was through the prime minister of the Jewish state, so he said to Ben-Gurion, "Tell me, is there anything I should do?"

Ben-Gurion answered: "You should do what is best for the free world." [1]

When Chuck Hagel, a known supporter of Israel and of the Jewish people, was nominated in 2013 to Secretary of Defense, he came under attack by the Jewish community for using the term "Jewish lobby" instead of "Israel lobby."

In broadcastings of the State of the Union speech, when a President makes reference to Israel, the cameras typically turn to Jewish members of the audience – such as a Jewish senator.

Defined by outside: In bad times, by adversaries

When waves of Jew-hatred emerged in Europe, and the question arose of "who is a Jew?", it was those haters who determined the answer to that question. Most notable is the case of Spain in the 15th and 16th centuries, where the Inquisition and agents of the monarch were to define "who is a Jew" even amongst those who converted. Jews who left Judaism and were practicing Christians, even for generations, were still stripped of an ability to self-define themselves as non-Jews. The outside world made this determination.

When Vienna's anti-Semitic mayor Karl Lugar was asked how come

1 – Michael Bar-Zohar: "Ben-Gurion", Volume II; Page 1394 (Hebrew), per his interview with Ben-Gurion.

he had contacts with certain Jews, he answered: "I will decide who is a Jew."

Around the same time, in 1896, Paul Pacher von Theinburg, a member of the Austrian parliament, demanded that anybody who had a Jewish father or grandfather would be denied citizenship.

In the same week that von Theinburg made his proposal, the editors of the Viennese newspaper *Neue Freie Presse* claimed that they were not a Jewish paper. This was met with ridicule. A local bank manager shared with Herzl: "It is funny that the *Neue Freie Presse* people think that they are not treated as a Jewish newspaper."

Similarly, the definition of "who is a Jew?" used by the Nazis and applied throughout Europe included anyone who had a Jewish grandparent.

In all these cases, Jews had a different definition of themselves than the outside did, but the Jews' definition was irrelevant. This was the recurring theme: Jews think of themselves one way, but it is the outside world who defines them.

3. Jews being viewed by the outside in a national context, not a religious context

Until the turn of the 19th century, no Jew or non-Jew would think there is any separation between the Jewish religion and Jewish nation. They were one and the same. Historically, the Jew would say "I am Jewish" or "I am Israeli" or "I am Hebrew," but not "I am Spanish" or "I am French."

In the 19th century, French Jews obtained citizenship, which came at the expense of shedding their national Jewish identity. Suddenly, a large group of Jews began to claim that they are French who are "members of the religion of Moses." (Français de confession mosaïque.) Yet, the French terminology remained "Israeliten." This is the term that was used in official French government documents through the turn of the 20th century to describe the Jews. Perhaps this demonstrated the skepticism of the French that Jews had really abandoned their national identity. It underscored that, for the French, the Israelite nation was still the Israelite nation.

The same terminology, Israeliten, was also the designation of the Jew-haters. Before the term anti-Semitism came around in the late 19th century, a commonly used term for such Jew-hatred was Israelite-eater (Israeliten-fresser). Herzl used this to describe the Jew-hatred that was widespread in the Boulangisme movement.[2]

There was an attempt to create a distinction between an "Israelite" – a polite French Jew, and a "Juif" – the collection of the "bad Jews" – Jewish beggars, Jewish moneylenders, German-Jewish nouveau riche, Russian-Jewish immigrants and Russian ultra-Orthodox poor Jews.

This good-Jew – bad-Jew distinction did not work. A Jew is a Jew. That was made clear through the Dreyfus Affair,[3] and certainly later on during World War II.

Friends of Jews were friends of the Jewish nation

Napoleon Bonaparte had no particular interest in the Jewish religion, but he took great interest in the Jewish nation. So much interest that at the turn of the century, as it became evident that France might conquer Palestine from the Ottomans, Napoleon was prepared to re-establish the Jewish state in Palestine. This interestingly followed a similar chain of events about 100 years later with Britain. As the British advanced through North Africa, and as conquering Palestine became a realistic possibility, the desire to establish a Jewish state grew.

The "Napoleon Declaration" preceded the British Balfour Declaration by 116 years. Historians debate the seriousness of Napoleon's intention, but from his declaration, we can learn how he, and therefore, his French superiors at the time, viewed the Jews. This is evident by the way he addressed his declaration to the Jews: "Bonaparte, Commander-in-Chief of the armies of the French Republic in Africa and Asia, to the rightful heirs of Palestine..."[4]

In his letter, Napoleon states that the Jews are a nation: "Israelites, a unique nation, whom, in thousands of years, lust of conquest and tyranny, have been able to be deprived of their ancestral lands, but not of name and national existence!"

Napoleon continued with treating Jews as a nation after he took power, most notably in establishing the Jewish Sanhedrin in 1806.

Ninety years later, an Anglican priest in Vienna showed up at the

---

2 – General Georges Ernest Boulanger, a hero of the 1871 France-Prussia war, led a diverse populist nationalist anti-establishment movement in France that was viewed as a threat to mainstream French republicanism. Amongst Boulanger's supporters were Jew-haters that later were instrumental in the Dreyfus Affair. For more on Boulangisme and Jew-hatred, see Theodor Herzl: "Die Boulangisten", Neu Free Press, Oct 14, 1891.

3 – See Michael Robert Marrus: "The politics of assimilation: a study of the French Jewish community at the time of the Dreyfus Affair".

4 – See Natan Shor: "Napoleon's journey in the Holy Land" (Hebrew).

doorsteps of Theodor Herzl. Reverend William Hechler gave Zionism its biggest breakthrough in its early days. Hechler was a religious Christian. His passion was not the Jewish religion, but the Jewish nation. He introduced Herzl to German nobility, and eventually to the German Kaiser himself – Wilhelm II. This demonstrated to the Jews that Herzl was received by world leaders, and this demonstrated to the world that Zionism was a real movement.

In the years that followed, many other Christians have shared this passion. When they thought of Jews, they thought of the Jewish nation and not the Jewish religion. This was evident by the choice of word in the London Times headlines a few days after the Balfour Declaration was issued: "Palestine to the Jews."

Adversaries of Jews were adversaries of the Jewish nation

As we see in episodes that follow, not only were Jews defined in terms of their national affiliation, but also attempts by Jews to self-define themselves, in terms of their religion, failed miserably. The outside world insisted on defining Jews as a Jewish nation.

SPANISH INQUISITION

During the time of the Spanish Inquisition, Jews believed they could be the ones to define themselves. Given the option to convert to Christianity or leave Spain, some decided to convert and hence, end their association with Judaism. But it was not up to the Jews to define themselves, or to decide if they left Judaism.

Being conversos had placed them under the auspices of the Church and the institutions of the Inquisition. That gave the legal grounds for facilitating persecution of the now-converted Jews and to the murder of many of them. Those Spanish Jews might have thought they had become Christians, but others defined them in terms of who they really were – members of the Jewish nation.

Throughout history, Europe has been using seemingly legal packaging to persecute Jews. This in turn gives Jew-haters the illusion of credibility, and that was indeed the case in one of the most notable cases of state-sponsored Jew-hatred, spanning multiple branches of the French government, media, military and social circles.

DREYFUS AFFAIR

If there was one place where Jews should have felt comfortable that they were no longer defined by their Jewish national affiliation, but rather by their Jewish religious affiliation, it was France in the late 19th century.

At last, Jews were citizens! Jews were French. Jews had equal rights.

After all, the Jews disavowed their national affiliation in a systematic and official manner. Napoleon gathered the Sanhedrin. The Jews welcomed it, accepted conditions to become French, which included the implicit shedding of their Jewish national affiliation, and becoming part of the French nation – or so they thought. The French public and its leadership did not really accept this.

A few decades later, the reactionary forces against such Jewish rights became organized and vocal. These forces still viewed the Jews as being part of the Jewish nation. The Jews took comfort in the false notion that such was only the works of a few, but soon, they would learn that the anti-Jewish movement went up and down the highest echelons of government, across the military, civil service, civil society and the entire republic.

This fact was reflected in Eduard Drumont's 1885 book *La France Juive*, which became one of the most popular and well-read books of the time. Drumont established and managed the newspaper *La Libre Parole* that instigated against the Jews and those non-Jewish politicians who were trying to defend them.

In referring to Jews, Drumont uses the common term "Israelites." For him, the focus was on the Jewish nation, the Israelites – "these people are the problem and they are the people who are taking over France." He went after those who gave rights to the Jews. In particular, Napoleon, who according to Drumont, was a Jew – not part of the Jewish nation, but part of that sociological ilk. So were Napoleon's Marshal Ney and Massena. (A similar accusation was repeated 150 years later in Erdogan's Turkey about Kemal Ataturk – the father of secular Turkey).

Drumont's voice was suppressed by the courts and liberal society, but similar voices were heard in the Boulanger movement. They, too, were silenced. But by the mid-1890s the silent voices found an outlet. On the surface, the Belle-Epoque was a joyful time (1871-1914) and euphoria ran high in anticipation of a new exciting century, and hence, the affair caught Jews by surprise.

Alfred Dreyfus, who certainly did not consider himself as part of the Jewish nation, was a proud Frenchman. As a French patriot and a member of the French nation, he joined the French army and excelled. In December 1894, he was arrested for treason, accused of giving secrets to the Germans. A decade later, he was exonerated and details emerged about the broad and wide conspiracy to take him down for one simple reason – he was a Jew.

The Dreyfus Affair was not just about a single-episode of anti-Semitism and a single victim. It showed the broad coalition that members of the government, military, civil service and society would build in order to express their disdain at Jews and rejection of the notion that the Jews were welcomed in the French nation, and even dare claim that they are part of it.

The Dreyfus Affair also exposed the popular hatred towards Jews. Even when facts became clear of his innocence, the opposition to Dreyfus was immense. Drumont and others took to the streets. For him and many others, the trial and exoneration of Dreyfus became a battle between France and the Jews.

HOLOCAUST

The definition of Judaism for the Nazis was based on the Jewish nation and not on the Jewish religion. This was not against practicing or non-practicing Jews, but against any person, of any age, associated with the Jewish nation.

Jewish babies, children, women, the elderly, those in hiding, those on the run, those whose families were once Jewish, those who had a Jewish grandparent, they were all forced to define themselves by their Jewish national affiliation and not by their religious affiliation.

ETHNIC CLEANSING OF MIDDLE EASTERN JEWS

The experience of Middle Eastern Jews underscores how artificial was the attempt to separate Jews from Israel, or reject the externally driven definition of Jews as a nation.

As soon as the State of Israel was declared, the local Arab governments and incited mobs ethnically cleansed the Jewish population and forced them to leave. This was for one reason only: they were Jewish; the Middle East viewed these Jews as part of the Jewish nation.

Analysis Of Conflict And Hate Shows That The World Is In Judaism 3.0

4. EVOLUTION OF JEW-HATRED

Jew-hatred has existed since the beginning of Jewish time. The form of hatred evolved with changing European circumstances as well as with Jewish developments. Through the Middle Ages, it was "easy" to hate the Jews, because they were a separate insular group. Jews were refugees in Europe – weaklings with no rights.

But since the French Revolution and gradually through the 19th century, Jews gained rights like everybody else. Suddenly, Jews were seen in cafes of Europe, in the workplace, in government, in theaters – everywhere.

Shifts in the relationship to Jews/Israel

The revolutionary idea of Jews as French was not accepted by many in France, just like Jews becoming German was not accepted by many in Germany. Therefore, granting Jews' rights was soon met with a counter-movement.

Anti-Semitism appeared toward the end of the 19th century and quickly rose in popularity to counter Jewish emancipation. It was a mainstream movement, perhaps somewhat akin to contemporary movements opposing the rise of Muslim immigrants in Europe.

Herzl wrote from Paris in 1892: "Till recently anti-Semitism in France has been something comfortable and polite, one can even say pleasant." At that time, Herzl sought to penetrate Parisian social circles and maintained contact with proud anti-Semites. One of them, novelist Alphonse Daudet, even advised him on the best way to get his Zionist ideas out – suggesting a novel would reach farther than a manifesto. (Herzl opted for the manifesto – *The Jewish State*.)

Herzl later wrote in his diary: "In Paris, I gained a more liberated attitude towards anti-Semitism, which I began to understand historically and to pardon."

But just like with today's socially driven Israel-bashing, Herzl recognized that this polite and pleasant fashion could turn dangerous. He wrote: "Anti-Semitism is a meeting point of the unsatisfied, sort of a salon of the deprived."

(i) Haters of Jews: From anti-Semitism (Judaism 2.0) to Israel-bashing (Judaism 3.0)

In the 1920s, German and Western European Jews lived in emancipation, in freedom. They had a sense of an "end of history," end of anti-Semitism. At last, they had rights. The aftermath of World War I made the emancipation widespread in Western Europe. A Jew became Germany's foreign minister and a Jew was soon to become France's prime minister (both were later murdered).

Similarly, in the 2020s Jews in Europe and around the world live in freedom and emancipation. But regretfully, Jew-hatred is alive and well.

In its current iteration it is not directed against the Jewish individual, as it is against the Jewish collective (Israel).

Indeed, the establishment of Israel in the 20th century allowed Jew-haters to funnel their hate to a tangible target. This came at an "opportune time" as expressing disdain towards the individual Jew – a European fashion until the 1940s – became unfashionable and taboo in the aftermath of the Holocaust. Indeed, the era where anti-Semitism was the popular expression of Jew-hatred has subsided and in its place Israel-bashing has become the new popular expression of Jew-hatred. Just like anti-Semitism which preceded it, after a few decades of brewing, Israel-bashing has now grown into a fashion and a culture, increasingly penetrating the mainstream of society. This is not just in Europe, but also in certain circles in the United States and around the world.

It should be made clear that most of the criticism against Israel is legitimate and must be protected and welcomed, even the harshest ones, even if viewed as misinformed or unfair. But equally, it is clear that the fashion of Israel-bashing is a new manifestation of Jew-hatred. This includes the attacks on Israel's right to defend itself, holding the Jewish state to radically different standards than other states, as well as blood-libels such as of Israeli genocide of Palestinians. Israel-bashing is turning into broad and socially acceptable fashion.

(ii) Putting distance has historically been ineffective and irrelevant

In each era, some Jews attempted to distance themselves from Judaism in order to protect themselves. This was proven ineffective – others were the ones to decide. In the 19th century, some Jews thought they were immune because they were secular and the hate was only directed against the Jewish religion. In 20th-century Germany, some Jews thought they were immune because they were perfectly assimilated Germans, and the hate was only directed against the Russian Jewish masses (not anti-Semitism, but merely anti-Russian-Semitism).

Similarly, in the 21st century some Jews might think that keeping a safe distance from Israel will immunize them from Israel-bashing. History shows that they are wrong, but more alarming is that so does the present – once again, demonstrating that whether they like it or not, Jews are defined externally by their Jewish national affiliation – Zionism.

(iii) Parallels between this and previous episodes

The parallels to previous episodes are alarming. Again, there is widespread dismissal. Like before, the denial is due to the focus on the previous incarnation of Jew-hatred. For example, in the 19th century, the notion that Europe had become secular and therefore, there was no such thing as Jew-hatred.

Like in previous episodes, there were accusations of paranoia, allegations that Jews have brought it upon themselves and rationalization that the hate was not directed at Jews, but merely at a subset of Jews. This was both by Europeans ("some of my best friends are Jewish") and by Jews themselves.

Another daunting parallel was how socially accepted and even fashionable the Jew-hatred movements became after those few decades of brewing. In the late 19th century, it took a few decades after the emancipation of Jews for the creation and popularity of the anti-Semitism movement. Today, it took a few decades after the establishment of the State of Israel for the creation and popularity of the Israel-bashing movement.

(iv) Jew-hatred came from Europe

Jew-hatred is a European concept. Jew-hatred throughout history originated and developed in Europe. This was to a large extent due to the fact that the vast majority of the Jews resided in Europe. That was the arena in which the world met the Jews during the last 2,000 years, and hence, that is where the world developed its opposition to the Jews. Even earlier, the opposition to the Jews came from Europe (Romans, Greeks).

Even episodes of Jew-hatred in the Middle East were instigated by Europe. Most notably, the Damascus blood libels of the 1840s were instigated by French diplomats.

Europe exported its opposition to the Jews, along with its other philosophies to its conquests and sphere of influence. Some historians claim Muslim brutality, expressed through terrorism, was possibly learned by the invading Europeans during the crusades, who deployed techniques never seen before in the region – such as outright massacring the entire population of a city once conquered by the Europeans.

(v) Europe – Jewish relationship – 2,300 years of conflict

As discussed, the transformation from Judaism 2.0 to Judaism 3.0 suggests that Zionism is a continuation of Judaism, certainly not a break from it. This is indeed the case when it comes to the relationship of Europe with Judaism. Its relation with Israel is a continuation of that relationship, not a break from it.

It would be dilettante and silly to pretend Europe-Israel relations began with the 1948 establishment of the State of Israel, just as it would be dilettante and silly to pretend French-German relations began in 1871 with the establishment of German Empire.

The European-Israeli conflict is the oldest conflict in the world, lasting for 2,300 years. The Palestinian-Israeli dispute is merely a footnote to the European-Israeli feud. While it had long periods of peace or containment (at times lasting for centuries), the Europe-Israel relationship has repeatedly cycled back to conflict following such periods.

The feud dates back to Greek and then Roman invasions to Judea. While other nations accepted the European invaders, the Jews rebelled. Centuries later, as a byproduct of those conquests, Europeans astonishingly accepted the Jews' monotheistic religion in the form of Christianity.

As Europe switched from paganism to monotheism, Europe and Israel enjoyed a brief period of acceptance. During this honeymoon of European-Jewish relations, Jewish life flourished. Europe did not stand in the way of Jewish accomplishment, such as the canonization of the Mishna. But shortly thereafter, the conflict re-emerged, this time in the form of a "brotherly feud," as Europe refused to contain the residual Jewish religion. Jewish refugees, expelled by Europe from their land, were subjected to persecution in Europe for the coming centuries.

In the 11th century, Europe's conflict with Israel escalated as the crusaders coerced European Jews to "kiss the cross" or die. They then proceeded to Jerusalem and slaughtered the city's Jews alongside their Muslim brethren. But the Jews were able to persevere.

In a period of great camaraderie between Europe and Israel, Jews thrived in places they were permitted to reside, such as in Spain. But the Jewish success led to competition, which served as the primary driver for their expulsion. Similar deportations occurred in England and France.

The religious persecution expanded through the centuries into new technologies and accusations. In the blood-libels, Jews were accused of using the blood of Christian children to make Passover matzah and perform religious rituals.

When the era of enlightenment arrived, and Europe turned secular, Jews again breathed a sigh of relief. Indeed, the mid-19th century were halcyon days in Europe-Israel relations and most Jews felt that Jew-hatred was a relic of the ancient past. But by the end of that century, Jew-hatred reinvented itself in the form of national and racial hatred, and a new term began to be used: anti-Semitism.

The period after the Holocaust and the establishment of the State of Israel mitigated anti-Semitism as an existential threat to Jews. But once again, Jew-hatred has come out of hiding. This time, towards the collective of Jews – the thriving State of Israel, demonstrating once again the common thread in the European-Jewish relationship: Regardless of how Jews like to self-define themselves, it is the outside world that ultimately defines the Jews.

(vi) An honest conversation about Jew-hatred

Jew-hatred is not the same as anti-Semitism

As mentioned in the introduction, there has been a confusion of terms. Anti-Semitism is new. It originated in the 19th century. Jew-hatred, on the other hand, has existed since the beginning of Jewish time. As the world evolved, so did the reason (or excuse) for Jew-hatred. When the world (led by Europe) was religious Christian, the hatred was funneled into the differences between Christianity and Judaism. When Europe turned secular, a new form of Jew-hatred emerged, based on national and racial grounds and was later named anti-Semitism.

Anti-Semitism became the term used for Jew-hatred, in a similar manner that Xerox became the term used for making a copy, and Rabbinic Judaism for Judaism. Yet, one needs to be careful not to confuse anti-Semitism, which is a form of Jew-hatred, with the actual concept of Jew-hatred. Similarly, one needs to be careful not to address Jew-hatred through anti-Semitism or to assume that if anti-Semitism goes away, so does Jew-hatred. That was exactly the false assumption made in the 18th and 19th century as Europe became secular. Jews thought that since religious-based hatred had been massively reduced, so had Jew-hatred. They were wrong.

Religious-based hatred was reduced, but Jew-hatred remained strong. Indeed, the haters in Europe have historically adjusted based on the prevailing fashion of Europe: religion, secularism, liberalism, human-rights, post-nationalism, post-colonialism. There is room for Jew-hatred in any one of these constructs.

Like in the 19th century, a reduction in anti-Semitism, or commitment to fight it, does not mean a reduction of Jew-hatred. It could simply mean a switch of form of hatred due to a switch in European circumstances. Indeed, in today's construct this hatred is directed through Zionism and the State of Israel.

Anti-Semitism analyzed only through the eyes of the Jews

Analysis of Jew-hatred and anti-Semitism tends to be done through the eyes of the Jew. Political correctness and mostly the shock of the

Holocaust prohibits any other points of view.

Asking if Jews brought this upon themselves is considered an anti-Semitic question by itself. It is akin to the "battered wife syndrome" – where the abused wife rationalizes the violence of her husband through her own deeds.

Both the Jewish and the non-Jewish world today are united in rejecting anti-Semitism – e.g. anti-Judaism 2.0 – but not in rejecting anti-Zionism and Israel-bashing.

So while the question "did Jews bring anti-Semitism upon themselves" is considered anti-Semitic, such questions are accepted as legitimate and indeed often asked when it comes to other forms of Jew-hatred.

Does legitimizing anti-Judaism 3.0 (Israel-bashing) also legitimize anti-Judaism 2.0 (anti-Semitism)?

This is indeed the case with Israel-bashing. The suggestion that Israel invites terrorism because of its own actions is a common claim, and not just by radicals or others in the fringe. World leaders, professors, journalists all suggested the same.

As long as Israel-bashing is not viewed as Jew-hatred, such accusations of Jews bringing it upon themselves are considered legitimate. But Israel-bashing is indeed the current iteration of age-old Jew-hatred and is certainly not analyzed from the point of view of the Jews. Therefore, if it is okay to apply the question if Jews brought Israel-bashing upon themselves, then perhaps it is time to also apply this question back to anti-Semitism and other forms of Jew-hatred that existed in the past. Did Jews invite anti-Semitism? Did Jews invite Jew-hatred?

Is Zionism anti-Semitism?

When Herzl asked that exact question – he concluded that the answer was yes! Hence, Herzl was bestowed with the title given to him by his supervising editor as an "honorary anti-Semite." In fact, Herzl was accused of inviting anti-Semitism himself, by "raising his head" and supposedly suggesting that Jews are members of the Jewish nation and therefore cannot be viewed as French patriots, or British or Germans – something he never argued. In addition, he was accused that he essentially joined the anti-Semites' call "out with the Jews" by making the exact call (i.e. to Palestine). Moreover, by elevating his stature and the stature of his movement, meeting with world leaders and spreading his vision, he created a perception that he represented the Jews. He therefore, by this argument, gave a "kosher certificate" to anti-Semitism.

Was Biblical Jew-hatred caused by the Jews?

Herzl was not the first person who was accused of bringing on anti-Semitism. Possibilities of Jews bringing it upon themselves date back to the very beginning of Judaism, raising the age-old question: Is Jew-hatred "justified?"

Indeed, the two most commonly used demonstrations of the prototype of Jew-hatred in the Bible are in the case of Egypt and of Persia. When rabbis, professors and politicians discuss anti-Semitism and Jew-hatred, they often point to those cases as evidence that Jew-hatred is organic, ancient and deep. But also in those cases, if one is brave enough to apply the same framework used with Israel-bashing today, then the answers might be surprising.

EGYPT

If one claims that Israel brought Israel-bashing upon itself, then this person inevitably must also understand the Egyptian's perspective. Joseph, a Hebrew, came in from outside. He quickly amassed power and promoted the sectoral interests of his family. It was Joseph who deprived the Egyptians of their assets and eventually of the land on which they lived on for generations (in exchange for subsidy). This, while bringing his own people and providing them a large chunk of land in Goshen. Generations later, as displaced Egyptian refugees recovered from the shocking events surrounding the famine, they saw the Israelis prosper and multiple. Not only that, the Egyptians saw the Israelis proceed to launch an ideological rebellion against Egypt and the Pharaoh, exactly as Egyptian intelligence warned. This included the deaths of the Egyptian firstborn, and to add insult to injury, the "borrowing" of Egyptian equipment as they left Egypt. Was it not the Israelis who brought upon themselves the misery inflicted on them by the Egyptians?

PERSIA

Similarly, if one claims that Israel brought Israel-bashing upon itself, then this person inevitably must also understand the Persian perspective. In the Book of Esther, Mordechai the Jew refused to bow to the deputy to the King – as if not accepting the rule of the kingdom he lived in, as if not being grateful for all that the Persians did for the Jews. This is stunning, considering that the Persians did something unprecedented – they allowed the Jews to return to their land, reclaim their capital Jerusalem, and even rebuild the Jewish Temple.

Was it not Mordechai who brought upon the Jews that horrible decision to eliminate the Jews? Persia had a right to self-defense, and when Mordechai started a rebellion by not bowing, was it not him forcing Persia to act?

SAME TODAY: JUDAISM 2.0

Indeed, if one claims that Israel brought Israel-bashing upon itself, then this person inevitably must also understand today's perspectives of the anti-Semites: Jews are wealthy, Jews are pioneers of globalization, and are clearly on the beneficiary side of the digital-divide. Jews are influential and have a disproportionate amount of power – they hold key positions in governments and media outlets, worldwide.

The Egyptian, Persian and anti-Semite cases show that when Jew-hatred is viewed from the point-of-view of the hater, it can be rationalized. Indeed, same in the case with Israel-bashing. If one argues that Israel-bashing is "understandable" given Israel's policies, one must argue the same with the other iterations of Jew-hatred, including 20th-century anti-Semitism. Or in reverse, since the behavior of Jew-haters in these episodes is considered inexcusable, so is that of the Israel-bashers.

Perhaps a key lesson from the previous episodes of Egypt and of Persia is to know when it is time to go home! The failure to go home when that path was available led to entrenchment, to addiction to the fleshpots of Egypt and Persia. That in turn led to opposition to Judaism. Same was the case in Europe, but then came two disrupters that altered the course of history.

5. DISRUPTERS TO JEW-HATRED

Until the 20th century, Europe dominated the world. Not only the preponderance of the global "GDP" and power structure was in Europe, but Europeans also influenced much of what was happening in Asia, Africa and America. This was both through dominating trade and later through their colonies. But the shift of power from Europe to the United States, followed by decolonialization that was forced on Europe and its eventual loss of its global leadership and economic strength, all contributed to the disruption in Jew-hatred. To say it bluntly, the shift of global power away from Europe was also a shift away from chronic Jew-hatred.

While on the one hand, a less Euro-centric world is a world with less Jew-hatred, on the other hand, the loss of relevancy and power is by itself a source of new European frustrations that should worry individual Jews, the Jewish nation and the Jewish state. That is in particular because Europeans have historically dealt with new frustrations they encountered by blaming the Jews.

The loss of European dominance is not the only cause for a reduction in Jew-hatred. There are two primary disputers that dramatically altered the evolution of Jew-hatred:

(i) First Disrupter – creation of the United States (new Zion)

America came to the world through a revolution of ideas – rebelling against European dogmas. Americans gained freedom of religion, freedom of worship, freedom of creativity and freedom from deeply rooted European perceptions and notions. This included freedom from European opposition to Judaism.

Europe's conflict with the Jews spanned a broad range of fronts and has lasted for centuries. It was so rooted in the core ethos of Europe that only a revolution in the magnitude of the American Revolution could liberate the human mind from the shackles of European opposition to the Jews. First and foremost, through the values of the American Revolution, Americans liberated themselves from the eternal European practice of blaming the Jews for Europe's own problems. That was the practice that had been deployed by Europe when it encountered a new woe: wars, Black-Death, famine. The American Revolution countered this European blame-game by replacing it with a strong notion of self-determination and accountability – concepts foreign to Europe, long living in a feudal system and under monarchy.

Indeed, core to the American Revolution was taking control of one's destiny. This is a sharp departure from European dependency on the monarch who was believed to be God's representative on earth and hence, the source of prosperity and the one Europeans must depend upon. This revolutionary idea meant that Americans no longer needed to thank the monarch when things were good, nor blame the Jews when things were bad.

America had a direct relationship with God. They rebelled against the Divine-right monarchy, and created a Divine-right republic instead: one nation, under God. Indeed, a cornerstone of the new American nation was Judeo-Christian values. That has been core to the American narrative since it was founded and remains so through today.

This is also a sharp break from Europe, where there was never such a thing as Judeo-Christian values. Europe simply had Christian values while "Judeo" was perceived as a "problem" (or later, at better times, a "question").

Not only that, but as America solidified its unison around such Judeo-Christian values, Europe moved away from Christian values and into deep secularism. This disruption was paramount to the attitudes towards the Jews:

The American Revolution was about the rebuilding of Jerusalem, about Zionism. Europe, in many ways, has been about moving away from Jerusalem, about negating Zionism.

As will be discussed, the American Revolution was about a shift from Divine-right monarchy to Divine-right republic. The Europeans have pivoted from Divine-right monarchy to no Divine at all.

(ii) Second disrupter – creation of the State of Israel (old Zion)

The establishment of the State of Israel served as a radical disrupter to European Jew-hatred:

(a) European Jew-haters can no longer bully the weakling. The weakling now has its own state, its own army, its own might.

(b) The imbalanced equation that existed for centuries was violated. The Jews were no longer "a guest who never hosts." Jews turned from being refugees into "homeowners."

The establishment of the Jewish state caused not only a linear disrupter in the European attitude towards the Jew, it also forced the European to rethink his philosophy, core beliefs and prejudices towards the Jew.

Re-examination of the relationship with the Jews – the Suffering Remnant

The European relations towards the Jew have been deeply rooted since the beginning of European-Christian civilization in the core notions of Replacement Theology and the Suffering Remnant.

For centuries, Europeans were taught that the misery of the Jews was due to their sins and their subsequent rejections of Jesus. A notion was instilled that Jews would stay in such misery forever, as a reminder for what happens to those who reject Jesus – the so-called Suffering Remnant.

Indeed, for Europeans, Jewish misery has reaffirmed one's own European existence. It has been core to the philosophy of a European's own being. Replacement Theology suggests that the Jews did wrong, and hence, the baton was passed to the Christians as the chosen people. The Jews themselves provided support for this notion with one of the key principles of Rabbinic Judaism (Judaism 2.0): We Jews were exiled due to our sins.

Consequently, for Europeans, a weak Jew has been a natural core aspect of life. Moreover, any sign that the Jews are no longer weak would run in sharp contradiction to this core notion, and hence, the Jew gaining strength would present an existential crisis for the European. In other words, European Christians as the chosen people can only be relevant while the Jew is weak. That was the case for centuries – in the Roman era, in early European Christianity, the Middle Ages and through to modern times. Yet, in recent centuries, the Church moved away, 180 degrees, from this notion.

The Protestant and then Catholic Church reversed course and disavowed previous beliefs, as well as the Church's desire to keep the Jews weak. Therefore, religious Christians today not only have the tools to deal with a strong Jew, but by their own belief and Church guidance, are supportive of such strengthening of Judaism. For them, a strong Jew is now an expression of their own Christian faith; A strong Jew generates Christian pride.

Secular Europe stuck in Replacement Theology of the Middle Ages

Secular Christians do not have the tools of the religious Christians. For many of them, there is this distant memory, some notion deep inside that for some reason, a strong Jew is a negation of their own existence. Such secular Europeans ended their religious evolution when their ancestors turned secular and hence, were not beneficiary to the shift in the Church's thinking. They "froze in time" when it came to the Christians' treatment of Jews, as a result of their religious "arrested development."

Hence, in a sense, such secular Europeans are today's baton-carriers of the Middle Ages' Church treatment towards the Jews. Secular Europeans are the baton-carriers of the residual notion of Jews as the Suffering Remnant – of Jews needing to stay weak as a prerequisite for the Europeans' own existence.

A religious Christian, hearing a sermon about the Jews rejecting Jesus, would use it to strengthen his ties to Judaism and mostly to Zionism. A secular Christian passing by and overhearing that same sermon, even with a degree of skepticism and agnosticism, would use it to reaffirm his disdain for the Jews.

At some subconscious level of the secular European, the Jew being mighty and the Jewish state thriving is an outright negation of his own core-being. It is a zero-sum game.

Jewish success happened too soon

The Jewish state's astonishing success over the last 20 years came too soon. Israel's sudden success – in security, economy, innovation, technology – was simply too fast and too difficult to swallow for the secular European. After centuries of indoctrination, a much longer adjustment period is needed. This too is consistent with European past behavior: Europeans could tolerate the weak Jew ("digestible element"). They could contain the presence of the weak Jew in the Middle Ages, in modern times, through the Holocaust and in the early days of Israel when the Jewish state was struggling.

When Jewish success happens too rapidly, Europeans produce a dangerous counter-reaction. This was the case in the 19th century when Jews suddenly became strong as a result of the emancipation. In reaction to that strengthening, Jew-hatred mushroomed. The hate was directed towards the rich Jews who amassed wealth in the aftermath of obtaining citizen rights. Later, the hate was also directed at the so-called "Stock-exchange Jews" who profited immensely at the end of the 19th century and early 20th century. And the hate continued towards Jews that were taking European jobs and doing well – in law, medicine and journalism.

Now for the first time, it is not individual Jews, but the entire Jewish nation that is prospering – having economic, ideological, political and military might.

Can the European who was able to tolerate the weak Jewish nation also tolerate the strong Jewish nation? So far, indications show that he cannot.

As the Jewish state began to prosper in the 21st century, the European political onslaught against it increased. Some of it is running to the absurd. (Jews have no historic connection to Jerusalem?) This seems to be a reminder that Europe is not ready and maybe will never be ready to accept a strong Jew.

A strong Israel with prosperous and successful Israelis is a tangible representation of a Jew that is problematic and indigestible for such Europeans. No longer the bent down weak Shylock-looking Jew, the image of today's Israeli is a proud, tall, muscular Israeli soldier, or an attractive Israeli woman carrying a machine gun. It's no longer Barbara Streisand as Yentl in a poor Jewish shtetl. It is Gal Gadot as Wonder Woman in saving the world.

(iii) Disrupters change the essence of Judaism

Jew-hatred is a European concept. As discussed, the Europe-Jewish relationship had long periods of peace, or at least containment, but after some time they returned to conflict. The two disrupters in this cycle of hatred are game-changers in the way the world perceives the Jews, and therefore in the way Jews view themselves.

Jews are no longer on a "damage minimization" mode with Europe – a status in which they have been ever since their first encounter with Europe 2,300 years ago – awaiting the next conflict with Europeans. Similarly, the world is no longer Europe-centric.

The two disrupters to age-old European Jew-hatred are clearly occurring on the Jewish national level, and not the religious level – they are not centered on theological disrupters, such as ones that were deliberated in the 13th century Disputation of Barcelona or Vatican edicts. They are national disrupters – the establishment of the United States and of the State of Israel. Hence, this strengthens the reality that Judaism is indeed transforming and Zionism is becoming its organizing principle.

6. Europe's frustrations contribute to conflicts with the Jews

(i) Historical pattern of European frustrations directed at Jews

History shows that when a society in Europe felt humiliated, the Jews were often the ones who paid the price.

In Herzl's time, it was France's humiliating defeat by Prussia in 1870. France's loss in the French-Prussian war was devastating. It lost territories as well as its pride. The young and fragile republic was shaken to its core. This led to extreme frustrations in France, which were subsequently consumed with an ethos of Revengism. The Jews paid the price for this frustration, as was demonstrated in the events around the Dreyfus Affair and the broad anti-Semitic coalition that emerged in France during this time. In Germany itself, its subsequent humiliation in World War I led to a series of events that ended with its campaign to exterminate all the Jews.

But humiliation was not the only trigger. Hate and disdain towards Jews was amplified whenever there were frustrations of any kind in Europe. The black death was a time of great horror in Europe. After some percolating, it was the Jews who paid the price. Similar realities existed after other European pandemics.

What is more telling is that in between those periods of European frustrations in which there were attacks on Jews, there were long periods of European flourishment in which there were no broad-scale attacks on Jews. During those good European times, Jews in Europe did well.

If there was no trouble in Europe, there was no need to blame the

Jews for anything. The fact that Jews thrived when there was no trouble is highly worrisome in the context of today.

Certainly since World War II, Europe has been thriving and Jews in Europe and around the world have been living in yet another golden age. Yet, the cycle seems to be shifting. New troubles are emerging for Europe, and early signs are already there that frustrations are being taken out once again on the Jews.

Even though Europe is still early in the cycle of its built-up frustrations, it seems that some in Europe are already choosing to address their misfortunes by entering that same "salon of the deprived" that Herzl described. It is clear from early indications that the new set of frustrations developing in Europe are this time directed at Judaism through Israel. This too is indicative that Judaism has transformed, at least in the eyes of those European aggressors.

(ii) Europe's existing frustration and the future of Europe

Some in today's Europe have been amassing built-up frustrations, humiliations and anxieties. The shift of global political and economic leadership to the United States, the sudden European fall from grace and loss of its colonies, the rise of Islam in Europe, the trench war against Islamist terrorism and the emerging debate over Europe's character all have elevated such frustrations to alarming levels.

The future of Europe is under a dark cloud. On a growing number of fronts, there is anxiety and even fear. This was amplified in 2020 when Europe was hit hard with the Coronavirus, leading to thousands of deaths.

Historically, civilizations came and went. Well-learned in history and still remembering the travesty of war in their own lifetime, many in Europe are terrified. History shows that as Europeans become terrified, Jews should be worried – in this cycle – the Jewish state.

European Challenges And How They Affect The Jewish Transformation

Trench war against Islamic terrorism

Terrorism is not new to Europe. In fact, terrorism has been a permanent fixture in Europe for a long time: Anarchists of the 19th century, right-wing terrorists of the early 20th century, left-wing terrorists of late 20th century and Islamic terrorism in the turn of the 21st century.

Now, however, the threat is more potent, frequent and ubiquitous.

Europe is now in its early stages of a trench war against Islamic terrorism. This trench war has forced this generation of Europeans, who grew up in peace, into challenges they have never faced.

European response and how it affects Judaism 3.0

Europe's traditional well-tested practice to blame Jews for its woes has already been applied to the early stages of its trench war against Islamic terrorism. For a long time, European governments and the European establishment have openly promoted a narrative that if the Jewish state could solve its conflict with the Palestinians, terrorism and other Middle Eastern issues could also be resolved.

Or more bluntly, the Israeli-Palestinian conflict is a cause, or at a minimum, a contributor to the terrorism that Europeans are enduring. This is not being promoted by fringe or anti-Semitic circles. It is mainstream European policy.

Another derivative of the same myth, also broadly supported by politicians, pundits and journalists is that Europe is paying a price for its political and military support of the Jewish state. As terrorism intensifies, the notion that "we are dying for Israel" is certain to take prominence in one way or another. Indeed, the notion that if we address a "Jewish problem," we would solve Europe's woes has been a staple of European history.

In the 17th century, France established the "office of beggars and Jews." Just by the sheer act of establishing that office, the French government had created an equation that was meant to direct frustrations against the Jews. Clearly, establishing the office and directing resources towards dealing with the Jews did not end beggary. After the emancipation, there were still beggars. After the Dreyfus Affair, there were still beggars, and after World War II's extermination of French Jews, there were still beggars.

It is clear that a solution to the Jewish state's conflict with the Palestinians will have no effect on Europe's war against Islamic terrorism. Israeli or Jewish action has nothing to do with the tragedy of terrorism in Europe. Yet, an outlet is needed to direct this European frustration, as there will be a sharp rise of horrific human suffering. With such broad buy-in to the linkage of the actions of the Jewish state and European suffering, they will point their finger towards Israel.

Christianity vs. Islam

"Europe is a Christian Club" – that was the statement of the Director-General of the German foreign ministry in the early 2000s, when

Turkey was applying for membership in the European Union, reflecting European public sentiment at the time. [5]

Such European rejection of Islam was very much in the European consensus. That was when a peaceful, polite request to be included was made.

European rejection of Islam has only escalated since. Europe now prohibits Muslims from dressing as they choose, praying as they want and even speaking as they prefer (for example, coercing an Arabic radio station with an all-Arabic audience to incorporate French). [6] If European suppression of Muslims is not enough, they even engage in an attempted forced Europeanization of Muslims. While such coerced Europeanization is against the spirit of international law, which was put in place by the Europeans themselves, it has broad support throughout Europe and, in particular, in France.

Many Muslims do not want to be Europeanized. They see what is happening in European societies: Secularization, childlessness, promiscuity, obesity, depression, alcohol consumption, drugs. These are not values Muslim families want to aspire to.

While it is perfectly legitimate for the many Muslims who choose to Europeanize to do so, it is equally legitimate for Muslims not to Europeanize if they so choose.

Facing the losing arguments of logic, Europeans resort to suppression of those Muslim communities. This suppression occurs as some in Europe fear that they are in the early days of a population replacement in Europe – something that happened throughout the history in Europe (for example, in France in the 5th century and Spain in the 15th century).

Not only is there a retail component (demography) and a philosophical component (narrative), there is also an institutionalized mechanism to enable the replacement: Muslim governments funding parallel communities in the heart of Europe. [7] In a sense, this is a form of reverse-colonialism.

Following this logic, it is not too much of a stretch to ascertain that we might be in the early stages of "the War of European Succession," with the seeds of its institutional, financial, philosophical, military and political infrastructure already in place.

5 – Per Amb. Uri Bar-Ner interviewed in my article: "Europe's anti-Israel sentiment", *The Jerusalem Post*, July 2, 2016.
6 – "Radio stations rebel over French music quota", BBC, September 30, 2015.
7 – European Parliament, "Motion for a European Parliament resolution on foreign funding of radical Islam in Europe", January 21, 2020, B9-0087/2020.

European response and how it affects Judaism 3.0

The extreme frustration of inevitable conflict in Europe between Christians and Muslims poses a dire danger to Judaism. This danger is already materializing in the form of inciting the Muslims against the Jewish state as a way to "appease" the Europeans Muslims.

Every constituency has a list of things it wants to accomplish. If we can serve Israel to the Muslims, the logic goes, perhaps they will be more in cahoots with us Europeans and loosen their demands.

In addition to taming Muslim disdain towards Europe, this is viewed as a way to score political favors for a growing electoral body. Given that Muslims are approaching 10% of certain European countries, and that they are concentrated politically on the left, Labor and liberal candidates now perceive attacking Israel as an attractive way to pander to Muslim voters. This came to bear in January 2020 when French President Macron, in Israel for the World Holocaust Forum, yelled at Israeli police assigned to protect him, in what analysts claim was an orchestrated show to pander to his Muslim voters. Macron's predecessor Jacques Chirac pulled a similar stunt during his 1996 visit to Jerusalem.

Ironically, for the vast majority of French Muslim voters, Israel is not a priority, or even on their radar screen.

Seemingly, the process of Europeans inciting the Muslim population against Israel is already in advanced stages. This is in addition to the more traditional European stance of Israel as the cause for conflict in the Middle East – that if Europe pressures Israel, it will score favors with its Arab allies. This of course ignores the changes of recent years and the alliance between the Jewish state and its Sunni Arab neighbors.

Some believe that the Muslims are used as an outlet by the white Europeans to express the European anti-Semitic stance. For a white European to say something negative about the Jews or Israel is not politically correct, but if he can co-opt the Muslim to do so, then that is not just politically correct, but would even be considered politically incorrect to deny the Muslim the means to vet "his" frustrations against Jews or Israel.

Europe, throughout its history, has applied the concept of "the enemy of my enemy is my friend." They applied it in their network of alliances and treaties in the 19th century that led to World War I. They applied the concept in their colonial era, and they have instinctively applied it here. Just like before, this is riddled with falsehoods. Europeans seem to believe that if Muslims in Europe are led to believe that Europe is the "enemy" of their "enemy" – Israel, then Muslims would become the "friends" of Europe.

The European strategy has proved effective in other areas. Before shifting strategies and accepting Israel, Arab dictators tended to incite their own population against Israel as a way to deflect their own woes: The economy might be bad, freedoms are in low supply, but we have no choice since we are threatened by Israel, we are at war with Israel, we must be prepared to fight and die against Israel.

Deflecting the issues (here, the oppression of European Islam) through finding a source to "draw fire" (in this case, the Jewish state) has been used broadly in the past and will probably be used here too.

A related concept is the "sacrifice of interests." In the wake of a greater threat, a lower priority must be thrown under the bus. Such was the case with Czechoslovakia in the lead-up to World War II.

Europeans are under threat from Islam. The Jewish state needs to be sacrificed. What makes this even more alarming is that the mechanism for such sacrifices exists. Unlike in the past, Europe now has a centralized authority to direct all of the earlier deflections – the European Union. The EU is significantly less supportive of Israel than any of the governments that compose its union.

This is further enabled through the lack of transparency and accountability of the European Commission. Having a lower accountability to the public allows the EU to pursue policies that are in theory against the will of Europeans. This is akin to the "benevolent dictatorship" concept, whereby the monarch does what is really good for the people, not what the people think is good for them. The monarch sees the bigger picture, the monarch is the expert.

The existence of the EU and the highly correlated foreign policy decisions of individual European governments (such as frequently indexing UN votes to one another), makes the impact of such deflection stronger and more effective.

The Europeans' deflection and the blame is not directed at individual Jews, but rather at the Jewish state. This is further evidence that Judaism has transformed. Even in this arena, European behavior suggests it is no longer in Judaism 2.0, but in Judaism 3.0 – Zionism.

Secularism vs. Religion

Europe has been a religious society since the Middle Ages. Only in the last 200 years did a move towards secularism begin to emerge. At first, secularism was felt strongest in France. By the 21st century, secularism became Europe's "new religion."

Like in the past, this new European religion is oppressive and attempts to force its views on the remaining "heretics" (e.g. church-goers, believers and other "primitives").

If secularism is viewed as the only acceptable "religion," then Muslims being "religious" are "legitimately" left out of the European club. Moreover, with the politically correct revolution, it is much easier for Europeans to say they are against religion, than to say they are against Islam.

Along the lines of "some of my best friends are Jewish," many in Europe today are saying they have nothing against Islam, but against the burka, against the oppression of women, against the education of children to religious values, as opposed to liberal secular values.

European response and how it affects Judaism 3.0

Jerusalem is the flagship of religion. Holy to Christianity, Judaism and Islam, and the birth of Europe's legacy religion, no city is more associated with religion than Jerusalem, and hence, no country is more associated with religion than Israel.

Europe reacted to the threat of Islam with a battle against religion. The politically correct environment mandated this: "There is no problem with Islam, there is a problem with religion." Thus, if Europe is in a battle against religion, it is in a battle against Jerusalem, it is in a battle against Israel. This underscores a shifting attitude of Europe towards Zionism as it becomes more associated with religion. Support for Zionism in the past that came from the European left was based on a perception of Zionism as a liberal secular society, the perception that Zionism is secularism. This is most noted by the kibbutz, the European volunteers who went there and the romanticism around it. But as it becomes evident that the kibbutz and the secular liberal narrative is now a feature of the past, so did the European embrace of Zionism.

No longer a "secular brethren" (or perceived as such), Zionism is now an easy target in secular Europe's war against religion, and by extension against Jerusalem. This played out in the astonishing European reaction to the UNESCO resolution suggesting Jews and Christians have no historic connections to the city of Jerusalem (in addition to inciting through a new form of libel: "The continuous storming of Al-Aqsa Mosque/Al-Haram Al-Sharif by Israeli right-wing extremists and uniformed forces").

Some European countries supported or abstained on those resolutions. This not only delivered an unexpected blow to Judaism, but it also negated its churches and Christian worshipers. Europe implied that there is no Jesus, there is no Christianity. What a difference 200 years make. What is more troubling is that in order to take a swipe at Israel, Europe was willing to take a swipe at its own Christian roots. This is a powerful demonstration that Europe is at Judaism 3.0.

The issue at hand is Zionism (Judaism 3.0), and hence, Europe is willing to completely negate Judaism 2.0 (Jewish religion, and by extension, Christianity). In other words, opposition to Judaism 3.0 is so strong that Europeans were willing to take a swipe at Jesus and Christians.

Federalism / Neo-Monarchy vs. Republic

Monarchy provided stability. The knowledge that one could never be king allowed one to never aspire to topple the government. Under republicanism, there is a sense that "everybody wants to be prime minister," which creates instability.

Over the last 250 years, a destabilizer occurred in Europe – the rise of liberal democracies and of republics. This started in France at the end of the 18th century and expanded to the rest of Europe through the Napoleonic wars in the early 19th century. But then came resistance and counter-reaction.

By the mid-19th century, restitution of monarchies to one degree or another was prevalent throughout Europe, and a debate on the two forms of government, as well as various other models, was in full swing. Most of Europe seemed to have been on the side of monarchy. This is both in terms of the number of countries that restored monarchy and the support it garnered from its respective public.

The idea of a republic is not only new (250 years old), but it was also forced on most of Europe. It did not come organically. It was "shoved down their throats" by the Napoleonic wars, and hence, the repeated counter-revolution and resentment. The objection to the system of republic is as natural as objection to any other form of conqueror/ occupier trying to force his way.

France, as the outlier, being a republic, was itself going through a debate internally, and at the turn of the 20th century, it seemed that the notion of a republic was losing steam with more and more voices calling for the restoration of monarchy. The debate on the right form of government and the natural affinity to monarchy was natural and legitimate. But the debate stopped artificially and abruptly through an unrelated event: the unexpected outbreak of World War I in 1914.

As the war came to an end, as a byproduct, monarchies were abolished and republics were established throughout Europe. This was in part due to the nature of the victors of the war: USA, UK and France. Champions of democracies were on the winning side. This while monarchies lost: the German Empire, the Austro-Hungarian Empire and the Ottoman Empire were all on the losing side. The set of arrangements, forced on the parties, was of liberal democracies. That did not work too well.

Austrian author Stefan Zweig describes the period prior to World War I as the Golden Age of safety and security: "In our Austrian monarchy which was 1,000 years old, all seemed as if it was established to last, and the state served as a supreme guarantor to this stability." The 20th century wars ended this stability. Yet in the second half of the century, in the wake of the atrocities of war, Europe internalized the dangers coming out of totalitarian regimes, and a consensus emerged that democracy was the only acceptable system.

But the war ended 75 years ago. The vast majority of Europe's population today, including its leadership, was not born yet, and once again we have a generation in Europe who grew up in peace. The shock of the war has faded and the debate in Europe is set to resume. But the form of debate is different this time. With the emergence of a neo-monarchy of sorts, the European Union, which has been accumulating more and more power, the political alliance of the pro-monarchy (typically those more on the right) and pro-republic (typically those more on the left) has also evolved.

The big difference goes into the source of the right to govern for the monarchy. Until World War I, the broadly accepted notion that kings were appointed by God (Divine-right monarchy) contributed to the stability and buy-in of the people into their government. A subject of a monarchy could view himself as a servant of God.

As discussed, the American Revolution was amongst other things a rebellion against such Divine-right monarchs, but not against Divine right. It resulted in a Divine-right republic – "One nation under God." This, while the European Revolution against the Divine-right monarchs was also against the notion of Divine-right – against God. Hence, by the 21st century, a non-Divine-right neo-monarchy emerged – the EU.

Counter-reaction

Brexit and the Trump election in 2016 led many in Europe, especially associated with the EU "neo-monarchy" to conclude that the "people simply do not know how to vote." People vote wrong – they do not know what is good for them. Hence, Brexit, Trump and other "bad choices," the logic goes.

Perhaps people should not have the right to make such monumental decisions, the thinking goes, and let sophisticated leaders do so. Same applies to other so-called "deep-state" bureaucracies that at their core subscribe to the notion that the people's power must be checked and professionals should make decisions for the people.

European response and how it affects Judaism 3.0

The stronger the European neo-monarchy is, the more troubling it is for Israel. The "House of the EU" has been consistently less sympathetic to Israel relative to the individual state governments that comprise the EU, and relative to the majority of its citizens. For example, in the height of the Coronavirus crisis, while nations were struggling and looking toward Israel for a cure and vaccine, the House of the EU found time to intervene in internal Israeli coalition negotiations and issued a statement regarding a political party's position about the Jordan Valley.

The increasing federalization of Europe and rise of the secular neo-monarchy is further indication that the battleground for Europe's age-old feud with Judaism has shifted from the religious aspect of Judaism (Judaism 2.0) to the national aspect of Judaism – Zionism (Judaism 3.0).

Paganism / Atheism vs. Monotheism

A primary narrative of the Bible is the war between monotheism and paganism. In Biblical times, the battle was inconclusive. The Biblical narrative ends with paganism staying alive and well. It was only with the spread of Christianity and then of Islam that the entire western world, Europe at its center, turned to monotheism, and paganism was eradicated.

But 1,500 years since the paganism vs. monotheism war ended with the outright victory of monotheism, paganism is back.

Arguably, Europe is in an era of "revisiting" previously decided wars. Just like in the case of its renewed debate of monarchy vs. republic, there is a renewed debate of monotheism vs. paganism, and both of these seem to be found in one arena: The EU.

The European neo-monarchy is no longer a Divine-right monarchy, but it has some features that arguably resemble a paganic-right monarchy. It derives its rule to govern from itself. It promotes the worship of values such as secularism, universalism and various new "sacred" liberal values. More so, it has strong elements of being anti-religious, or more precisely, anti-monotheistic.

Europe's Supremacist Ideology

Europe is promoting a supremacist ideology, which has a hint of white supremacism, residual of suppressed national supremacism. This is manifested in its relations with Islam, in the arrogance of the EU, such as in its condescending attitudes towards the Palestinians,[8] in the promotion of European universalism values, and other values Europe feels it must instill on the non-enlighten world. Mostly it manifested in the aggressive promotion of Europe's new zealous religion – Secularism.

Every few centuries there is a regression to old practices, a counter-revolution of sorts. Today, it seems like the world is going through a "retro on turbo" wave:

- Russia: Going back 100 years into symptoms of its old monarchy of the Czar.
- Turkey: Going back 100 years to the time before Ataturk. In a sense, an attempt to renew the days of the Ottoman Empire.
- Europe: Going back 1,500 years into paganism and renewing the Biblical battle between monotheism and paganism.

Since Israel is so much associated with monotheism, the European resumption of the old battle of paganism vs. monotheism is a long-term issue of grave concern to Judaism, which has a profound effect on the state of Judaism.

It seems the stage is set for a renewed conflict between Rome and Jerusalem, Paganism and Monotheism, Europeanism and Zionism – e.g. the renewed age-old conflict is now clearly with Judaism 3.0.

Analysis Of Embrace And Love Shows That The World Is In Judaism 3.0

7. The Zionist ideal as a European role model

European attitudes towards Judaism are indicative of the inevitability of a Jewish transformation, but this is not only due to its frustrations and the form of opposition to Judaism. Increasingly, Europeans are looking at Zionism as a role-model for Europe!

---

8 – See my article, "Europe's Cultural Occupation of Palestine", *The Jerusalem Post*, April 6, 2016.

Israel as scion of true European liberalism

As discussed, after World War II, Europe has pivoted towards a post-nationalist ethos and towards European integration. Yet, today, more and more Europeans want to reverse this process. The Eurosceptic movement has many flavors – some seek reforms in the EU while others outright abolishment. As evident in European elections in the late 2010s, Eurosceptics of various degrees gained power and took control of some of their respective country's governments. As they do so, a narrative and counter-EU philosophy has emerged. Some of those crafting this narrative have identified Israel as a role-model for Europe.

For example, Michael Modrikamen, leader of The Movement, an organization that promotes Eurosceptic parties said: "There are those in Europe who look at Israel as an aberration, but there are also those who look at Israel as a model. They look at Israel as a value. And that is the one thing we are missing in Europe – common values. Israel is the example for Europe because it is a nation-state concept that fights for its values and concentrates on the future. It affirms exactly what we are and where we are heading." Other Eurosceptic leaders echoed similar messages. [9] To some, Israel represents a scion of true European liberalism.

Herzl envisioned a more perfect Europe in Israel

Indeed, when Theodor Herzl was crafting his vision for the Jewish state in the late 19th century, he viewed it as the most exact application of European liberalism. He spent years in Palais Bourbon carefully observing French democracy. He analyzed Bismarck's audacious state-building during German reunification and noted the challenges of Austria's pluralistic approach to liberalism. Herzl studied political philosophers, internalized the imperfections of European liberalism and planted the seeds for a more perfect Europe in Israel.

Herzl envisioned a Jewish state which would serve humanity. Indeed, Israel has been blessed with a string of astonishing successes. Nations in Asia, Latin America, Africa and the Middle East are now seeking to share this blessing and partner with the Jewish state. This is even the case amongst a growing number of Palestinians – some of whom are sick and tired of the European-sponsored dictation of conflict perpetuation.

As the debate about the core essence of Europeanism shapes up, more and more Europeans, on both sides of the European divide, are now

---

9 – Interviewed in my article: "The Battle for Europe", *The Jerusalem Post*, April 6, 2019.

calling for Europe to join the world's nations, and rather than oppose the Jewish state, view Israel once again as a light to Europeans.

Counter-reaction to Europe's obsession with Israel

Through the UN, EU, NGOs and actions of its own governments, European taxpayers continue to participate in Europe's escalation of anti-Israel rhetoric and actions. This and other European actions led to a counter-reaction.

More and more Europeans are calling for Europe to more warmly embrace Israel and the Zionist ideal that Israel is rooted in – rather than obsessively oppose it. It is both overt, such as in the case of the European right, and below the surface, amongst many in the European left. Some European politicians behave in a similar dichotomy once familiar in the Arab world – express support for Israel quietly – not in front of the cameras. Indeed, there are those in Europe who are repelled by the European obsession with Israel, and some are beginning to come out, take action and proclaim, "not in our name." For those Europeans, the "Jewish Question" that was so prevalent in Europe in the 19th and early 20th century has once again resurfaced, but it is now funneled through the State of Israel. Europe's "Jewish Question" has turned into Europe's "Israel Question". Hence, further evidence that Judaism has transformed.

8. FROM PHILO-SEMITE TO ISRA-PHILE

Embrace of Zionism is not only driven by political forces in Europe. There is an increased interest in Israel and Zionism around the world that is much deeper than tactical political considerations.

In the 19th century there was a growing trend in Europe of Philo-Semitism. This included people who were organically interested in Judaism, as well as those who did so in reaction to the rising opposition to Judaism of the time – as Friedrich Nietzsche self-described himself, the anti-anti-Semite.

In the 20th century, as much of the geographical core of Diaspora Jewry moved to America, such interest in Jews continued, especially in geographical areas where Jews lived. Philo-Semitism was expressed through participating in Jewish events, using Yiddish jargon, and consuming Jewish experiences – from eating gefilte fish to watching *Fiddler on the Roof.* This was also reflected in the popularity of the TV show *Seinfeld* – and its non-Jewish Philo-Semite characters such as Elaine – an "honorary Jew." Over the years Philo-Semitism was expressed through various experiences, including attending Kabalah classes like Madonna famously did. Other non-Jews engaged in other types of Jewish learning. Such Philo-Semites displayed a strong affinity to Jews and Judaism, but did so without having any desire or plans to convert to Judaism.

Yet, in the 21st century, this interest in Judaism has begun to shift, and has increasingly been directed towards Israel and Zionist experiences. The "honorary Jews" today consume Israeli experiences such as Israeli music, Israeli TV shows, Israeli art, Israeli wines, Israeli cuisine, Israeli innovations, Israeli strength, Israeli success and indeed, interaction with Israelis. This new global culture of Isra-Philes is emerging and replaces the old Philo-Semitism.

Israeli innovations are more interesting than engagement with the Holocaust and victimhood. Arab and Muslim influences in Israel (Judaism 3.0) are more attractive for such non-Jews than Eastern European influences of Judaism (Judaism 2.0). This too is reflected by the broad consumption of Israeli TV shows such as *Tehran* and *Fauda*. Furthermore, those around the world who choose to express affinity to Judaism, more and more do so through expressing affinity to Israel.

It is safe to say that by today there are not many Philo-Semites who are not Isra-Philes, but there are certainly plenty of Isra-Philes who are not Philo-Semites. The love side follows a similar path to the hate side described earlier: Just as Israel-bashing is replacing anti-Semitism as the primary vehicle of opposition to Judaism, so does Isra-Philia replace Philo-Semitism as the primary vehicle of love to Judaism.

9. Christians Yearning to Engage with Judaism – only possible through Judaism 3.0

Much of the Christian teaching, learning and philosophy stems from the Jewish rejection of Jesus. There is an innate desire to undo this rejection. Indeed, many Christians want to get closer to Jews and closer to Judaism. But that is not possible from a religious point of view. Hence, under the existing organizing principle of Judaism, Christians getting closer is an all-or-nothing choice – either convert or stay out. Clearly, therefore, the only available option is "nothing." But as Judaism transforms to Judaism 3.0, it allows Christians to get much closer to Judaism, while staying devout Christians. Judaism 2.0 rejects Christianity (as it did from the outset). Judaism 3.0 invites Christians to get closer.

Zionism welcomes outside support. One does not need to be a "member" in order to be a friend. Under Judaism 3.0, such friends are not only welcomed, but are indeed core to the Zionist ideology.

Friends of Zionism (Judaism 3.0) is much easier than Friends of religious Judaism (Judaism 2.0). After all, the Jewish rejection of Jesus and his teaching stemmed from religious reasons, not national reasons.

Jesus never intended to leave the Jewish nation. Christians of all denominations agree that Jesus felt very much a part of the Jewish nation. Likewise, today's Christians feel a natural affinity to the Jewish nation (Judaism 3.0). The Jewish religion's rejection of Jesus is the issue of contention (Judaism 2.0). While Jesus' teaching was rejected by the Jews, it was strongly accepted by the outside nations, who ultimately converted to what later became known as Christianity.

(i) Coming home

Many Christians want to "go home" – to Judaism. But not in a conversion manner. That is not possible: Neither from the point of view of "demand" – Christians do not want to convert, nor from "supply" – Jewish law prohibits it. Christians want to go home to Judaism while staying Christians.

Such "coming home" is without compromising any theological or faith-related aspects of Christianity. Certainly, there is no desire to abandon Jesus, or to accept any aspect of the Jewish laws. On top of it all, the crave of "coming home" is certainly not about joining the Jewish nation! Christians want to go home in the same way a brother wants to go home and be with his siblings, but keep his own unique identity.

Indeed, Christians for a long while have been looking for a way to say "shalom." This too is an expression of the concept of symbiotic particularity, which is now core to Israel and to Zionism.

The *Saturday Night Live* character of Stuart Smalley, portrayed by former US Senator Al Franken, was known for the phrase: "I just want to be loved; is that so wrong?" Under the old template of Judaism, the answer was yes – that was indeed "so wrong."

Judaism 2.0 makes it very difficult, if not impossible, for Christians to be loved by Jews. It makes it very difficult for Christians to say "shalom." This is certainly reflected in Jewish law – not allowing Christians to attend synagogues, not allowing them to choose Judaism a la carte, even strongly discouraging them from converting. This is the way Judaism 2.0 looks at non-Jews. The degrees of particularity in the Jewish religion are so high that there is an outright discouragement to engage with the Goyim (non-Jews). It therefore makes it very difficult to accept the love of the Goyim.

Such an attitude is conducive to an era where there is a war of religions on the one hand, and when there is unison of the nation-religion on the other. This was the case in the Biblical era through the Middle Ages. But in a Western, postmodern world, this is highly problematic. Judaism 2.0's Goyim-phobia is out of place with current world realities.

Under a transformation to Judaism 3.0, the Jewish particularity mentioned earlier is not at all compromised. The Goyim-phobia remains, but is limited to the religious aspect of Judaism, while welcoming engagement on the national level, which is turning to be the organizing principle of Judaism. Indeed, the transformation provides a framework for non-Jews to say "shalom."

(ii) Friends of Zion

This positive relationship with non-Jews is already happening with various organizations such as Friends of Zion, the League for Friendship, Christians for Israel and various other organizations that are not engaging in being pro-Judaism 2.0, but indeed actively engaging in being pro-Judaism 3.0. Recognizing the transformation allows such friendship not only with the State of Israel and to Israelis but also to the Jewish nation and hence, to Judaism as a whole.

(iii) Creating the language of saying Shalom

If Judaism would give Christians the tools and create the language, Christians will indeed come to say shalom. This could be the case not only for practicing Christians but also faithless Christians for whom traces of Middle Age opposition to Judaism translates to obsessive opposition to the Jewish state.

The language needs to be genuine and truthful. The language should certainly not be about surrender, compromise or concession – not tactical political "concessions," nor theological "concessions." It is not about policy demands from the world's nations, such as ending the settlements or withdrawal from the West Bank, just like it is not about the demand for the sudden acceptance of Jesus. This would not be a language of engagement, but a language of conflict milestones – a form of "conflict management" between Judaism and the world's nations.

The Jewish transformation creates a different language of interaction with Christians and therefore with many of the world's nations.

As described, in the old language, absent a transformation, Judaism is bound to lose, since even if Judaism or Israel takes actions – for example, freezing the settlements, it would be digested in the context of conflict – a measuring stick on just where on the occupation scale Israel is – it would be assessed in the framework of the 2,300 years of conflict with Judaism.

The new language has nothing to do with policy or the State of Israel. It is about synchronizing the language to the world's realities.

Engagement with the non-Jews could be a pinnacle of Judaism – peace! It could be viewed as a fulfillment of the Biblical prophecies. It is not the "end of history," since history does not end, but it certainly could offer a monumental point of stability, whereby Jews and non-Jews accept and even embrace one another for centuries to come.

(iv) Christian Zionism in the 19th century, interrupted

The world's implicit support of a transformation from Judaism 2.0 to Judaism 3.0 began in the mid-19th century, if not earlier.

The Protestant Revolution and later the American Revolution were forerunners for such world support for Zionism. This had not only philosophical aspects, but practical aspects as well.

In the UK, a broad support for the return of the Jews to Israel captivated mainstream society through the 19th century and into the 20th century. British Zionism was so strong that it reached all the way to the prime minister level and the higher echelons of society. Zionism was intertwined with Christianity. Prime Minister, and later Foreign Secretary, Arthur Balfour reflected that he could name the kings of Judea and Israel, but not the Kings of England.

The British historically were at the forefront of advocating for Jewish settlement in their old land. They were early to open a consulate in Jerusalem in 1838 and took the Jews under their wing. They issued the Balfour Declaration, and they ultimately conquered Palestine, replacing the Turks.

Indeed, it was not clear until the spring of 1917 that the UK forces would invade Palestine. Their operation in Egypt could have been viewed as "defensive" to protect the Suez Canal. The War Cabinet decided to conquer Jerusalem and clear the Turks out of Palestine. Lloyd George wrote in his memoirs years later that for him, the issue of Jerusalem and of Palestine was of personal interest.

A century earlier, Napoleon declared, as he was conquering Palestine, that he intended to re-establish a Jewish state in Palestine.

The Jews' return to their ancestral homeland served as an inspiration broadly – not just to religious Christians, but to other non-Jews, including Muslims and Arabs.

There is no reason why such inspiration should not continue. It was artificially suppressed by world events – by the European genocide of the Jews in the 20th century, and later by European political hostility to the Jewish state, due to various diplomatic and political calculations. But as the fog of such disruptions dissipates, Zionism – 19th century – was interrupted, it is ready to be resumed.

If Judaism accepts what the world seemed to have already accepted over 150 years ago – that Zionism is the current manifestation of Judaism – European Christians can embrace Judaism by embracing Zionism.

10. CHRISTIANS AS JEWS?

As Christians get closer to Judaism, a challenge arises. Just like there is a danger to Judaism due to hate, there is also a challenge to Judaism due to love.

In recent years, more and more Christians practice their religion in a similar manner to Judaism. Famously, when Donald Trump was running for the office of president and spoke at an African American church, the pastor covered Trump with a Jewish prayer shawl. Similarly, some Christians now observe the Sabbath on Saturday as opposed to Sunday.

This Christian yearning to come back home to Judaism is not possible from a religious point of view. Hence, under existing Jewish architecture, Christians stay away. But a number of notable changes are taking place that makes a Jewish transformation even more relevant.

(i) Back to Jesus

There is an intra-Christian trend, primarily in America and in Protestant circles – to recenter Christian practice on Jesus – understanding his life in Judea better, trying to feel what he felt.

Jesus was Jewish. Scholars and clergy agree that Jesus did not try to create a new religion, but to reform Judaism. He was Jewish and intended to stay Jewish. In fact, Jesus was a Jewish reformer, just as the Jewish sages were. Therefore, Jews should have no problem with Jesus.

Paul and the disciples took the teachings of Jesus to the next level. That next level became an integral part of Christianity. And no doubt there was a need to create meaningful distinctions between Christianity and Judaism, from which it was a spin-off. But in recent years, there has been a trend amongst many Christians to redirect the emphasis from those aspects of Christianity back towards Jesus the Jew.

This is somewhat akin to Israel's movement "from the Tanach to the Palmach" [10] – from the Bible to the Military – from Judaism 1.0 to

---

10 – The Palmach was the elite military force that helped re-establish the Jewish state.

Judaism 3.0, skipping Rabbinic Judaism in the middle, a form of "Jewish fundamentalism."

As a result of those processes, Christians who center Jesus in their faith, at the expense of the disciples and later interpreters, are reducing the differences between the two religions. Such closeness makes the Jewish transformation to Judaism 3.0 a necessity in order to draw a difference and keep Judaism distinct, but more so, it makes a transformation a greater reality given how Christians view Jews.

The return to Jesus naturally results in a greater admiration for Jews – as Jesus was Jewish. But that admiration is reflected in admiration of the Jewish nation! Jesus was part of the Jewish nation (Judaism 3.0). But Jesus was not part of today's Jewish religion in the way it evolved after his time to Rabbinic Judaism (Judaism 2.0). In Jesus' time, Judaism was still in Judaism 1.0.

"I work for a Jewish carpenter," many Christians proclaim. That Jewish carpenter is certainly not part of today's Rabbinic Judaism. But because he is certainly part of today's Jewish nation, such dedication to Jesus leads to extreme admiration for the State of Israel.

The Christian return to Jesus supports the Jewish transformation, and makes it necessary, but a bigger blurring of the lines is occurring with the popularity of a new movement, which is only a few decades old – Messianic Judaism.

(ii) Jews accepting Jesus? The emergence of Messianic Judaism

What started in the 1970s as "Jews for Jesus," and perceived to be a cult, has now developed into a very small, yet noticeable denomination. Its worshipers are respectable educated Jews who, each for his own reasons, decided to accept Jesus as their Messiah.

Many are former flower-children on a spiritual search, others are rational theologists. While this group is small, it has grown and is no longer a fringe. Most importantly, they view themselves as Jewish. They claim that they did not convert out of Judaism, but simply added Jesus to their Judaism.

A group consisting of a fraction of a percentage of world Jewry may not be of much interest when it comes to assessing Jewish transformation, but the beachhead they created for non-Jews could have a daunting effect on Judaism.

(iii) Christians joining Messianic Jews

More and more Christians, being made aware of such Jewish congregations in their community, choose to worship with the Messianic

Jews. Now that the Jesus issue is neutralized, then why not worship in a synagogue?

Looking at it from the reverse view, sure enough, a growing percent of worshipers in Messianic Judaism synagogues are now non-Jews; by some estimates, the vast majority. Hence, Messianic Judaism has turned into a gateway for Christians into Judaism.

(iv) Christian missionary

An important part of the Christian religion is the spread of the Christian faith and the teachings of Jesus around the world. The Mormon Church is the most known for that, but other denominations have done the same.

Jesus was Jewish; Christianity came from Judaism. It successfully spread around the world, but the one nation that does not accept it are the Jews. This is akin to a successful musician or artist who gets recognition from all over the world for his skill, except from his parents who still view his music or art as shallow and him as a failure.

Christian missionary activity towards Jews encounters various problems. One is the Jews' rejection of the mere missionary task, including aspects of it being illegal in Israel. Another is the change in relationship to the good between Christians and Jews. The strong friendship and closeness have put the missionary task at a low priority. Yet, suddenly there is an opportunity for a "reverse-merger" of Christianity into Judaism; into the Jewish religion – into Judaism 2.0.

(v) Reverse-merger into Judaism 2.0?

If Messianic Judaism prevails, and given it has no conversion requirements (the founders were Jewish, but anybody can join regardless of their background), Messianic Judaism has unlimited growth capacity. It can be the vehicle by which Christians numerically "take over" Judaism. This is not by ill-intention. This is simply by choosing to come home to Jesus by joining Messianic Judaism. It is an act of love. The back door to Judaism, that can result in its takeover, only exists under Judaism 2.0. Recognizing the transformation of Judaism would shut that door. Once it is underscored that Judaism is a nation, this reverse merger cannot occur.

The vitality of the reverse merger route is not just due to individual Christians worshiping in Messianic Jewish synagogues. The bigger issue is if entire churches or entire denominations join Messianic Judaism, or simply declare themselves to be "Jews who believe in Jesus."

(vi) Judaism 3.0 preserves Judaism through the Jewish nation

As stated, getting closer and merging are two separate things. While the vehicle to get closer to Judaism is via its national aspect (Judaism 3.0), not its religious aspect that rejects such closeness (Judaism 2.0), the vehicle to merge Judaism out of existence is through the religious aspect (Judaism 2.0) and not through the national aspect (Judaism 3.0).

This is just like one can convert to Catholicism but not "convert" to become part of the Irish nation (irrespective of residency and citizenship), just like a Chinese person living in China cannot suddenly "convert" to become Swedish. He can adore Swedish heritage, be a friend of the Swedish culture, but not just "convert" to Swedish. He perhaps can immigrate to Sweden or attain Sweden citizenship through some process and join the Swedish nation that way, but simply by declaring "I am Swedish" while staying in China does not mean that this Chinese person is now part of the Swedish nation.

Similarly, while a Christian can find a door to the outskirts of Judaism through Messianic Judaism, this does not mean that he is now part of the Jewish nation. That Christian can feel that by his religious practices he is a part of the Jewish religion, just like that Chinese can feel part of the Swedish Church, but that Christian is not likely to feel part of the Jewish nation, just like that Chinese is not part of the Swedish nation. Suggesting otherwise has enormous implications: If a Chinese person can "convert" to the Swedish nation while staying in China, just by saying so, then the Swedish nation will shortly be reverse-merged out of existence. It will be Chinese!

While not many Chinese want to "come home" to Sweden, many Christians want to "come home" to Judaism. This underscores the imperative to recognize the transformation. The potential pool of "new Jews" is in the billions. The "existing Jews" are less than 20 million. They would be a drop in the bucket, and failing to transform, Judaism could be merged out of existence through a bear hug.

A related event happened in the 16th and 17th centuries. "New Christians" – Jews who were forced to convert to Christianity – possibly outnumbered Christians in certain Spanish communities, leading to the prospect of Judaism "reverse merging" into Spanish Christianity. This was likely a contributor, or an excuse, to the genocidal policies of the Spanish Inquisition.

Christians do not want to take over Judaism. The "hug" therefore is better received as a warm fuzzy hug by Judaism 3.0 – the Jewish nation, than as a bear hug by Judaism 2.0 – the Jewish religion. If it is recognized that the organizing principle of Judaism is now its national aspect, then Judaism is safe.

11. Conclusion: The world is already in Judaism 3.0

The world has been in Judaism 3.0 long before the Jews themselves have. Both friends and foes today simply do not make a meaningful distinction between Jews and Israel. Given that historically it was the outside that defined Judaism, a recognition that the world is already in Judaism 3.0 supports a reality that Judaism itself is transforming to Judaism 3.0.

As discussed earlier, developments in the United States are indicative of a transformation to Judaism 3.0. So are developments in the rest of the world.

(i) Europe is in Judaism 3.0

Europeans have long viewed the Jews in a national context and continue to do so today, as they direct age-old opposition to Judaism through Zionism and funnel their frustration to the Jewish state as opposed to individual Jews. But even the nature of threat against individual Jews is indicative of Jewish transformation.

In Europe, and in particular in France, many Jews feel under a sudden physical threat, after decades of safety. This has led to a significant migration out of France to Israel, as well as to the spike in purchases of second homes in Israel. Anti-Jewish terrorism, such as the 2012 Toulouse shooting of Jewish children, and the 2016 Jewish Deli attack served as a wake-up call. It became evident that French and European Jews once again are not safe. But these attacks against Jews have nothing to do with their Jewish faith (Judaism 2.0), it simply has to do with their Israel connection (Judaism 3.0).

The French Jews fully acknowledge this. They respond, not by attempting to distance themselves from Judaism, which having studied history, they know is utterly ineffective and even silly, but by embracing Israel.

Hence, the result of the attacks on Jews in France is the French Jewish community strengthening its connection to Israel.

This is natural, as European Jewish communities themselves tend to be more connected with Israel than the North American Jewish communities. They tend to visit more often and they tend to have stronger family ties. The intertwining of Jews and Israel is occurring throughout Europe.

Jews are targeted by Europeans when it comes to the boycotting campaign. For example, the Labor party anti-Israel campaign that followed the 2015 election of Jeremy Corbyn as party leader and the rise of his young followers (The "Corbynistas") has quickly morphed into well-documented Jew-hatred. The Corbynistas are clearly in Judaism 3.0 – their issues with the Jews are because of Israel. Hence, British Jews are forced into Judaism 3.0 as well.

Activities of anarchists and far-left activists in other parts of Europe include desecrating synagogues in revenge for Israeli policy. On the European far-right as well, myths that "Israel controls the world" or "Zionists control the world" are by now much more prevalent today than "Jews control the world." For example, as manifested in widespread conspiracy theories about the Bilderberg Group as an outlet of Zionist global domination.

Europe and the United States are certainly in Judaism 3.0, but the rest of the world is even more so.

(ii) Arab and Muslim world is in Judaism 3.0

The Arab and Muslim world have long been in Judaism 3.0. This is true in both centers of Islam: The Middle East and Europe.

Arabs/Muslims in the Middle East are in Judaism 3.0

From the very beginning of the Arab nationalist movement in the early and mid-20th century, there was no distinction between the Jewish religion and Jewish nationalism, and rightfully so.

On the positive side, the Arab support for Zionism was synonymous with the support for Judaism. When Emir Faisal appeared before the powers in the 1919 Paris Peace Conference, he did not appear as "Southern Syrians" or "Arabian Peninsula." He appeared as an Arab. And symmetrically, he did not support Jewish Zionist leader Chaim Weizmann's effort for a Jewish homeland in Palestine as an "Israeli" effort. This was obviously perceived as a Jewish endeavor.

Similarly, Weizmann and his Zionist colleagues appearing on the same commission, in effect served as a recognition by the world powers that Zionism was de facto representing Jewish interests.

Faisal and other Arab leaders had a three-week meeting in London at the end of 1918 leading to an agreement on January 3, 1919 in which Faisal solidified his support for Zionism.

On the flip side, when Saudi Arabia restricted Jewish entry to the kingdom through the 20th century, it was not because of an issue related to American Jews or the Jewish religion; it was due to the Saudi feud with the State of Israel.

Similarly, Arabs who have been fighting Israel have not viewed it as fighting "Israelis" – but rather fighting the Jews. This is evident, for example, in the infamous Arab call to battle: *Itbah al Yahud* – kill the Jews (not the Israelis).

Anti-Semitism in the Islamic world is well documented. From efforts to deny the Holocaust in Iran, to the screening of an original series on the Protocols of Elders of Zion in Egypt. The context of this Arab anti-Semitism is without a doubt in relation to Israel.

Arabs/Muslims in Europe are in Judaism 3.0

Similarly, in the anti-Semitic incidents in Europe by Muslims, there is no separation between Israel and Jews. This is evident in Muslim attacks on European synagogues and cemeteries – targeting Jewish symbols and institutions as a way to express frustration at Israel. This is not new – the PLO did the same going back to the 1970s. In fact, current PLO chairman and president of the Palestinian Authority, Mahmoud Abbas' (Abu Mazen) PhD dissertation was not anti-Israel, but outright anti-Semitic: Holocaust denial.

(iii) The rest of the world is in Judaism 3.0

Israelis traveling in Asia, Latin American and around the world often encounter people who react to hearing a person is from Israel by saying "Oh, Jewish."

For much of the world, Jew and Israeli are interchangeable terms. Just like for Jews, Judaism and Rabbinic Judaism are interchangeable terms. This is because that is how most non-Western societies work. The tribal-national-clan organizing principle often goes hand-in-hand and is inseparable from religion.

Here too, conspiracy theories used in admiration, rather than in hate, are centered around Israel's domination of the world and not the Jews' domination of the world.

(iv) Inevitability of Judaism 3.0

The world is in Judaism 3.0. This is true when it comes to friends, and this is true when it comes to opponents of the Jews, who are now funneling their Jew-hatred through the collective of the Jews – the Jewish state of Israel.

A Jew's instinctive attempt to distance himself from Israel is irrelevant. The outside world still associates this Jew with Israel. There is only one possible response by the Jews to such opposition – to strengthen their Jewish identity around Israel and around Zionism (Judaism 3.0).

Jews around the world are forced to confront their Judaism vis-à-vis criticism of Israel directed at them openly or subtly by association. They are forced into the "fight or flight" response – defend Israel or put distance – perhaps even join anti-Israel movements. But the one thing that is not available to the Jews is an option to ignore their connection to Israel. For the Jew, denying the connection might seem logical, but for the outside this would simply be ridiculed.

This is similar to past episodes, when the Jews' attempts to put distance from their Jewish national affiliation was proven irrelevant: In 16th and 17th-century Spain (as evidenced by the Inquisition), in 19th-century France (as evidenced by the Dreyfus Affair), in the 1930s and 1940s throughout Europe (as evidenced by the Holocaust), and in the late 1940s and 1950s throughout the Middle East (as evidenced by the deportation of Jews). All of those attempts were proven ineffective. Same is the case today.

In an August 14, 1895 diary entry, Herzl wrote that he explained to a friend who wished to convert to avoid anti-Semitism that "when five thousand like him become baptized, the watchword would simply be changed to Dirty Converts."

German poet Henriech Heine thought that putting distance between himself and Judaism would allow him to prosper in German society. It did not work. As he reflected on this, he said that the only difference was that now both non-Jews and Jews hate him.

Jews trying to put distance from Israel is laughable. It does not work. Jews are and will always be defined by the outside world in terms of their Jewish national association, in terms of their affiliation with Israel, in terms of Zionism (Judaism 3.0).

And yet, the inevitability of the Jewish transformation may not stem from the way the world perceives the Jews, nor from the way Jews relate to their Judaism, but rather from an existential necessity to transform.

IX

Existential Threats To Judaism

Transformations rarely occur without an existential threat. One can recognize that changes or improvements are necessary, but a radical transformation typically occurs only when the option of keeping things as they are is no longer available – when there is no choice. This is true across the board: for organizations, movements, companies, countries, religions, nations and even for individuals.

This is the case today with Judaism. The emergence of three potent existential threats necessitates a Jewish transformation. In escalating order, they are:

1. Internal threat of assimilation of American Jews (affecting less than 50% of worldwide Jews).

2. Internal threat of post-Zionism in Israel (a single bullet that can eliminate 100% of Judaism).

3. External threat of Israel-bashing (the 2,300-year-conflict with Judaism).

The architecture of Judaism 2.0 that was suitable for dealing with the threats of the last 2,000 years is not relevant to addressing today's three existential threats to Judaism.

Not only that a Jewish transformation is necessary to address contemporary threats to Judaism but those same threats also serve as a propelling force that would prompt the completion of a transformation. This is just as when Herzl launched the Zionist movement, he identified anti-Semitism and the misery of the Jews as the propelling force that would lead Jews into Zionism.

It is imperative to internalize that the core nature of the threat to Judaism has shifted.

1. SHIFT OF EXISTENTIAL THREAT TO JUDAISM FROM SECULARIZATION TO DENATIONALIZATION

(i) End of secularization threat

Secularization is no longer an existential threat to Judaism because Judaism is already secular. The pool of Jews that could be secularized has been depleted:

- American Jews are already secular. An estimated 85-90% of American Jews are non-observant.

- The majority of Israeli Jews are either religious or traditional and they make up the potential "pool" for further secularization of Judaism. But even if mass secularization of those groups occurred, they would turn to be secular Israelis, and unlike their American counterparts, secular Israelis are not at risk of evaporation. As discussed, they are very much connected to Judaism through Zionism.

Furthermore, the overwhelming majority of Israeli seculars are not atheist, agnostic or anti-religious. The rise of the Datlaf, and it becoming the primary stream of secular Israeli Judaism, has essentially neutralized the threat to Judaism stemming from further secularization. Even if mass secularization of Israeli Jews occurs, it would be to a religious-friendly secularism that is anchored in Jewish particularism.

However, denationalization *is* the process through which secular Judaism could cease to exist, and hence, Judaism would cease to exist.

(ii) Rise of the Denationalization threat

When Jews were a close-knit nation-religion, either of those two pillars of Judaism were sufficient to hold the Jews together. A Jew could have stopped observing religious laws and practicing Jewish rituals, but he would still stay confined by the walls of the Jewish ghetto – physical or social. Jews had no option to leave, and hence, even secular Jews would stay Jewish. But since Jews are now emancipated and most of them are now secular, the loss of their ethnological national affiliation could mean the elimination of the remaining connector to Judaism.

As discussed, community activities, the mission of Tikun Olam (repairing the world), shared history or other low-octane non-particular connections are insufficient and on their own mostly irrelevant to the survival of Judaism as a distinct entity.

The threat of Denationalization manifests itself in three ways:

Denationalization threat in the Diaspora: Assimilation

Jews in America are on a trajectory of evaporation because of assimilation. This is a result of a process of denationalization that occurred shortly after the Jews arrived in America, reducing the Jewish nation-religion into the "Jewish Church."

Absent a transformation, most American Jews can quickly turn into Americans of some Jewish ancestry. Paradoxically, if that threat materializes to its fullest, then Judaism would automatically transform to Judaism 3.0, since then the vast majority of Jews would be in Israel, where the connecting thread is Zionism.

American Judaism's evaporation track is not surprising. As discussed, other immigrant groups that came to America around the same time as the Jews have also evaporated and turned into pan-American brands: the Irish, the Germans, the Italians.

The Jewish evaporation path is a function of forces described earlier: the exit from the ghetto, the secularization of American Jews, the low place of Judaism in one's hierarchy of identities, the passing of the generations, the fading of cultural glues that held the Jewish community together and the failure to connect Jews through other means. The evaporation has been manifesting in the high intermarriage statistics. But it is not only due to intermarriage. Jews assimilate out of Judaism even as couples and as individuals. In fact, historically, whenever an assimilation option was available, the Jews exercised that option. Such was the case for Western European Jews in the late 19th century and early 20th century. For example, the intermarriage reached 56% in Copenhagen in the 1880s, over 50% in Germany in the 1910s, and 70% in Amsterdam in the 1930s. [1]

Assimilation was not an option for most Eastern European Jews, and that was where the majority of European Jews lived at that time. Nor was it a viable option for Middle Eastern Jewry, estimated to be about 10% of world Jewry at the time.

European Jewry survived the early 20th century because of this dual reality: Jews assimilated wherever they could, but for the overwhelming majority of Jews, the assimilation option was not available legally or socially.

Today, assimilation in America is available, and unlike in 19th-century Western Europe, it is socially accepted and very easy: no need to convert, no need to be judged, no need to be condemned. Indeed, the threat of assimilation is a core ethos of today's American Jewry.

Denationalization threat in Israel: Post-Zionism

The State of Israel is rooted in a bedrock of solid ideology – Zionism. The only raison d'etre for Israel's establishment in the first place, and for the legitimacy of the Jewish people living in Israel, is acceptance of Zionism's core assumption: Israel is the national homeland of the Jewish nation.

Absent Zionism, there is no justification for millions of Jews to have immigrated to Israel since the 20th century. Moreover, the negation of Zionism would make it clear that a person who has proven ancestry

---

1 – Walter Laqueur: "A History of Zionism: From the French Revolution to the Establishment of the State of Israel".

to the land from 80 years ago (estimated by the UN to be about 7-10 million) has a superior right to move to Israel than a person who has conceptual claims to the same land from 2,000 years ago. [2]

Zionism is the reason Israel exists as the homeland of the Jewish people. Negation of Zionism would be the negation of Israel. That is not only conceptually but also practically, as it would remove an ideological hurdle for those 7-10 million Palestinians to immigrate back to Israel. Since Europeans and other world powers have artificially and cruelly kept many of those Palestinians as refugees, as well as actively blocked opportunities for them to integrate in their host countries, the prospect of such mass returns is real and rooted in the Palestinian national ethos. A German today is not likely to come back home to Sudeten, even if allowed, same for a Jewish refugee from Iraq or a Pakistani refugee from India. But given the dire conditions of many of those Palestinian refugees, a mass move back to Israel is likely, leading to Jews being a minority in Israel and losing their state. If Israeli Jews stop believing in Zionism, this would mean they have stopped believing in their own collective raison d'etre.

The risk of Israelis embracing post-Zionism is considered minor and is perceived to exist only in the fringe of Israeli society. Indeed, an estimated 99% of Israelis vote for Zionist parties (including Haredi parties). The left and the right are united in strong support of Zionism.

Yet, undercurrents in Israeli society and aggressive outside intervention can lead to a rapid rise of post-Zionism. A post-Zionist philosophy has been developed by Israeli intellectuals and academics, which includes well-developed concepts and doctrines expressed through books, articles and cultural packages. It is deployed and ready to be spread to the broader Israeli population. In addition, some believe that a well-funded ground operation is in place to hijack unrelated protests, demonstrations and civic actions, and to recruit these into the post-Zionist cause. Therefore, those 99% of Israeli Jews who are Zionists are indeed vulnerable to post-Zionism.

Post-Zionists argue that Zionism has run its course; that its purpose was to establish the Jewish state and for Jews to immigrate to the state. Now accomplished, they argue that Zionism's role has been completed. Israel as a political entity should be like any other country, and not be viewed as the national homeland of the Jewish nation, but rather the

---

2 – Descendants of Palestinian refugees who fled in 1948. Five million of them are eligible for UNRWA services. Other estimates of the number of refugees, such as from Al-Awada and INSS, range from 5 million to 10 million.

national homeland of its citizens – the Israelis.

Another more extreme version of this is that, granted, the Israelis originated from the Jews, but have since created something new and are now their own distinct entity, separate from the Jews. This concept was introduced in Israel's early years by a group of artists and intellectuals called "the Canaanites", but it has gained more traction as Israeli culture has developed. [3]

The Israelis are akin to the Americans; the logic goes – just as the Americans originated from the British, the Israelis originated from the Jews. Just like in the American case, where individuals from other ethnicities later joined, same with Israel when it comes to the Arabs. Just because America was founded by the British, it need not stay British, and just like Israel was founded by Jews, it need not stay Jewish.

Post-Zionists will point out that indeed many Israeli Jews feel closer to an Arab-Israeli than they do to an American Jew. Taking it a step further, just like British-ancestry Americans are a minority today, so could Jewish-ancestry Israelis be a minority in Israel in the future. It is a natural evolution by this logic.

The end of Zionism in Israel has broader implications. If an Israeli Jew no longer feels part of the Jewish nation, and given his lack of religiosity, he is likely to experience similar patterns of evaporation that is experienced by American Jews. Such Jews are at a greater likelihood to move out of Israel, and to have lower motivation to defend Israel, given lower morale and the fading raison d'etre. In addition, such Israelis are at risk of marrying non-Jews in Israel, especially if peaceful conditions ensue.

Today, in addition to the national particularity of Jews and Arabs, it is the Israeli-Arab conflict that prevents broad intermarriage between secular Jews and secular Arabs in Israel. But what if there is no conflict, and no Zionism?

The case of the American Jews can serve as an indicator of what could happen if the post-Zionism threat materializes. Denationalization of secular societies could be a fatal blow to their continuity. Indeed, given American Jewry's survival challenges, post-Zionism is essentially post-Judaism.

External Denationalization threat: Israel-bashing

The two internally generated threats – evaporation of American Jewry and post-Zionism – pale in comparison to a looming danger

---

3 – See Yaakov Shavit: "From Hebrew to Canaanite" (Hebrew).

steaming from the outside. Israel-bashing is the current manifestation of centuries-old Jew-hatred.

As discussed, historically, the evolution of Judaism was not dictated organically by the Jews, as much as in the Jewish response to actions by outside actors, such as the decisions by the Babylonians and Romans to expel the Jews from Judea, or by the Persians to allow exiled nations in their empire to return.

Jews do not control the nature of the threat to their existence. For example, in 20th-century Europe, a Jew could not have converted out of the threat, nor claimed that he is a proud German or a proud French who has long left Judaism.

When most Jews were in Europe, the anti-Semitism ideology became a potent threat. It was an ideology that was developed in response to the Jews' emancipation and success. Indeed, this ideology matured into the systematic genocide of European Jewry.

Now that Jews are out of Europe, the same underlying hatred has followed them to Israel. A new ideology has emerged. Like anti-Semitism that preceded it, after a few years of brewing, Israel-bashing is gaining popularity and acceptability in mainstream European circles and around the world, in particular with young audiences.

The threat does not just put the State of Israel in danger. Israel is merely the vehicle that the Israel-bashing movement uses to direct its frustration against the Jews. On the individual level, the Israel-bashing ideology puts every Jew in danger, regardless of his views about Israel. This is especially true since the Israel-bashing movement has both a retail component and an institutional arm that can serve as effective mechanisms to destroy Israel.

The strengthening of those mechanisms over the past decades that could in theory be deployed towards Israel's destruction, such as the UN, the International Criminal Court, and other multinational organizations and coalitions, makes this threat a tangible one.

Such mechanisms were instrumental in destroying other "pariah" states such as South Africa and Baathist Iraq. [4]

While it is true that strong allies of the Jewish state are found in mainstream European leadership, the increasing mainstreaming of the Israel-bashing movement in Europe should be worrisome. Moreover,

---

4 – Apartheid South Africa collapsed in 1994 and was forced to dismantle its nuclear weapons after intense international pressure. Baathist Iraq collapsed in 2003 after international pressure that was followed by international military action.

one of the key lessons of the 1973 Yom Kippur war, when Israel faced the threat of military destruction, is that one must not analyze the enemy's intentions, but assess its capabilities. As the arsenal of mechanisms, such as international sanctions and binding multinational resolutions are strengthening, the danger of political destruction of the Jewish state becomes more viable.

Political destruction through outside institutions is not the only ammunition of the Israel-bashing movement. Demoralization and attrition can be equally lethal. As the Israel-bashing movement gains popularity and penetrates Jewish society, and Israel itself, the higher the risk becomes that some Israelis would "give up" and opt to move elsewhere, or alternatively, defend their country with less vigor.

(iii) Relation between the magnitude of the threat and likelihood of materialization

The three existential threats to Judaism progress in inverse order: the most immediate threat is the least damaging, and the most far-fetched is the most lethal.

- The threat of evaporation of American Jewry is the least potent threat to the survival of Judaism, since it merely affects half of the Jewish nation. This threat, though, is already in the process of being materialized. The core of the American Jewish community is on a path towards evaporation. If this threat fully materializes, then by default, Judaism would turn to Judaism 3.0, since nearly all Jews would live in Israel, where Zionism is the connecting thread. The most imminent threat to Judaism is one that Judaism can sustain.

- In the middle, post-Zionism is a fringe movement affecting only those on the outskirts of Israeli Jewish society. But undercurrents in Israel and its aggressive promotion from outside make this latent threat real and viable.

- The threat of Israel-bashing is the most lethal threat to Judaism. Just like previous episodes of popular institutional Jew-hatred, if this threat materializes in its full potency, it could lead to the eradication of Judaism. The vehicle for the fulfillment of this threat is powerful – the political extinction of the state of the Jews. The third exile may be even more lethal than previous ones, since Jews in the first two exiles were able to survive by remaining as a distinct community in exile – something that is less likely today in an integrated global environment. Yet, the strength of Israel and of the Zionist ideology, as well as the solid support it gets from those countries who currently control those lethal mechanisms, makes this threat the least likely to be fulfilled.

Judaism 3.0 Addresses Today's Existential Threats To Judaism

While the three existential threats to Judaism are serious and potent, there is a symbiotic solution to all three: transformation of Judaism to Judaism 3.0. The mere recognition that Judaism has transformed would provide an effective defense against these threats.

2. JUDAISM 3.0 MITIGATES THE EVAPORATION OF NORTH AMERICAN JEWS

The most common characteristic of American Jews today is that they tend to marry non-Jews. As discussed, intermarriage now accounts for 72% of non-Orthodox Jewish marriages. The intermarriage "epidemic" of the last decades has served as a primary path towards assimilation and the eventual evaporation of American Judaism.

With Judaism 3.0, the non-Jewish spouse has a home. That is because the organizing principle is not the religious aspect of Judaism, where the non-Jewish spouse is both excluded from and likely not interested, but the national aspect of Judaism – where the non-Jewish spouse is both welcomed and interested.

In many cases, the pro-Israel attitude amongst non-Jews who intermarry "in" is higher than it is amongst the under-engaged or unaffiliated Jews who intermarry "out." Judaism 3.0 connects to the intermarried spouse's past and tradition, since, as discussed, the predominance of the intermarriage "in" pool in the United States is Christian. They themselves might be secular, but many of them have religious Christian parents or grandparents and they retain a strong emotional affinity to Israel. The connection to Israel may not be something they ever think about, but it is rooted at some deep level. Once marrying a Jew, that connection inevitably gets awakened.

The predominance of the intermarriage "out" pool are liberal Jews. They often have a more critical approach towards Israel than America's non-Jewish population. Hence, intermarriage, while no doubt weakens the religious Jewish aspect of the new couple, augments the Zionist aspects. When visiting Israel, the non-Jewish spouse feels welcomed (unlike in synagogue – the litmus test of inclusion for him/her under Judaism 2.0). Indeed, such spouses often report a strong desire to repeatedly visit Israel.

Similarly, the intermarried spouse can relate to Judaism through values that are relevant and appealing to him/her: Israeli culture, Israeli wine,

Israeli entrepreneurship, Israeli fashion, Israeli dance. The belongingness to Judaism that is generated through those Israeli connections is later passed to the children, who are more likely to stay in the Jewish tent.

The under-engaged Jew marrying "out" is often some place on the trajectory of evaporation out of Judaism regardless of who he marries. If he marries another under-engaged Jew, such trajectory would still be towards evaporation. But by marrying a non-Jew that can connect through Israel and through Zionism, he increases the chances of staying (and his children staying) in Judaism – in Judaism 3.0 (Zionism).

Marrying another evaporation-track Jew makes Judaism less of an issue – there is no "Jewish question" for the couple, and hence, the ambivalence continues, and so does the evaporation-track. Marrying a non-Jew forces the "Jewish question." Judaism 3.0 provides a change in direction for the previously evaporation-track Jew.

(i) Judaism 3.0 turns assimilation into an enabler of Jewish survivability

On a summer afternoon in 1895, Theodor Herzl and Max Nordau sat in a Parisian cafe and had a beer. As they were drinking, they engaged in a philosophical debate about what kept Judaism together. They agreed: anti-Semitism! That is, as Herzl phrased it, "what has made Jews of us." They agreed that it was an existential threat which indeed turned out to be the enabler of survivability. But how does this impact the Jews' pursuit to reclaim their land? On this point, Herzl and Nordau parted ways. Nordau viewed anti-Semitism as "a hurdle to achieve a Jewish state," but Herzl had a different view: "We will be compelled by anti-Semitism to create the Jewish state." Herzl viewed the threat not only as an enabler of survivability till now, but as a secret weapon that would end the Jewish exile.

Similarly, today the threat of assimilation can turn into an enabler of survivability and a mechanism to fulfill the Jewish transformation for which Herzl planted the seeds.

To do that, one needs to apply the thinning of Herzl to the issue of assimilation. That is to understand assimilation in the same depth and nuance that Herzl understood anti-Semitism: The assimilation of Jews is not, as it was in the 19th century Europe, assimilation into being a German Protestant or a French Catholic (that indeed would mean "the end").

The assimilation of an American Jew today is not an assimilation into a religion, or into another political nation. It is an assimilation into Americanism (not into Christianity). Decades ago, assimilation

Existential Threats To Judaism

to Americanism could have meant "the end" because shedding the remaining hint of the Jewish nation and religion would have meant the end of being Jewish. But as discussed earlier, Americanism has changed.

Ethnological national identity is not just accepted in today's American narrative, but highly encouraged. This is given societal trends in America already discussed of heritage-identity, multi-identity realities, and cultural pluralism, as well as Americanism's strong embrace of Zionism.

Indeed, on a philosophical level, Americanism is a form of abstract Zionism. Today, a Jew marrying a non-Jew does not mean he has assimilated out of Judaism. Assimilation into Americanism means "assimilation" into a Zionism-friendly concept. Hence, the intermarried couple and their children can stay Jewish as long as they center their Judaism around Zionism – i.e. as long as there is a recognition that Judaism is in Judaism 3.0. This is the same with an intra-married couple who is assimilating out due to lack of interest in religion, synagogue or Jewish culture.

Assimilation to Americanism enables Jews to strengthen their Zionist identity. With Judaism 3.0, the Jew connects back to his Judaism (Zionism) through his assimilation to Americanism. It would not only allow an assimilated Jew to stay Jewish, but such a connection could also indirectly strengthen his Jewish religious identity!

Just like with anti-Semitism, which normally would be viewed as a threat, but can also be viewed as an enabler of survivability, so is assimilation. Under the transformation to Judaism 3.0, the assimilation threat is not only addressed but also becomes a mechanism for Jewish continuity.

Furthermore, even in an extreme scenario of complete assimilation of the non-Orthodox American Jewish community, the unassimilated "refugees" will likely lean on the surviving Orthodox structures, perhaps adopting the Israeli model of "secular Orthodox" Datlaf.

(ii) Judaism 3.0 could stop the evaporation of American Jewry

As discussed earlier, Judaism 3.0 makes Judaism relevant for the American Jew, and hence, it will probably limit intermarriage to some extent. Connecting through a relevant conduit to Judaism – Zionism – whether in positive or negative, or both, would likely lead to more Jews choosing naturally to marry another Jew. But recognizing the transformation would not only provide a remedy that could stop the threat from materializing, it also provides a safety-cushion for those far out on the evaporation path.

Recognizing the transformation would also fuel a counter-reaction by

• 289 •

Jews down that evaporation path who might want to "prove it wrong" by showing they are indeed connected to Judaism through a conduit other than Zionism. Just as Herzl pontificated – the power of an idea is not just through those who support it, but also by those who oppose it.

3. JUDAISM 3.0 PROTECTS JUDAISM FROM POST-ZIONISM

The mere acknowledgment that Zionism is the organizing principle of Judaism gives a significant boost to the Zionist ideology and provides a solid defense from the emerging existential threat of post-Zionism. Judaism 3.0 recruits Judaism, along with its history, tradition and sustainability into Zionism. It underscores the reality that post-Zionism equals the end of Judaism.

Similarly, recognizing the transformation would point the Israeli to the arena where the contemporary battle to save Judaism is fought. When the threat to Israel's survival was militarily, the call to arms was increased determination of Israelis to physically defend their country. Now that the threat is ideological, the call to arms needs to be an ideological one. Therefore, it is imperative to strengthen Zionism. The mere recognition of the transformation to Judaism 3.0 does exactly this.

Recognition that Zionism is the organizing principle of Judaism would up-the-ante for those in Israel sympathetic to the post-Zionist narrative. It would essentially strip them of the ability to pretend that they can be post-Zionist and still be Jewish. It would prevent those potentially new post-Zionists from doing something they do not intend to do – end Judaism. On the contrary, it would likely infuse them with a sense of duty – of Jewish responsibility.

Herzl not only argued that we "now have Judaism in our hand." He also argued that certain Jewish behavior would not come along. Such behavior "was all right in the time of our captivity. Now we have the duties of freedom."

Recognizing the transformation to Judaism 3.0 would call to the duty of freedom even those sympathetic to the post-Zionism cause.

(i) Zionism turns into a "starting-point"

Mostly, recognizing the transformation of Judaism will address the post-Zionism existential threat by ending the debate about Zionism. The debate will shift from a debate about Zionism, to a debate within Zionism. Just like today, there is no debate about the Jewish religion. Judaism is accepted as a religion and the debate is within Judaism. That was not the case in the early stages of the transformation to Judaism

2.0. Rabbinic Judaism had competition from the Karaites and those not recognizing the transformation. But once the transformation to Judaism 2.0 was fully recognized, it ended the debate about Rabbinic Judaism, so much that Rabbinic Judaism and Judaism became one and the same. Rabbinic Judaism became the "starting point" and from there on, the debates occurred within the contrast of Rabbinic Judaism.

Similarly, recognizing the transformation to Judaism 3.0 would leave no room for the rising doubts about the viability of Zionism, and Zionism would no longer be a "dirty word" in certain circles as it is now. By definition, in Judaism 3.0, "Zionist" would only be a dirty word if "Jew" is a dirty word.

(ii) Diaspora Jews infuse Zionism with vitality

Acknowledging that Judaism has transformed would also deploy American Jews and other Diaspora Jews to the battle against the post-Zionism threat in Israel.

Many of those American Jews are often more enthusiastic supporters of Zionism than Israelis themselves. Even those who are sharp critics of Israel are typically also engaging with Zionism with high passion and enthusiasm. Many of them claim that their harsh criticism of Israel's policy is in order to improve Israel. Indeed, even the harsher ones are not true anti-Zionists. Hence, recognizing the transformation would not only address the threat of evaporation of American Jewry, but it would also address the threat of post-Zionism through the renewed vitality American Jews would give Zionism.

Transformation turns Diaspora to Babylon

Indeed, Diaspora Jews playing a role in developing Zionism and protecting it from post-Zionism can be as crucial to Judaism 3.0 as the role played by Diaspora Jews in Babylon in the early stages of Judaism 2.0.

Back then, the realities under Roman rule in Judea were very different from the realities outside. The Talmud was developed in Jerusalem, but another Talmud, with different perspectives, was developed in Babylon. Both turned into core staples of Rabbinic Judaism (Judaism 2.0). [5]

Same with today. The one-nation market of Israel, combined with its herd mentality and history of "party voice" messaging, could present potential risks.

An Israeli reading an Israeli newspaper in the cafe, listening to Israeli

---

5 – See Rabbi Jill Jacobs: "Tale of Two Talmuds: Jerusalem and Babylonian", myjewishlearning.com

radio news in his car and watching Israeli TV at home is biased. There are ample examples of Israelis arriving at a view that is bizarre, and could use an external point of reference. For example, when the train between Jerusalem and Tel Aviv opened in 2019, it had an astonishing 95-99% on time arrival rate. Yet, through 2019, Israelis viewed the train as a "national disaster:" unreliable, frequent cancellations, late arrivals and delays due to getting stuck in tunnels. [6] This happened because Israeli news outlets made a point of reporting every time a train was canceled or delayed. Can one imagine a news headline like "The 10:30 a.m. bus got stuck in traffic?" but that was the reality through 2019 and early 2020 when it came to the new Tel Aviv-Jerusalem train.

There are many other examples of Israelis acquiring "negative knowledge" about Israel. Hence, there are times that someone living outside of Israel would have a better perspective of Zionism – just like someone living in Babylon had at times a better perspective on Judaism than someone living in Judea.

This is an important point. While the messaging in Israel today is clearly compatible with Zionism, what if it changes at some point due to this or that interest or development? With Zionism as the organizing principle of Judaism, Diaspora Jews can serve as defenders of Zionism. This is already happening in a very real and meaningful way.

Lone Soldiers

A fascinating phenomenon has emerged in recent years. American and other Diaspora Jews are increasingly volunteering to serve in the Israeli army. In the past, such volunteering often consisted of a support-function, such as through Sar-El and Mahal programs, which placed hundreds of volunteers every year on military bases. But in recent years there has been a tidal wave of Diaspora Jewish men and women volunteering for full service, including the elite combat units, being known as "lone soldiers."

Before college or after college, more and more Jewish youth are coming to Israel and joining the army. There is also a smaller sub-trend of US military veterans who, upon completion of their service in America, come to Israel and volunteer with the Israeli army.

The lone soldier phenomenon is one of the stronger expressions of the transformation to Judaism 3.0. It is not only indicative of the ultimate bond between the Jewish Diaspora and the Jewish state, but

---

6 – See my article: "The Jerusalem fast-train vs. the powerful media", *The Jerusalem Post*, May 11, 2019.

it is indicative of the acceptability that Judaism is a nation, and not only a religion. Certainly, for a Diaspora Jew, serving in the Israeli army is an act of Jewish nationalism, an act of Zionism, as opposed to merely an expression of Jewish religiosity. Moreover, it is central to the Diaspora Jew's Jewish experience. This is given the great sacrifices and commitment these Jews undertake when volunteering to serve.

In addition, it serves as a potent response to post-Zionism. An Israeli notices those who come from outside in the name of Zionism and are willing to sacrifice so much. Perhaps even more than Aliya, lone soldiers provide to the Israeli the ultimate proof that the Zionist narrative is alive and well.

Israel is a small country whose soldiers are no more than a few hours away from home. It is not easy being a soldier, and family support is paramount. Diaspora Jews who come to Israel to serve do not have this support. Organizations such as the Michael Levin Lone Soldier Center and Chayal el Chayal provide support, and so do the "Israeli parents" that the military assigns to each lone soldier. But mostly it is the virtual group hug provided by the entire country. [7] Embedded in this hug is the essence of Judaism 3.0, and through it the negation of post-Zionism.

Meeting young Jewish students in Paris in 1896, Herzl said: "I am not asking you to march yet, I am only asking you to rise." Now, 120 years later, the Diaspora youth are not just rising – they are marching!

(iii) Recognizing the Transformation addresses post-Zionism's breeding grounds

The simplification that on the surface, 99% of Israelis vote for Zionist parties is countered by a subterranean ecosystem that promotes post-Zionism. Recognizing the transformation would disrupt this ecosystem.

End of the sacred cows era opens doors

In recent years Israel has finally begun to break away from the glorification of the status quo on religious-secular relations. This, on the one hand, removes a hurdle to the transformation, but on the other, presents new risks. Once the status quo is broken, once the file of Israel's Jewish nature is opened, sacred cows are under threat – amongst them, the sacred cow of Zionism.

An example of a sacred cow that is on the table as a result of the

7 – Jacob Magid and JTA: "Over a thousand Israelis attend funeral for American lone soldier", *The Times of Israel*, 28 March 2019; also Noa Amouyal: "Israel pays tribute: Honoring a warrior", *The Jerusalem Post*, May 1, 2017.

relaxation of the status quo involves the Holocaust. A few years ago, as Israelis united in spirit to mark Holocaust Memorial Day (a day of somber consensus in Israel – cafes and restaurants close and the entire country stops for a moment of silence), a former Speaker of Israel's Parliament, published an op-ed calling for the cancellation of the day, stating Israel had "overdrawn its historical account."[8]

This example is not isolated. Other symbols and core beliefs are "on the table" once the country breaks from its status quo. This includes the core belief that Israel should remain the Jewish state.

The Mainstreaming of post-Zionism

As mentioned, post-Zionism was until recently, and to a large extent still is, a fringe and negligible view within the Israeli dialogue. But a dangerous mainstreaming of the post-Zionist narrative is now embedded in Israel's internal political and social dialogue.

Zionism's core narrative, Israel as the homeland of the Jewish people, is being increasingly challenged by the competing narrative suggesting that Israel, just like any other country, is merely the home of the Israelis ("A state for all its citizens"). While there are various flavors of post-Zionism, it boils down to this simple question – Is Israel the homeland of the Jewish nation?

Debate about the path to peace has inadvertently strengthened the post-Zionism threat

The internal challenge to Zionism has been magnified in the last decade by two aspects of the Israeli-Palestinian peace process.

A key demand by Israel in its negotiations with the Palestinians is to be recognized as a Jewish state. This has prompted an ancillary internal debate in Israel about the importance of such recognition. While the opposition is mostly about the policy of making such recognition a demand, as opposed to being about the merit of the recognition, inevitably the debate results in some doubt of "just how important is it" to be recognized as a Jewish state?

The other aspect is the shift in advocacy strategy and rationale for the two-state solution. Proponents of the two-state solution have, in the past, advocated it to Israelis in terms of peace ("land for peace"), then in terms of justice, then in terms of end of terrorism, then in terms of avoiding the threat of international isolation. In recent years, the

8 – Avraham Burg: "In ten years will Holocaust Remembrance Day be marked on Tisha b'Av?", www.walla.com, April 12, 2013.

primary promotion of the two-state solution has been in terms of the viable threat to the Jewish nature of Israel.

A broadly accepted narrative in Israel's mainstream is that if Israel fails to achieve a two-state reality, it will transition into a one-state in which Jews will soon become the minority, and hence, lose their state.

The notion is so strong that significant portions of the Israeli mainstream have even been calling for a unilateral withdrawal to a border that would assure a Jewish majority (to the 1967 lines, or with some adjustments). Proponents even acknowledge that the withdrawal could result in terrorism and weaken Israel's ability to defend itself, but that it is worth the risk given that one state could mean the end of Zionism and the end of Israel.

The high volume of the message "one state = the end" is certainly not intended for Israelis to start getting used to the idea of post-Zionism, or of defeatism. It assumes that the threat of an end to Israel would be strong enough that it would persuade Israelis to support the two-state solution.

Inevitably, a byproduct of the message of a looming end is the early seed of an acceptance that such a possibility exists. End of Israel is on the table again, just like it was in Israel's first two decades prior to the 1967 war.

Political debate about the Nation-State Bill inadvertently turned into a debate about the Jewish nation-state

Similar dynamics came to bear in the 2018 debate of Israel's Nation-State Bill, which reaffirmed that Israel is the nation-state of the Jewish people. While there was a robust internal debate in Israel about aspects of the law, its wording and message, the essence of the law has been deeply rooted in the Israeli consensus since its founding. Yet, the debate over the law quickly spilled to issues beyond wording and implication, and into the core essence of what the law was reaffirming – should Israel really be the national homeland of the Jewish people? The law was introduced on the eve of an election year, and the opposition to it was loud and broad, capturing daily headlines.

The camp opposing the law, which included most of the Zionist left and center-left, claimed that Israel is indeed the nation-state of the Jewish people, but that the law is not needed or offends Israel's non-Jewish population or that they opposed specific aspects of the law, such as the section about the Hebrew language being the only official language. Instead, it was falsely perceived by some, especially those not paying close attention, that the objection to the bill was about opposition to Israel being the nation-state of the Jewish people. Suddenly, the 99% consensus about Israel being the national homeland of the Jewish nation, about Zionism – was dented. The transformation to Judaism 3.0 provides a backstop to this denting – Zionism is not on the table – that is as long Judaism is not on the table.

Israeli Jews increasingly vote for non-Zionist parties

While still about 99% of Israeli Jews vote for Zionist parties, there has been a rapid increase in the small Jewish minority that supports the Arab Joint List, a non-Zionist party. It is estimated that it increased by 100% between the September 2019 election and the one in March 2020 – though still less than 1% of the Jewish electorate. (As discussed, the Haredi parties are de facto Zionist and are not at all exposed to the risk of the post-Zionist threat.)

The March 2020 vote to the Joint list was not likely a referendum on Zionism but rather a result of other aspects in Israeli Jewish voting patterns: Meretz, the natural home of many on the Jewish left merged with the Labor party, which was led by figures that some on the left were uncomfortable with (including Orly Levy-Abekasis, who till recently was member Yisrael Beiteinu, viewed till then as a far-right party). The other party left-wing voters could have voted for was Blue and White, which lacked ideological clarity, and even included self-proclaimed right-wingers. In addition, the Joint List leader Ayman Odeh, unlike his predecessors and some of his colleagues, is a relatable and a likable figure to Israeli Jews.

There were also some Israeli Jews who voted for the Arab Joint List in support of its coexistence messages and as an expression of their opposition to the Nation-State Bill.

The shift of an estimated 20,000 or so Israeli Jews that historically voted for Zionist parties, and in 2020 voted for a non-Zionist party should not be overstated. It is merely a fraction of a percent, and driven by reasons other than Zionism, which was not "on the table" in this round of elections.

And yet, a line has been crossed. While "Zionism" was not "on the table" in the March 2020 elections, it might be in future elections, and those voters are already in. A non-Zionist party is being mainstreamed, and with it rises the risk of the mainstream of post-Zionism.

Such mainstreaming is also driven by political interest. Until now, it was clear that non-Zionist parties were off-limits when it came to forming a government. How can a party that does not endorse the basic tenet of the Jewish state be a member of government? But since the support of the Joint List could have put the center-left Blue and White party in power, its mainstreaming turned into the interest of about half of Israel who wanted Blue and White to take power.

A similar pattern emerged a year later in the March 2021 election. This time, another non-Zionist party that got elected, Raam, indicated they might lend their support for Prime Minister Netanyahu's Likud party. This contributed to the broad process of legitimizing those parties as potential partners despite an anti-Zionist stance. Indeed, in June 2021, Naftali Bennett became prime minister, thanks to the support of Raam, who joined his government coalition.

The examples given of post-Zionist dangers – through the peace-process, opposition to the Nation-State Bill and the vote for non-Zionist parties – can be dismissed on their own merits as too far-fetched. But in a soundbite headline-driven era, with limited attention span, there is a natural risk. The two-step process of adapting a behavior pattern is a known human trait. "Just one puff" creates a precedent and gateway to heavy smoking, and "just coming in for one drink" can lead to other things. Hence, the existential risk of post-Zionism is real and dangerous. Recognizing the transformation to Judaism 3.0 provides the defense from that risk.

(iv) Recognizing the Transformation defends Israelis from intense post-Zionism pressures from Europe and NGOs

The two threats of post-Zionism and Israel-bashing are different, but they feed on one another, and often come from the same source. One is an internal threat that is aided by the outside, and the other is an external threat. Indeed, post-Zionism is enjoying a strong tailwind from the increasingly mainstreaming of the Israel-bashing fashion in Europe, and its rapid spread to more and more European-influenced social circles.

Given globalization and Israel's integrated economy, such fashion has trickled into Israel as well. Some Israelis feel they need to distance themselves from Zionism in order to participate in European circles.

An entry ticket to Europe's academic, media and social circles might indeed be proving that even though you are Israeli, you are one of the "good guys." For example, some in European academia are believed to quietly be assured before inviting an Israeli professor to speak at a conference that the speaker is not a Zionist, rather, that he is a "righteous Israeli."

This is consistent with the conventional European falsehood that the Israeli-Palestinian conflict is due to extremists on both sides, and that there are indeed good Israelis and good Palestinians.

A bookend of that is the equation that "not every Israeli is a Zionist," just like "not every Palestinian is a Hamas supporter." Europeans bring that notion into their work in NGOs, the UN and the EU as well as express this notion to Israelis in Europe. This notion provides support for the fringe presence of post-Zionism in Israel. This is evident in the glamor and "hero status" that Israeli post-Zionist and anti-Zionist authors receive in Europe and around the world.

Israelis want to succeed, be accepted and included. The external encouragement of post-Zionism gives substantial support and amplification to the internally generated existential threat of post-Zionism. This is honed in through a series of specific European-dictated messages that smooth the road of the Israeli into post-Zionism.

Judaism 3.0 protects Israelis from portrayal of Zionism as Colonialism

In recent years there has been a rise in the number of leaders who on the one hand openly label Zionism as colonialism and on the other hand voice a call to once and for all end colonialism. Jeremy Corbyn and the "Corbynistas" in the UK are prime examples of this. They are not on the European fringe. This was the leader of one of the UK's two largest parties and a credible candidate for prime minister.

Similar attitudes can be found with supporters of Bernie Sanders and the Progressive movement in the United States, as well as various elements of the European left. Those groups are in search of a common narrative and have identified anti-colonialism: rebelling against Europe's colonial past and fighting it where it exists today.

To those groups, Zionism is a golden gift. It remains the last bastion of colonialism according to their narrative, and hence, a tangible cause to unite against. For them, Zionism is about a group of white people (the Jews) coming into a region not their own (or at least not theirs for 2,000 years), and displacing the local inhabitants. To add to the gross injustice, the white Zionist then engages in additional land grab, illegal settlements, displacement and abuse of the local population.

Many of those who carry such messages are not radicals, anarchists or anti-Semites. In fact, many of them maintain contact with Israelis, many of them have visited Israel. Being part of the mainstream, their message carries greater credibility, and therefore their narrative inevitably trickles to Israelis, and provides a boost to the post-Zionism narrative in Israel.

Israelis are vulnerable to the message that Zionism is colonialism and that therefore Zionism should be negated. Recognizing the transformation would provide a firewall against such charges, since it would then suggest that Judaism is colonialism – a message that these mainstream voices would not dare say and Israelis would certainly not be receptive to hear.

Judaism 3.0 protects Israelis from portrayal of Zionism as counter-universalism

The European Union and much of Europe carries the message of universalism. In its extreme version, universalism means "no nation, no religion, no country." These, according to prevailing European views, were the causes of wars in the past. In the 20th century alone, hundreds of millions of Europeans died because of nationalism, because of a narrative, because of an ideology.

Here comes Zionism and, according to such thinking, reverses the course of humanity – reverses the move towards peace and universalism and goes back to nationalism, to ideology, to particularity. Don't the Zionists know that this is what caused wars in the past? Sure enough, the Zionists are now at war with the Arabs. Case proven! As a result of this logic, for many Europeans and those in its sphere of influence, objection to Zionism is essential to preserve the universalism point of view.

Moreover, the European promotion of lack-of-narrative is negated by Zionism, which is all about a narrative. Zionism has emerged as a counter-thesis to the contemporary European ethos.

This is becoming even more potent with recent European elections – in Britain, France, Germany and Austria – where a substantial group of Europeans are rebelling against the extreme universalist approach. In the May 2019 European elections, such parties won the plurality of the vote in both France and Great Britain, and this is spreading throughout Europe.

Germans are suddenly saying, "we are indeed German nationalists." British are saying, "we are not just pan-Europeans, we are British." And not surprisingly, nationalist and ideological parties in Europe tend to be strong supporters of Zionism.

This further antagonizes Europeans against Zionism, now associated with the loathed populist rebelling European parties. Israelis' social connection with Europeans as well as their own instinctive opposition to such European populist parties, some of which house anti-Semitic elements, further contribute to the promotion of post-Zionism within Israel. Yet, recognizing that Zionism is the anchor of Judaism would mitigate such a narrative.

Judaism 3.0 protects Israelis from charges that Zionism is counter-Patriotism

Zionism is a national movement. In recent years, especially after the election of Donald Trump in 2016, there has been an attack on the concept of nationalism. This came to new heights as French President Emmanuel Macron, during World War I memorial ceremonies, proclaimed that nationalism is a betrayal of patriotism: "Patriotism is the exact opposite of nationalism."

Zionism is a form of nationalism, thus the words President Macron used, and which got support from mainstream circles in Europe, inadvertently strengthens post-Zionism.

Indeed, Israel's friends are involved in a campaign that has nothing to do with Zionism or Israel. The popular themes in Europe – anti-colonialism, universalism and anti-nationalism, are not reactionary to Zionism. They are organic views, but lead to the inevitable opposition to Zionism.

Israelis spending time in those European circles adopt those themes and then without any outside encouragement, naturally apply these ideas to the environment which is most familiar to them: Israel. Hence, post-Zionism can grow organically and almost subconsciously as a secondary side-effect of Israelis' global interactions.

Judaism 3.0 protects from demoralization of Israeli society

Along with the pressures from the outside and the threat of post-Zionism from the inside, comes a rising degree of "fatigue" in small, yet vocal circles of Israel. A large part of this fatigue is "war fatigue" – the notion that we have had it with of 70 years of war, and that it is time to end this state of living, no matter what. This is understandable – just as Israel recovers from one wave, here comes another wave of terrorism, another wave of rockets, more sirens, more trauma, more tears. Simply put, "we are sick and tired of fighting; we are sick and tired of wars."

This kind of demoralization can lead to a legitimate "surrender" option. While not as damaging if done on an individual level (a family leaves the country to a more peaceful life outside of Israel), it is brutally damaging if done as a group. This is on the fringe, but there is a risk of mainstreaming the notion of putting an end to Jewish sovereignty and "giving them what they want." For example, the idea of "just let us live peacefully as individuals and forget about the national thing." This philosophy seems to have been "trial ballooned" in "Judas", one of the last books by Amos Oz. The main character raises the simple question – "Is it all worth it?"

Gradually, the "is it all worth it" question is on the table, or at least on the margins of the table. This is in sharp contrast to the previous wall-to-wall consensus that, of course, it is. Demoralization of this kind is getting support by re-working the equation around "worth it."

In the past, the notion was that one lives in Israel despite the difficulty and hardship. Such feelings were romantic, strong and filled with conviction.

There was a common saying in Israel, "We wish we were in Switzerland" that was accompanied with a resolute sense that unlike Switzerland, we needed to fight for our survival and prevail. But in recent years, in some circles of Israeli society, people have begun to say, "Why should I wish for Switzerland? I can actually move to Switzerland."

The notion of "This is the situation and we will make the best of it" has been replaced with a question: "Where am I better off?" An answer came to light with the "Milky criteria." A broadly publicized analysis showed that it was cheaper to buy an Israeli company's popular Milky brand of yogurt in Berlin than it was in Israel. This analysis gave support for the notion that one is better off living in Berlin than in Israel. [9]

Cumulative and repeated assaults on the quality of life in Israel with exaggerated and misleading cost-of-living data contribute to the post-Zionist narrative by demoralizing the population.

In addition, the outside attempts to hijack the term "Zionism" and portray Zionism as a term that represents immorality and racism contributes to the demoralization of Israeli society. Once the transformation is recognized, Zionism can only be considered immoral and racist if Judaism is considered immoral and racist.

(v) Negating the Alternative Response to the post-Zionism threat: Diversification

Jewish transformation to Judaism 3.0 could mean that the elimination of Zionism would also mean the elimination of Judaism. Thus, some would argue that the recognition of the transformation would put Judaism's survivability at a greater risk. But that is only theoretical.

It is already true today that there is no feasible path to the survival of Judaism without Zionism, and hence, a threat of post-Zionism is a threat

9 – "The Milky Way", *The Jerusalem Post* Editorial, October 6, 2014, also see "Olim Le Berlin" (Ascending to Berlin) Facebook page.

of post-Judaism. Not recognizing the transformation would not change the existence of the threat, just like not diagnosing a disease does not change the existence of such an underlying disease.

One could mistakenly argue that a response to post-Zionism being a threat to Judaism should be the escape from Zionism for "diversification purposes." Developing a non-Zionist Jewish alternative, the logic goes, could assure Jewish continuity in the unlikely event that Zionism is eliminated. Creating a non-Zionist Jewish alternative is not only non-sustainable, but even if it would be created, it would not be able to survive a demise of Zionism.

One could create non-Zionist Jewish alternatives that could cling to something else. That has already happened. In a sense, the emergence of Christianity is the non-Zionist Jewish alternative, incorporating key aspects of the Jewish religion without the Jewish nation. But for Judaism to survive as Judaism, Zionism is essential.

As discussed, the answer to the existential threat of post-Zionism is not the escape from Zionism, but the doubling-down on Zionism. Moreover, if one were to look for diversification, it should not occur outside of Zionism, but from within. American and Diaspora Jewry having Zionism as their anchor would create a much-welcomed diversification. As discussed, the one-nation market in Israel and the herd mentality can place Israelis at risk to distorted messages. Having a thriving Zionist center that is outside the one market, where most people read the same newspaper or listen to the same radio stations, could be of utmost importance to Zionism and hence, to Judaism.

In the previous transformation of Judaism from Biblical Judaism (Judaism 1.0) to Rabbinic Judaism (Judaism 2.0), diversification was not done outside of Rabbinic Judaism – for example, through the Karaite – but rather within Rabbinic Judaism, such as through the thriving Jewish community in Babylon. Similarly, the insurance policy for Judaism is not by having diversification outside of Zionism, but from within.

Post-Israel scenario: Better-off in Judaism 3.0

Even in a horrendous case where Israel would be eliminated, Judaism would be more likely to survive if it had been already recognized that it has transformed its organizing principle.

Rabbinic Judaism being Judaism's organizing principle in a post-Israel world would require secular Jews to be connected through an ethos that existed 2,000 years ago – through longing for the old Temple. But under the transformation, that connection would be more recent, more viable, and indeed with greater global support – the longing for Zion would be the longing for Zionism.

4. JUDAISM 3.0 ROBS THE ISRAEL-BASHING MOVEMENT OF ITS STARTING POINT

Key to the Israel-bashing movement's success is the fortification of the Judaism 2.0 narrative: Judaism's organizing principle is its religious aspect, and moreover, Judaism is merely a religion. Since Israel-bashers are attacking Israel and not the Jewish religion, the logic goes, their efforts are legitimate and do not represent Jew-hatred or any sort of hatred.

The argument that anti-Israel attacks are not anti-Jewish attacks are accepted not just by the attackers, but also by a meaningful portion of the defenders, not to mention observers. The more it becomes accepted that Judaism is merely a religion and not a nation, the stronger the legitimacy of the Israel-bashing movement is. Or in reverse, if it is made clear that Judaism's anchor is its national aspect – Zionism, then the Israel-bashing movement would lose much of its legitimacy.

Moreover, Judaism staying in Judaism 2.0 enables the Israel-bashers to make their movement into one of love and liberation: It is not an attack on Jews, it is an attack on Zionism, and an attempt to liberate Jews from the malaise of the occupation and colonialism that was inflicted on Judaism through Zionism. According to this narrative, Israel-bashing helps the Jews and Judaism, since it eradicates a rogue anomaly that occurred in Judaism a century ago – Jewish nationalism.

Recognizing the transformation to Judaism 3.0 robs the Israel-bashers of their starting point. It also underscores the built-in hypocrisy. Most of those who make such arguments "in defense of the Jewish religion" are secular and even anti-religious. It is illogical that Israel-bashers suddenly turned into defenders of religion. Even by their own logic, consciously or subconsciously, willingly or unwillingly, Israel-bashing is Jewish-bashing. The response must be on the national level, since that is the only arena that concerns the attackers.

Increased Jewish religiosity, revival of Jewish literature and culture, greater emphasis on bagel and lox or on Tikun Olam are all irrelevant to the attempts of the Israel-bashers and even supports their cause by showcasing the strength of Judaism outside Zionism.

(i) Where does the lethal Israel-bashing threat lie?

Many dismiss the Israel-bashing threat as an existential threat to Judaism, claiming that it only lies on the fringe. Part of it is a confusion of terms. Most notably when it comes to BDS. The Boycott, Divestment, Sanctions movement is only a fragment of the amorphous Israel-bashing coalition. While it is true that BDS and other extreme expressions of Israel-bashing originate mostly in the fringe, realities are more complex:

- This fringe has been successful at mainstreaming its message. The BDS movement, for example, has sympathizers with various degrees of enthusiasm through the European mainstream, and within far-left circles in the United States. Even the Israel-bashers' term for Israel – "the genocidal colonialist Zionist entity" – gets traction with some mainstream critics of Israel's policies, who are exposed to the Israel-bashers' messaging on social media. This is especially the case in times of military conflict, such as the one with Hamas in May 2021, when media coverage is focused on Israel and emotions run high. Then, the Israel-bashers' messages are not viewed as "fringe," but rather as a component in the pro-Palestinian side of the conflict.

- This fringe is attaining more and more political power. This was reflected in the rise of Jeremy Corbyn in the UK, a candidate for prime minister in 2019, and the rise of the so-called "squad" in the US Congress in 2018. [10] The prospects of a 2022 Democrat primary between incumbent New York Senator Chuck Schumer, who at times refers to himself as "Shomer Israel" (guardian of Israel) and Congresswoman Alexandria Ocasio-Cortez, a member of the squad who called Israeli defense operations in Gaza a "massacre," could symbolize the inflection point when the fringe becomes the mainstream.

- More alarming is that the core of the existential threat from Israel-bashing is not even in the fringe. The most lethal expression might come from those who are not part of the movement, but are influenced by it. They are friends of Israel in the heart of the European mainstream and by extension in Europhile circles in North America. Those are not merely sympathetic to some of the fringe's messages but are actually influenced by the Israeli-bashing culture. When media outlets describe Israeli defense operations against Hamas in Gaza as "Israel attacks Palestinians" and when they rationalize Hamas firing indiscriminate rockets into Israeli

10 – The squad consists of young progressive members of the US Congress: Alexandria Ocasio-Cortez of New York, Ilhan Omar of Minnesota, Ayanna Pressley of Massachusetts and Rashida Tlaib of Michigan. In 2021, Jamal Bowman, who defeated Rep. Elliot Engel, became the newest member.

cities, the Israel-bashing poison inevitably trickles into the global mainstream. That is particularly the case with younger audiences who have a more active social media presence and are more vulnerable to social pressure. There are social circles whose entry point is acknowledgment that Israel engages in massacre, ethnic-cleaning and genocide in Palestine (just as in the past, there were social circles whose entry point was the acknowledgment of the widely accepted belief that Jews use the blood of Christian children to prepare Passover Matzos). This happened in the May 2021 conflict, when the Israel-bashing message carriers were no longer on the fringe. Respectable news personalities, late-night comedians, business leaders, and even some politicians and diplomats labeled Israel's actions against Hamas military targets as "murder," "bombing Gaza indiscriminately," and "targeting civilians." Some suggested Israel should not take any measure to strike back at Hamas, and instead rely on its Iron-dome rocket defense system. (There were 12 Israeli casualties from Hamas rockets, as well as hundreds of injuries and thousands of trauma injuries of various degrees.) Similarly, the notion that the eviction of eight Palestinian families in a civil property dispute amounts to "Ethnic Cleansing" was adopted by some mainstream friends of Israel who were merely "expressing criticism." Indeed, when a ceasefire was announced after 11 days of fighting, the rockets stopped, but the poison that infected the mainstream has stayed. This is just like through the centuries, after seven days of Passover, Jews were no longer making Matzos, but the poison spread by the blood-libels resonated in the mindset of the European mainstream.

These three factors amount to a frightening reality. Just like anti-Semitism that preceded it, and nearly eradicated Judaism a few decades after it first appeared as a fringe movement, Israel-bashing has spread and is now present throughout the spectrum of the world's touch-points with the Jews.

Just like anti-Semitism, it has moderate "polite" elements, as Herzl called them, and extreme elements, such as those who were calling for outright negation of Judaism in Herzl's time, and of Israel today.

Where does the danger to Judaism lie? Is it from the outspoken, outright BDS activist who is openly calling for an end to Israel? Or is it in the "polite elements," such as a European government official who packages his criticism in the context of friendly words to an ally, and has both legitimacy and the fulfillment mechanism?

(ii) The path to destruction through Israel-bashers-lite

The path to Israel's destruction was, until recently, a military one. As recent as in 1973, this path nearly materialized. But today, the threat of a military invasion from Arab armies has greatly subsided, due to a number of factors: Those strong armies that served as the path to Israel's destruction have been severely weakened – such as the Syrian and Iraqi armies. It is also due to the changing interests of the Arab nations, who no longer want to destroy Israel. In fact, most Arab countries view a strong Israel to be in their strategic interest and some of them have recently struck peace treaties with the Jewish state. Finally, it is due to the further fragmentation of the Arab world, and the further strengthening of the Israeli military and intelligence capabilities.

Now that the military path towards the elimination of Israel has subsided, another path to Israel's destruction has opened up – the political path. Israel's adversaries recognize this.

Hence, the vehicle to end the Zionist endeavor is no longer through military means, but through influencing multinational organizations: the UN and their various agencies, the International Criminal Court, the EU and even individual European governments.

The dream of the Israel-basher is that the UN Security Council will strenuously condemn, maybe even impose sanctions that will demoralize the Israelis. If the sanctions and isolation are strong enough, the thinking goes, the Israeli elite would simply leave, leading to a domino effect and the end of Israel. Same goes for actions of the International Criminal Court who could order mass arrests of Israeli soldiers and citizens living in the West Bank and in Jerusalem. The mere threat of arrest can paralyze Israelis' travel, business and freedom – akin to the threat of terrorism.

While some might even fantasize of upgrading the sanctions against Israel into intentional use of force like in Yugoslavia, the more realistic path to destroy Israel is a diplomatic war of attrition against the Jewish state. This path to destruction does not go through the hardcore of Israel-bashers, but rather through sympathizers of the Israel-bashing movement. While the hardcore Israel-basher might be in the fringe, the Israel-bashers-lite and sympathizers have spread into the core of European governments, the EU, multinational organizations, the media and hence, to public opinion. In particular, it has a strong presence in the young generations. It then percolates through Europe's sphere of influence into the United States – to college campuses, academic circles, civic groups, the media and the cocktail receptions in New York and Los Angeles.

The Israel-bashers-lite present an immediate existential threat to Israel and thus to Judaism. The threat is not to the religious aspects of Judaism, nor to the immediate safety of individual Jews (Judaism 2.0). It is funneled specifically through Israel and Zionism. Hence, recognizing the transformation would go a long way to confront the threat.

Ecosystem of frustration in Europe

What makes the threat from the Israel-bashers-lite even more dangerous is the ecosystem of frustration already described. Those built-up European frustrations are bound to find an outlet at one point or another, and if history is the judge – that outlet tends to be the Jews. This is already evident in the intensifying European political opposition to the Jewish state and the lack of public outcry to its outrageous actions, such as product labeling or implying that Jerusalem has no Jewish connection.

Such lack of public outcry to early symptoms of a massive anti-Jewish movement is a recurring phenomenon in Europe. In previous episodes of European assaults on Judaism, the public outcry was passive or at best weak.

Europe is in its early stages of dealing with its new frustrations. During the Coronavirus pandemic, anti-Semitic accusations in Europe went rampant, and many accusations were directed at Zionism. For example, in early 2021 as Israel became the world's leading vaccinator of its population and Europe was struggling, a new version of the good-old European blood-libel emerged: "Israel is vaccinating its people, while letting the Palestinians die of Covid." Ironically, this came from the same people who view the Palestinian Authority as a sovereign government and refer it as "the State of Palestine."

More alarming are the set of long-term European frustrations that are looking for an outlet. It has only been one hundred years since its unexpected fall from grace and abrupt shift of power to the United States, yet European deniability is still paramount. Similarly is the European radical shift from a religious society to aggressive secularism as well as the extreme shift from monarchies to liberal democracies that occurred over the last two centuries. As discussed, there is increasing evidence that Europeans are not sufficiently prepared for such shifts. Same goes for Europe's conflict with Islam and its dealing with new domestic-generated terrorism. These new and growing European frustrations mean that there will be a receptive ear to the menacing Israel-bashing movement.

(iii) External threats push Jews towards one another

In the past, the mere existence of a threat was not sufficient for the Jews to transition or transform. The threat needed to mature and even materialize in order for Jews to reluctantly transform.

As long as there is plausible-deniability, the Jews will linger in the old frameworks (along the line of the Biblical narrative of the "Egyptian watermelons" as a sign of stability of Israeli life in Egypt).

Herzl recognized this human behavior pattern and hence, along with identifying the threat to Judaism, he also recognized a positive aspect of the threat: "There, in anti-Semitism lies the will of God to benefit [the Jews] – for it pushes us towards one another and unifies us. Its pressures unite us and such unity liberates us."

Applying Herzl's logic to today, it is possible that Israel-bashing today may be the will of God to push Jews towards one another and unite around their Zionist identity, to liberate Jews from their past and unify under Judaism 3.0.

How should Judaism adjust to the new existential threat of Israel-bashing? First and foremost, to recognize that it exists as an existential threat to Judaism. So far, this has not happened.

Israel-bashing tends to get diminished into the limited category of BDS – the movement to Boycott, Divest and Sanction Israel. As discussed, the BDS movement tends to be associated with fringe elements and is generally viewed as an outlier. BDS is certainly not an existential threat to Judaism, but Israel-bashing is – it has the mechanism, philosophy, popular support and resources to eradicate the Jewish state and hence, to eradicate Judaism.

Acknowledging that Israel-bashing is an existential threat which is alive and real goes a long way. This is especially given the errors of the past.

When anti-Semitism emerged in the late 19th century, it was treated in a similar way to BDS today – just a little movement on the fringe. There was a failure to recognize that anti-Semitism was the current manifestation of the centuries-old Jew-hatred. It even took Herzl time to do so. As mentioned, he first developed what he described as a "liberal attitude" towards anti-Semitism. Once he recognized the magnitude of the threat, Herzl tried to alert the Jews, but he encountered widespread ambivalence. Being rejected early on by a group of French rabbis and intellectuals, he concluded: "French Jews look at my idea in hostility. I did not expect it to be anything else. It is too good for them here. Too good for them to think that a situation can change." Indeed, when the situation changed for the worse for French Jews, it was too late.

Today, a danger looms, but it is still not too late to recognize and counter this danger. And yet, the danger of Israel-bashing is often dismissed, since just like for the French Jews of 1895, there is sufficient plausible-deniability that allows today's Jews to enjoy the "Egyptian watermelons."

5. Conclusion: Threat as the Propelling Force to the Transformation

Theodor Herzl identified anti-Semitism as a key enabler of Jewish survivability. Jews being rejected by Europeans forced them to stay insular and led to the unlikely preservation of Judaism.

Today, the threat of Israel-bashing forces Jews into their Zionist identity, while the threat of post-Zionism awakens latent Zionist sentiments in Israel. Similarly, the reality of evaporation of American Jewry forces the "Jewish Question" upon American Jews.

The mere recognition of the transformation to Judaism 3.0 goes a long way in providing protection from those new existential threats to Judaism. It strips Israel-bashers of the false argument that the assault is not against Judaism, but merely against Zionism. It neutralizes much of the lethal diplomatic capability of the Israel-bashers, and in particular the Israel-bashers-lite. Keeping in mind the politically correct culture of the organizations that are at the forefront of the Israel-bashing movement, a recognition that Zionism is the organizing principle of Judaism, would deny them the luxury of claiming Israel-bashing is not Jewish-bashing – it would turn Israel-bashing into a profound non-politically correct activity. That is in particular in Europe.

Europe's last go at the Jews is audaciously now used as a weapon against Israel. The diabolic narrative that is increasingly trickling into mainstream circles suggests that saving the Palestinians from Israel is applying the lessons of the Holocaust.

Recognizing the transformation would put an end to the Israel-basher's shameful attempt to recruit the battle against anti-Semitism into their own cause.

Recognizing the transformation would also defend against the threat of demoralization of Israeli society. If Jews are led to believe that indeed the attacks against Israel are semi-legitimate and are not against the Jews, this could lead to attrition of Zionist ideology in Israel and the strengthening the post-Zionism narrative described earlier.

The nascent narrative in Israel that suggests that "we are sick and tired of fighting" also has a diplomatic branch: "We are sick and tired of being condemned by the UN." It also has a self-esteem branch: "We are sick and tired of being scolded by the BBC and rejected by Europeans."

All of those applications of externally inflicted fatigue present an existential threat to Judaism due to attrition, due to surrender. But the transformation to Judaism 3.0 further emphasizes the reality that there is no "surrender option." At best there are illusions that a surrender option exists. The 2005 Gaza withdrawal and aftermath provided strong evidence for the existence of this illusion. The widespread notion at the time that "if we only get out, we will be loved by the UN" and that Israel would have the "moral high-ground" should it encounter terrorism from Gaza was shuttered three years later. Israel's defending itself from a barrage of Hamas missiles was met not only with condemnation from the UN, scolding from the BBC and rejection by Europeans, but with an unprecedented escalation in the age-old saga of Jew-hatred, labeling Israel's self-defense actions as a "crime against humanity!"

Under the transformation, it would be clear that labeling Israel's right to self-defense as a crime against humanity is the same as labeling the Jews' right to self-defense as a crime against humanity. (Jews killed over 100 Germans in the Warsaw Ghetto Uprising.) Such labeling puts Europeans and other Israel-bashers back in a position that they are not comfortable with. Hence, it would curtail such Israel-bashing capabilities.

More importantly, the transformation would underscore that one cannot "convert" out of the problem of Israel-bashing. The recognition that there is no "surrender option" to Israel-bashing is similar to past episodes of Jew-hatred where there was no surrender option, only illusions of surrender. And hence, recognizing there is no "self-correcting" or "surrender" option would push Jews into their Judaism, and in particular would block the effort to demoralize Israeli society.

(i) Threat as condition to change

Research shows that people are less likely to make a change in order to obtain a gain, than they are to make a change in order to avoid a loss in the same magnitude. Therefore, a transformation from an existing state of affairs is not likely, unless there is a real and tangible risk of losing what currently exists. This happens when there is a recognition that things are about to change for the worse unless a transformation occurs.

Netflix transformed from an online DVD rental store since it had no choice. People were no longer renting DVDs. It realized that if it kept its current state of affairs, it would go out of business. It recognized that it had to transform in order to survive. Same with an individual who neglects his cavities until there is a threat that he will lose his teeth. Same with an individual that does not change his bad eating or smoking habits until diagnosed with a life-threatening disease.

In the early stages of the 2020 Coronavirus crisis, it became evident that certain behavioral patterns had to change – such as hugging and group gatherings. But it was not until there was a viable threat of horrific danger that populations began adhering to what they knew was necessary to do. The magnitude of the threat in the Coronavirus pandemic has already led to more long-term changes – both on personal and collective levels.

The Ottoman Empire in the 19th and early 20th century needed to change. There was no doubt about this – internally and externally. The system of bribes, the ubiquitous corruption, the lack of controls as well as the decentralized and unaccountable style of management, all produced a situation where the empire could no longer survive under those conditions. While the writing was on the wall for decades, the changes that the so-called "sick man of Europe" needed to undertake, did not occur. It was not until there was an existential threat – a real viable fear of the end of the empire that a transformation began to occur – the Young Turks were able to launch a revolution with the intention to change things. The revolution came too late in the case of the dying empire.

The previous Jewish transformation 2,000 years ago was also driven by an existential threat.

(ii) Transformation from Judaism 1.0 to 2.0 was due to a threat

There were many debates, protests and calls for a change in the centuries leading to the destruction of the first Temple and the end of the Biblical Judaism era. However, while it "made sense" to make changes to Judaism, there was no transformation of Judaism during that time.

The core ideas of Judaism 2.0 were already on the table, but Judaism continued to operate under the architecture of Judaism 1.0 well into the 1st century: the centrality of the Temple, the sacrifices, the dependency on Jerusalem and of the Land of Israel in the Jewish narrative.

Looking backwards, that transformation of Judaism had already shown its signs before the destruction. There was a gradual shift of power from the *kohens* (the priests) to the rabbis; there was a democratization of power away from the elite. There were even local temples (later called synagogues) that sprung up and reduced the power of the Temple. The institution of the Temple itself was weak, relative to what it used to be. But there was no transformation. Judaism stayed in its familiar architecture of Judaism 1.0. It required an existential threat to Judaism 1.0 for Judaism to transform.

Judaism 1.0 revolved around the Temple, the ritual of the sacrifices, Jerusalem, and the Land of Israel. When those four elements were no longer applicable and Judaism was therefore on an inevitable path towards evaporation, then a transformation occurred.

(iii) Examples of Jewish evolution due to external threats

Indeed, the deportation of the Jews from Jerusalem and then from Judea had forced Jews to develop Judaism 2.0 (rituals, halacha, canonization of Oral Torah).

But the evolution of Judaism 2.0 and Jewish life itself was also in response to specific threats:

– Internal Jewish politics: The deportation of Jews from Jerusalem and burning of the Temple forced a seismic shift in Jewish politics away from the Sadducees to the Pharisees. The Sadducees included the priests in the Temple, whose power base had now been destroyed. The shift to the Pharisees, who were more liberal and relied on developing Judaism beyond the Temple, was the cornerstone of the foundation of Rabbinic Judaism (Judaism 2.0). This response to a threat – to the destruction of Temple – defines Judaism until today.

– The rise of Christianity: The acceptance by Rome and then the pagans of Europe of Monotheism in the form of Christianity also came with a series of threats to Judaism. Reaction to the threat and the redirection of Judaism to serve as a de facto counter-religion to its new sister religion also defined Judaism until today. Suddenly, Judaism was a counter-religion to Christianity and not to paganism.

– Ghetto life: The ghetto life in Europe forced Jews to be limited to certain behavioral codes and professions as well as develop patterns that affect Judaism until today. "We are what the ghetto made us," as Herzl said.

– Professional prohibition: The prohibition of land ownership and employment led the Jews to turn to banking and entrepreneurial activities. This was the case in Europe and this has been the case in the United States also, as Jews were excluded from the large investment banks (such as JP Morgan). Moreover, some non-Jewish banks would not finance Jewish businesses. This threat to the Jewish economic viability in turn contributed to the rise of Jewish investment banks such as Goldman Sachs, Salomon Brothers, Lehman Brothers.

Judaism today is a function of the Jewish response to the threats. Rabbinic Judaism carved a path in between the dangers to evolve into what it is today.

(iv) Threats to Judaism necessitate a Jewish transformation

"Only anti-Semitism made Jews of us," said Herzl. Indeed, anti-Semitism forced European Jews into their Jewish identity. Some were forced into it early on, by agreeing with Herzl and recognizing the dangers of European anti-Semitism. Others – those Jews who took comfort in having "anti-Semite-lites" as best friends – were forced into their Jewish identity later on through the diabolic actions of the anti-Semites.

Today as well, the threat of Israel-bashing forces Jews into their Jewish identity. It does so through the element of Judaism that is being attacked – the Jewish nation, Zionism. This is in a similar manner that if the attacks were military, Jews would unite in spirit to support the defense from the military threat. This is a basic human trait, as it is an animalistic trait – unite in order to defend!

This is the same with post-Zionism: Israel has an overwhelming Zionist majority. Paradoxically, the post-Zionism threat is a great contributor to the strengthening of the Zionist identity, and hence, to the transformation to Judaism 3.0. More so, such threats infuse the rather "boring" and obvious identity of Zionism with a strong sense of purpose and urgency.

Similarly, the threat of evaporation of American Jewry contributes to a renewed focus on the topic of Judaism – it leads to discussions, symposiums, debates and books. The mere acknowledgment of a problem generates a conversation about Judaism that would otherwise not have occurred. It prompts the Jew to think about his identity, and as he does so, he would do it through contemporary realities and his existing circumstances as an American. Therefore, the threat leads the Jew to recognize that whether positive or negative, his true conduit to Judaism runs through Israel and by doing so, validating the transformation to Judaism 3.0.

The human tendency to focus on the threats of the past could be dangerous when new threats emerge. Recognizing the transformation to Judaism 3.0 will go a long way in defending against those new looming existential threats to Judaism.

X

Judaism 3.0

Just like Herzl's original idea 120 years ago, the transformation of Judaism is not based on a new discovery and its existence is already a reality. It is the result of an inescapable conclusion rather than a flighty imagination. [1] The vision is the presence.

The transformation does not presume, or require legislation, Halachic changes, immigration, accords, agreements, the creation of new movements or seeding of new entities. It is happening in one's consciousness – in one's basic approach to Judaism. Indeed, the historic transformation of Judaism is already occurring. Recognizing it would be its fulfillment.

Jews in Judaism 3.0

With the recognition that Zionism is its organizing principle, Judaism would be more organic to secular and religious Jews alike. It would no longer be associated with a rabbi or a grandfather.

In addition, recognizing the transformation would lead to an "adulting" experience of Zionism and Israelis – living up to the responsibility that comes with being the de facto custodian of Judaism.

This, in turn, would allow for greater inclusiveness of all groups in Zionism, such as of Haredi Jews and of Diaspora Jews. It would also allow greater acceptability of a broader range of relationships between Jews and the Jewish homeland, such as through vacation home ownership and Cloud-Zionism.

Jews in the Diaspora, having a solid, attractive conduit to Judaism, would inevitably be more mindful of their Jewish affiliation. Judaism 3.0 is not only more relatable than Judaism 2.0, it is also more tangible. Recognizing the transformation would allow Diaspora Jews to feel more integral to policy discussions involving Israel – their Jewish state. This would turn criticism of Israel to a more constructive, and less angry one. The mere recognition of the transformation to Judaism 3.0 would make

---

1 – In the opening paragraph of *The Jewish State* which launched Zionism, Herzl stated: "I want it to be clearly understood from the outset that no portion of my argument is based on a new discovery. ... If, therefore, this attempt to solve the 'Jewish Question' is to be designated by a single word, let it be said to be the result of an inescapable conclusion rather than that of a flighty imagination."

such criticism more welcomed on the one hand, and more loving on the other. It would make clear that such criticism is an expression of one's Judaism.

The connection of Jews to Judaism would also naturally be augmented, since it would be less of a "chore" – a list of duties and connections through sadness and the past (Holocaust, Eastern Europe, annual synagogue visit). Instead, it would be a connection through happiness and the present: Israeli vibrancy, success, innovation, fun. The Jew would also wear his Judaism badge with pride, since it would be respected and admired by his non-Jewish friends. He would no longer self-perceive himself with the apologetic image of an old Jew (Judaism 2.0), but rather as a member of a relevant and dynamic success story (Judaism 3.0).

Day-to-day life in Judaism 3.0 is exactly what it is today, but recognizing that Judaism transformed would inject a greater sense of ownership and pride. It would incentivize Jews to want to stay as Jews. It would also likely lead to increasing the connection with the Jewish religion. As the Jew feels a greater sense of belonging, he would likely seek additional points of contact with his Judaism – the synagogue and the Jewish religion would be such natural points of contact. Indeed, all streams of Rabbinic Judaism are likely to benefit from the recognition of the transformation to Judaism 3.0.

Outside world in Judaism 3.0

The rest of the world will be looking at Jews without the built-in ambiguity that stems from wondering who the Jews are or how they are different. Are they are a religion or a nation and how should they be addressed properly without offending them?

Such built-in ambiguity exists today to some depth or another and clouds the relationship of the world with the Jews. But once the transformation is recognized, it will dissipate. For example, a Welsh person will look at his Jewish Welsh neighbor with greater respect and camaraderie when it will be clear that this Jew is carrying in his heart a third flag – not just the Welsh flag and the Union-Jack, but also the Israeli flag – the Star of David.

In reality, that is exactly how the Welsh person looks at his Jewish neighbor today, but the ambiguity that stems from the Jews' insistence on staying in Judaism 2.0 will be removed. The relationship with the Jew will be more genuine and thus stronger. This is also true because there will be a greater recognition that the Jew is part of a group that contributes enormously to humanity.

1. Zionism as a "light to the nations"

Strong evidence that Zionism is succeeding Rabbinic Judaism as the organizing principle of Judaism is provided by the core Jewish concept of a "light to the nations." This concept was manifested in each era of Judaism by that era's anchor. In Judaism 1.0, it was the Temple that served as that light, as described in the book of Kings and through the prophecies of Isaiah. In Judaism 2.0, after the Temple was destroyed, Rabbinic Judaism developed the concept and emphasized that the light that is spread to the nations is monotheism.

(i) Judaism's objective of "light to the nations" is no longer fulfilled by Judaism 2.0

Indeed, early in its development, Judaism set up a core principle – to spread monotheism to the world, and in doing so, to be a "light to the nations." This principle is rooted in the Biblical prophecies of Isaiah and expanded in the Mishna and Talmud and through Biblical interpreters and thinkers. Three times a day, Jews end their prayers by reciting their hope that all human beings would recognize God, call His name and worship Him. This mission was extraordinarily successful – one nation was able to beam the light of monotheism through much of the pagan world.

The war on paganism and polytheism has been won! The objective of spreading monotheism to the nations has been accomplished. That is thanks to the success of Christianity that emerged out of Judaism and spread monotheism to then paganic Europe, and through the success of Islam, which later spread monotheism to the then paganic Middle East. In a sense, "they did the job for Judaism." Thus, the result is that there is no longer a need for Judaism to spread monotheism. The specific mission set by Judaism of spreading "light to the nations" through monotheism has been fulfilled.

If there is an active front, it is probably not the original "offensive mission" to further the spread of monotheism's geographical footprint, but the "defensive mission" of defending monotheism from atheism which has emerged in Europe in recent centuries and has been spreading to the rest of the previously monotheistic world.

This is best demonstrated by the rise of the EU, which took the relatively new concept of a secular government that emerged over the last 100 years a step further. Like any other government, the EU has been spending millions of Euros to spread its messages. Amongst those messages is a secular mission of sorts: From a religious point of view it can be perceived to be well-financed secular propaganda – spreading "dark to the nations" if viewed from the monotheistic perspective.

In this example and in other fronts where one sees erosion of religion and monotheism, the question becomes – Is spreading the "light to the nations," or more accurately, preventing the spread of "darkness" best fulfilled by Judaism? Of course not – such a defensive front is best handled by Christianity since Christianity is "on the ground" in areas where atheism has been rising. In other words, it is Christianity which is the likely monotheistic alternative to atheism, not Judaism. It is Christianity that can stop the counter-monotheistic revolution, not Judaism.

The vast majority of atheists are Christians (or former-Christians). Therefore, if there is a front of spreading light to them and accepting monotheism again, it would be in the form of return to Christianity rather than to accept a new version of Judaism. In a sense, this is a repeat show of centuries prior when Christianity pitched to the atheist/ paganic audiences in Europe its monotheistic views. When it comes to the defense of monotheism as a "light to the nations," it is an intra-Christian battleground.

From both the perspectives of offense and defense, if "light to the nations" is a core Jewish objective, Judaism 2.0 is no longer needed or relevant for that. But Zionism is!

(ii) Judaism 3.0 is the "light to the nations" – Israeli soft-power

Within a few decades, Israel has emerged from being a developing country to becoming one of the world's leading technology-driven economies. Israel is considered by many to be home to one of the world's three most prominent centers of Innovations: Silicon Valley (Palo Alto), Silicon Alley (New York), Silicon Wadi (Israel).

Humanity is advanced from Israel. When it comes to medical breakthroughs, new technologies, safety innovations, productivity and lifestyle advances, Israel has rapidly ascended to the forefront. This even came to bear in the Coronavirus pandemic, when many around the world carefully studied the early actions Israel took to confront the crisis, and some emulated them – from restricting incoming flights, to deploying aggressive technological techniques to contain the spread. Moreover, friends and foes alike made no secret in the early days of the crisis that their eyes were towards Israel to develop a cure or a vaccine. The founder of the BDS movement told his fellow Israel boycotters that if Israel developed a vaccine, boycotters should take the vaccine. In Iran, one of the leading clerics approved taking a vaccine from Israel, should it develop one.[2] What was telling about all this is that it is done without any knowledge that Israel was on track to develop a vaccine, but in anticipation that it would – implicit in it a recognition that Israel is a "light to the nations." When a vaccine became available, Israel quickly became the world's #1 vaccinator per capita, and the first to offer a booster shot. Nations around the world are studying Israel's actions and learning from its experience.

The light emanating from Israel is expected to increase in the coming years. Trends around the world support segments within the technology sector in which Israel is particularly strong: Artificial Intelligence, robotics, drones, internet-of-things, agricultural internet-of-things, industrial internet-of-things, connectivity.

Even in the side effects of technological innovation such as cyber-security, Israel is at the forefront, housing 25% of the world's cyber start-ups and being the recipients of the world's 20% of cyber-security investments.[3]

Israel's burdens turn to assets

"I am the man who makes aniline dyes out of refuse," Herzl wrote in his diaries. He proceeded to write a play called the "Inn of aniline" showing how one can turn waste into the most remarkable accomplishments. The Jewish state that he envisioned is doing exactly that – turning burdens into power.

The Israeli military does not only provide the blanket of security that enables its economy to grow, but it is essentially one large incubator of ideas. Technologies used for intelligence and defense are converted to civilian use and have led to the establishment of some of the more successful high-tech companies. Beyond technology, the military puts in one place, in one ecosystem, a variety of young ambitious Israelis who are interacting, talking and learning from one another.

Nowhere in the world does such a fountain of soft-power exist, and it is juxtaposed to Israel's hard-power. Nearly all Israeli Jews in the 18-21 age group (except the ultra-Orthodox), as well as Israeli Druze, serve in the military or related organizations – men and women alike. Combined with the ambition and innovative culture of young Israelis, this is turning service in the Israeli army from a "sacrifice" of a few years of one's life into a spiraling generator of advances in humanity.

2 – "BDS founder: No problem cooperating with Israel if it develops a coronavirus vaccine.", i24, April 6, 2020; "Top Iranian cleric okays buying future Israeli coronavirus vaccine", *The Times of Israel*, March 12, 2020.
3 – Start-Up Nation Central.

Entering the army in Israel can be compared to entering college in America for people in the similar age group. They meet interesting people, expose themselves to knowledge, inspiration and accretive experiences. However, in the Israeli case it is done with a radically greater sense of purpose, seriousness, mission and creativity. The culture of the military is an enabler of Israel's soft-power revolution. Indeed, the Israeli military is akin to a feeder school to Israel's high-tech industry.

The Israeli high-tech industry can be viewed as a fulfillment of multiple prophecies about the good things that will come out of Zion, and about turning swords into plowshares. Israeli military technology converted to civilian use is improving the lives of millions of individuals all over the world, including those in countries that were, and even still are, Israel's adversaries. An Iranian doctor participating in an online training workshop of an Israeli medical education startup is benefiting from light coming out of Zionism (Judaism 3.0), and not out of Rabbinic Judaism (Judaism 2.0).

Global trend-setter

Zionism as a "light to the nations" does not just come to bear in technological innovations and medical breakthroughs, but also in social innovations, setting trends adopted later by the rest of the world.

For example, as mentioned earlier, the Israeli anti-establishment movement of 1977 occurred 40 years before a similar wave engulfed Europe and the United States.

Israeli Coronavirus measures were taken at the time when other nations thought such measures would not be feasible. Nations around the world studied the Israeli actions and then adopted them. Similar to this is the astonishing speed in which Israel vaccinated its population.

In another aspect of light it sheds, Israel's respect and even admiration for Muslims is unique in the Western world. Israel understands that Muslims do not need to be "westernized," and accepts the Muslim faith and tradition as it is – symbiotic particularity. This is also a trend that will need to be studied by Europe and the rest of the world as they address their relationship with their own Muslim population.

Israel is also a global trendsetter when it comes to its leading-edge acceptance and respect for others: for gays, for minorities, handicap-accessibility, and more so through dehandicapping the handicaps.

Such rapid change is noticeable in Israel. What would attract stares in one year seems routine in the next years. For example, seeing a young lady on the beach or in the Shuk with a machine gun (an off-duty soldier) is no longer an uncommon occurrence as more and more female soldiers assume combat roles in the military.

In many respects, Israel is a model society, and its actions are often emulated in other societies. This underscores that Zionism has picked up the role of being the "light to the nations" from Rabbinic Judaism.

Israel is a future-driven society, comfortable with its deeply rooted past, akin to a grounded, secured explorer whose freedom to explore is enabled by his grounding and security. This is in contrast to Europe, which is a past-driven society, milking the reserves of a much shorter and checkered history. Indeed, here too Israel can serve as a light to Europeans (though this would require a change in European attitudes).

Israel excelled and became a "light to the nations" while it has negotiated through extremely challenging situations, including war and terrorism. It is moving forward even under fire and tries to do so with a positive attitude.

In addition, Israel continues to prosper and move forward while under assaults by multinational organizations and entities aiming to harm it politically (such as elements in the UN, EU and the International Criminal Court). This skill to make progress under intense political fire is also something that will likely be emulated by other societies. This especially since the list of "bad-behaving pariahs" that are under fire by those organizations is growing, and now includes the United States, which is under investigation by the International Criminal Court and the United Kingdom, which is a target by the EU given Brexit. In addition, moving forward under fire might turn into a global mantra if the Coronavirus crisis persists. It might be the only way to move forward, and Israel's proven ability to do just that could serve as another source of light emanating from Zionism to the world.

Civilized engagement with adversaries

Another aspect of Zionism being a "light to the nations" is in Israel's encouragement and embrace of dissent. The proliferation of human rights organizations, civil society organizations, frequent demonstrations and protests are a welcomed feature of the Israeli democracy. This culture of dissent exists while maintaining unison and a strong buy-in around the core uniting ideology of Zionism. This was reflected in the 2020 protests calling for the resignation of Prime Minister Netanyahu. Those demonstrations were loud and at times aggressive, yet the most common banner displayed was the Israeli flag. The dissent was not against Zionism. On the contrary, it was about the improvement of Zionism.

Similarly, the nuanced way Israel engages with its adversaries is also a source of "light to the nations." This is reflected in the deployment of de facto understandings as opposed to de jure agreements, such as in Israel's relationship with Hezbollah in Lebanon and Hamas in Gaza. It is also demonstrated in the Israeli innovation of "knocking on the roof" and "real estate bombing" – Israeli tactics that send a message to the terrorists without killing the terrorists. The same can be said for cyber warfare. The general objective to minimize the enemy's casualties is a departure from traditional warfare. [4]

Israel, after all, is a country where the families of the same terrorists that seek to kill its citizens are treated in Israeli hospitals. Similarly, Israel treats injured fighters and civilians from the Syrian war, including ISIS terrorists.

Herzl: The Jewish state will exist because it is the need of the world

Israeli success is not a luxury. It is a prerequisite for its existence.

Herzl recognized that the Jewish state would not be established due to the goodwill of the nations. He wrote: "The Jewish state will exist because it is the necessity of the world."

Indeed, the innovations that are produced in Israel today are improving the lives of billions of people around the world. Whether it is addressing famine and drought by turning air into water, increasing longevity through biotech innovations and saving lives through tele-medicine and through cutting edge medical research, Israel has turned out to be the necessity of the world.

Israel is ranked #1 in the world in terms of Research and Development per capita. Israel is also ranked #1 in the world in terms of venture capital per capita. Israel has more startups than anywhere in the world outside of Silicon Valley – Israel is also ranked #1 in terms of startups per capita. [5]

The Israeli technological success is synergistic with other success stories in Israel (such as Israel wine) that give Israel the stature it is known for – The Start-up Nation. And that Start-up Nation has turned out to be the necessity of the world. Indeed, Zionism is not just the "light to the nations", but the necessity-of-the-nations! This is just as Herzl predicted.

---

4 – Adam Withnail, Steven Viney: "Israel-Gaza conflict: Israeli 'knock on roof' missile warning technique revealed in remarkable video", The Independent, July 13, 2014.
5 – Start-Up Nation Central.

2. Zionism as a "light to Judaism"

But Zionism is not just the "light to the nations." Zionism has also become the "light to Judaism."

Israel is the draw for world Judaism. When a Diaspora Jew feels a moment of Jewish pride, it is often because of an accomplishment by an Israeli that has touched his heart – whether hearing about an Israeli innovation, Israeli humanitarian aid, or an accomplishment in sports or in the arts. When a Jewish American achieves an accomplishment, the Jew does not view the fellow Jewish American with such particularity. In the mindset of the American Jew, the accomplishment of a Jewish American athlete is an American accomplishment, but the Israeli Jewish athlete's accomplishment is a Jewish accomplishment.

Those Jews who are critical of Israel's policies would take issue with the notion that Zionism is the "light to Judaism", yet at the same time they too benefit tremendously from this light. Their criticism of Zionism does not detract from the light it emanates. This is not any different from Judaism's previous organizing principle of Rabbinic Judaism – Jews certainly have had plenty of criticism about various aspects of the Jewish religion, while benefiting from it being the anchor of Judaism.

Israel is not just the geographical manifestation of Zionism, it is also the cultural manifestation of Zionism. Jewish cultural rays of light are emanating from Israel far more than they are from the Diaspora. This is reflected in a shift of Jewish icons.

(i) From Barbara Streisand (Judaism 2.0) to Gal Gadot (Judaism 3.0)

When the film *Wonder Woman* came out to the screens in May 2017, it immediately became a source of controversy due to the casting of Wonder Woman: Israeli actress Gal Gadot.

Wonder Woman in the film was indeed very Israeli: Gal Gadot speaks in her normal Israeli accent. Moreover, Wonder Woman behaves very Israeli: having an enormous amount of chutzpah, defying conventional wisdom, doing what she sees right, being anti-establishment, being utterly ambitious and entrepreneurial and not letting anything get in her way.

Like with Judaism, Wonder Woman was defined by the outside. The film was boycotted. Boycotters labeled the movie "The Israeli soldier film" because of Gadot's service and support of the Israel Defense Forces. Suddenly, the outside world has turned Wonder Woman into "Israeli Wonder Woman."

Like with Judaism, this criticism of the film that came from Israel's adversaries affected how the Jewish world itself viewed the film and Gal Gadot's role. Gal Gadot as Wonder Woman soon became a Jewish icon, a Jewish hero. With that, the long journey was completed from Barbara Streisand as Yentel (icon of Judaism 2.0 – Rabbinic Judaism) to Gal Gadot as Wonder Woman (icon of Judaism 3.0 – Zionism). This shift is also indicative of the shift in the threat to Jews: a shift from the threat of anti-Semitism of the 20th century to the threat of Israel-bashing of the 21st century.

The shift resulted in a different type of Jewish icon: a strong Jew who takes a stance and fights back. The Jewish icon is no longer a Jew who is subject to the mercy of host nations and forced to endure pogroms, deportations, and worse, but a proud Jew.

Today's Jew is not a weak Jew begging the Hamas terrorist not to shoot, but a Jew who takes a stance and fights back. (Judaism 3.0). Similarly, today's Jew is not a weak Jew begging the European diplomat to allow him to defend himself against Hamas terrorism, but a strong Jew who chooses to protect his life and be scolded by Europeans, rather than to die and be sympathized by the Europeans. (Judaism 3.0). Equally, today's Jew is not a weak Jew who is apologetic about the actions of other Jews (beggars, bankers, moneylenders), but a proud Jew who supports his people with vigor, takes a stance and fights back.

Wonder Woman is symptomatic of the process that world Judaism is going through: cultural Israelization alongside de-Yiddishization. Gal Gadot is a successor to Barbara Streisand; Wonder Woman is a successor to Yentl as a Jewish icon; Zionism is a successor to Rabbinic Judaism as the organizing principle of Judaism. Judaism 3.0 is a successor to Judaism 2.0.

(ii) Zionism as the light to Israelis

Absent a constitution, Zionism became the lowest-common-denominator that connects Israeli Jewish society. It is the safe ground in which Israeli society is rooted and hence, an enabler of the passionate arguments and disagreements. As discussed, this is demonstrated amongst other things, by the consistent pattern that most Israeli Jews vote for Zionist parties. It is also manifested by the high level of community volunteering and certainly by the Israeli's strong motivation to serve in elite units of the military.

Israeli success and pride occur in the realm of Zionism and not in the realm of Rabbinic Judaism. This is true for religious Israelis and for secular Israelis alike.

The values that unite Israelis are associated with Zionism – both in happiness (such as Israel's Independence Day) and sadness (such as Israel's memorial day for the fallen soldiers).

Irrespective of one's religiosity level, it is Zionism that has become the primary beacon of light to Israelis.

3. Prerequisites To A Successful Transformation

As discussed, the transformation of Judaism to Judaism 3.0 is already evident. Yet, there are certain conditions that are necessary for its success.

(i) Israel stays as the Jewish state

Israel staying as the Jewish state is not intuitive and is dependent on the outcome of the battle of narratives in Israel between the incumbent narrative of Israel being the homeland of the Jewish people vs. the challenging narrative of Israel being the homeland for the Israelis. ("State for all its citizens.")

Israel staying as the Jewish state should not be taken for granted, but, as discussed, vectors and trends in Israel strongly support it: Demographic trends, increased leadership of the religious community, immigration patterns, strengthening of Jewish identity amongst seculars, greater transparency, democratization of Israel, growing acceptance by Israel's Arab population (symbiotic particularity), as well as moving away from "the party voice" and "the media voice."

(ii) Zionism – pluralistic but still Zionism

Zionism is getting upgraded. Having received Judaism in its hands, as Herzl put it, means that Zionism is the mechanism by which Judaism will be preserved, thrive and flourish. To do so, it needs to be pluralistic and embrace a wide range of relationships between Jews and the Jewish homeland.

Being the organizing principle means that Zionism now needs to contain all of Judaism – with all of its diversity and richness. To do so, it will need to expand into a broader tent.

Most-favored-nation status enables Zionist pluralism

There can certainly be "most-favored-nation status" for various aspects of Zionism without negating the other alternatives. [6]

---

6 – Most-favored-nation status is a term used in trade agreements, granting a nation best trade terms relative to other nations. The term is also applied to other international agreements and in business.

For example, residing in Israel (making Aliya) should retain its "most-favored-nation status" in the menu of alternative geographical relationships between Jews and Israel. But this does not mean that other relationships, such as owning vacation homes, visiting occasionally, or never visiting, should be negated. Such alternatives should be fully embraced and welcomed under the Zionist tent.

In other words, a Jew living in America who has never been to Israel is still a Zionist. This does not negate a preference that the Jew should move to Israel.

Similarly, Orthodox Judaism could keep its "most-favored-status," given its interconnection with Zionism, historically and today. But this does not mean that other streams of Judaism such as Reform, Conservative, Reconstructionist, non-denominational, unaffiliated, atheistic, secularistic or agnostic, should be negated. They should be fully embraced and welcomed under the Zionist umbrella.

A Reform Jew today might feel that he is rejected from Judaism since he is not allowed to pray at the main section of the Wailing Wall alongside his wife (due to separate male-female arrangements) or that some of his fellow Jews do not embrace his non-Jewish spouse. But under Judaism 3.0, it is Zionism which is the organizing principle of Judaism. Hence, he is no longer "rejected" from Judaism. He is embraced by Judaism.

His inability to practice the way he chooses to at the Wailing Wall now moves from being perceived as rejection by Judaism to a more low-octane dispute about balances and policies.

Indeed, a debate can ensue about topics such as prayers at the Wailing Wall, conversions and other issues on the Orthodox-Reform divide, but those now become tactical. Recognizing the transformation would reduce those disagreements and remove them from being at the core of Judaism. That is because the core of Judaism is now its national aspect – Judaism 3.0.

As described, Israelis are outright Orthodox, including secular Israelis. After all, the synagogue the Israeli secular chooses not to go to is clearly Orthodox, and the synagogue the Haredi, National-Religious and traditional Israeli frequent is also Orthodox. Hence, a "most-favored-status" of Orthodox Judaism in Zionism should be viewed as logical and accepted by the non-Orthodox as well.

With those understandings, the tension between elements in the American Jewish leadership and Israel around religious topics would be defused. Just as an American Jewish visitor to Paris accepts (perhaps reluctantly) that the predominant language there is French and not English, so does he accept today's reality that Orthodox Judaism has the "most-favored status" in Israel. Just as he understands that a street sign in French in Paris does not represent a rejection of his American identity, so does he understand that Orthodox arrangements at the Kotel do not represent a rejection of his Jewish American identity.

Such attitudes should trickle up to Reform and Conservative leadership. In fact, Reform leadership would be wise to embrace the Orthodox's "most-favored-status," since disputes such as those surrounding the Wailing Wall would no longer be viewed as a litmus test of Reform Judaism's viability.

Full acceptance of Orthodox Judaism as "most-favored-status" in Zionism enables greater pluralism and hence, a stronger embrace of Reform and Conservative Judaism!

(iii) Slight de-Israelization of Zionism

For the transformation to be successful, Zionism should slightly "de-Israelize." In doing so, more broadly embrace the notion that Zionism is not only about Israel but also about the national aspects of all Jews. Conceptually (as opposed to politically), Israel is not just the national homeland of its citizens, but also the national homeland of Diaspora Jews.

There is a distinction between a political home (right to vote) and a national homeland. For American Jews', political nationality in the United States is not in conflict with also having a national homeland in Israel. At the same time, Israeli citizens being the only ones who can vote in Israel are not in conflict with sharing the national homeland with Diaspora Jews.

Uncompromising equal civil rights in Israel for non-Jews is not in conflict with the Jewish nation's exclusive national rights. Similarly, it is not in conflict with a non-Jewish Israeli citizen feeling national affiliation with another political entity. This is just like the American Jew remains a patriotic American while feeling a national connection to another political entity – Israel. Same for the Mexican American and the Korean American.

Zionism is no longer a fringe movement that it was in its first decades. It is now the anchor of world Judaism. Zionism and Israel need to adjust in recognition of this. This is similar to companies that turn from being a start-up to becoming a multinational firm.

There is a celebration of Israeli culture, character and language in Israel. This includes celebration of its diversity. No doubt that such Israeli culture is indeed the dominant Zionist culture, but it is not the exclusive culture of Zionism.

There is room in Zionism for a Jew who lives in Israel and does not speak Hebrew; there is room in Zionism for a Jew who wants to wear a suit to a wedding instead of jeans; there is room in Zionism for a Jew who does not want to reside in Israel, and never visits. Indeed, there is room in Zionism for Diaspora-like, exile-like behavior that was once negated. It is now time for a correction: To negate the negation of the Diaspora.

With Israel-related culture and language so strong and dominant, Zionism has the room to slightly de-Israelize and allow the Diaspora back in. The slight de-Israelization of Zionism would go hand-in-hand with the increased pluralism of Zionism. In that context, it should be made clear that notwithstanding slight de-Israelization in Zionism, the Israeli culture must keep the "most-favored-status" of Zionism.

Israeli culture could evolve, be diverse, and turn to be a hybrid of various subcultures, but whatever this Israeli culture turns to be – it is this version of Israeli culture that has the "most-favored-nation status." It is important to note that "whatever Israeli culture turns out to be" does not necessarily need to be the legacy Israeli culture or the founders' culture. Wearing khaki shorts and a tembel hat is not "most-favored-status" – unless Israeli culture evolves back to that. This is a market-force concept and not a guiding concept.

(iv) Owning it

A prerequisite to the success of the transformation is being in that frame of mind. For any item a person owns, he can have varying degrees of enthusiasm about owning it. In other words, there are multiple degrees of "ownership." Jews should internalize that the Jewish state, which was established in 1948, has survived both military and economic challenges, and that the Zionist endeavor has so far been an astonishing success. Israel exists, Jews live in it.

While always striving to improve and encourage criticism and debates, Jews should not engage in a wild goose chase for fatal faults with existing realities, nor to obsessively seek opportunities to talk foul about their land. Jews should keep on "doing what they are doing."

The famous call – *Am Yisrael Chai* (the people of Israel are alive) – is not just a slogan, it is a depiction of day-to-day life in Israel and around the Jewish world. Recognizing, embracing and "owning" these new realities is a prerequisite for a successful transformation.

(v) Accepting non-Zionists into Zionism

Taking it a step further, the confidence bandwidth of Zionism now being the anchor of Judaism allows Zionism not only to include under its tent all forms and relationships of Jews to Zionism, but also to accept non-Zionists. This is just like Judaism 2.0 has accepted under its tent even those who feel that they are not Jewish.

For example, a Jewish person who is an atheist and has no connection to Judaism is still considered Jewish by Rabbinic Judaism (Judaism 2.0). Similarly, Judaism 3.0 accepts under its tent those who feel they are not Zionist. A Jewish person who does not believe that Israel is the homeland of the Jewish people or does not self-identify as Zionist is still "in the tent."

Similarly, under Judaism 2.0, a person who demonstratively says "I am not Jewish" is still designated by the outside world as Jewish and is still considered by Jews as Jewish. Under Judaism 3.0, a person who says "I am not Zionist," would still be designated by the outside world as Jewish (Judaism 3.0 – Zionist), and would still be considered by Jews as such.

4. NEW RISKS AS A RESULT OF THE TRANSFORMATION

The transformation to Judaism 3.0 is not without risks. When Herzl began the process of planting the seeds for this transformation, he was confronted by his superiors at the *Neue Freie Presse* newspaper: "No individual has the right to take upon himself the tremendous moral responsibility of setting this avalanche in motion – endangering so many interests," he was told.

Herzl proceeded despite the warnings. Yet, it is important to recognize that changing the global consciousness about what Judaism is, presents new risks to Judaism. In assessing those new risks, there needs to be a clear understanding of what is Judaism 3.0 and what it is not.

The following pages present the new risks that are associated with Judaism 3.0 and explain why they are benign.

(i) Concern of mass immigration to Israel ("give us your poor")

Until recently, Israel was perceived as a poor country at war. The notion of life in Israel was of a difficult one. Hence, someone who is not Israeli and not Jewish would not be likely to ever choose to immigrate to Israel. But this has changed.

Israel is now a thriving country. Given global migration trends, and the popularity of Israel amongst young Europeans, there is now an emerging demand by non-Jews to move to Israel.

For example, the Israeli modern-dance company, Bat-Sheva, attracts some of the best dancers from around the world. Once done with their tenure in the company, some of the group's European dancers seek creative ways to stay in Israel, including actively seeking to marry Israelis. They are not Jewish. They are not refugees, nor are they poor. They are Europe's elite.

A broader-scale application of this phenomenon can happen with university students. In recent years, more and more English-language programs are offered by Israel's academic institutions, which in turn attract non-Jewish students. Some students who come to study "fall in love with Israel" and over time some might seek ways to stay after their program ends.

The idea of non-Jews moving to Israel became even more pronounced during the Coronavirus crisis and in particular in early 2021 as Israel became the world's leading country in vaccinations per capita.

If one accepts that Zionism is the organizing principle of Judaism, is there a risk that a person can argue that even if he is not converting to Judaism, he can "convert" to Zionism (by merely declaring that he is a Zionist), and hence, should be able to move to Israel under the country's Law of Return?

The Law of Return allows immigration to the Jewish state for anybody who is at least a quarter Jewish by ancestry (having at least one Jewish grandparent).

Does the transformation suggest that so many Zionists could now immigrate to Israel? Especially given the sharp rise in past decades of intermarried couples, inter-dating couples, friends and relatives of such couples, as well existing people with a lower degree of Jewish ancestry who do not qualify under the Law of Return.

Could the gates to Israel be flooded?

The answer – Judaism 3.0 has nothing to do with Israel's immigration laws.

The transformation is about what Judaism is. It is not about Israel's immigration laws. Recognizing the transformation should not have an effect on the Law of Return or other internal Israeli laws and regulations. Just like today, there are separate definitions of Judaism for rabbinical purposes (such as marriage) and citizenship / immigration purposes, same with Judaism 3.0.

This transformation is a reflection on the state of Judaism. It is agnostic to changes in laws. It is taking place regardless of whether such laws change or not. This is just as it is agnostic to changes in Jewish law (halacha), and agnostic to changes in conversion practices.

But still, if it is determined that the transformation to Judaism 3.0 poses an immigration problem or threat due to its misinterpretation, or due to the transformation taking a life of its own (one cannot "control" a transformation), then in such a scenario, the Law of Return can be modified.

Laws get changed all the time, and in Israel it is relatively easy to do so, given the government structure and that there is no constitution. Immigration laws changed in the United States. Most notably was the 1924 Johnson-Reed act, which radically limited immigration, and yet, America is still today an immigration nation. Similarly, in 2017, President Trump stopped immigration from certain countries with the stroke of a pen.

Such a hypothetical change of the Law of Return would also be a recognition that the threat to world Jews from which the Law of Return was enacted to protect, is no longer against those with "Jewish blood" (as it was at the decades around Israel's establishment), as much as against those having an affiliation with Israel, by being Jewish.

Separate from the immigration question related to unaffiliated people (such as in the example of the Bat-Sheva dancers and university students) and to loosely affiliated people (such as relatives of intermarried couples), a bigger immigration question pertains to affiliated people who are not Jewish.

What if those people who are not Jewish – not by self-definition, and not by Halachic definition – decide to move to Israel? This happens today, and Israel permits it under its existing Law of Return. The criteria is a Jewish grandparent, but not proof of practicing Judaism. One can be a practicing Christian wearing a cross and openly stating that he is not Jewish, and he would still be fully qualified under Israel's Law of Return to get Israeli citizenship as long as one of his grandparents was Jewish.

Israel, as homeland of the Jewish people and geographical manifestation of Zionism, can be comfortable with the notion of non-Jews in the midst of Israeli communities (for example, daughters of non-Jewish mothers), as well as non-Jews living in distinct non-Jewish communities in Israel (for example: foreign workers, Druze or Arabs). The natural increase in Israel's Jewish population allows Israel to "contain" this theoretical influx of non-Jews. Since Jews in Israel have reached critical mass (7 million), it seems that, mathematically, there is no real threat of de-Judaizing the Israeli Jewish community through such "non-Jewish" immigration.

(ii) Concern of mass "conversions" to Judaism (even if not moving to Israel)

If Zionism is the organizing principle of Judaism, then could people "convert" to Judaism simply by becoming Zionist? Many people have sought to get closer to Judaism, and some have sought to become a part of Judaism. JDate, the Jewish dating site, even created a category of "non-Jewish" for those seeking to marry a Jewish spouse.

Conversion is a lengthy and difficult process. Could the transformation be mistaken to suggest that one can become Jewish simply by pledging support for Zionism? Especially since under this template described in this book, it seems so easy. There are no Zionism acceptance committees or a Zionism test. There are no Zionist rituals one is asked to perform.

But this is not what the transformation is suggesting.

The answer – this has nothing to do with "conversions"

Zionism is the national expression of Judaism. One cannot enter the Jewish nation just by stating so, or expressing support, just like one cannot enter the Irish nation just by stating so or expressing support.

If one wants to convert to Catholicism, there is a process. If one wants to convert to Judaism, there is a process for that as well (for which this transformation is agnostic and expresses no view). If a non-Irish person wants to immigrate to Ireland, there is a process for that as well – subject to the laws and customs of Ireland. If a non-Jew wishes to immigrate to Israel, there is a process – subject to the laws and customs of Israel (for which this transformation is agnostic and expresses no view either).

Simply declaring, "I am Irish" does not result in an automatic inclusion in the Irish nation, just like simply declaring, "I am Cuban" does not result in an automatic inclusion in the Cuban nation. Similarly, such a statement does not give a person an automatic conversion to Catholicism nor Irish or Cuban citizenship.

The transformation to Judaism 3.0 does not deal with conversions to Judaism, just like it does not deal with Israel's Law of Return.

Being Jewish is subjective, based on objective criteria

Under Rabbinic Judaism, the previous organizing principle of Judaism, it was clear that the test for inclusion in Judaism was objective: Being born to a Jewish mother or converting through a rabbinical process. But what about under Zionism as the organizing principle of Judaism? Is it subjective or objective? It is subjective under objective criteria.

If a person from Iran would suddenly declare "I'm Irish" with no ancestral, matrimonial or any other context, this person would be ridiculed. Same with a person wishing to join the Jewish nation without such context.

(iii) General confusion on "who is a Jew" given subjective criteria

Subjective tests based on objective criteria open doors to confusion. When Rabbinic Judaism was the organizing principle of Judaism, then it was clear that a Jew is someone who is born to a Jewish mother (or parent in the Reform case) or went through rigorous conversion. If under the transformation, the test is subjective, is there risk of confusion about who is a member of the Jewish nation?

The Answer: The transformation helps to clarify who is a Jew

Political entities, institutional religions, and well-defined clubs can have objective criteria. They are the gatekeepers in deciding who gets into their entity. An application to a club, organization, country, or religious institution can be accepted or rejected. But for a more abstract grouping, this is not the case. While there are objective inputs, the ultimate decision is subjective. Though if there are no objective backups, your subjective decision would simply be ridiculed and not very relevant.

For example, "Are you a New Yorker?" is an abstract enough question to require a subjective answer. Yet, it is backed by objective criteria. How long does one need to live in New York in order to self-designate himself as a New Yorker? What about people who left New York – can they still call themselves New Yorkers? This is up for debate. But what about someone who has never been to New York? If such a person chooses to call himself a New Yorker, he will simply be ridiculed. What about someone who visits New York once a year? Probably the same.

While the question "Are you entitled to a New York City library card?" is answered objectively based on objective criteria, the question "Are you a New Yorker?" is answered subjectively based on objective criteria.

Same under Judaism 3.0, it is seemingly subjective – there is no "committee" to accept / reject inclusion in the Jewish nation (Zionism) but it is backed by objective criteria such as someone born to Jewish parents or someone who halachically converted to Judaism. As to what exactly constitutes a Jewish parent or halachically converted can be left vague. That is beyond the scope of transformation.

Judaism 2.0 is also subjective, based on objective criteria

Inclusion in Judaism is subjective today as well! When a person says, "I converted to Judaism," who is checking that he indeed converted? However, when it comes to getting citizenship or rabbinical court matters, such as marriage, there is a check to validate the person's status. When it comes to his general claim to be Jewish – in a casual conversation, in a dating context, in a sense of belonging – being Jewish is completely subjective today! Yet, it is based on objective criteria – such as his stating that he or his mother converted to Judaism.

While it is today subjective and will remain so under the transformation, the transformation provides clarity to the underlying objective criteria.

Even if in error, low consequences

The downside of this confusion is limited. As discussed, there are no practical consequences: this does not deal with the Law of Return or opinions on the religiosity of conversions. In reality, in Israel most people do not attempt to validate the Jewish status of a social acquaintance. Indeed, errors occur today when a man of questionable halachic status is being counted as one of the ten in a prayer quorum.

If there might be confusion as to who is halachically Jewish, that would be akin to the confusion about a kosher certificate a particular restaurant might have. Some kosher restaurants are "Glatt" kosher, some are "Mehadrin" kosher, some are "Rabanut" kosher, some by their own statement ("the honor system"). Indeed, kosher status too is subjective based on objective criteria.

What if a Liberal Rabbi converts 50 million people to Judaism?

While the transformation is agnostic to discussions about conversions, one cannot ignore the possibility that exists, regardless of the transformation.

In Orthodox conversions, the people accepted for conversion proceed through a strenuous multi-year process and there is a rabbinical court to approve or reject the applicant to Judaism.

Conservative and Reform conversions are more lenient. Similarly, there is a growing debate in the Orthodox community about the ease and requirements of conversions (most notably relating to soldiers in the Israeli army).

It is not inconceivable that at some point a rabbi might offer "drive-through" conversions. Similarly, it is not inconceivable that a rabbi might convert a whole church, or even whole denomination. In fact, this would be along the lines of Herzl's brief thought about a mass conversion of the Jews on a given Sunday in front of the main church in Vienna. This scenario would raise the possibility of Judaism "merging itself out of existence."

It was discussed earlier how such events can be easily neutralized with respect to the Law of Return and Israeli citizenship. Similarly, it was discussed how people can make their own choices – such as if they want to marry the daughter of someone converted through a "drive-through" conversion – in the same manner they choose what level of "kosher" they need in order to dine in a given restaurant.

But what about mass conversion of a group? Market forces will reject ludicrous conversions. The discussion about the individual level can be relevant to the collective level as well. If a random group in the Pacific Islands suddenly announced that they are Irish, and expected to be included in the Irish nation, they would be ridiculed. Same with a group claiming to have "converted" to the Jewish nation.

With the advent of social media, big data and free flow of information, the power of market forces gets augmented. A line will be drawn organically somewhere between full Orthodox conversions and "drive-through conversions."

Internet-conversions fail the objective criteria

It is clear that a person who subjectively claims to be part of the Jewish nation because he was converted by a Reform rabbi is indeed part of the Jewish nation. Similarly, it is also clear that a person who subjectively claims to be part of the Jewish nation because he was converted by an instant conversion app is not. It fails the objective criteria.

As for the in between? It falls under the same guidelines of "Is this restaurant kosher?" Absent a certificate, the determination is subjective, based on objective criteria. A consumer can choose to dine there or not.

The transformation is not about individuals; it is about the state of Judaism and the continuity of Judaism. Hence, there are no "certificates."

Infinite ideal – adjusting

If there are confusions or problems associated with the transformation, Zionism will know how to adjust. That is because Zionism is an infinite dynamic ideal.

Judaism, with Zionism as its organizing principle, will know how to evolve to address all sorts of risks and challenges – be it the rabbi who converts 50 million people, a conversion app, confusion of terms or some other unforeseen circumstances.

The transformation makes Judaism more particular, not less particular, hence, more protected. By broadening the tent and including much more inside, one is protected from what is not meant to be inside.

(iv) Blending of Judaism and Christianity – both are Zionist

Would the transformation risk blending the lines between Christianity and Judaism? After all, many of the trends mentioned are applicable to Christians as well. If one takes it a step further: Can Zionism be the architecture that binds both Judaism and Christianity?

Some would argue those lines are less clear today. There are now Christians who keep Shabbat and wear a talit. At the same time, American Jews have set up "Jews for Jesus" chapters and established "Messianic Judaism" – Jews who believe Jesus is the Messiah. Some Christians worship in these congregations.

Would a transformation to Judaism 3.0 blur the lines between the two sister religions? What would this mean for Jewish survivability?

The answer – a good friend is not the same as oneself

Friends of Zion are not the same as the nation of Zion. Just like today, under Judaism 2.0, friends of the Jews are not Jewish. There is no shortage of Philo-Semites, but still, the Philo-Semites do not convert to Judaism. They stay non-Jews, while admiring the Jews, just like being a friend of one's family does not make that friend a family member.

Risk of confusion of terms

Risk of "term confusion" as a result of a transformation certainly exists. Once a process takes place, it is hard to control it. That is true for any process.

Therefore, despite the risk-mitigating factors mentioned, the risk remains that people would start self-designating themselves as Jewish, simply because they are Zionists or because they support Zionism or because they support the State of Israel.

While that risk exists, it is arguably mitigated, not enhanced, by this transformation. Once the transformation is recognized, it provides the clarity that the Jews are a nation, and the public discussion is therefore more likely to dispel the risk of confusion.

Am I a Zionist? Or Am I a "Friend of the Zionists?"

In the New Yorker analogy, the context of the conversation provides clarity. If a conversation takes place in Manhattan, it is relatively clear that when someone says that he is a New Yorker, it means from New York City. If someone from Buffalo says he is from New York or even that he is a New Yorker, it is relatively clear it means something else – that he is from New York State.

When a Christian says "I am Zionist" it is clear what it means – he is certainly not implying he is part of the Jewish nation. The transformation to Judaism 3.0 is not going to change that. This is not about changing terms. Just like now someone says "I'm Jewish" and not "I'm a Rabbinic Judaism Jew;" same under the transformation. Someone will say he is Jewish because he is part of the Jewish nation. But if an "outsider" says, "I am Zionist," it would mean something else. If at some point this leads to debilitating confusion, terms can change. The terms used here are meant to diagnose the transformation using existing contemporary terms.

Terms change all the time, and mean different things to different people at different places at different times. For example, in the United States, the term "Oriental" was the commonly used term through the 1990s for someone from East Asia. It then switched to "Asian," which is used till today. Yet, the term "Asian" in the UK is in reference to someone from Pakistan or India.

In 19th-century France, when people wanted to make a distinction between Sephardi Jews of Southern France, who were more palatable for the French than those from closed Ashkenazi Jewish communities in Alsace, the term for a Jew was bifurcated – Juif for one and Israeliten for the other.

If Zionist and Jewish terminology causes confusion in the future, it could be changed, just as it had in various places, in various circumstances, in various times. Yet in today's world, the context provides sufficient clarity. A Christian Zionist referring to himself as Zionist may not mean the same as Jew referring to himself as Zionist – one is clearly a "Friend of Zion" while the other is clearly a member of the Jewish nation.

(v) Outbreak of anti-Semitism as a result of the Transformation

If the Jews themselves say that Judaism is Zionism, then they can no longer hide behind the claim that they have nothing to do with Zionism, and hence, feel safe in areas where anti-Zionist sentiments are high.

Would Jews be targeted by anti-Israel protesters due to the transformation? Is there a risk that those who despise Israel would now more easily target Jews, since Zionism is the anchor of Judaism?

This risk is fictional.

The answer – there is nowhere to hide today

There are no such places today where a Jew can be safe from anti-Zionist sentiments. There is no ability for a Jew today, regardless of the transformation, to put sufficient distance between himself and Zionism that would immunize himself from such anti-Israel forces.

As discussed, the outside world does not make this distinction. With the possible exception of certain liberal Jewish circles, all other arenas of anti-Zionist hostility translate to anti-Jewish hostility.

(vi) Concerns of "pulling the Jewish rug" from under Judaism

Some might argue that placing the Jewish religion on a seemingly lower level on the Jewish hierarchy would put the Jewish faith at risk. Given that the new organizing principle of Judaism is a secular principle – Zionism – people in Judaism 3.0 could feel very much Jewish while completely ignoring the Jewish religion, and hence, could become agnostic to the Jewish faith.

After all, it is not so simple to be a Halachic Jew, but it is easy to be a Zionist. One requires a long list of actions, such as going to synagogue three times a day, fasting six times a year and observing the commandments. The other does not even require a declaration.

Would observant Jews become secular since the transformation allows them to stay Jewish while not observing the mitzvahs and the halacha? Does the transformation risk pulling the rug from under Judaism?

The answer – the Jewish faith will be strengthened

An observant religious Jew does not stay religious to stay Jewish. He is well aware that even if he turns secular, he would stay Jewish.

It is clear that religiosity today is not a requirement to be Jewish under Judaism 2.0, and hence, it would simply remain clear that it is not a requirement under Judaism 3.0 either.

The transformation actually strengthens the Jewish faith, as Zionism helps people feel a higher belonging to Judaism, and while at ease and not "under pressure," it would make them more likely to exercise their faith freely and embrace religious aspects. If a person feels a stronger sense of being Jewish due to his national affiliation, he is more likely to deepen that sense of being Jewish through religious practice.

A prerequisite to the transformation is that Zionism stays Jewish. There is no Zionism absent Judaism, and that includes the Jewish faith. The transformation is not about "from the Tanach to the Palmach" – the idea of skipping Rabbinic Judaism and going from the Biblical era to the Zionist era (from Judaism 1.0 to Judaism 3.0). Such a notion is contradictory to the core principle of the Jewish transformation. Zionism is inseparable from Rabbinic Judaism.

5. Implication: Zionism – the Golden Era of Judaism

The return of Jews to the Land of Israel is not only the most under-estimated event in Jewish history but also in Jewish theology. It is not only that the Jewish religion needs to be adjusted to accommodate the new realities of residing in the ancestral land on which much of its religion is based on. Similarly, it is not just that the Jewish religion needs to be modified to the reality of renewed sovereignty and Jewish governance.

Indeed, this is not about adjustments to Judaism. The return of the Jews to their land is a transformative event in Judaism. This return represents a seismic shift. Applying the old architecture that successfully bound world Judaism for two millennia could be dangerous, as it may not be able to bind Judaism given current realities. The basic fundamental approach to Judaism needs to change.

While on the micro-level, details of adjustments are convoluted, debatable, and might require long processes of making decisions [7] on various levels and jurisdictions, the shift in the fundamental approach to Judaism is simple – it takes place in people's consciousness. Indeed, such a shift is already occurring.

(i) The Utopia has turned into prophecy

Herzl wrote a Utopian novel called *AltNeuLand* – Old-New-Land, in which he outlined how the Jewish state would look and how the world's nations would accept it and even be inspired by it. Sprinkled through his various speeches, letters, diary entries, articles and conversations, Herzl crafted a vision which has become today's Zionism. A close, slow read of Herzl would unveil Judaism 3.0.

---

7 – For example: Is rice now kosher for Passover?

"There are those who do not understand us properly and believe that the goal of our effort is to return to our land," he said in 1899. "Our ideal goes further than that. Our ideal is the vision of eternal truth. It is an ideal that always moves forward. It is an ideal that is infinite."

Indeed, Zionism is a dream that is continuing to move forward. In the epilogue to *AltNeuLand*, Herzl wrote a message to the book, and perhaps to his entire movement – a note to its future custodians: "Now, dear Book, after three years of labor, we must part, and your sufferings will begin. You will have to make your way through enmity and misrepresentation as through a dark forest. When, however, you come among friendly folk, give them greetings from your father. Tell them that he believes dreams also are a fulfillment of the days of our sojourn on earth. Dreams are not so different from deeds, as some may think. All the deeds of men are only dreams at first. And in the end, their deeds dissolve into dreams."

The dreams of Herzl turned into a deed – Zionism. Now this deed is turning into a Dream – Judaism 3.0 – a transformation of Judaism.

The Book of Herzl

It is possible that if Herzl wrote in Biblical times, his writings would have been included in the Biblical canon. This is purely hypothetical and certainly a loaded and debatable question. But what is safe to say, is that "the book of Herzl" is akin to that of other post-Biblical Jewish figures – those who shaped Rabbinic Judaism (Judaism 2.0).

Just like with other Jewish thinkers such as Yehuda Halevy, Maimonides and Nachmanides, Herzl's writing as well, is to some extent, an abstract interpretation of the Torah and of the relationship of the Jewish people with God.

For the Jewish thinkers in the Middle Ages, during the time of Rabbinic Judaism (Judaism 2.0), the overall environment, language and code-of-communication was a religious one. Hence, their writings are classified as such and deemed religious.

Herzl wrote at a different time, but his concepts are similar. Furthermore, one can say that in retrospect, many of Yehuda Halevy's, Maimonides' and Nachmanides' thoughts and concepts were not religious, but national concepts – akin to Herzl. Judaism has been a nation-religion since its inception. It is only after the 19th century that a separation has been made between the national and religious elements. Indeed, those Middle Age thinkers' call for a return to Israel would be viewed in today's bifurcated framework as a national concept – not a religious one. Extrapolation of this to Zionism can show that Herzl's words are not only about Jewish nationalism, just as Yehuda Halevy's are not only about the Jewish religion.

With Zionism as the organizing principle of Judaism, it is becoming more clear that Herzl's thoughts are first and foremost building blocks of Judaism.

The Exodus from Europe vs. Arrival in Israel

Indeed, Herzl studied Moses and understood that transformations of the magnitude that both Moses and he were undertaking take time. "A new generation will arise whom we must educate for our purposes," he wrote. According to Herzl's own interpretation of the Biblical story of the Hebrews' wandering in the desert, it was less about the arrival in the Land of Israel (the destination), and more about the transformation of the nation through the wandering (the journey). He called the 40 years in the desert "education through migration."

Both Moses' Judaism and Herzl's Zionism were drawn only in general terms at first. Moses did not delve into details or into the depth of the religion at the onset. This was done gradually, later on through a monumental event in Sinai and indeed through the 40 years in the desert.

Both had an analogous rhythm: An exodus from Egypt/Europe, where the majority of Jews lived (estimated 100% in Egypt's case and over 80% in Europe's case), re-education of the nation (de-exile), and then a prolonged process of development of Judaism 1.0/Judaism 3.0. Just as the Exodus from Egypt is core to Judaism, the 20th century exodus from Europe is core to Herzl's Zionism. Both Judaism and Zionism are expressed in contrast to what we were in Egypt/Europe.

While Egypt and Europe are admired both in Moses' Judaism (Judaism 1.0) and in Herzl's Zionism (Judaism 3.0), nothing can be more counter to Moses's Judaism as the return to Egypt, just like nothing can be more counter to Herzl's Zionism as the return to Europe – both physically and metaphorically.

The threat of such a return to Egypt dominates a significant portion of the 40 years in the desert and continues long after Moses' death. Being an astute student of Moses, Herzl recognized that the same danger also existed in an exodus from Europe. He wrote: "In the first 25 years of our existence we need, for our development, some rest from Europe, its wars and social complications."

Herzl identified the primary vehicle to safeguard against a return to Europe: the Passover Seder. It is a powerful tool to remind the Jewish nation: Do not return to Egypt! Neither physically nor mentally. Indeed, an astonishing 93% of Israeli Jews are estimated to participate in the Passover Seder.

In *AltNeuLand*, after the story of the Exodus from Egypt is recounted, the story of the 20th century exodus from Europe is then told: "First we shall finish our Seder after the manner of our forefathers, and then we shall let the new era tell you how it was born. Once more there is an Egypt, and again a happy exodus."

Herzl claimed the exodus from Europe was more complex than the exodus from Egypt, noting in his diary that Moses' Exodus resembled the one he is leading from Europe in the same manner that a simple song written by an amateur poet from the Middle Ages relates to a complex, multi-layered, extended modern opera. Moses planted the seed for Judaism 1.0, but it only became the nation's organizing principle long after his death – even the building of Jerusalem and the inauguration of the Temple occurred centuries later. Similarly, Herzl planted the seeds for Judaism 3.0, but it took over a century after his death for Zionism to become the organizing principle of Judaism.

The inescapable conclusion

Herzl maintained that his Zionism ideas were not a product of a flighty imagination; rather they were a result of an inescapable conclusion.

Same is the case with the Jewish transformation he seeded. Not only that transformations are not linear, but they also tend to have a blurry line between what is a vision, and what is an analysis of today's reality. Indeed, as Herzl said, "dreams are not so different from deeds."

Those dreams have morphed into a new golden-age for Judaism – into Judaism 3.0. All that is left for us is to recognize it.

(ii) Greater religious freedom and easing of secular-religious tensions

Paradoxically, by recognizing that the organizing principle of Judaism has shifted from its religious aspect to its national aspect, rabbis would be at greater liberty to make halachic rulings, including being stricter.

The issue of balancing religious law with realpolitik is paramount to rabbinic rulings. With the transformation to Judaism 3.0, rabbis would be able to rule based on their understanding of the halacha and God's will, without fearing that they would adversely affect the Jewish people. That is because under the transformation, the Jewish nation exists and thrives independent of their ruling.

This would allow greater religious freedom not just for the rabbis, but to Torah learners and religious Jews in general, who could delve into the richness of Rabbinic Judaism in a more pure and holy manner. This is precisely what Herzl envisioned in his manifesto, *The Jewish State*: "We shall keep our priests within the confines of their temples in the same way as we shall keep our professional army within the confines of their barracks." Rabbis having the luxury of "being kept within the confines of their temples" significantly strengthens Rabbinic Judaism, in the same way that soldiers, having the luxury of "being kept within their barracks," as opposed to doing police or rescue work, strengthens the military.

Strengthening of Rabbinic Judaism

Indeed, the transformation helps, and does not hurt Rabbinic Judaism. None of the religious aspects of Judaism are compromised, and the engagement with the Torah becomes more free.

But the strengthening of Rabbinic Judaism goes much further. Under Judaism 3.0, Jews more strongly embrace Judaism. This not only generates Jewish pride, but it also leads to associating the dynamic Israeli-related experiences with Judaism. A Jew who celebrates Israel as the start-up nation, or enjoys Israeli wine, certainly does not associate this experience with Rabbinic Judaism. Yet, under Judaism 3.0, embracing Zionism is embracing Judaism. And by embracing one aspect of Judaism, a Jewish person is much more likely to engage with other aspects of Judaism, including the religious aspects.

All streams of Rabbinic Judaism are likely to benefit tremendously from the recognition that Judaism has transformed and is now in Judaism 3.0. Under-engaged Jews will have the opportunity to become more religiously connected through Reform or Conservative synagogues once the transformation is recognized and Judaism becomes more relevant to them. Indeed, Rabbinic Judaism is likely to experience a revival from recognizing the transformation, both in message and in engagement.

This is just like Judaism 2.0 enhanced aspects of Judaism 1.0. Until today, Rabbinic Judaism heavily engages with the Temple, the sacrifices and the centrality of Jerusalem – tenants of Biblical Judaism (Judaism 1.0). For example, the prayer of Musaf, recited on Shabbat and other days of significance, is based on the additional sacrifices that were made during those days. Similarly, the daily morning prayer includes a recap of the order of the sacrifices that were made in the Temple. In addition, the Mishna, a tenet of Judaism 2.0, has an order called Kodashim that deals with the details of the worship in the Temple. It is therefore likely that many Jews living during 2,000 years of Judaism 2.0 were more knowledgeable about the details of worship in the Temple than those Jews living during Judaism 1.0 and actively engaging in such worship in the Temple. Judaism 2.0 saved Biblical Judaism, just like Judaism 3.0 saves Rabbinic Judaism.

Neutralizes the debate about conversions

A prime example of rabbis reluctantly compromising with their own values to accommodate realpolitik exists in the realm of conversions. Making accommodations is inevitable. Rabbis know that their actions, such as rejecting conversion applicants, have far-reaching consequences. What if the applicant is eight-months pregnant from a Jewish father? She would be giving birth to a non-Jewish child. They would be excluding her and her child from the Jewish nation. But under the transformation to Judaism 3.0, from the view of the Jewish nation, the child grows up feeling "in," so the rabbis have more liberty to decide.

Similarly, with respect to the debate about Reform and Conservative conversions, are the people they have converted Jewish or not? Today that depends on the stream of Judaism a person belongs to, and the rabbis they adhere to. The transformation sidesteps this question. It does not deal with any halachic issues.

Neutralizes the debate about Israel's Law of Return

As discussed, the transformation is agnostic to any debate about Israeli citizenship and linkage of one's Judaism. In fact, just like it takes away from the rabbinical authorities the ability to determine who is a Jew, it also takes away that power from the Israeli government.

Under the transformation, those two bodies would only make determinations that are relevant to their jurisdiction – they will be confined to the issue at hand – halachic issues for one, immigration for the others. The priests in the confines of the temple, the soldiers in the confines of the barracks, and by extrapolation, government officials and judges in their respective confines as well. Judaism 3.0 means that Judaism belongs to the Jews!

Herzl's principle allows each jurisdiction to prosper in its own domain, but to no longer serve as "excluders" of individuals who feel part of the Jewish nation. And yet, if the clarity provided by the transformation about who is a Jew is deemed to clash with the Law of Return, or if there will come a time where there would be tens of millions of subjective Jews claiming citizenship, or converted by a "drive-through liberal rabbi," then the transformation is even more important in providing maneuvering room for the state.

Mechanisms could be put in place to dodge a flooding of the immigration gates. One could be a "generational test." For example, someone who has at least one Jewish parent, as opposed to the way it is now – at least one Jewish grandparent. This would postpone the discussion by at least 50 years, as today there are not tens of millions of converts or self-described Jews at the gates of Israel. And if in 50 years, the problem is so grave that tens of millions of children of loosely-converted or self-designated Jews are applying for Israeli citizenship, one can simply cancel the Law of Return, as opposed to just modifying it. It would take a few weeks, if not days. [8] An array of options are there, and recognizing the transformation to Judaism 3.0 just makes the ability to exercise such options more plausible.

Indeed, when the organizing principle of Judaism is the Jewish nation and not the Jewish religion, the intensity of debate about religious issues will be significantly reduced.

(iii) Jewish Clarity

Judaism is more clear and simple under Judaism 3.0. Its simplicity allows it to be effective. Debates on Jewish questions will continue: who can immigrate, which rabbi can convert, is this restaurant kosher? But with Zionism as the organizing principle of Judaism, there would be more clarity about the essence of Judaism.

Backward-looking concept unsustainable

Rabbinic Judaism is an organizing principle of Judaism that is backward-looking. Since over 90% of Jews are not religiously observant, applying a religious concept as a conduit to one's Judaism implies reliance on tradition, heritage, reverence to grandparents, ancestors and Jewish history. Same when it comes to memory of the Holocaust and Yiddish culture. These are connectors that are not based on present circumstances of the life of the Jew. They are based on "customer loyalty."

Zionism, on the other hand, is an organizing principle of Judaism that is forward-looking. It is the arena where the Jew meets his Judaism,

---

8 – For example, in May 2020, the Israeli Knesset (Parliament) changed a number of Basic Laws, which enabled the formation of a new type of government. Basic Laws are more rigid laws (step closer towards a constitution, as opposed to a simple law), and yet, the process to change a few of them at once only took a few weeks from the time the changes were even thought about, until they were approved and enacted as new laws.

positive or negative, and it is where change can occur moving forward. It is a connection that is based on "consumer demand."

A backward-looking concept is rigid – the past cannot be changed, only looked at through different angles, frameworks and spins. A forward-looking concept is flexible and can be adaptable to changing realities. The Coronavirus crisis underscored that this is an era when one needs to be ready to adapt to new circumstances that are unpredictable. Zionism, the Infinite ideal that Herzl seeded, is exactly this concept.

This is reflected in the culture of Israel, in its politics and industry. For example, in wine: A Bordeaux winemaker must adhere to strict rules including the use of four varieties of local grapes in order to keep his Bordeaux designation. If his Merlot grapes that year were bad, he must use those bad grapes. An Israeli winemaker, on the other hand, can do what is right based on existing reality. It is building from the ground up, and not drawing on traditions, brands and other past caches.

Judaism has gone through radically changing circumstances in the last 150 years and is likely to continue going through more changes. Therefore, it is important that its organizing principle is forward-looking.

Zionism - giving and receiving

Zionism is a breathing organism. It was never "canonized." Any religion or movement that wishes to survive needs to be able to adjust.

The Jewish nation is one of travelers, businesspeople, Zoom-trollers, open-minded, accepting people who interact with the world, and opt to adjust as needed. Yet now with the existence of a solid Israeli culture, there is the confidence bandwidth to stay true to the Zionist core while incorporating outside influences. Zionism, by both its nature and nurture, gives to, and receives from, the outside.

Zionism is a "light to the nations" because it also receives light from the nations. Taking this even further, Zionism could serve as a better model of universalism in a postmodern era. Not the notion that all are the same, but the notion that distinct and particular entities indeed give to, and receive from, one another with the shared goal to promote the greater good – symbiotic particularity. (Symbiotic particularity as neo-universalism?)

Indeed, that is exactly the relationship Herzl envisioned between the Jewish state and the world: The Jewish state will be a resource through which the world's nations would be blessed. It will export to the world a wide range of social and technological innovations, from the seven-hour work day to agricultural breakthroughs. Those innovations would be generated in the Jewish state, in part thanks to the blessed concepts that would be imported from Europe and the rest of the world.

In Herzl's vision, the mechanism by which the world would benefit from the Jewish state is certainly not by joining it. On the contrary – nations will apply the blessings they receive from the Jewish state in their own particular context.

This Herzlian concept is akin to the Abrahamic one that those who bless Abraham will be blessed, and those who curse him will be cursed. The mechanism through which all families of the earth are blessed through Abraham is not by joining Abraham ("universalism"), but by blessing Abraham. [9]

Zionism's machine-learning

In a dynamic world quick to change, human-driven adjustments are not enough. Concepts need to change organically through experiences.

A backward-looking concept that is based on tradition cannot do that. Yet, Zionism, as drawing and understanding from others, is the ultimate 'big data" concept. It can adjust without a committee or government – just by the strength of the ideal.

One cannot predict the circumstances that can come one's way, such as the 2020 Coronavirus crisis. But by Judaism having a dynamic ideology as its organizing principle, Judaism can adapt to the unexpected circumstances simply through "concept learning" – a form of autonomously generated organic artificial intelligence.

After all, Zionism was designed by Herzl as "an ideal that is infinite, that forever grows, in such a way that with every step forward, our horizon expands in front us, and in its perspective, we see an even greater and more noble purpose to which we strive."

(iv) Interdependence of the Jewish nation and religion

Judaism has been a nation-religion since its inception. But in recent centuries an attempt has been made to reduce it to one or the other – that has failed. Zionism (Judaism 3.0) does not exist absent the Jewish religion. It is indeed a religious concept because Judaism is a religious concept. This is just as Rabbinic Judaism (Judaism 2.0) does not exist absent the Jewish nation. Rabbinic Judaism has always been a national concept because Judaism is a national concept.

The attempt in America to denationalize Judaism and turn it into a mere religion has failed, and consequently, the American Jewish

---

9 – Genesis 12:3.

community is on a trajectory towards evaporation. Similarly, the attempt in Israel to strip out the religious element of Judaism and turn Zionism into a purely secular national movement has also failed. Increasing numbers of secular Israelis are now reincorporating aspects of the Jewish religion into their individual secular lives. There is no national Israeliness that can prevail independent of the Jewish religion. (This exists on the individual level, but not on the group level.)

Absent the Jewish religion, Zionism would be new, invented, and would lack legal, cultural, and structural foundations. Individual Zionists can be atheist, believers, seculars, Haredi or anything in the middle – certainly, Zionism is agnostic to one's religiosity. Yet Zionism as an ideology is an expression of Judaism, not a break from it.

(v) Jews embrace Judaism

Judaism cannot prevail without Jews. Similarly, Judaism cannot prevail without a substantial portion of Jews that are engaged to one degree or another with their Judaism. The transformation allows for that to happen. Thanks to the recognition of the transformation, Jews will once again embrace Judaism. It will be relevant. Hence, Judaism will survive.

Jewish pride

A nation needs pride in order to survive. When a nation loses its narrative, gets less excited about its culture, turns agnostic about its distinction and turns unfaithful to its own core being, it is in danger of disappearing, hence, European frustrations.

Universalism, which influences the current state of Judaism 2.0, advocated for such agnosticism. Zionism refutes this notion.

Zionism is Jewish pride. It is pride even for those who disagree with its core aspects or with Israel's policies. This is just like those waving a gay flag in a gay pride parade are not endorsing gay leaders. They might put distance between themselves and certain aspects of the gay movement and stereotypes, but they are still proud! They still wave the flag. Zionism is the Jewish flag – it is what generates Jewish pride.

Hence, the transformation to Judaism 3.0 is an injection of pride, energy and optimism to Judaism.

Neo-Karaites

Not everybody will accept this transformation. As discussed, Judaism 3.0 is designed to fully encompass Jews who are not Zionists, including anti-Zionists! This is just like Judaism 2.0 today is designed to fully encompass Jews who are not religious, including Jewish atheists.

But still, some Jews will resent it, fight it, and deny the realities of the transformation. That too is legitimate, and that indeed is what happened in the previous transformation of Judaism, from Judaism 1.0 (Biblical Judaism) to Judaism 2.0 (Rabbinic Judaism). Back then, a group of Jews decided to stay in the old architecture of Judaism, and not to transform. Those were the Karaites who exist till today. They did not accept Rabbinic Judaism and the developments of the post-Biblical era of Judaism. They stayed in Judaism 1.0 (Biblical Judaism).

Like the Karaites in the previous transformation, there will be those, likely amongst American Jews, who will choose to stay with a legacy version of Judaism. Though unlike the Karaites, who clung to a thousand years of rich engaged Jewish traditions, the neo-Karaites of today merely cling to a century of weak, under-engaged denationalized Judaism.

Unlike the Karaites, the sustainability of neo-Karaites is highly doubtful. In most likelihood, they will continue on the evaporation track American Judaism is on today, and within a few generations will become extinct. This is especially true since, to begin with, the neo-Karaites are typically people for whom Judaism is low on their hierarchy of identities.

What is and how big would the neo-Karaites movement be is a topic for a future discussion, but it is important to note that they too are legitimate and indeed, their existence would support the transformation to Judaism 3.0. By showcasing what's out, they would help solidify the notion that Judaism has transformed.

This is just as the transformation from Biblical Judaism being the organizing principle of Judaism (Judaism 1.0) to Rabbinic Judaism serving in that role (Judaism 2.0) occurred without the Karaites and yet, this did not hinder the success of the transformation. Indeed, the terms Rabbinic Judaism and Judaism are today interchangeable. Similarly, once the transformation to Judaism 3.0 is recognized, it is possible that the terms Judaism and Zionism will become interchangeable. Just like there is no need to say Rabbinic Judaism when talking about Judaism today, there will be no need to say Zionism when talking about Judaism in a few years – it will be obvious.

(vi) The world nations accept Judaism at last

Europe did not and could not accept Judaism in the past. Given its global domination, this rejection of Judaism trickled into the world's nations. That changed thanks to the American Revolution, which accepted the Jewish religion, and more importantly, warmly embraced Zionism as an abstract philosophy, even before the birth of the organized Zionist movement.

Political Zionism was synergistic with Americanism. While other nations had yet to fully accept Judaism at the time, most have done so indirectly and inadvertently through accepting Americanism.

Herzl claimed that the establishment of the Jewish state would lead to the nations' acceptance of Judaism. But for this to happen, the transformation Herzl seeded needs to be recognized. As long as there is the ability to carve out Judaism, there is room to mask opposition to Judaism as political opposition to Zionism. Once the transformation to Judaism 3.0 is fully recognized, opposition to Judaism will subside.

Indeed, in recent years, the success of Zionism has led world nations to accept it directly. By centering their engagement with Judaism nearly exclusively in the arena of Zionism, world nations have reaffirmed that the transformation of Judaism is occurring.

Peace through strength with Europeans

The broad recognition of a transformation and moreover, the recognition that world Jewry has accepted Zionism as its organizing principle, would make Europeans realize that Zionism is an "affair-complete."

As discussed, there have been multiple attempts throughout history by Europeans to eradicate Judaism – sometimes it was overt and sometimes latent. The notion that Zionism could be defeated is a primary driver for those Europeans who are engaging in the contemporary battleground with Judaism.

A Jewish transformation, whereby Judaism is intertwined with Zionism, would gift Europeans a firm consciousness that Zionism cannot be defeated. The triumph of Zionism would allow Europeans to make the inevitable call: "If you cannot beat them, join them," and at last make peace with Judaism.

There is a broad acceptance of the world's need for the Jewish brain, for Jewish ingenuity. Recognizing the transformation would allow the European brain and Zionist brain to join forces without the debilitating European-generated noise. This is achievable.

Europeans recognized transformations of such magnitude in the past. For example, after World War I, Austria was not held accountable for its role in the war in the same manner that Germany was. This was primarily since the European allies (the coalition of the war's winners) recognized that Austria had transformed from the Austro-Hungarian

Empire with which the European allies had a conflict, to the Austrian Republic – a new state.

European recognition of the Jewish transformation could mark the end of its 2,300-year feud with Judaism.

Peace with Arabs

Recognizing the transformation to Judaism 3.0 would not only advance peace with Israel's Arab neighbors, but it would also make such peace nearly inevitable. It would provide clarity and would dispel any myth that Zionism is a passing phenomenon that is soon to disappear. Such myth serves as the fuel that enables the Israeli-Arab conflict to continue.

Given the culture of long-term perspectives prevalent in the Muslim and Arab world, a recognition that Judaism is Zionism would lead to an inevitable conclusion: What could not have been done in 2,300 years by the Europeans, and in 100 years by the Arabs, is not going to be done now. Judaism survives, hence, Zionism survives.

Moreover, the notion that Jews have power and influence around the world – a notion highly prevalent in the Arab world – would now be applied fully to Zionism. This would promote a desire to be on the side of Zionism. Here too, "if you can't beat them, join them" – e.g. Peace!

In addition, the peace through strength with the Europeans would eliminate a primary hurdle to Israeli-Arab peace. There are numerous conflicts around the world that are by far more difficult than the Israeli-Arab one. The high volume of the Palestinian issue is not only generated by the merits of the conflict, but also by its artificial inflation including by the Israel-bashing movement. As discussed, Israel-bashing needs to stay in Judaism 2.0 in order to succeed.

Recognizing that Zionism is the organizing principle of Judaism would eliminate its ability to mask its opposition as "friendly criticism." Hence, Judaism 3.0 would release the Arabs from debilitating European dogmas that have occupied their true character for the last 100 years. It would indeed give Arabs some rest from Europe, its wars and social complications. This in turn would allow Arabs to regain their own character, which by its nature bears respect to Jewish nationalism. After all, it was the Emir Faisal who lobbied European powers for a Jewish state in Palestine and was a staunch Zionist himself.

This is already happening. The 2020 Abraham Accords between Israel and the United Arab Emirates, Bahrain, Sudan and Morocco are a reaffirmation of Zionism and of Arab particularity – a celebration of symbiotic particularity. There was immediate engagement: travel, business partnership, trade and friendship. This is a leading indicator that once there will be a broader recognition that Zionism is the organizing principle of Judaism, the Israeli-Arab feud will end and be reduced to a tactical dispute.

Indeed, recognizing the transformation to Judaism 3.0 will bring back the Israeli-Arab dialogue to an organic, local and truthful one, which in turn will lead to the inevitability of peace.

Zionism and America unison

Recognizing the transformation to Judaism 3.0 will rectify noise that exists between Judaism 2.0 and aspects of the American ethos. As discussed, secular, universalist American Judaism is at times perceived by some to be in tension with the American ideal. But recognizing the Jewish transformation will create a unison: the sacred trinity of religion-Americanism-Zionism. It would showcase the Jewish inspiration of America's founding fathers, who were building a new Zion in America.

Moreover, once recognized as the organizing principle of Judaism, Zionism can serve as a uniting value in America, especially at a time of polarization.

The events of the summer of 2020 and the disagreements that followed the November 2020 elections underscore just how badly America needs uniting values. Indeed, "America is an idea" as President Biden stated. Zionism is an idea as well, and those two ideas are in unison. Zionism and Americanism are sister-ideologies that are about particularity, freedom, self-determination and faith.

Peace dividends: The world would benefit from recognizing the transformation to Judaism 3.0

The world would not only accept the Jews at last, but once the transformation is recognized, the world would greatly benefit from Judaism.

The transformation of Judaism enables the opportunity to "join them" – be a partner in the success of Judaism – something that was not available until now, but that is deeply desired by the world's nations.

Herzl alluded to the power of this latent desire by the world's nations: "I did not know until I came into this movement that the Christians, just as Jews, view our return as the beginning of the era of wonder. The wonder of this era will be expressed through our aspiration for our infinite ideal – to the elevation of humanity."

Indeed, French thinker Ernest Laharanne predicted in 1860 that the Jews' return to their land would lead to a dramatic advancement of humanity. "March forward, because you are a generous nation...You (Jews) will be the triumph-arch of the era of the future – that is – the era of peace and unity." [10]

That era seems to have arrived. Exactly as Herzl predicted, the Jewish state today is making "extensive experiments which benefit the other nations of the world" – technological and medical breakthroughs, political and cultural creativity, innovative ideas and social ingenuity.

Once the transformation of Judaism is recognized, the world will no longer be hindered by debilitating constraints of boycott movements that stand in the way of human progress and of peace, nor by the limitations that stem from its checkered history with the Jews. The world will at last be free of its opposition to Judaism and hence, humanity will be elevated through the wealth of good that is coming out of Zion.

10 – Ernest Laharanne: "The New Question of the East: Empires of Egypt and Arabia: reconstitution of Jewish nationality" (French), 1860. Excerpts appeared in 1862 in Moshe Hess's "Rome and Jerusalem" – a book that Herzl brought with him on his 1898 trip from Europe to Jerusalem.

XI

Conclusion

"Infinite, infinite is our ideal," Herzl stressed. Indeed, Zionism is an ideal without constraint. It is not canonized nor limited in any way. Hence, with Zionism as its organizing principle, Judaism is now resuming its infancy and entering a golden era, perhaps never experienced before, even in Biblical times.

Indeed, Zionism is still in its early days. It takes a long while for transformations of such magnitude to settle. It took centuries for the previous transformation of Judaism from Biblical Judaism to Rabbinic Judaism. After some time, the terms Judaism and Rabbinic Judaism became synonymous – so much that nobody even uses the term Rabbinic Judaism now when talking about Judaism. Same will likely be with Zionism and Judaism.

Zionism is not only the purest expression of contemporary Judaism, but it is also the most obvious one. Zionism is relatable and simple, given that it has a relevant tangible expression – the State of Israel. Israel's success, its contribution to humanity, its culture, its people, as well as its controversies and flaws, all dictate how nations view the Jews and how Jews relate to Judaism. Indeed, Zionism is the one aspect of Judaism that evokes passion, engagement and belongingness.

Judaism 3.0 provides the unison under which Judaism thrives. The richness of Judaism is now funneled through the prism of Zionism, including when it comes to morality, spirituality, giving, learning, relationship to the land, to Jews, to the world's nations and indeed to God.

Hence, Zionism has turned into the anchor of Judaism. It succeeds Rabbinic Judaism as the organizing principle of Judaism, not by replacing it, but by incorporating it. This is just like in the previous transformation, Rabbinic Judaism succeeded Biblical Judaism as the organizing principle of Judaism by incorporating its concepts – certainly not by replacing it. On the contrary, Rabbinic Judaism thrives under Judaism 3.0 to a higher level than it had under Judaism 2.0, when it was burdened with being the organizing principle of Judaism.

Yet, Zionism is not just any ideal. As Herzl underscored, it is an infinite ideal. It is a breathing organism. Hence, Zionism too must develop over time. One day in the future it is possible that Zionism itself will be transformed-out and a new ideal of Judaism will succeed it as the organizing principle (Judaism 4.0-?).

This is built into Zionism, because Zionism is not a political party or a view. It is designed to be the essence of Judaism – an ideal that optimizes the Jewish nation-religion's thriving under contemporary circumstances. "We indeed received Judaism in our hands," Herzl stated.

In his final days, recognizing that the flag he was now carrying would soon be carried by others, Herzl stressed that Zionism "will not stop being an ideal even after we arrive in the Promised Land, because in Zionism," as he wrote in an April 1904 article called "Our Hope", is embedded "not only the aspiration to the Promised Land...but also the aspiration to moral and spiritual completion."

That same article was republished later that month in the Zionist bulletin *Die Welt*, but with a new title: "Journey's Blessings". Three months later, Herzl died.

The blessing Herzl gave to the Zionist journey continues until this day. More than 120 years since that journey began in Basel, the vision Herzl carefully articulated has indeed turned into a powerful reality: Zionism is the return to Judaism.

Glossary Of New Terms

Some terms in the book are original or applied in unconventional ways. Visit the book's website: www.judaism-zionism.com for expansion and related articles about these concepts.

Cloud-Zionism – accessing Israel-related experiences from one's own home. For example, lectures on Zoom, Israeli TV series on Netflix, Israeli music on YouTube. A shift from Zionism's previous mantra of Aliya.

Concept Learning – applying the idea of machine-learning to concepts, such as Zionism, designed by Herzl as an Infinite ideal.

Counter-Intersectionality – the reactionary embrace of particularity that results from the overreach of the Intersectionality movement, which has racist, homophobic and counter-individualism themes. Counter-intersectionality represents the ability of individuals to be themselves, as opposed to being defined by outside "authorities" based on sexual orientation, race or groupings.

Cultural Occupation of Palestine – The European occupation of Palestinian minds, done through promotion of the victimhood narrative, perpetuation of the refugee status, aggressive blocking of Palestinian participation in the Israeli economy, and opposition to the development of a free and entrepreneurial Palestinian mindset.

Datlaf – Hebrew acronym for "sometimes religious" – secular Israelis who consume religious experiences a la carte, while staying secular. Datlaf has become the primary stream of Israeli secularism.

Haredi-Spring – the inevitable boost to the Israeli economy that would occur once the Ultra-Orthodox enter the workforce and the high-tech sector. Akin to the boost received in the 1990s from the Russian immigration.

Israel-bashing – Funneling hate to Judaism through Israel (Judaism 3.0), as opposed to through the Jewish religion or individual Jews (Judaism 2.0). It is the current manifestation of age-old European opposition to Judaism, replacing anti-Semitism which was that manifestation in the 19th and 20th centuries, and religious hatred that preceded it. Not to be confused with criticism of Israel, which must be protected, and even encouraged.

Isra-Philia – People who admire Israeli culture, achievements, vibe and people. This is regardless of one's political opinion about Israel and its government's policies. It replaces Philo-Semitism as the primary expression of admiration for the Jewish people.

Neo-Karaites – those who would not recognize that Judaism has transformed and stay in Judaism 2.0. This is just like the Karaites who did not recognize that Rabbinic Judaism had become the organizing principle of Judaism back then, and stayed in Judaism 1.0.

Neo-Universalism – Applying symbiotic particularity to the idea of universalism, defined as loyalty to the other regardless of his national allegiances. Neo-Universalism argues that such loyalty to the other would be augmented if an individual celebrates his own national particularity.

Open-architecture of worship – the worship outside one's own stream of Orthodox Judaism, such as National-Religious worshiping in ultra-Orthodox synagogues, Ashkenazis in Sephardic synagogues or vice versa. A subtle shift towards pan-Orthodoxy.

Reverse-Colonialism – Just as Europeans created parallel European societies overseas, drawing on the resources of the occupied land, reverse colonialism is the creation of parallel Muslim societies in Europe, drawing on the resource of Europe, such as welfare, municipal services, and health-care.

Second act of the American Revolution – rebelling against European values that negate the ideological aspects of the American Revolution. Europeanism vs. Americanism is becoming the global philosophical divide of the 21st century in a similar manner that communism vs. capitalism was in the 20th century and monarchy vs. republicanism was in the 19th century.

Symbiotic Particularity – the recognition that optimal contribution to society occurs when an individual chooses his own level of national/ethnic particularity. This is in contrast to universalism (all the same) and European multiculturalism (parallel societies in competition; zero-sum game).

War of European Succession – the fear that absolutist rejection of Islam in Europe on the one hand, and European childlessness on the other, could lead to a cold or violent war between the two competing claimants to Europe. This is particularly alarming, considering that Europe has persistently gone into war for unexpected reasons in every century.

Acknowledgments

I would like to thank all who helped me write this book, challenged my thinking, critiqued my writing, and gave valuable advice. In particular, to the following people who spent their valuable time reading the book and giving comments: Sara Bard, Rainer Barzen, Ourit Ben-Haim, David Brummer, Daniel Chertoff, Steven Cohen, Moshe Dann, Ariel Ganz, Alex Grobman, Yishai Haetzni, Tamar Krieger, Steve Linde, Yisrael Medad, Bennet Ruda, Ellie Rudee and Gina Ross.

I want to thank Chaim Mazo, whose publishing house brought this book to life and was so patient with me during the editing process, as well as to Maor Tzfira for the creative book cover design.

Also to the members and staff of the AIFL Think Tank, who for the last decade helped me deliberate the ideas in the book.

To the readers and editors of *The Jerusalem Post*, who through interacting with my articles, allowed me to fine-tune the ideas.

To my family, who provides the deep roots and support that enables such thinking.

I am so grateful for the astonishing gift I received: to live in this era, at home, in freedom, amongst my people, who I am so blessed to walk alongside in the desert, through unpaved roads.

The conversations continue on the book's website:
www.judaism-zionism.com

Index